THE STATISTICAL STUDY
OF
LITERARY VOCABULARY

THE STATISTICAL STUDY
OF
LITERARY VOCABULARY

BY

G. UDNY YULE, C.B.E., M.A., F.R.S.

ARCHON BOOKS
1968

First Published 1944
Reprinted by Permission of
The Cambridge University Press
in an Unaltered and Unabridged Edition

SBN: 208 00689 3
Library of Congress Catalog Card Number: 68-8027
Printed in the United States of America

CONTENTS

1.1–1.3. The inception of this work was due to interest in the vocabulary of the *De Imitatione Christi*: previous work seemed too much concerned with details. 1.4. I wanted a general picture, which would only be obtained by tabulating separately words used once, twice, thrice, etc. 1.5. The work was carried out, with a concordance, for nouns only, and 1.6, results were sufficiently interesting to lead to further work, by sampling, on the miscellaneous works of Thomas à Kempis and the religious works of Gerson. 1.7–1.9. But this work showed how ignorant one was of the nature of such statistics: the special investigation was laid aside and general investigations undertaken to solve problems essential to the understanding of what one was doing. 1.10. Thus the bulk of this work is devoted to problems quite unforeseen at the start, and the original investigation only takes a minor place as an illustration at the end. 1.11. Statistics of literary vocabulary are of a respectable antiquity, as instanced by the statistics of the Masoretes. 1.12. A note on references. References. *Pages 1–8.*

2.1. The word-distribution, showing how many words are used once, twice, thrice, etc. is important in this work: 'words' may include all words or any special class. 2.2–2.6. Illustration 2.1. Nouns in the *De Imitatione Christi*: detailed analysis: mean, standard deviation etc. 2.7. Illustration 2.2. Nouns in samples from the works of Thomas à Kempis. 2.8. Illustration 2.3. Nouns in samples from religious works of Gerson. 2.9. Illustration 2.4. Nouns in Macaulay's essay on Bacon. 2.10. Illustration 2.5. A limited class: non-Vulgate nouns in the sample of Illustration 2.3. 2.11. Illustration 2.6. Adjectives in the *Imitatio*. 2.12. Illustration 2.7. Verbs in the *Imitatio*. 2.13. Was the choice of nouns for the first investigations a wise one? Comparative neutrality of adjectives and verbs, especially the latter, as regards subject. 2.14–2.15. Illustration 2.8. Approximate distribution for nouns in the Vulgate, as an example based on a much larger sample. 2.16–2.18. Illustration 2.9. Nouns in St John's Gospel in Basic English, illustrating effect of a limited vocabulary and, 2.19, Illustration 2.10, in St John's Gospel, A.V., for comparison. 2.20–2.23. Some general deductions from the tables. 2.24. Terminology: 'vocabulary' and 'occurrences'. 2.25. The tables of Zipf are not comparable with those given, since he enters separately every inflection of a word etc. References. *Pages 9–34.*

3.1–3.5. General notions on sampling, practical methods of random sampling, the standard error of a mean. 3.6. Difficulties of random sampling for vocabulary. 3.7–3.9. Spread sampling as an alternative: advantages and disadvantages. 3.10–3.11. The word-distribution is a distribution of 'multiple happenings' or 'accidents', but 3.12, differs from a distribution of personal accidents in as much as (1) time is not specifically involved, (2) the distribution is decapitated, the number of words that have not met with the accident of being used being unknown: 'size of sample' in the personal-accident case means number of persons at risk: the number of words at risk is unknown, and 'size of sample' inevitably comes to mean the total number of occurrences, an equivalent of total number of accidents or of time. 3.13. For the accident-distribution we know a function of mean and variance which is (in the ideal case) independent of time, measuring the variance of members of the group for liability to accident. 3.14. Words also vary in liability to the accident of being used, and, 3.15, a quantity K derived from the expression for accidents is a characteristic of the decapitated word-distribution which is independent of size of sample: but, 3.16, constancy will not be exhibited if the sample is extended, not by further random sampling from the same field, but by taking successive contributions to the sample from different portions of the author's works.   3.17–3.24. More complete development and discussion of the preceding general notions.   3.25. Possibility of characteristics of a higher order.   3.26.   The problem of standard errors in relation to word-distributions.   3.27.   An equation that fitted well some distributions for personal accidents failed, so far as tested, with word-distributions: a formula given by Zipf also fails.   References.   *Pages 35–56.*

CHAPTER 4.   The Characteristic K: Practical Problems   57

4.1.   Desirability of a practical test of the constancy of the characteristic for different sizes of sample: values of the characteristic for distributions of Chapter 2.   4.2–4.12. An experiment in sampling, testing the constancy of the characteristic for samples of 2000 to 8000 occurrences of a noun from Macaulay's essay on Bacon.   4.13–4.23.   Attempts at estimating the order of magnitude of W, the total number of words at risk: further discussion of the meaning of the term.   4.24.   Hence estimates of the value of v_λ. 4.25–4.31.   An empirical relation between characteristic and mean for samples of the same size: discussion.   4.32.   The range of variation of K to be expected in different but similar works of the same author is an important practical question: see Chapter 6. References.   *Pages 57–82.*

CHAPTER 5.   Certain Difficulties and Sources of Fallacy   83

5.1–5.13.   The ratio of the vocabulary of author A to that of author B in samples of the same size is a function of size of sample. For a small sample the limit of the ratio is unity in all cases, for a large sample W_2/W_1. The course of the ratio between these limits may be very varied.   Difficulty of interpreting an impressionist judgment.   5.14–5.23.   Proportions or percentages. Two forms of statement are in use for assessing the proportion of some class of words to the whole: (1) the proportion p_w of occurrences of words of the special class to all occurrences, (2) the proportion p_v of words in the special list to the total of words in the vocabulary. The first, p_w, is independent of size of sample: the second, p_v, is a function of size of sample.   5.17.   Illustration 5.1.   Nouns not in Lewis and Short's *Dictionary* in the data from the *Imitatio*, etc.   5.18.   Illustration 5.2.   Once-nouns in Macaulay's essay on Bacon.   5.19–5.23.   Illustration 5.3. Romance words in Chaucer. 5.24–5.26.   The proportion, p_c, of special vocabulary to total occurrences or some statistical measure thereof, such as lines or pages, tends continuously to decrease with increasing size of sample.   5.27–5.28.   Applicability of these conclusions in fields other than vocabulary.   5.29.   The reason for this exceptional trouble, the various proportions being functions of size of sample, is that we are not using that expression in its usual sense— but such usage seems quite unavoidable: Lutoslawski over forty years ago wrote of 'samples' of text.   5.30.   Note on a paper by G. H. Thomson and J. R. Thompson.   References. *Pages 83–116.*

CHAPTER 6.   Word-distributions from different Works of the same Author   117

6.1.   The desirability of tests to see how far word-distributions based on different but similar works of the same author are consistent with one another.   6.2–6.6.   First test: data for three additional essays of Macaulay, making four in all.   6.7.   Distribution for the pool of the four essays: the characteristic reduced.   6.8–6.13.   Second test: data for four of Bunyan's works.   6.14.   Distribution for the pool of the four works: the characteristic reduced.   6.15 *et seq.*   On certain classes of nouns in Bunyan and Macaulay: 6.16–6.18, Verbal nouns in *-ing*; 6.19–6.20, Monosyllabic nouns; 6.21–6.24, Biblical nouns.   6.25–6.26.   Conclusion.   References.   *Pages 117–147*

CHAPTER 10. The *De Imitatione Christi*, Thomas à Kempis and
   Gerson, continued   251

10.1–10.7. Correlations and contingency coefficients.   10.8–10.14. 'Frequent'
nouns, occurring twenty times or more in the samples from the respective works: nouns
characteristic of the *Imitatio* (or Thomas à Kempis) on the one hand and of Gerson on the
other.   10.15–10.17.   Association tables between the presence of a noun in the samples
from one author and its presence in the samples from another.   10.18.   Alphabetical
distributions of nouns in the *Imitatio* and the sets of samples from Thomas à Kempis and
from Gerson: similarity of the three distributions.   10.19.   First supplementary
investigation: the distributions of 'non-classical' nouns, not in Smith's *Smaller Latin-
English Dictionary* (1933).   10.20–10.23.   Second supplementary investigation:
distributions and characteristics K for four of the minor works of Thomas à Kempis.
10.24.   Consensus of the evidence from vocabulary with prior evidence obtained from
sentence-length.   10.25.   The argument that the *Imitatio* cannot be the work of
Thomas, since it is so much better than anything known with certainty to be his.
References.   *Pages 251–280.*

CHAPTER 11.   Valedictory   281

11.1.   Incompleteness of the present work: need for more work on adjectives and verbs.
11.2.   For safety the work on nouns required a sample of some 2000 occurrences of a noun
or about 10,000 words, a larger sample than is always available: the use of adjectives and
verbs, and possibly other words as well, may reduce this requirement, but the best rules
for practice need investigation.   11.3–11.4.   The methods given are methods for
studying language-in-use, and it is hoped they will not be used solely or mainly for matters
of controversy.   Some further problems for investigation by the student of language or
literature, and, 11.5, some problems for the theoretical statistician.   11.6.   It is hoped
that the methods and ideas suggested may prove fruitful.   11.7.   Postscript: Theorem
on the Characteristic.   *Pages 281–283.*

NOTE ON THE NUMERATION OF PARAGRAPHS, EQUATIONS, ETC.

Each paragraph in the book is distinguished by a number consisting of the number of
the chapter in which the paragraph occurs prefixed to the number of the paragraph in
that chapter, and separated from it by a period, e.g. § 6.10 means the tenth paragraph
Chapter 6. A similar system of numeration is used in all other instances: thus 'equation
(3.9)' means the ninth (numbered) equation in Chapter 3, 'fig. 5.1' means the first figure
in Chapter 5, 'ref. 3.4' means the fourth reference in the list of references at the end of
Chapter 3

PREFACE

My first chapter is so largely of the nature of a preface that here I may be brief. This book arose from a desire to study a particular vocabulary in a case of disputed authorship. When I had advanced some way in that particular study, it became only too clear into how thorny a field of statistics I had strayed. Statistics of literary vocabulary proved to have their own special problems, their own peculiar difficulties and sources of fallacy, which no one apparently had made any attempt systematically to explore. The special study was accordingly laid aside for later use as little more than an illustration, and other investigations were taken up with the aim, not of throwing light on this or that problem of literature, but of illuminating the way in which statistics of the kind behaved and exemplifying methods which could be used in discussing them. As is inevitable in any such case, problem after problem arose that was not foreseen at the start. The book therefore was not and could not have been planned: if the reader find in it any logical development, it is simply the logic of the natural growth of the investigations.

I have found the work of such absorbing interest that the reader, I hope, may be interested too. If he find any novel ideas, I trust he will use them: if errors, let him amend them and judge mercifully. Neither old age nor the anxieties of war are favourable to continuity or clarity of thought.

In conclusion I have to thank the Controller of H.M. Stationery Office for permission to reproduce the data of Tables 3.1 and 3.2 from the Reports cited, Mr C. K. Ogden, Mr H. Sykes Davies and Mr G. Herdan for several references that I have used, and the Syndics of the Press for the spirit they have shown in risking the issue of such a book as this at such a time.

G. U. Y.

May 1943

Chapter 1

INTRODUCTORY, PERSONAL AND APOLOGETIC

1.1.   Words are to the writer what paints are to the painter, the materials at his disposal for the purpose of creation. Carefully selecting, arranging and re-arranging words from his treasury, he shapes a poem or a tale for our delight, a history or some grave tractate for our edification. To those who write, many of us owe more than to almost any other class of men. How kind, how more than kind, they have been thus to create for our pleasure, and what a magical work they have done. The Word, by a sacred metonymy, symbolises the eternal spirit of Creation: the word *spoken* by the lips of humanity is a very emblem of the fleeting, gone down the wind with the breath that uttered it—

> Nam et ipsi qui loquuntur,
> ecce omnes nihil;
> deficient enim cum sonitu verborum.

> Thee too the years shall cover; thou shalt be
> As the rose born of one same blood with thee,
> As a song sung, as a word said.

But the writer takes these emblems of the fleeting and endows them with life, a life it may be outlasting many generations of men, a life that on rare and happy occasions audaciously we term immortal.

1.2.   To pin down such creations and dissect them is but a sorry business, work for the second-rate, a job for the uncreative. For the uncreative can at least ask questions, and very foolish questions they may ask at times: Did Thomas à Kempis really write that little volume which passes under the title of its first chapter, the *De Imitatione Christi*?* Did Shakespeare write the plays that are generally attributed to him, or such and such a particular play? Did St Paul write the Epistle to the Ephesians? What is the probable chronological order of this, that and the other work of Plato? In endeavouring to obtain an answer to any such question every element of that highly complex quality the author's style may and should be taken into account, but amongst those elements his *vocabulary*—the aggregate of words he uses—takes an important position. It is a definite characteristic, and

* 'Non quaeras quis hoc dixerit sed quid dicatur attende.' *Imit.* 1. 5.

certain aspects of it at least are susceptible of definite numerical treatment, treatment by what we now term statistical methods.

1.3.   It was no mere desire to get another field in which to exercise my craft that led me to take up the present work. Interest in the *De Imitatione Christi* provided the initial stimulus. The controversy on the authorship of that book seemed to me mostly quite foolish, a matter of historical and pathological rather than actual interest, but I had read some few of the works relating thereto and in these, from comparatively early days, the vocabulary and diction of Thomas à Kempis are discussed as evidence. These discussions left in my mind a sense of inadequacy. They did not tell me what *I* wanted to know. They dealt with such details as his use of words and idioms taken literally from the Dutch—like the well-known *exterius* in the sense of *by heart* in Lib. i, cap. i of the *Imitatio*; of words used in unusual, non-classical senses; of italianate words, and so forth. All these are mere details, details certainly quite useful in relation to the controversy, providing valid evidence (if they are rare elsewhere) when we find them occurring both in the *Imitatio* and in other works admittedly by Thomas; *but they give no faintest notion as to what his vocabulary is really like as a whole.* To tell me that there is a small mole on Miranda's cheek may help me to identify the lady, and may in conceivable circumstances be quite useful information to the police, but it hardly amounts to a description of her alluring features.

1.4.   What I felt I wanted in the first place, prior to any detail, was some summary, some picture of the vocabulary *as a whole.* Surely the colour and flavour of a text, if I may be permitted to mix my metaphors, are determined not by the exceptional words, unless these words taken together form a large class, but in the main by the common words used by the author, the words used by him over and over again? This was the question I asked myself. The sort of picture I wanted could only be given by a list of the words used classified by the number of times they were used; words used once, words used twice, words used thrice and so on.

1.5.   I am no linguist: I was wholly ignorant of what had been done in the way of applying statistical methods to the study of vocabulary, and know very little of that 'literature' now. Rashly no doubt in the circumstances, but purely for my own interest, I started an exploratory investigation on the lines suggested, an investigation of which full details are given in Chapters 9 and 10. Naturally enough the investigation was devoted to the work which had excited my interest in the question, the *Imitatio*: it is a conveniently short work, of some 42,000 words only, and the fact that there is a complete concordance available is a further convenience. To limit material,

I decided to confine myself to a single class of words, viz. nouns. The concordance was worked through page by page and every noun entered on a card together with the number of times it was used. From these cards it was easy to book up a table, the 'frequency distribution' to use the statistical term, showing the numbers of nouns used once, twice, thrice, etc., and also a list showing the actual nouns used once, twice, thrice, etc. This second classification was what I set out to obtain, and it presented many points of interest. But one never knows what one is going to find in the course of such a bit of exploration, and quite unexpectedly the simple frequency distribution showing merely the *numbers* of nouns used once, twice, thrice, etc. proved to have considerable interest of its own. It showed that little less than half—some 45 per cent—of the nouns were used only once in the whole work, some 15 per cent twice, 9·5 per cent thrice, and so on in a very long gradually and irregularly decreasing series, only terminating with a word which occurred 418 times—very appropriately the noun *Deus*. The large proportion of nouns used only once was a complete surprise, and the whole form of the distribution at once raised the question how far peculiarities of form might be characteristic of one author as compared with another.

1.6.   The interest of the results was quite sufficient to encourage me to proceed, and I decided to draw up comparative vocabularies for (1) the miscellaneous works of Thomas à Kempis other than the *Imitatio*, (2) the works of Gerson—one of the competitors, with many supporters in former days and even in the latter part of the last century, for the authorship of the *Imitatio*. But here there could be no question of completeness. Even if there had been concordances available to the other works of Thomas and to the works of Gerson they would have been of little use, for the material would have been unwieldy, and the great length of the works as compared with the little *Imitatio* would have rendered many comparisons difficult or almost impossible. It was decided accordingly to proceed by way of sample and, for convenience of comparison and avoidance of possible fallacies, to make the sample taken from each of our authors of about the same size as the *Imitatio*, that is to say a sample of rather more than 8000 occurrences of a noun. Passages were taken well spread over the miscellaneous works of Thomas and the theological works of Gerson, and the occurrences of nouns booked up on to cards, using the same cards as for the *Imitatio* in so far as the nouns were the same. When the work was done, every card had an entry for (1) the number of times the noun occurred in the *Imitatio*, (2) the number of times it occurred in the sample from the miscellaneous works of Thomas, (3) the number of times it occurred in the sample from the theological works

of Gerson. The results were summarised in the same way as before, and of
course there were now many further points of interest, since not only were
comparisons possible, but other statistical methods could be used. The two
new frequency distributions resembled in general form that for the *Imitatio*,
but were more contracted, not extending into so long a 'tail' of words used
many times: *Deus* remained the substantive most frequently employed, but
it occurred only 369 times in the sample from the miscellaneous works of
Thomas and 256 times in the sample from Gerson, as against 418 times in
the *Imitatio*.

1.7.   But all this work had raised one question after another of a purely
statistical kind, questions some of which, so far as I know, had never either
been asked or answered. What is the nature of these frequency distributions
showing the numbers of nouns used once, twice, thrice, etc.? It is evident
that if we go on extending the size of sample taken from a given work, or a
given author's 'works', the distribution will itself continually extend. If in
2000 occurrences of a noun taken at random from the given work the most
frequent noun occurs some 50 times, in 4000 occurrences of a noun taken at
random from the same work it will probably occur some 100 times, more or
less. Everything about the distribution—or apparently everything—will in
fact alter as the size of sample is increased: the mean number of occurrences
of a noun will go up; its reciprocal, the number of distinct or different nouns
per 1000 occurrences of a noun, will go down; any measure of scatter or
dispersion will rise rapidly; the percentage of nouns used only once will fall
slowly. Are not some of the statistical measures or percentages that have been
used in practice fallacious for these reasons? Can one throw any further
light on such fallacies, or possible sources of fallacy? Is there no characteristic
of the distribution that is independent of size of sample?

1.8.   In quite the early days of the work, the analogy had forced itself
on my mind between these data showing the numbers of words used once,
twice, thrice, etc. and data showing the numbers of persons out of a given
number at risk who have met with 0, 1, 2, 3, ... accidents during a given
period of exposure. Both are data respecting 'repeated events' or 'multiple
happenings' as they have been termed. But there are two important points
in which the verbal case differs from the case of personal accidents. In the
first place, the case of personal accidents involves time: it presents time-
problems. Given say the numbers of persons out of 2000 at risk who have
met with 0, 1, 2, 3, ... accidents during a year, we can ask ourselves for
example how many will have met with 0, 1, 2, 3, ... accidents during a
longer period of exposure, 2 years or 5 years. Time in the personal case is

replaced in the verbal case by the total number of occurrences of a word (or noun or whatever it may be) on which we have based our table, i.e. the amount of material, roughly the number of pages of the author, that we have used. We are not in the least concerned to know how long the author took to write those pages. And it may be noted that this change of aspect almost inevitably leads to a certain change of nomenclature. It is hardly possible to avoid terming the amount of material on which we base our table, viz. the total number of occurrences of a word, the *size of sample*, but in doing so we are using the term in a sense wholly different from that which it would normally carry in the case of personal accidents, viz. number of persons at risk. Our 'amount of material' or 'size of sample' is most nearly equivalent to 'time of exposure to risk' in the accident case, for the total number of accidents is, within the limits of fluctuations of sampling, directly proportional to time. This first point of difference is an essential, but not a very troublesome distinction. In the second place, while in the case of personal accidents we know the number of persons at risk and consequently the number who have not met with any accident during the period of exposure, we do *not* know the number of words 'at risk', that might have been used by the author, and cannot insert in our table the leading figure 'words occurring 0 times'. We may be able to make a very rough guess whether the total vocabulary is nearer 5000, or 10,000, or 20,000, or 50,000, but that is about all. Our table for words is, therefore, compared with its analogue, incomplete, lacking its head, decapitated. This is not only an essential but an emphatically troublesome distinction.

1.9.   The theory of accident-distributions has received a great deal of attention during the past twenty-five years or so, and that theory was familiar to me. A certain characteristic of the distribution which, in greatly simplified hypothetical circumstances not strictly valid for any real case, is independent of the period of exposure to risk, was known. It proved possible to transform this characteristic into a form applicable to the decapitated table for words. One had therefore now got that obvious desideratum, a figure characterising the word-distribution which was independent of size of sample within the limits of mere fluctuations of sampling. This seemed an important result, so important that it was worth an experimental test. The test was accordingly carried out, by taking a series of samples spread over one and the same work, and gave satisfactory verification. The 'characteristic' remained the same within the limits of fluctuations of sampling whether the distribution was based on some 2000, 4000, 6000 or 8000 occurrences, and one was therefore able for the first time to compare two distributions

without regard to the numbers of occurrences on which they were respectively based. Full details of the experiment are given in Chapter 4. The
results gave one confidence in the general notions on which the theory was
based, and led one to apply them to the consideration of possible fallacies
(Chapter 5). In this work the experimental data again came in useful as
illustrations. Next, the 'characteristic' having been obtained, it was
obviously desirable to find out the extent to which it would be likely to vary
in data drawn from different but similar works of one and the same author.
This information could only be got by actual trial, and the trial was duly
carried out, using four of Macaulay's essays as one example and four of
Bunyan's works as another (Chapter 6). This again raised further questions.
The data provided by the work on Macaulay and Bunyan showed certain
striking similarities as regards the relative numbers of words peculiar to each
separate work or common to any specified two, three, or all four of the
works. To what are these similarities to be ascribed? The answer to the
problem, discussed in Chapter 7, is that they depend simply on the form
of the word-distribution—the proportionate numbers of words that are
used by the author once, twice, thrice, etc. Again, when the first card
drawers for the Bunyan data and for the Macaulay data happened one day
to be standing open together, it leapt to the eye that while in Macaulay
nouns beginning with A were much more numerous than those beginning
with B, in Bunyan matters were exactly reversed, nouns beginning with B
being by far the more numerous. Other more or less conspicuous differences
between the alphabetical distributions were then noticed, and this led
finally to a long investigation (Chapter 8), including an analysis of the
respective vocabularies into words of Old English-Teutonic and of Latin-
Romance origin. The difference between the two alphabetical distributions
is mainly due to the much larger proportion of Latin-Romance nouns in
Macaulay.

1.10.   It is evident from this very summary account that my work proceeded very much as such a piece of research work is apt to proceed, opening
up problems that were quite unforeseen at the start and inevitably changing,
to a greater or less degree, one's point of view. As the work advanced my
original notion of simply trying to obtain a picture of the vocabulary by
means of the classified word list, though remaining important, faded in
some degree into the background, and purely statistical problems took its
place—for their solution was essential to the understanding of what one was
doing and to the interpretation of results. Indeed I might add their solution
was essential to the understanding of what *other* people had been doing and
to the interpretation of *their* results. There remain many bits of investigation

which I should like to undertake to fill in obvious gaps and illuminate obscure points, but work of this kind takes a long time and they might occupy years. Years are fleeting, and I am old. I have thought it best to give some account of results reached at the present stage, hoping that, however incomplete, they may at least be suggestive, and that errors may be corrected, omissions supplied and further advances be made by others. This is no logically ordered text-book, but a collection of notes. All that I have been able to do in the way of logical ordering is to give an exposition of more theoretical and general notions first, and postpone to the end the investigation into the vocabularies of Thomas à Kempis and Gerson which actually initiated my work. Publication of that investigation does, I know, require apology, and I have already apologised, for I am no linguist. But after all neither the statistician without training in linguistics, nor the linguist without training in statistical method, is properly equipped for work in this field, and the latter has charged in quite cheerfully, not always without disaster.

1.11.   It seems almost strange that no statistician, so far as I am aware, should have specially devoted himself to this branch of work during the past half-century of rapid advance in statistical method. It is full of interest, and is of the most venerable antiquity and august associations, for the earliest examples that one can give relate to the Hebrew text of the Old Testament. To cite first from Dr Wheeler Robinson (see References at the end of the chapter) :

After the destruction of the Jewish state in A.D. 70, it obviously became necessary to ensure the preservation of this consonantal text [of the Bible] and the correct tradition of its pronunciation. This became ultimately the work of the *Masoretes*. The name ' Masoretes ' is derived from the Hebrew word *Masora*, in the sense of ' tradition '.

. . .in general they were meticulously careful guardians of the consonantal text *as it reached them*. This is seen from the general character of the Masora, i.e. the textual notes which are found written above, below, and in the margins of Biblical manuscripts, as well as in separate treatises. These are largely concerned with the indications of *hapax legomena*, or of the number of instances in which a particular form occurs. Everything countable seems to be counted, and if such work seems to us often futile, it was not so to men deeply concerned with the literal accuracy and the 'plenary inspiration' of the Scriptures; moreover, its practical usefulness for copyists is apparent.

The writer in Hastings's *Dictionary of the Bible* somewhat expands this statement as to the work of the Masoretes:

They *counted* the verses and the words of each of the 24 books and of many sections; they reckoned which was the middle verse and the middle word of each book; nay, they counted the letters both of particular sections and even of whole books.

Thus they could specify the middle word and the middle letter in the Torah, the middle verse and the middle letter of the Psalms:

> They counted also the frequency of occurrence of words, phrases, or forms, both in the whole Bible and in parts of it.
>
> They collected notabilia into groups, and thus not only helped the recollection of these, but also facilitated the control of the MSS. . . . There is a great fondness for anything alphabetical; e.g. we have an alphabetical list of words which occur only twice in the O.T.—once with and once without [the conjunction] *waw* at the beginning.

Much of this, it must be confessed, does seem 'futile', and its 'practical usefulness for copyists' is not very apparent. Surely counting the number of times a given word occurs (by no means an easy task to perform with accuracy) or the number of letters is a strangely indirect and insufficient way of checking the accuracy of a copy? The whole process seems odd and puzzling, but a passage in the *Jewish Encyclopaedia* makes a very plausible suggestion as to its origin:

> In classical antiquity copyists were paid for their work according to the number of stichs. As the prose books of the bible were hardly ever written in stichs, the copyists, in order to estimate the amount of work, had to count the letters. Hence developed, in the course of time the Numerical Massorah, which counts and groups together the various elements of the text.

This suggestion also accounts in a very natural way for the practice of determining the middle letter, or word, or verse of a book, which otherwise seems quite pointless. The tired copyist would always be glad to know when he had completed half of his task.

1.12. The average non-mathematical student of literature will, I am afraid, find much of this work very difficult. I have endeavoured to help him, so far as may be, by explanations in general terms, by practical examples, and by giving at the end of each chapter, where it is necessary, references to a text-book on statistical method. Regarding the numeration of references, paragraphs, etc. the reader is referred to the note on p. viii.

REFERENCES

My citations in § 1.11 concerning the Masora and Masoretes are made from:

(1.1)   Wheeler Robinson, H., Editor (1940). *The Bible in its Ancient and English Versions*. Oxford: Clarendon Press. (See pp. 26, 29.)

(1.2)   Hastings, J., Editor (1898–1904). *The Dictionary of the Bible*. Edinburgh: T. & T. Clark. (See the article 'Text of the Old Testament', especially Section iii, The work of the Mas(s)oretes.)

(1.3)   Singer, I., Editor (1901–6). *The Jewish Encyclopaedia*. New York and London: Funk & Wagnalls. (See the article 'Masorah'.)

Chapter 2

THE WORD-DISTRIBUTION: ILLUSTRATIONS

2.1.   The reader will have gathered from Chapter 1 that in the present work a position of importance is assigned to the table showing the number of words used once, twice, thrice, etc. by an author in any given writing or sample from his writings. The 'words' in question may include all words, or nouns or adjectives or verbs only, or those words only that fall within some special class defined by the investigator. Let us look at some specimens of such tables.

2.2.   *Illustration* 2.1. Columns 1 and 2 of Table 2.1 give the data for nouns, Latin nouns, in the *De Imitatione Christi*. The table was compiled from Storr's *Concordance* (ref. 2.2): fuller details, references and notes on the practical difficulties encountered will be found in Chapter 9. It will be seen that on my reckoning there are 520 nouns that occur once only in the whole work, 174 that occur twice, 111 that occur thrice, and so on. The figures tail away very slowly, naturally with slight irregularities here and there, and the table only terminates with a noun that occurs 418 times, the noun *Deus* as already mentioned in Chapter 1. In all there are 1168 separate and distinct nouns in the table (see figure at the foot of col. 2), or a *vocabulary* of 1168 nouns to put it briefly. The number f_x of nouns that occur X times is called in statistical terms the *frequency* of X, and the manner in which the frequencies are distributed over the scale of X is spoken of as the *frequency distribution* of X. In form this frequency distribution shows a maximum at the bottom end of the range (the top of the table) for words occurring once only, and from this point the frequencies decrease at first rapidly and then more and more slowly.

2.3.   Let us study this first illustration in some detail. In col. 3 of the table are given the products $f_x X$: each such product evidently gives the number of occurrences of a noun due to nouns of the class X (nouns that occur X times). The total number of occurrences, as given at the foot of the table, is 8225. Col. 4 gives the sum of the figures in col. 2 added up step by step from the bottom, so that the figure on line X gives the number of nouns occurring X times *or more*. Col. 5 similarly gives the sum of the figures in col. 3 added up step by step from the bottom, so that the figure on line X gives the number of occurrences due to nouns occurring X times *or more*.

TABLE 2.1. Showing the number f_x (col. 2) of nouns occurring X times (col. 1) in the *De Imitatione Christi*: compiled from Storr's *Concordance* (ref. 2.2). For explanation of cols. 3–7 and data at foot see text. Note that to save space blank rows are omitted in this and all similar tables

1	2	3	4	5	6	7
X	f_x	$f_x X$	$S(f_x)$ from bottom	$S(f_x X)$ from bottom	Col. 4 reduced to total 10,000	Col. 5 reduced to total 10,000
1	520	520	1,168	8,225	10,000	10,000
2	174	348	648	7,705	5,548	9,368
3	111	333	474	7,357	4,058	8,945
4	70	280	363	7,024	3,108	8,540
5	37	185	293	6,744	2,509	8,199
6	33	198	256	6,559	2,192	7,974
7	20	140	223	6,361	1,909	7,734
8	28	224	203	6,221	1,738	7,564
9	11	99	175	5,997	1,498	7,291
10	14	140	164	5,898	1,404	7,171
11	10	110	150	5,758	1,284	7,001
12	9	108	140	5,648	1,199	6,867
13	11	143	131	5,540	1,122	6,736
14	5	70	120	5,397	1,027	6,562
15	4	60	115	5,327	985	6,477
16	7	112	111	5,267	950	6,404
17	7	119	104	5,155	890	6,267
18	4	72	97	5,036	830	6,123
19	5	95	93	4,964	796	6,035
20	2	40	88	4,869	753	5,920
21	5	105	86	4,829	736	5,871
22	1	22	81	4,724	693	5,743
23	1	23	80	4,702	685	5,717
24	7	168	79	4,679	676	5,689
25	2	50	72	4,511	616	5,484
26	1	26	70	4,461	599	5,424
27	4	108	69	4,435	591	5,392
28	3	84	65	4,327	557	5,261
29	2	58	62	4,243	531	5,159
30	3	90	60	4,185	514	5,088
31	1	31	57	4,095	488	4,979
33	2	66	56	4,064	479	4,941
34	2	68	54	3,998	462	4,861
36	2	72	52	3,930	445	4,778
37	5	185	50	3,858	428	4,691
38	4	152	45	3,673	385	4,466
39	3	117	41	3,521	351	4,281
40	1	40	38	3,404	325	4,139
41	1	41	37	3,364	317	4,090
43	2	86	36	3,323	308	4,040
44	2	88	34	3,237	291	3,936
46	2	92	32	3,149	274	3,829
48	1	48	30	3,057	257	3,717
50	1	50	29	3,009	248	3,658

TABLE 2.1 (*continued*)

1	2	3	4	5	6	7
					Col. 4 reduced to total 10,000	Col. 5 reduced to total 10,000
X	f_x	$f_x X$	$S(f_x)$ from bottom	$S(f_x X)$ from bottom		
51	1	51	28	2,959	240	3,598
52	1	52	27	2,908	231	3,536
53	1	53	26	2,856	223	3,472
54	1	54	25	2,803	214	3,408
56	1	56	24	2,749	205	3,342
57	2	114	23	2,693	197	3,274
58	1	58	21	2,579	180	3,136
61	1	61	20	2,521	171	3,065
62	3	186	19	2,460	163	2,991
63	1	63	16	2,274	137	2,765
69	1	69	15	2,211	128	2,688
76	2	152	14	2,142	120	2,604
79	1	79	12	1,990	103	2,419
92	1	92	11	1,911	94	2,323
94	1	94	10	1,819	86	2,212
102	1	102	9	1,725	77	2,097
104	1	104	8	1,623	68	1,974
135	1	135	7	1,519	60	1,846
146	1	146	6	1,384	51	1,683
172	1	172	5	1,238	43	1,505
196	1	196	4	1,066	34	1,296
210	1	210	3	870	26	1,058
242	1	242	2	660	17	802
418	1	418	1	418	9	508
Total	1,168	8,225	—	—	—	—

$S_0 = 1168$; $S_1 = 8225$; $S_2 = 577,665$; $M = 7 \cdot 042$; $\sigma^2 = 444 \cdot 987$; $\sigma = 21 \cdot 095$; $v = 3 \cdot 00$.
Percentage of nouns occurring once only = 44·5. Vocabulary per 1000 occurrences = 142.

Thus, reading the line for $X = 102$, we see that there are only 9 nouns occurring 102 times or more (we may say actually 100 times or more since there are no nouns occurring 100 or 101 times) but these 9 nouns contribute 1725 occurrences or over one-fifth of the total. Again, reading the line $X = 30$, there are only 60 nouns occurring 30 times or more, but they contribute in all 4185 occurrences or over half the total. The last two columns, 6 and 7, have been drawn up to enable such figures to be read directly as proportions of the total vocabulary (1168) or the total occurrences (8225) respectively: col. 6 gives the figures of col. 4 multiplied by 10,000/1168, and col. 7 the figures of col. 5 multiplied by 10,000/8225. If we want to read the figures of these two columns as percentages instead of proportions per 10,000, the last two digits must be cut off. Thus, starting right at the bottom of the table,

the most frequent noun constitutes by itself less than one-tenth of 1 per cent
of the vocabulary but contributes over 5 per cent of all occurrences of a
noun. Words of 102 occurrences or more (or 100 occurrences or more)
form only some three-quarters of 1 per cent of the vocabulary, but contribute
nearly 21 per cent of all occurrences. Words occurring 56 times or more
form little more than 2 per cent of the vocabulary, but contribute over
one-third of all occurrences. Words occurring 30 times or more form little
more than 5 per cent of the vocabulary, but contribute over half the occurrences. Such figures show how enormously preponderant the more frequently occurring words must be in giving the special colour to the text. It
is astonishing that so few as 9 nouns should account for one-fifth of all the
occurrences of a noun in the *Imitatio*, 24 nouns for one-third, and the mere
handful of 60 nouns for a full half. The use of the vocabulary is concentrated
very heavily on to a relatively very small proportion of the whole.

2.4.   Some of the characteristics of the frequency distribution can be
quantitatively defined in the usual way by such measures as averages and
measures of dispersion, and by other measures of interest in our particular
case. Of the ordinary measures I shall only use the mean, standard deviation and coefficient of variation. As some of my readers may have little
knowledge of statistical method I give here a brief explanation; text-book
references will be found at the end of the chapter. The mean M is a quantity
with which everyone is familiar: if we have N values of some varying quantity X, say $X_1 X_2 \ldots X_n$, M is defined by the equation

$$M = \frac{X_1 + X_2 + \ldots + X_n}{N} = \frac{S(X)}{N}, \qquad (2.1)$$

where $S(X)$ denotes 'the sum of all quantities like X'. In our illustration the
values of X are grouped into a frequency distribution: N is the sum of the
frequencies f_x or $S(f_x)$, which we will briefly denote by S_0, and for $S(X)$ we
must read $S(f_x X)$, which we will briefly denote by S_1. In this notation the
mean number of occurrences of a noun is

$$M = \frac{S_1}{S_0}. \qquad (2.2)$$

The standard deviation σ is a measure of the scatter or *dispersion* of the
distribution about the mean. If $x_1 x_2 \ldots x_n$ are the deviations of $X_1 X_2 \ldots X_n$
from the mean M, σ is defined by the equation

$$\sigma^2 = \frac{x_1^2 + x_2^2 + \ldots + x_n^2}{N} = \frac{S(x^2)}{N}. \qquad (2.3)$$

That is to say, the standard deviation is the square root of the mean deviation squared, deviations being measured from the mean. As a matter of arithmetic, however, it is simplest, especially in tables like our own, to calculate the standard deviation directly from the values of X without working out the deviations x. Since

$$x = X - M,$$

we have

$$S(x) = S(X) - NM,$$

and therefore by (2.1)

$$S(x) = 0, \tag{2.4}$$

i.e. the sum of the deviations from the mean, giving them their proper signs of course, is zero. Now

$$X^2 = x^2 + 2Mx + M^2.$$

On summing, the sum of the central terms on the right vanishes by equation (2.4) and we have

$$S(X^2) = S(x^2) + NM^2,$$

or dividing through by N,

$$\sigma^2 = \frac{S(X^2)}{N} - M^2.$$

In our case of the grouped frequency distribution we must read $S(f_x X^2)$ for $S(X^2)$ and will denote this sum by S_2 for the sake of brevity; N will be denoted by S_0 as before. In this notation

$$\sigma^2 = \frac{S_2}{S_0} - M^2. \tag{2.5}$$

The sums S_1 and S_2 are sometimes termed the first and second *moments* of the distribution about zero as *origin*. Finally, the coefficient of variation v is the ratio of the standard deviation to the mean,

$$v = \frac{\sigma}{M}. \tag{2.6}$$

In other fields of work v is most usually expressed as a percentage, but in our work the coefficients of variation are so large that it is more convenient to use the simple ratio.

2.5. S_0, the total number of separate and distinct nouns in the distribution, is given directly by adding up the column of f_x's. If a calculating machine is available, and it is essential for anyone who is doing much statistical work, the sums S_1 and S_2 can be run off very rapidly on the machine, allowing the products to accumulate on the slide: the squares for S_2 can be taken from Barlow's *Tables* (see refs.). The work should always be checked. In the absence of a calculating machine, multiplication tables can be obtained up to 1000×1000 and may be found useful, but the products must be written down and added, as in col. 3 of Table 2.1 for $f_x X$.

2.6. The values of S_0, S_1 and S_2 are given at the foot of Table 2.1 together with the values of the derived constants. Thus we have at once

$$M = S_1/S_0 = 8225/1168 = 7 \cdot 04195;$$

we keep more digits than will finally be retained in order to ensure accuracy in the standard deviation. For the standard deviation itself,

$$S_2/S_0 = 577,665/1168 = 494 \cdot 57620$$
$$M^2 = 49 \cdot 58906$$
$$\sigma^2 = \overline{444 \cdot 98714}$$

whence $\sigma = 21 \cdot 0947,$

the value being obtained by interpolation in Barlow's *Tables*. Finally,

$$v = \sigma/M = 21 \cdot 0947/7 \cdot 04195 = 2 \cdot 9956,$$

or $3 \cdot 00$ if we round off to a couple of decimal places. In addition to these standard measures I have given the percentage of nouns in the vocabulary that occur only once:

$$100 f_0/S_0 = 100 \times 520/1168 = 44 \cdot 5,$$

and also a figure which has been given by other writers, I think, viz. the number of nouns in the vocabulary per 1000 occurrences of a noun. This is actually 1000 divided by the mean, or

$$1000 S_0/S_1 = 1000 \times 1168/8225 = 142$$

to the nearest unit. It measures the *apparent* richness of the vocabulary *in the given sample*, but as we shall see later (Chapter 5) any wider interpretation is dangerous. Summarising, a noun is repeated on the average some 7 times: the standard deviation is roundly 21 (the reader may note that a range of 6 times this or 126 covers all but the 7 most frequent nouns) and is roundly 3 times the mean; the percentage of nouns occurring only once is $44 \cdot 5$ or little less than half, and there are 142 nouns in the vocabulary per 1000 occurrences of a noun.

2.7. *Illustration* 2.2. Table 2.2 shows the number of Latin nouns occurring once, twice, thrice, etc. in a sample spread over the miscellaneous works of Thomas à Kempis other than the *De Imitatione Christi*. The way in which the sample was taken is fully described in Chapter 9: it was arranged to be of approximately the same length as the *Imitatio*, i.e. to contain about the same number of occurrences of a noun. Actually the number of occurrences is 8203 against 8225. It will be seen that the distribution is distinctly more contracted than the last: the most frequent noun (*Deus*) occurs only 369 times, not 418; the mean is only 5·8 against 7·0; and the standard deviation 16 against 21—the reader may note that a range of 6 times the standard deviation or 96 again covers all but the 7 most frequent nouns.

TABLE 2.2. Showing the number f_x of nouns occurring X times in a sample of 8203 occurrences of a noun spread over the miscellaneous works of Thomas à Kempis other than the *De Imitatione Christi*

X	f_x	X	f_x	X	f_x	X	f_x
1	621	17	7	36	4	68	1
2	216	18	4	38	3	69	1
3	122	19	5	39	3	91	1
4	90	20	6	40	1	93	1
5	66	21	5	42	1	95	1
6	46	22	3	43	3	102	2
7	28	23	2	44	1	115	1
8	30	24	3	45	1	116	1
9	21	26	5	47	3	162	1
10	15	27	4	48	1	200	1
11	11	28	2	50	4	369	1
12	8	29	3	52	1		
13	8	30	3	53	1		
14	7	32	3	56	1	Total	1406
15	10	33	1	59	3		
16	6	34	1	65	1		

$S_0 = 1406$; $S_1 = 8203$; $S_2 = 409{,}619$; $M = 5{\cdot}834$; $\sigma^2 = 257{\cdot}298$; $\sigma = 16{\cdot}045$; $v = 2{\cdot}75$. Percentage of nouns occurring once only $= 44{\cdot}2$. Vocabulary per 1000 occurrences $= 171$.

Corresponding to the more contracted distribution and lower mean number of occurrences, the vocabulary per 1000 occurrences is of course higher, viz. 171 against 142, there being 1406 nouns in the vocabulary as compared with 1168 in the *Imitatio* alone. These changes are perhaps in the direction that might be expected when we pass from one small work, and a very homogeneous work with the exception of Lib. iv, to a sample spread over a number of works of more or less varying character. The percentage of nouns occurring once only is, however, almost exactly the same as before, viz. 44·2 against 44·5. I have not thought it necessary to give, in this and the following cases, the equivalent of cols. 3 to 7 of Table 2.1: the reader can work them out if he likes to see the data in full. But we can give a couple of comparative figures. Interpolating in cols. 6 and 7 of Table 2.1 it will be found that approximately 0·70 per cent of the vocabulary accounts for 20 per cent of the occurrences, and 4·93 per cent of the vocabulary for 50 per cent of the occurrences in the *Imitatio*. For Table 2.2 the corresponding figures are: 0·91 per cent of the vocabulary accounts for 20 per cent of the occurrences, and 6·09 per cent of the vocabulary for 50 per cent of the occurrences. The more frequent nouns are less heavily stressed, as is clear from the form of the distribution.

2.8.   *Illustration* 2.3. Table 2.3 shows the number of (Latin) nouns occurring once, twice, thrice, etc. in a sample spread over the voluminous theological works of Jean Charlier de Gerson (1363–1429), sometime

TABLE 2.3. Showing the number f_x of nouns occurring X times in a sample of 8196 occurrences of a noun spread over the theological works of Gerson

X	f_x	X	f_x	X	f_x	X	f_x
1	804	17	3	35	2	64	1
2	318	18	2	36	1	66	1
3	164	19	5	38	1	67	1
4	98	20	7	39	2	68	1
5	71	21	4	40	3	74	1
6	46	22	4	41	3	86	1
7	34	23	6	42	2	92	1
8	27	24	1	44	2	94	1
9	25	25	2	45	1	102	1
10	16	26	5	46	1	105	1
11	11	27	7	47	1	256	1
12	8	28	2	52	2		
13	10	29	3	56	1		
14	9	30	2	57	1	Total	1754
15	6	32	4	58	1		
16	10	34	4	63	1		

$S_0 = 1754$; $S_1 = 8196$; $S_2 = 248{,}984$; $M = 4·673$; $\sigma^2 = 120·118$; $\sigma = 10·960$; $v = 2·35$.
Percentage of nouns occurring once only $= 45·8$. Vocabulary per 1000 occurrences $= 214$.

Chancellor of the University of Paris, and one of those to whom the authorship of the *De Imitatione Christi* has frequently been ascribed. Particulars of the way in which the sample was taken will be found in Chapter 9: it was again intended that the sample should be of approximately the same size as the *Imitatio*, and actually it will be seen that the number of occurrences is 8196 against 8225, a difference of only 3 or 4 parts in 1000. The distribution is obviously even more contracted than the last. The most frequent noun (*Deus* as before) occurs only 256 times, against 418 and 369. The mean number of occurrences of a noun is only 4·7 roundly, against 7·0 and 5·8; the standard deviation only 11 roundly, against 21 and 16. Correspondingly, the total vocabulary is raised to 1754, against 1168 and 1406, and the vocabulary per 1000 occurrences to 214, against 142 and 171. A range of 6 times the standard deviation, just under 66, covers all but 10 of the most frequent nouns, that is all but 5·7 per thousand: the corresponding figures for Tables 2.1 and 2.2 are 6·0 and 5·0 per thousand. Such figures may help the reader unaccustomed to this measure of dispersion to realise a little better its physical significance. The percentage of nouns occurring once only is a very little higher than for the two previous tables at 45·8. Construction of columns like 6 and 7 of Table 2.1 shows that in this distribution for Gerson it takes 1·25 per cent of the vocabulary to account for 20 per cent of the occurrences, and 7·15 per cent of the vocabulary to account for 50 per cent. Both these figures are higher than those for Table 2.2, and still more exceed those for Table 2.1.

2.9. *Illustration* 2.4. Table 2.4 shows the number of nouns—English nouns this time—in a sample of 8045 occurrences from Macaulay's essay on

TABLE 2.4. Showing the number f_x of nouns occurring X times in a sample of 8045 occurrences of a noun covering the greater part of Macaulay's essay on Bacon

X	f_x	X	f_x	X	f_x	X	f_x
1	990	14	10	27	3	40	1
2	367	15	13	28	4	41	1
3	173	16	3	29	1	45	2
4	112	17	10	30	3	48	1
5	72	18	7	31	2	57	1
6	47	19	6	32	1	58	1
7	41	20	5	33	1	65	1
8	31	21	1	34	1	76	1
9	34	22	4	35	1	81	1
10	17	23	7	36	1	89	1
11	24	24	2	37	1	255	1
12	19	25	1	38	2		
13	10	26	5	39	4	Total	2048

$S_0 = 2048$; $S_1 = 8045$; $S_2 = 183,963$; $M = 3·928$; $\sigma^2 = 74·395$; $\sigma = 8·625$; $v = 2·20$. Percentage of nouns occurring once only = 48·3. Vocabulary per 1000 occurrences = 255.

Bacon. Though strictly speaking a sample, actually it covers the great bulk of the essay apart from Latin quotations, which were excluded: particulars will be found in Chapter 4. Though the actual range of numbers of occurrences is practically the same as in the last case, for the most frequent noun occurs 255 times against 256, this is actually the distribution with the lowest dispersion, as measured by the standard deviation, that we have yet encountered. The standard deviation is only 8·6 roundly, against nearly 11 for the distribution of Table 2.3, and the mean only 3·9 against 4·7. Correspondingly the total vocabulary has risen to 2048, and the vocabulary per thousand occurrences to 255. In comparing Table 2.2 with Table 2.1 we commented that the change to a lower mean and lower standard deviation seemed consonant with what we might expect on passing from a homogeneous work to a sample from heterogeneous works: but here we have a still more contracted or condensed table, based on a number of occurrences only some 2 per cent lower than before, and founded on a single essay. The percentage of nouns occurring only once is a little higher at 48·3. If columns corresponding to cols. 6 and 7 of Table 2.1 are formed, they show that 1·62 per cent of the vocabulary will account for 20 per cent of occurrences and 9·66 per cent of vocabulary for 50 per cent, figures more than double those for the *Imitatio*. As the four tables are all fairly comparable as regards size of sample (total number of occurrences S_1), we may bring together these figures which exemplify so clearly the extent to which the more frequent nouns must colour the style.

The percentage of the vocabulary stated below accounts for:

	20 % of the occurrences	50 % of the occurrences
De Imitatione Christi	0·70	4·93
à Kempis, *Miscellanea*	0·91	6·09
Gerson's theological works	1·25	7·15
Macaulay's essay on Bacon	1·62	9·66

2.10. *Illustration* 2.5. As stated in § 2.1, the words tabulated may be those words only which fall within some special class defined by the investigator, for example, Romance words in Chaucer or other writers of the period. I take as an illustration the nouns which occur in the sample from the theological works of Gerson on which Table 2.3 is based, but which do *not* occur in the Vulgate. Table 2.5 gives the results. As might be expected such nouns show relatively low numbers of occurrences: the three at the extreme tail of the distribution are *theologus* (19 occurrences), *theologia* (34), and *consideratio* (42). In all, the 447 nouns of the class account for only 823 occurrences, and just over 70 per cent of them occur only once in the sample. Further details will be found in Chapter 9, § 9.15.

2.11. *Illustration* 2.6. So far all the tables have been based on nouns, and all my own work has been based on them. Simply for the sake of illustration I have, however, compiled a couple of distributions for adjectives and for verbs respectively in the *De Imitatione Christi*, compiling them from Storr's

Concordance as before. As the tables were formed simply as examples, the words were not booked on to cards, but the scale of X was written down along one side of sheets of foolscap, the number of occurrences in the concordance

TABLE 2.5. Showing the number f_x of non-Vulgate nouns occurring X times in the sample on which Table 2.3 is based

X	f_x	X	f_x	X	f_x
1	315	7	4	19	1
2	69	8	1	34	1
3	28	9	2	42	1
4	14	10	1		
5	6	13	1	Total	447
6	2	16	1		

$S_0 = 447$; $S_1 = 823$; $S_2 = 5517$; $M = 1 \cdot 841$; $\sigma^2 = 8 \cdot 952$; $\sigma = 2 \cdot 992$; $v = 1 \cdot 63$. Percentage of nouns occurring once only $= 70 \cdot 5$. Vocabulary per 1000 occurrences $= 543$.

TABLE 2.6. Showing the number f_x of adjectives occurring X times in the *De Imitatione Christi*: compiled from Storr's *Concordance* (ref. 2.2)

X	f_x	X	f_x	X	f_x	X	f_x
1	203	16	4	33	3	56	2
2	75	17	2	34	1	58	1
3	49	18	5	35	1	60	1
4	30	19	3	36	1	64	1
5	18	20	1	37	1	66	2
6	20	21	2	38	2	83	1
7	18	22	2	39	1	87	1
8	12	23	4	40	2	146	1
9	11	24	1	41	1	147	1
10	4	26	2	42	1	171	1
11	6	27	1	44	1	210	1
12	6	28	2	45	1	227	1
13	3	29	2	48	1	586	1
14	1	30	1	49	1		
15	5	32	2	54	1	Total	529

$S_0 = 529$; $S_1 = 5053$; $S_2 = 609{,}121$; $M = 9 \cdot 552$; $\sigma^2 = 1060 \cdot 217$; $\sigma = 32 \cdot 561$; $v = 3 \cdot 41$. Percentage of adjectives occurring once only $= 38 \cdot 4$. Vocabulary per 1000 occurrences $= 105$.

counted, and a tick made against the corresponding value of X. These ticks were grouped in fives and could be rapidly counted up when the distribution was finished. But no checking of the classification is possible on this method, and consequently the accuracy of the distribution cannot be completely trusted, though it is not likely that any mistakes have been made which will appreciably affect the results. Working in this way, of course it is not possible to give the actual vocabulary, but a few of the more frequent words were noted as the work progressed. Table 2.6 shows the distribution for adjectives. The number of separate adjectives counted is less than half that of the nouns, only 529, but mean and standard deviation are both higher. The distribution is of the same general form, but the percentage of adjectives occurring only once is lower than for nouns, viz. 38·4 against 44·5.

2.12.   *Illustration 2.7.* Table 2.7 gives the corresponding table for verbs: participles, sometimes entered separately in the concordance, were counted in with the verb, and the passive voice with the active. The verb *esse* is not

TABLE 2.7. Showing the number f_x of verbs occurring X times in the *De Imitatione Christi*: compiled from Storr's *Concordance* (ref. 2.2). The verb *esse* not included

X	f_x	X	f_x	X	f_x	X	f_x
1	407	17	11	34	1	75	1
2	175	18	4	35	3	76	1
3	99	19	7	36	3	77	1
4	74	20	7	41	1	79	3
5	77	21	7	42	1	95	1
6	43	22	5	43	2	97	1
7	34	23	2	46	1	108	1
8	27	24	2	47	1	111	2
9	26	25	2	49	2	155	1
10	15	26	1	51	1	196	1
11	18	27	2	53	1	206	1
12	13	28	4	54	1	225	1
13	13	29	1	56	1		
14	10	30	6	58	1		
15	12	31	3	60	1	Total	1157
16	11	33	2	65	1		

$S_0 = 1157$; $S_1 = 8116$; $S_2 = 356,654$; $M = 7\cdot015$; $\sigma^2 = 259\cdot052$; $\sigma = 16\cdot095$; $v = 2\cdot29$. Percentage of verbs occurring once only = 35·2. Vocabulary per 1000 occurrences = 143.

entered completely in the concordance and is consequently not included here. It is interesting to compare this table with Table 2.1. The values of S_0 and S_1 are only slightly higher for the nouns than for the verbs and the two means are almost the same (7·042 and 7·015), but the standard deviation for the nouns is much larger than for the verbs, viz. 21 against 16. The result is that the frequencies f_x are smaller for the verbs than for the nouns at the beginning and end of the table, and larger over the central portion, thus:

	Frequencies	
X	Nouns	Verbs
1–3	805	681
4–25	293	420
26 upwards	70	56
Total	1168	1157

2.13.   My object in limiting myself to nouns for the investigation into the vocabularies of Thomas à Kempis and Gerson was in part simply the limitation of material and the exclusion of words of little or no significance as regards style, such as prepositions, pronouns, etc. Of the three principal parts of speech, nouns, adjectives and verbs, I thought nouns would probably be the most significant or characteristic. My few notes on Tables 2.6 and 2.7 seem, at first sight at all events, to bear out this conjecture. The adjectives with greatest numbers of occurrences from $X = 54$ onwards are *unus*, *devotus*, *nullus*, *malus*, *caelestis*, *humilis*, *proprius*, *solus*, *aeternus*, *verus*, *totus*, *sanctus*, *multus*, *magnus*, *bonus* and *omnis*. The only adjectives in this list at all clearly suggestive of a religious work are *devotus*, *caelestis*, *humilis*, *aeternus* and *sanctus*, with perhaps *malus* and *bonus*. The remaining adjectives seem neutral or indifferent words that might well occur in any writing by any author on any subject. In the case of the verbs I only noted unfortunately the few that occurred 95 times or more. These are *quaerere*, *videre*, *dare*, *debere*, *dicere*, *velle*, *facere* (including *fieri*), *habere* and *posse*. There is not a single one, with the possible exception of *debere*, clearly indicative of the fact that we have to deal with a Christian religious work. This is in sharp contrast with the nouns; the 25 most frequent nouns in the *Imitatio* are *desiderium*, *tempus*, *tribulatio*, *virtus*, *tentatio*, *caelum*, *crux*, *res*, *veritas*, *filius*, *gloria*, *anima*, *spiritus*, *verbum*, *pax*, *amor*, *consolatio*, *mundus*, *vita*, *nihil* (*nil*, *nihilum*), *cor*, *gratia*, *dominus*, *homo* and *Deus*. Here the neutral words are conspicuous by their rarity: *tempus*, *res* and *nihil* seem the only three. Nevertheless caution is necessary in drawing any conclusion. The frequency with which such neutral or indifferent words are used by any author may be just as characteristic of his writing as the frequency with which he uses words more definitely allied to his subject; they may point quite clearly to habits or tricks of style. My first notion in fact involved a confusion of thought between characteristics of subject and characteristics of style. The nouns *consideratio*, *pars* and *modus*, for example, are quite neutral words: but the frequency with which they are used by Gerson is distinctly characteristic of his writings as compared with those of Thomas à Kempis (cf. Chapter 10, § 10.12). The point calls for further investigation, since I have used nouns alone for comparison of style. It is possible that the very 'neutrality' of verbs and adjectives, their relative independence of subject, might render them a better basis for investigation. Only trial can show. It must be remembered, however, that choice of subject within the given field is also characteristic of the author. *Theologia* and *theologus* are words to be expected in religious writings: neither occurs in the *Imitatio*; the second alone occurs but once in the sample from the miscellaneous writings of Thomas à Kempis; the first occurs 34 times and the second 19 times in the samples from Gerson.

2.14.   All the tables that we have given, without a single exception, have one characteristic in common, viz. that words occurring only once are the most frequent. There is no immediately obvious theoretical reason for this, and the question arises whether the rule is really universal or no. The tables given relate to relatively small samples: it is true that Tables 2.1, 2.6 and 2.7 refer to an entire work, but that work may be regarded as a small sample —though anything but a random sample—from the totality of the works of Thomas à Kempis, if for the moment we admit his authorship. Now it was pointed out in § 1.7, and it will do no harm to repeat the passage, that if we go on extending the size of sample from a given work, or a given author's works, the distribution itself will continually extend. If in 2000 occurrences of a noun taken at random from the given work the most frequent noun occurs some 50 times, in 4000 occurrences of a noun taken at random from the same work it will probably occur some 100 times, more or less. Everything—apparently—about the distribution will in fact alter as the size of sample is increased: the mean number of occurrences will go up; its reciprocal, the vocabulary per 1000 occurrences, will go down; any measure of scatter or dispersion will rise rapidly; *the percentage of nouns used only once will fall slowly.* This suggests that, if only we take a long enough work, words used twice or even thrice may prove to be the most frequent. The Bible suggested itself as a much longer work on which trial might be made. Cruden's well-known concordance is available for the Authorised Version, and a concordance (ref. 2.3) is also available for the Vulgate. It seemed to me that Cruden would prove rather inconvenient owing to the way in which some words are split into sub-sections, and I decided, perhaps mistakenly,* to use the concordance to the Vulgate. It proved most troublesome. In addition to the texts listed, many articles lead off with a series of references to some 60 pages or more of preliminary Synoptic Tables: for careful work all these references should be checked, both to make sure that they do not overlap with texts cited and to see whether they contain only one mention of the word or more. Many articles again are not complete in themselves

* No, not mistakenly. Later experience has convinced me that the use of Cruden's *Concordance* would have been not merely inconvenient (see remarks in § 6.21) but wholly unsafe as the foundation of a word-distribution. Some words are actually missing, and lists of references seem not infrequently defective or the necessary cross-references that would complete them to be missing: e.g. under *way* no cross-reference is given to *go* or *went*, under which phrases like *Go thy way*, *Went his way*, etc. are listed, and not under *way* itself. My experience is based on the old edition used (ref. 6.8), but it may be doubted if recent editions are better.

but refer the reader to other articles for further citations. As a striking instance, the article *plăga* (region, quarter) contains only 7 references: but it leads off with 'Vide *australis, meridianus, occidentalis, orientalis,* et *septentrionalis*'. From these articles I made up a total of no less than 60 references in all. References to duplicate texts before or after the main text are a minor vexation: they will be picked up by a careful reader, but are very liable to be overlooked in a hasty count. These are all sources of trouble which could be overcome by anyone willing to give sufficient time and care to the work. But the fact that some articles are simply incomplete rules out the possibility of compiling from this concordance any complete and accurate table at all. With entries like *et alibi passim, passim, multa omittuntur* one can do nothing, and the articles *Deus* and *dominus* (with the articles to which cross-references are given under these heads) seem to be particularly afflicted in this way. The concordance was, of course, never intended to be used for our purely statistical purpose and the fact that it is imperfect for that end implies no reflection on those who gave so much labour to its compilation. But, in the circumstances, any table based on it must be taken as the roughest approximation, sufficient only to show the general form of the distribution and to answer the question whether once-used words are still, in a work of this length, the most frequent.

2.15.   *Illustration 2.8.* As my previous work had dealt for the most part with nouns, it was decided to confine the investigation to nouns in the Vulgate. Merely to get a notion of the general form of the distribution it was obviously needless to attempt a complete tabulation, and in fact a little experience showed that the attempt would be futile, for the reasons stated in the preceding paragraph. It was accordingly decided to proceed by way of sample and begin with nouns under the initial A; nouns with initial D were then chosen, because from the experience with Thomas à Kempis and Gerson it was thought that *Deus* and *dominus* would be amongst the most frequently occurring nouns and so would give some notion of the range; and finally nouns under P and S were taken, as it was known from the previous work that these letters would provide large numbers of nouns. Altogether these four letters cover some 38 per cent of the pages of the concordance proper. Table 2.8 shows the results. The work was done rapidly and cannot pretend to accuracy as has already been emphasised, but there is no doubt at all as to the general result. The distribution is just of the same form as before, nouns occurring once only being still the most frequent. The percentage of once-occurring nouns is, however, lower than in Tables 2.1 to 2.4, viz. 24 per cent against 44 to 48 per cent. The corresponding percentages for nouns under the several initial letters are very consistent: A's, 22·8 per cent; D's, 23·6 per cent; P's, 25·0 per cent; S's, 24·1 per cent—deviations

TABLE 2.8. Showing the number f_x of nouns beginning with A, D, P or S occurring X times in the Vulgate: compiled from *Concordance* (ref. 2.3): for difficulties see § 2.14

X	f_x	X	f_x	X	f_x	X	f_x
1	317	41	1	87	2	218	1
2	172	42	4	88	1	222	1
3	121	43	6	90	2	228	1
4	74	44	4	92	1	251	1
5	58	45	2	94	2	253	1
6	38	46	3	95	1	255	1
7	38	47	4	96	3	257	1
8	35	48	4	97	1	276	1
9	28	49	4	99	2	308	1
10	32	50	2	100	1	311	1
11	16	51	2	101	1	323	1
12	30	52	4	102	1	336	1
13	13	53	4	104	2	352	1
14	14	54	2	105	1	353	1
15	7	55	3	106	1	358	1
16	7	56	1	109	1	363	1
17	11	58	1	112	1	394	1
18	9	59	3	113	1	440	1
19	9	60	3	115	1	452	1
20	11	61	3	116	3	477	1
21	7	62	3	117	1	553	1
22	7	63	2	122	1	573	1
23	10	64	3	124	1	634	1
24	8	65	1	125	1	658	1
25	9	66	1	133	1	720	1
26	5	67	2	135	1	727	1
27	2	68	1	138	1	758	1
28	2	69	1	139	1	848	1
29	5	70	2	140	1	853	1
30	5	71	1	143	1	1521	1
31	7	73	2	158	1	1969	1
32	8	75	2	169	1	2055	1
33	3	77	1	181	1	2474	1
34	5	78	3	185	1	4500*	1
35	4	79	2	186	1	7500*	1
36	2	80	1	188	1		
37	2	81	3	189	1		
38	4	82	1	206	1	Total	1321
39	1	85	2	212	1		
40	4	86	2	216	2		

* Figures uncertain, probably in defect: see text.

being well within the limits of random sampling. The Vulgate, at a very rough guess, I should put at some 17 or 18 times the length of the *Imitatio*, and the effect of this great increase in 'size of sample' has been just about to halve the percentage of nouns occurring once, no more, and to leave them by far the most frequent: nouns occurring twice are only 13 per cent of the total. The dispersion of the distribution is naturally very high: there are six nouns with well over 1000 occurrences each: *pater*, with 1521 occurrences counted—but I do not expect any of these figures to have great precision; *domus*, 1969; *populus*, 2055; *dies*, 2474 are the first four. *Deus* I counted up to 4363 and *dominus* to 7378 but am sure these figures are in defect for the reasons stated in § 2.14, so have rounded them up to 4500 and 7500 respectively. Even so these numbers may be considerably below the truth: a special count would have to be made to arrive at correct figures. Since the data must be regarded as so rough I have not given the mean, standard deviation, etc. of this distribution.

2.16.   *Illustration 2.9.* It seemed possible that a distribution with a maximum frequency not at 1 but at 2 or 3 occurrences might be obtained by a method other than that of increasing the size of sample, namely by greatly limiting the vocabulary at the writer's disposal. This is readily done by compelling him to write in Basic English. I therefore decided to draw up a table based on the Gospel according to St John in Basic English (ref. 2.4). The normal Basic vocabulary lists 600 nouns, viz. 400 'Things-General' and 200 'Things-Pictured'. In addition to these, for this special book there is a list of 49 'Bible' nouns and also 90 under the heading 'Verse'. The writer is, however, permitted to form other nouns from these by rule, e.g. agent-nouns in -*er* like *changer, teacher, worshipper, sinner, gardener*, and nouns of action in -*ing* like *saying, offering, cutting, planting*, to cite examples that actually occur in the Gospel. But there is a number of other nouns used in the Gospel but not in the lists. *King* is not in the lists, though *kingdom* is given in the 'Bible' list; *outlaw* is not listed but is perhaps justified as a compound of *out* and *law*. *Police* will be found in chap. 18, vv. 3, 12 and 22, but is not listed and the justification for this baffles me. Weights and measures (*gallon, mile, yard*) again are not listed, nor such words as *Passover, Synagogue* and *Temple*, nor plant names like *palm* and *fig*. As I wished to form a table based on a specific vocabulary, I decided to ignore all such additional nouns, and adjectives used substantivally, and confine myself to those nouns alone which are specified in the lists. Even from these I omitted one, viz. 'evil' in the 'Verse' list, regarding it as an adjective used substantivally. This makes the total number of 'nouns', so defined, at the writer's disposal $600 + 49 + 89 = 738$.

2.17.   As these 'Basic' books are inexpensive, it was possible to adopt the simplest process for booking up the data: each noun as it occurred was entered on a card and the first and subsequent occurrences booked up by ticks or strokes in groups of five: after it was entered, every word was struck through in pencil in the text. Even with this simple procedure, as those who have done any such work will know, it is only too easy for errors to be made. It is quite easy to overlook a noun. If the page is re-read to amend such omissions—and I did re-read it—well, it may have happened that the word

TABLE 2.9. Showing the number f_x of nouns (in lists 'General', 'Pictured', 'Bible', 'Verse', see text) occurring X times in the Basic English version of the Gospel according to St John (ref. 2.4)

X	f_x	X	f_x	X	f_x	X	f_x
1	72	14	3	27	2	64	1
2	49	15	2	28	2	67	1
3	32	16	1	31	2	69	1
4	23	17	2	32	1	71	1
5	18	18	2	34	1	75	1
6	5	19	2	37	1	85	1
7	8	20	1	38	1	87	1
8	4	21	4	40	3	90	1
9	6	22	3	43	1	139	1
10	5	23	2	44	2	149	1
11	8	24	2	60	1		
12	7	25	2	62	1	Total	296
13	1	26	3	63	1		

$S_0 = 296$; $S_1 = 3088$; $S_2 = 137,982$; $M = 10 \cdot 432$; $\sigma^2 = 357 \cdot 320$; $\sigma = 18 \cdot 903$; $v = 1 \cdot 81$. Percentage of once-nouns = $24 \cdot 3$. Vocabulary per 1000 occurrences = 96.

was entered but not struck through, and now gets entered twice. It is highly unlikely, however, that errors will have been so numerous as appreciably to affect the results. These are given in Table 2.9. It will be seen that, notwithstanding the great limitation of the vocabulary and the fact that 296 out of the 738 permitted nouns (or 40 per cent of them) have been used, the table is still of the usual form with once-occurring nouns, or once-nouns as we may perhaps term them for brevity, again the most frequent. But the percentage of such nouns is only about half that of Tables 2.1 to 2.4 although the sample is a much smaller one, some 3000 occurrences against 8000: there are 72 once-nouns out of 296, or 24·3 per cent. This is almost exactly the same as the percentage of once-nouns in the whole of the Vulgate, as estimated by the sample of Table 2.8, viz. 24 per cent.

2.18. Comparison with these earlier tables may, however, be a little dangerous if we interpret differences as due solely to Basic English. It is possible that they may be due in whole or in part to the essential style of the Gospel. No one, in fact, can read the Gospel with any attention without noticing how highly *repetitive* is that style. More especially in the long discourses attributed to Jesus one noun may be repeated over and over again within a few verses. Thus in chap. 15, vv. 18, 19 (I quote the A.V.) we have:

18. If the *world* hate you, ye know that it hated me before it hated you. 19. If ye were of the *world*, the *world* would love his own: but because ye are not of the *world*, but I have chosen you out of the *world*, therefore the *world* hateth you.

Or again in chap. 6, vv. 31–35:

31. ...He gave them *bread* from heaven to eat. 32. Then Jesus said unto them, Verily, verily, I say unto you, Moses gave you not that *bread* from heaven; but my Father giveth you the true *bread* from heaven. 33. For the *bread* of God is he which cometh down from heaven, and giveth life unto the world. 34. Then said they unto him, Lord, evermore give us this *bread*. 35. And Jesus said unto them, I am the *bread* of life.

And these phrases and ideas are taken up and repeated later in the same discourse:

48. I am that *bread* of life.... 50. This is the *bread* which cometh down from heaven, that a man may eat thereof, and not die. 51. I am the living *bread* which came down from heaven: if any man eat of this *bread*, he shall live for ever: and the *bread* that I will give is my flesh, which I will give for the life of the world.

58. This is that *bread* which came down from heaven: not as your fathers did eat manna, and are dead: he that eateth of this *bread* shall live for ever.

In the first passage 'world', in the second group of passages 'bread', is repeated again and again and, as it is hardly necessary to add, the English in this respect directly follows the Greek. It seemed very possible that this tendency to repetition would in itself tend to reduce the percentage of nouns occurring only once, and it was therefore thought desirable to draw up a comparative table based on the Authorised Version. This was done in exactly the same way. To get a fair comparison any 'omitted noun' of the Basic Version (e.g. nouns in -*er* and -*ing*; *Synagogue*, *Temple*, *Passover*, etc.; weights and measures; plant names; *king*, *police*, and a good many others) was omitted also in the A.V. work if occurring in the same passage: but if one of these 'omitted nouns' occurred in the A.V. where it was represented in the B.V. by some other noun or phrase it was included. A noun of an 'omitted' *class* in the A.V. (e.g. a noun in -*er* or -*ing*) was similarly included if represented in the B.V. by an included noun or by some periphrasis.

2.19. *Illustration* 2.10. Table 2.10 shows the results for nouns in this restricted sense, in the Gospel according to St John, A.V. It will be seen that the table differs remarkably from Table 2.9 for the B.V. There are 353 nouns in the vocabulary against 296; but *per contra* there are only 2248 occurrences of a noun in the A.V. against 3088 in the B.V. The B.V. is *much* more substantival in its style than the A.V., notwithstanding the limited vocabulary. This arises largely no doubt from the periphrases used in Basic English as a substitute for verbs, e.g. 'have love for' in place of 'love' (*vb.*), 'his answer was' or 'make answer' in place of 'answer' (*vb.*), and such phrases as 'put the question' or 'make request' for 'ask', with the result

Table 2.10. Showing the number f_x of nouns (limited to correspond with Table 2.9, see text) occurring X times in the Authorised Version of St John's Gospel

X	f_x	X	f_x	X	f_x	X	f_x
1	151	11	3	22	2	80	1
2	54	12	4	23	1	82	1
3	27	13	5	24	4	83	1
4	24	14	3	26	1	137	1
5	14	15	1	38	1	145	1
6	10	17	1	42	1		
7	8	18	5	43	1		
8	8	19	2	47	1	Total	353
9	4	20	3	64	1		
10	5	21	2	76	1		

$S_0 = 353$; $S_1 = 2248$; $S_2 = 92,164$; $M = 6\cdot368$; $\sigma^2 = 220\cdot532$; $\sigma = 14\cdot850$; $v = 2\cdot33$. Percentage of once-nouns = 42·8. Vocabulary per 1000 occurrences = 157.

that 'love' (*sb.*) occurs only 7 times in the A.V. but 40 times in the B.V., 'answer' (*sb.*) twice only in the A.V. but 67 times in the B.V., 'question' once only in the A.V. but 21 times in the B.V., and 'request', which does not occur at all in the A.V., is used 15 times in the B.V. To continue the comparison, the mean for the A.V. is down by some 40 per cent as compared with the B.V., but the standard deviation down by little more than 20 per cent, so that the coefficient of variation is raised from 1·8 to 2·3. The vocabulary per 1000 occurrences is raised from 96 to 157 and finally the percentage of once-nouns is raised from 24·3 to 42·8. Even this last is a very low figure for so small a sample: the experiment described in a later chapter (Chapter 4, see especially Table 4.5, col. 9) shows some 60 per cent of nouns occurring only once in samples of some 2000 occurrences and round about 54–55 per cent in samples of some 4000 occurrences. The conjecture that the low percentage of once-nouns in the Basic Version is due in part not to the Basic English, but simply to the style of the original, seems accordingly quite justified. The contrast between Table 2.9 and Table 2.10, however, exhibits very clearly the peculiarity of Basic as against normal English, and shows how effectively this method of tabulation can bring out such differences. The most frequent noun in these tables is *man* and the second *father*:

the small differences between the numbers of occurrences recorded may be due to errors. The restriction on nouns included in Table 2.10 renders it, of course, not fully comparable with other tables for nouns.

2.20. The facts shown by the preceding tables throw a good deal of light on the difficulty of acquiring the vocabulary of a new language simply by reading a book in that language: for it is clear that relatively few words out of the whole vocabulary are repeated sufficiently often to enforce their meaning on the memory. Thus, suppose someone with no previous knowledge of Latin, but desirous of acquiring sufficient knowledge of that language to read mediaeval works, decides to begin his reading with the *De Imitatione Christi*, an excellent choice since its style is extremely simple. He is getting on in years; his verbal memory is no longer what it was, and it is quite likely that he will come across a noun a dozen times before its meaning is fairly driven into his rapidly hardening brain. How many nouns will he really know at the end of a first reading of the *Imitatio*? Reference to Table 2.1 shows that only 140 of the 1168 nouns occur a dozen times or more, so that will be the extent of his acquirements. Would he have done any better to read varied passages from the miscellaneous works of Thomas à Kempis, totalling to the same length as the *Imitatio*? No: Table 2.2 shows that in the sample from those works there are again just 140 nouns occurring a dozen times or more. Or again, would he have done better to read varied passages from the theological works of Gerson, amounting in all to the same length as the *Imitatio*? No: for once more, by a remarkable fluke, the number of nouns in Table 2.3 occurring a dozen times or more is exactly 140. And if our student had been a foreigner who started learning English by tackling Macaulay's essay on Bacon, *he* would find in a length of it equal to our sample of Table 2.4 again 140 nouns occurring a dozen times or more, or something near that number.

2.21. The illustration is, of course, an over-simplification of the case. The meanings of words are not learned, separately and individually, merely by repetition alone. The learning of one noun helps the learning of related nouns, or verbs or adjectives; the learning of a verb helps the learning of related nouns; the knowledge of derived English words may help; some phrase or aphorism may stick in the mind and enable it to retain the meaning of a word seen for the very first time—and so forth. But the tables do show very well the fundamental source of trouble. I myself was not very far from the position of the imaginary learner when, at an age a few years short of sixty, I decided to try to build up again some knowledge of Latin, neglected since my schooldays; moved to the attempt mainly by the desire of reading the *De Imitatione Christi* and St Augustine's *Confessions* in the original.   I had, of course, a small but only a very small vocabulary remaining from what I had learnt in school, and the re-acquirement of even a moderate vocabulary took a surprisingly long time. Now I understand why. That my verbal memory was not what it had been I knew very well: that I had to be introduced to a new word again and again before I really got to know it was soon forced on my attention. But I did not realise how small was the proportion of words repeated with sufficient frequency to be fairly driven into *my* rapidly hardening brain.

2.22.   The tables also show that notwithstanding the constancy of the general form of the distribution (words occurring only once being in every instance the most frequent) the various distributions differ largely from one

TABLE 2.11. Summary of the principal constants for Tables 2.1 to 2.4

Constant	Table 2.1 *De Imitatione Christi*	Table 2.2 à Kempis, *Miscellanea*	Table 2.3 Gerson's theological works	Table 2.4 Macaulay's essay
Vocabulary S_0	1168	1406	1754	2048
Number of occurrences S_1	8225	8203	8196	8045
Mean M	7·042	5·834	4·673	3·928
Vocabulary per 1000 occurrences	142	171	214	255
Standard deviation σ	21·095	16·045	10·960	8·625
Coefficient of variation σ/M	3·00	2·75	2·35	2·20
Percentage of once-nouns	44·5	44·2	45·8	48·3

another in other respects. We can only at present safely compare distributions based on approximately the same size of sample, i.e. number of occurrences, but Tables 2.1–2.4 serve very well in this respect. They are all based on some 8000 occurrences of a noun, S_1 ranging between 8045 and 8225. Table 2.11 brings together the principal constants or measures for these four distributions. The first and last distributions, Tables 2.1 and 2.4, are closely comparable with each other in so far as both are based on single works, though the first is in Latin (the *Imitatio*) and the second in English (Macaulay's essay on Bacon). Yet they are strongly contrasted. The vocabulary of the first (1168) is only 57 per cent that of the last (2048). The mean number of occurrences of a noun is roundly 7 in the *Imitatio*, only 4 in Macaulay's essay, or reciprocally the vocabulary of the *Imitatio* is only 142 nouns per 1000 occurrences, of Macaulay's essay 255. The standard deviation is roundly 21·1 for the first table, 8·6 for the last; the coefficients of variation are 3·0 and 2·2. Only in the percentages of once-nouns (the last line of

Table 2.11) do we fail to find any great difference, though as we should expect the percentage is the higher for Table 2.4. All the differences point to the author of the *Imitatio* concentrating his emphasis on relatively few words, too full of the vital things he has to say to be careful of variety of diction, while Macaulay exuberates in words. The reader may remember that anagram cited by Augustus De Morgan in the *Budget of Paradoxes* (p. 83 of the original edition of 1872):

> Thomas Babington Macaulay
> Mouths big: a Cantab anomaly,

and it is amusing to recall the tirade of *The Times* (26 September 1839, reprinted in the issue for the same date in 1939) on the 'anomaly's' appointment to the War Office:

> Mr Babington Macaulay—Mr Babington Macaulay—mighty in language— a deliverer of all but interminable speeches—busy yourself with aspirations— confine yourself to words—leave substances unmolested. Beware of *things*. Touch not the world of action. You are a machine for giving utterance to noises.

Very varied noises they are too, producing an astonishing diversity of words. Thomas of Cambridge and Thomas of Kempen are well contrasted, in their verbal styles as in their minds and their lives.

2.23.   Tables 2.2 and 2.3 are founded, not on single writings, but on samples widely spread over the collected works of the respective authors, Thomas à Kempis and Gerson. They do not differ so greatly as Tables 2.1 and 2.4, but the vocabulary of 2.3 (1754) is 25 per cent greater than that of 2.2 (1406), its mean is correspondingly lower, and the standard deviation is lower by over 30 per cent. While the percentages of once-nouns in these four tables only show relatively small differences, Tables 2.9 and 2.10 warn us that this percentage may be found considerably divergent in writings of a wholly different style. If the Gospel on which the two tables are based had been of such a length as to give a sample more nearly comparable with those of Tables 2.1 to 2.4, the Authorised Version would have given a percentage of once-occurring nouns much lower than 42, and the Basic Version a percentage much lower than 24, for as we have seen, and as is well illustrated by the sampling experiment described in Chapter 4, to which we have already referred, the percentage falls with increasing size of sample.

2.24.   A few words in conclusion on a point of terminology. In work of this kind one may state the proportion of words of some special class in two wholly distinct ways: (*a*) the proportion of such words in the complete list of separate and distinct words used by the author; (*b*) the proportion of such words in the author's text, every word being counted as often as it occurs. Joseph Mersand in his study of *Chaucer's Romance Vocabulary* (ref. 2.5) termed the simple word list the 'static vocabulary', the aggregate of words in the text (each word entered as often as it occurs) the 'dynamic vocabulary', though at times he uses other phrases. These expressions do not seem to me very happy. A statistician would more naturally use such expressions as 'the simple vocabulary' and 'the weighted vocabulary'. But brief terms are more convenient, and to me at least 'vocabulary' is primarily suggestive of the simple word list, a view supported by the dictionaries. I propose accordingly to confine it to this sense alone. By the *vocabulary* of an author I mean the list of words (or it may be nouns or other special class of words) that he uses. Elliptically one may also use the term *vocabulary* for the *number* of words in that list, the sum S_0, in the sense in which one may write 'the vocabulary of nouns in the *Imitatio* is 1168'. For the aggregate of words that occur it is often sufficient to use such terms as 'the text', 'the nouns in the text', as does Mersand himself on occasion: but more often one is only concerned with the *number* of such words and I find it more distinctive to speak of this as 'the number of occurrences', i.e. of a word or a noun or whatever it may be—the sum S_1. Thus we have from Tables 2.3 and 2.5,

Table 2.3. Sample of nouns from the theological works of Gerson:

$$S_0 = 1754; \quad S_1 = 8196,$$

Table 2.5. Non-Vulgate nouns in the same sample:

and hence, $\qquad S_0 = 447; \quad S_1 = 823,$

Percentage of non-Vulgate nouns in vocabulary $= 44{,}700/1754 = 25 \cdot 5,$
Percentage of non-Vulgate nouns in occurrences $= 82{,}300/8196 = 10 \cdot 0.$

The difference between the two percentages is due of course to the fact that non-Vulgate nouns, as pointed out in § 2.10, show relatively low numbers of occurrences, over 70 per cent of them occurring only once in the sample. The reader will find some warnings as to the first method of stating the proportion in Chapter 5.

2.25.   Not only while the preceding work was being done, but for long after, I was unaware that anyone had compiled word-distributions such as those given in the preceding tables. It was not until after the draft of the great bulk of this book had been completed that I was given a reference to the work of Zipf (ref. 2.6), in whose monograph will be found three somewhat similar tables for Latin, for English and for Chinese. His tables differ from mine, however, in two important respects: in the first place he includes *all* words, not limiting himself, as I have done for the most part, to a single class of words (nouns), and in the second place his definition of 'word' (for the purposes of his work) is entirely different from mine. Zipf enters every inflection separately, I do not. Every case, singular or plural, of *homo* was entered by me under the card for that noun. By Zipf each case is entered separately, so that we find in his data:

Word	Number of occurrences	Word	Number of occurrences
homo	67	*homini*	19
hominem	64	*hominis*	6
homines	26	*homine*	3
hominum	20	*hominibus*	3

yielding eight separate headings of entry where I would have had only one. But Zipf also goes further than this, entering separately such contracted forms as *hominist* and *homos*, as well as words with an enclitic such as *adulescentiaeque, bonasque, cumque*. The difference of practice is no doubt due to our difference of aim, for Zipf is solely concerned with linguistic problems, but it is obvious that it renders our tables wholly non-comparable, more especially for a highly inflected language like Latin. Zipf's table for Latin is based on over 34,000 occurrences, but shows 64 per cent of once-words, a figure far higher than any of mine, as might have been expected. For his (or Eldridge's) English table the difference is naturally less startling, as English is so much less inflected, but the percentage of once-words is 49·6 for a table based on nearly 44,000 occurrences. A table based on over 20,000 occurrences of a noun in Macaulay's essays, in my own work (Table 6.4), gives only 41·2 per cent of once-nouns, and a table based on over 16,000 occurrences of a noun in four of Bunyan's works (Table 6.7) gives 41·5 per cent.

REFERENCES

A. STATISTICAL METHOD

The reader with no previous knowledge of statistical method may find it of service to be given some references to a text-book. References will be given here to *An Introduction to the Theory of Statistics* by G. Udny Yule and M. G. Kendall, 11th edition, 1937 or 12th edition, 1940. London: Charles Griffin & Co. Ltd. It is cited briefly hereafter as 'Y & K'.

In Chapter 6 will be found a considerable collection of frequency distributions from other sources, illustrating the variety of forms which such distributions may take. Worked out examples of the calculation of the mean and standard deviation will be found in Chapters 7 and 8. At the end of the book, pp. 524–5, will be found lists of 'Tables useful in calculation' and 'Tables useful in statistical work'. The most useful in such work as the present is:

(2.1) Barlow's *Tables of Squares, Cubes, Square Roots, Cube Roots and Reciprocals of all Integer Numbers up to* 10,000. New edition, 1930. London and New York: E. F. & F. N. Spon.

B.   Citations in Text or Tables

(2.2) Storr, Rayner (1911). *Concordantia ad quatuor libros latine scriptos De Imitatione Christi editos* A.D. M.CCCC.XLI *a Thoma Kempensi.* Altera editio. Oxford: University Press.

(2.3) PP. Peultier, Étienne et Gantois (1897). *Concordantiarum universae scripturae sacrae thesaurus.* Parisiis: P. Lethielleux.

(2.4) Smith, Edwin W. (1938). *The Basic St John.* London: Kegan Paul, Trench, Trubner & Co. Ltd.

(2.5) Mersand, Joseph (1937). *Chaucer's Romance Vocabulary.* Brooklyn, New York: The Comet Press Inc.

(2.6) Zipf, G. K. (1932). *Selected Studies of the Principle of Relative Frequency in Language.* Harvard University Press. The data for English in this work are cited from the following, which I have not seen:

(2.7) Eldridge, R. C. (1911). *Six thousand Common English Words.* Privately printed at Niagara Falls, New York.

References to the texts used for Tables 2.2 and 2.3 will be found at the end of Chapter 9.

Chapter 3

THEORY OF THE WORD-DISTRIBUTION, WITH AN EXORDIUM ON SAMPLING: THE CHARACTERISTIC

3.1.   This chapter is really, as stated in the heading, concerned with the theory of the word-distribution, but in order to clear the ground I am going to start with an exordium on *sampling*. It has already been necessary to use the term *sample* a good many times. Table 2.2 is based on a *sample* from the works of Thomas à Kempis, Table 2.3 on a *sample* from the works of Gerson, Table 2.8 on a *sample* of nouns in the Vulgate. The comment has been made (§ 2.14) that although Tables 2.1, 2.6 and 2.7 refer to an entire work 'that work may be regarded as a *small sample*—though anything but a *random sample*—from the totality of the works of Thomas à Kempis, if for the moment we admit his authorship'. And finally (§§ 1.7 and 2.14) we have pointed out the difficulty caused by the change in form of the distribution 'if we go on extending the *size of sample*'. What do we mean by a sample, what conditions should it fulfil if it is to be of service to us, and how can we ensure that it will fulfil those conditions?

3.2.   To begin with the first question, what do we mean by a sample, the words *sample* and *example* (compare the now archaic *ensample* used in the Authorised Version of the Bible) are really the same, both derived initially from the Latin *exemplum* and hence (from *eximo*) meaning 'something taken out', a specimen. The purpose for which we 'take out' the 'specimen' is to save labour: we hope by studying this specimen to be able to draw some conclusions as to the character of the mass from which it is drawn, without the enormous or it may be practically impossible labour of dealing with the mass as a whole. If the 'specimen' is to serve this purpose, it is clearly necessary that it should be typical, representative, unbiased; otherwise it may merely mislead. That is the answer to our second question: if the sample is to be of service, it must be typical, representative, unbiased. One method of selecting a sample from an author's works, quite frequently adopted by the scholar who is not a statistician, is simply to pick out a few passages which are in his judgement typical—it may be even a single passage. His judgement as to the typical character may be perfectly sound, the conclusions he draws may be perfectly correct and such as would be borne out by a more extensive investigation: but the method is obviously bad, mainly because of its personal character. Dr Dryasdust may differ from Professor

Gusher as to the representative character of the *examples* chosen—the term seems more suitable than *samples*—and the issue can be definitely decided only by a method that is quite impersonal. The one method that is in general *completely* satisfactory from the theoretical standpoint is the method of *random sampling*, or *simple random sampling* as it may be better termed, the insertion of the adjective serving as a reminder that conditions other than mere randomness are implied.

3.3.   *Simple Random Sampling.* In technical terms we are said to form a sample by selecting 'members' or 'individuals' from the 'population' or 'universe' (the 'universe of discourse' of writers on logic) to be sampled. A sample is said to be a simple random sample when it is so made that each member of the universe has the same chance of being selected for the sample, *and the successive selections are independent of one another.* These are by no means easy conditions to fulfil: considerable trouble must be taken to ensure them. To obtain, for example, a random sample of words from some volume, it certainly would not do merely to open the volume at haphazard, jot down the first word that caught one's eye, and repeat the process until a sample of adequate size had been formed. Neither the page pitched on nor the word taken would be at all likely to be a truly random choice.

3.4.   The method usually employed now is fully adequate for its purpose and may be best explained by an example. I choose as an example a problem to which it can be applied very simply. Suppose we wish to estimate the number of words entered in a certain dictionary. Obviously all we have to do is to estimate the average number of words in a page, and multiplying this by the number of pages we will have an estimate of the total number of words. The problem is how to pick out a certain number of pages at random from which to make the estimate of average words per page. This is done very readily by means of 'tables of random numbers', that is of the digits 0 to 9 arranged in random order, of which two have been published (refs. 3.4, 3.5). The second, by Kendall and Babington Smith, are the more extensive tables, running to 100,000 digits, and the better tested: the digits were given by reading the number most nearly opposite a fixed mark on a continuously spinning disk with 0 to 9 evenly spaced round its circumference, when the disk was illuminated by an instantaneous flash from a neon lamp. The digits, both in these and Tippett's tables, are arranged in groups of four. If the number of pages in the dictionary exceeds 1000, four digits will be necessary to give the page number, numbers being represented as on a revolution counter or speedometer, i.e. 5 will be 0005, 15 will be 0015, 115 will be 0115, and so on. All we have to do to make a random selection of pages is to start in the tables at any point we please and note groups of four digits less than the highest-numbered page, simply omitting the others. The same group of digits may happen to recur more than once: if so the same page in the dictionary must be taken more than once as the 'random numbers' dictate, or the condition that successive selections must be independent of one another will not be fulfilled.

3.5.   For example, I wished to make an estimate of the number of *nouns* in the *Shorter Oxford English Dictionary*. The dictionary is in two volumes, paged continuously from 1 to 2475, but neither page 1 nor page 2475 is a complete page, so I decided to call it 2474 pages and take the first and last pages together if page 1 did happen to turn up in the sample. I used Tippett's tables, the only ones then available, and started on the page numbered (IV), the first column, which begins as on the right. The first pages to be sampled were accordingly 2002, 754, 1551, and 427, the remaining groups of digits all exceeding the limit 2474. Continuing the process, 50 pages were picked out in this way and the nouns on them counted. The mean number per page proved to be 23·28, which on multiplying by 2474 gives roundly 57,600 as an estimate of the total number of nouns in the dictionary. But now comes the important point. By using this method of sampling we can not only form an estimate but also a measure of the limits of trustworthiness of that estimate. Obviously, if we formed a number of such estimates as the above each based on 50 pages, they would vary more or less from each other, each sample giving a slightly different value for the mean nouns-per-page, say m. Let the standard deviation of such means be ϵ_m: then evidently ϵ_m, called the standard error of the mean, is a measure of the untrustworthiness of any one of our means. But it may be shown that if σ is the standard deviation of the number of nouns on a page ϵ_m tends to the value given by

$$\epsilon_m^2 = \frac{\sigma^2}{n}, \tag{3.1}$$

where n is the number of pages on which the means m are each based—50 in our example. And we have an estimate of σ from the data for our 50 pages and so can apply the formula. Actually I found

$$\sigma^2 = 76 \cdot 002, \quad \sigma = 8 \cdot 72,$$

the nouns-per-page being exceedingly variable and ranging from 9 to 45. Dividing σ^2 by 50 we have the estimate $\epsilon_m^2 = 1 \cdot 5200$, $\epsilon_m = 1 \cdot 233$, and the mean may often be written in the form

$$23 \cdot 28 \pm 1 \cdot 233.$$

Roundly we would expect, on repeating samples of 50 pages each, that some two-thirds of the means would lie within the limits given by the standard error. Multiplying both the above figures by 2474, our estimate of the total number of nouns may now be written as

$$57,600 \pm 3050,$$

or, considering the untrustworthiness of the figures, we may as well say

$$58,000 \pm 3000.$$

The estimate is 58,000 and the odds about 2 to 1 that the true figure lies between 55,000 and 61,000. The estimate was good enough for my purpose and it seemed no use going further, but it may be noted that if we wanted to halve the standard error it would be necessary to take four times the number of pages, since ϵ_m is inversely proportional to the square root of n, not to n itself. It should also be emphasised that the standard error refers solely to fluctuations of sampling, not to any other sources of error: other workers, for example, might diverge a good deal from the above figure because they started with a different notion as to what was to be included under the term 'noun'. That is one good reason for not attempting too high a degree of superficial precision.

3.6.   The above process is invaluable for taking a random sample from any 'population' that has already been enumerated, e.g. the 'population' of pages in a book, or lines in a text in which the lines have been numbered. But the enumeration is an essential preliminary, and if it has not already been done for him the experimenter must do it himself. Consider what this would mean if he wanted to take a random sample of words, say nouns, from the whole of an author's collected works. He would have to read through the works, very carefully, from beginning to end, and attach its number to every noun as he came across it. To record the number, if he didn't mind spoiling his edition of the works, it might suffice to enter in the right-hand margin the number of the last noun in the line: otherwise he would have, as he read, to write out a numbered list. Even in the works of Thomas à Kempis, seven small octavo volumes in Pohl's edition, there must be something like 500,000 words, of which about 100,000 are nouns. The works of Gerson in the edition I used are in four volumes folio, and I decline to estimate the number of words and nouns. It is obvious that the mere making of the initial numbered list of the words from which the sample was to be taken would be an almost impossible task. And when that list had been made, a list of some 8000 random numbers (if the sample were to be of the length of that used for my Table 2.2 or 2.3) each of five or six digits would have to be compiled for taking the sample, and then the word corresponding to each of these numbers turned up separately. The taking of a sample on these lines is hardly a practical proposition—certainly for one man working alone. Possibly something on quite different lines might be more workable: for example, a collection of random numbers might be used to give (1) the volume, (2) the page, (3) the line on the page, (4) the number of the word in the line, 2.224.20.3 denoting volume 2, p. 224, line 20, word 3 and so on, thus avoiding all making of the numbered list. But even this would be a very lengthy process and there would probably be a large wastage in the list of random numbers as first made, owing to the page given being a blank or contents page or page of prefatory matter and not text, or to there being no line of the assigned number on the given page owing to its being the first short page of a chapter, or no word of the given number on the line assigned. The tables of random numbers can be used in a great variety of ways, and it is possible that some ingenious worker may devise some practical method of taking a random sample of words from an author's works by their aid, but I have failed. In these circumstances there is nothing for it but to give up the notion of random sampling, and use some quite different method, founded on a different basic idea, for getting a sample that one may be reasonably confident will be 'representative'. There is nothing really novel about the method I have suggested, but I have christened it 'Spread Sampling', a term fairly descriptive of its character, to distinguish it briefly and clearly from random sampling.

3.7. *Spread Sampling.* The basic idea of the method is to spread the sample as uniformly as possible over the whole of the work to be sampled. Thus if we want a sample of about S_1 words and there are n pages in the work to be sampled, a sample of $S_1/n = r$ words (to the nearest unit) from each page will give the desired sample. The particular r words to be taken from each page must of course be determined impersonally. We may adopt some arbitrary numerical rule such as choosing the 1st, 3rd, 5th, etc., or the 1st, 6th, 11th, etc.; or we may at this point bring in random sampling and pick out the words by random numbers. A simpler and more rapid method than any of these is to determine first the number of *lines* from each page required to give a sample of the size desired, and take all the words in a continuous passage of so many lines from each page. This is an extremely simple process and seems, judging from an experiment (§§ 4.2 *et seq.*), to work fairly well; but one or other of the methods first suggested would probably be preferable if the additional labour were not too forbidding. Any continuous passage is very far from a random sample: the words hang together round the same sequence of ideas and particular words tend to be repeated, cf. the passages cited from St John's Gospel in § 2.18, and such passages as the following:

> ...a man of great *abilities*, whose *abilities*....

> ...in *this last situation*. Yet *this last situation*....

The *wise man* of the *Stoics* would, no doubt, be a grander object than a *steam-engine*. But there are *steam-engines*. And the *wise man* of the *Stoics* is yet to be born.

> ...the *difference* between his *school* and other *schools* was a *difference* so fundamental....

The Crown had not sufficient influence over the *Parliament* to procure an acquittal in so clear a case of guilt. And to dissolve a *Parliament* which is universally allowed to have been one of the best *Parliaments*....

(Macaulay, essay on Bacon.)

A sample of disconnected words from the page picks out individual words for the most part singly. A paragraph or other continuous passage is apt to catch pairs, triplets or even larger groups in its net: the sampling is 'clumped'.

3.8. The method can obviously be worked in all kinds of ways guided by the basic idea, some of these being clearly better than others. The method actually employed for Tables 2.2 and 2.3, described in detail in Chapter 9, was a rough and ready application of the notion, pages or longish passages being taken spread more or less uniformly over the chosen works. It may well be asked, could not random numbers have been used at least to determine the pages to be taken? The answer is, possibly: I had little experience of such work, and methods of sampling applicable to the particular case had hardly been thought out. At the same time there would be difficulties in any such application. The problem in my mind was not the simple one of getting a fairly representative sample of the whole of Thomas à Kempis's or Gerson's vocabulary in its entirety, but of throwing light on the controversy respecting the authorship of the *Imitatio*. It was therefore thought better to exclude certain of Thomas's works, e.g. verse and biographies, from the sample taken from his works, as belonging to a different type of literature from the *Imitatio*. Gerson's works required quite careful examination: some writings are included in the volumes his authorship of which is admitted to be doubtful; others have been translated into Latin from the vernacular by another hand; some are on purely legal questions. When the question is whether he is at all likely to have written the *Imitatio*, it is obvious that all such works must be omitted: the sample must be confined to writings of a religious character, and to writings more or less certainly by Gerson and composed in Latin by his own hand. It will be rarely in cases of this kind, where comparison and not merely description is in question, that personal judgement can be wholly excluded from the choice of the material to be compared. Only when that material has been delimited can problems as to the applications of random sampling or spread sampling in one way or another be properly considered.

3.9.   A 'spread sample' taken with care by a good method may be even more closely *representative* than a random sample of the same size. The trouble, is, however, that in general there does not exist any method for assessing its accuracy, such as can be used in the case of a random sample (§ 3.5). The reliance to be placed upon it must depend largely on the precise detail of the method used, and remains to a great extent a matter of personal opinion. This is obviously a very serious disadvantage.

3.10.   Now let us return to the difficulty already touched on in §§ 1.7 and 2.14, the difficulty created by the continuous change in the form of the word-distribution as the size of sample is increased. The mean, the standard deviation, the percentage of once-words, *everything* apparently about the distribution alters. But does not this seem a little paradoxical if we are careful to take our sample so that from beginning to end it represents one and the same work of one and the same author? If we use simple random sampling that condition is strictly fulfilled at every stage. If we use spread sampling, we can take a sample of say six lines from each page of the work and base our first distribution on this. We can then take a sample of the second six lines from each page and base a second distribution on the results of the two samples combined—and so on for as many sets of six lines as the page provides. All the successive distributions so obtained are representative samples of one and the same work. Does not common sense suggest that there ought to be *something* the same, or rather approximately the same within the limits of fluctuations of sampling, for all the tables, some numerical measure independent of the number of occurrences on which the table is based and *characteristic* of the material and author? The answer is that there is such a characteristic, but its form can only be obtained by a consideration of the theory of these distributions.

3.11.   Frequency distributions of the kind with which we are dealing belong to the class of distributions representative of 'multiple happenings' or 'repeated events': each of our tables shows the number f_x of words that 'happen' to have been used X times. The theory of such distributions has received much attention since 1920 (cf. refs. 3.1, 3.2, 3.3), mainly with reference to the theory of personal accidents, i.e. the theory of distributions showing how many out of a given number of persons at risk have met with

0, 1, 2, 3, ... accidents during a given period of exposure to risk. Table 3.1 shows three distributions of this type. In the first, 648 women were at risk for five weeks: 447 of them did not meet with any accident during that period, 132 met with one accident, 43 with two accidents, 21 with three, 3 with four, and 2 with five accidents—an 'accident', it may be mentioned, might be quite a trivial occurrence, anything sufficient to send the worker

TABLE 3.1. Three distributions showing the number f_x of persons meeting with X accidents in a given period of exposure to risk (ref. 3.8: used as examples also in ref. 3.1). A, 648 women working on 6 inch H.E. shells for five weeks. B, 414 machinists: three months' study. C, 198 machinists: six months' study

Number of accidents	Number of persons meeting with said number of accidents, f_x		
X	A	B	C
0	447	296	69
1	132	74	54
2	43	26	43
3	21	8	15
4	3	4	13
5	2	4	1
6	—	1	2
7	—	—	1
8	—	1	—
Total	648	414	198
M	0·468	0·483	1·318
σ^2	0·6934	1·0082	1·8735
σ	0·833	1·004	1·369

to the welfare room, though it might be serious. Distribution B gives data for 414 machinists exposed to risk for three months; one of them met with no less than eight accidents during that period. Distribution C gives the distribution for 198 machinists exposed to risk for six months. It is evident that all these distributions are of the same *kind* as our distributions for words. Table 3.1 shows the number of happenings of a certain sort to certain persons: Table 2.1 shows the number of happenings of a certain sort to certain words. Table 3.2 illustrates the matter further. The first distribution shows the number of omnibus drivers, out of 166, who met with 0, 1, 2, 3, ... accidents during the first year of work. The following columns continue the data, for the same group of men, showing the number who met with 0, 1, 2, 3, ... accidents during 2, 3, 4 and 5 years' exposure to risk respectively. As the length of the period of exposure to risk increases, the distributions continually extend: the mean increases, the standard deviation increases, the numbers of men who have met with few accidents drop off and the numbers who have met with more increase. The changes in form are precisely parallel to those we expect to take place in the word-distribution

TABLE 3.2. Showing for 166 London omnibus drivers the number who met with 0, 1, 2, 3, ... accidents, trivial or serious, in an exposure of 1 to 5 years (ref. 3.9, Appendix E)

Number of accidents	Number of drivers meeting with said number of accidents in an exposure to risk of				
	1 year	2 years	3 years	4 years	5 years
0	45	16	4	1	1
1	36	28	22	6	2
2	40	29	14	13	3
3	19	24	22	17	14
4	12	26	21	19	17
5	8	12	21	21	21
6	3	11	19	21	17
7	2	7	12	17	14
8	1	4	5	13	14
9	—	5	8	9	12
10	—	2	8	3	13
11	—	1	4	7	9
12	—	1	1	5	6
13	—	—	3	5	2
14	—	—	1	2	6
15	—	—	—	2	1
16	—	—	—	2	6
17	—	—	—	2	3
18	—	—	—	—	—
19	—	—	—	—	1
20	—	—	—	—	—
21	—	—	1	—	3
22	—	—	—	—	—
23	—	—	—	—	—
24	—	—	—	—	—
25	—	—	—	1	—
32	—	—	—	—	1
Total	166	166	166	166	166
M	1·813	3·355	4·970	6·476	8·012
σ^2	2·9109	6·4580	11·1376	15·0446	21·3854
σ	1·706	2·541	3·337	3·879	4·624

as the number of occurrences is increased. The three distributions of Table 3.1 are all of the form usual with word-distributions, so far as our present experience goes: persons who have met with only one accident during the period of exposure to risk are more frequent than those who have met with any single greater number. In Table 3.2 the distributions are rather irregular, owing to the small number of men at risk, but clearly as the period of exposure extends they are taking a form with the most frequent number of accidents at first round about 1 to 3 and finally round about 5. This is just the change we might expect in the form of the word-distribution if the number of occurrences were sufficiently increased, though we have found no instance in which the change of form has actually gone anything like so far.

3.12.   Notwithstanding the essential resemblances, the distributions of Tables 3.1 and 3.2 differ from our word-distributions in two important respects, briefly mentioned in § 1.8. In the first place the problem of the accident-distribution is a problem involving time, i.e. the time of exposure to risk. Our problem does not specifically involve time: the author must indeed take a certain time to write, exposing one word after another to the risk of being used, but we are not concerned with the rate at which he writes, only with the number of words he has in fact written. That is one point in which our distributions differ from distributions of personal accidents. But there is another and more troublesome point of difference. Our distributions are incomplete: they do not give the number of words that have *not* met with the 'accident' or 'happening' of being used. In other terms, since we do not know this number, they do not give the total number of words 'at risk', the number of words subject to the 'risk' of being used by the author. The distributions of words are so to speak *decapitated*, lacking the leading frequency f_0: the distributions of accidents are complete. For the development of any theory of the word-distribution we must, however, assume the total number of words 'at risk' to be known, as theory can only consider the complete distribution. Finally, attention may be redirected to the change of terminology, already mentioned in § 1.8, due to the change in the nature of our problem as compared with the case of accidents. In accident-distributions we understand by 'size of sample' the number of persons at risk: 648, 414, 198 and 166 in the respective distributions of Tables 3.1 and 3.2. The equivalent for the word-distribution would be the (unknown) total of words 'at risk'. But in the work on words we can hardly avoid using the term 'size of sample', as we have in fact used it, for the number of occurrences S_1. This *is* the size of sample in any ordinary sense, corresponding more or less closely to the number of pages of the author's work that we have covered. Its equivalent in the accident case would be 'total number of accidents' or approximately 'period of exposure to risk'.

3.13.   The development of theory necessarily involves some, if not very serious, mathematical work, but it may be possible to explain to the non-mathematical reader the general lines which the theory of personal accidents has followed, and the way in which it is proposed to apply similar notions to the word-distribution. If a number of persons exposed to the risk of accident all have exactly the same liability to accident, theory suggests that the frequency distribution resulting should be of a particularly simple type (Poisson's distribution) for which we have the remarkable relation

$$\sigma^2 = M, \qquad (3.2)$$

i.e. the square of the standard deviation, or *variance* as it is sometimes termed, is equal to the mean. Actual investigation of many accident-distributions shows on the contrary that in the vast majority of instances we have

$$\sigma^2 > M, \qquad (3.3)$$

the variance often greatly exceeding the mean. It will be seen, by reference to the figures at the foot of Tables 3.1 and 3.2, that this rule holds for all the distributions of those tables. In Table 3.2, for example, the distribution for a single year's exposure gives a variance more than one and a half times as big as the mean, and the distribution for five years' exposure a variance more than two and a half times as big as the mean. What is the explanation of this? The simplest explanation that suggests itself, and a very natural one, is that in actual fact the liabilities of different individuals to accident are *not* the same, that they vary in 'liability' to accident just as they vary in intelligence or in stature. The 'liability' of an individual might be ideally defined as the *mean* number of accidents he would tend to meet with in the given period of exposure to risk, say unit time. Let us call this liability λ, and let us suppose the liabilities of the persons at risk to be known and grouped into a frequency distribution—just as we might group their statures or weights—and that this distribution has mean $\bar{\lambda}$ and standard deviation σ_λ. Then from the mean and standard deviation of the accident-distribution, M and σ, we can calculate $\bar{\lambda}$ and σ_λ. Now if we extend the period of exposure to risk from one unit into two units, *and all individuals retain their relative liabilities*, $\bar{\lambda}$ becomes $2\bar{\lambda}$ and σ_λ becomes $2\sigma_\lambda$. Therefore the coefficient of variation of λ, $v_\lambda = \sigma_\lambda/\bar{\lambda}$, remains the same and is independent of the period of exposure to risk: in the highly simplified conditions assumed it would be just the same for five years' exposure as for one year. Expressing $\bar{\lambda}$ and σ_λ, in v_λ^2, in terms of M and σ, we then have a 'characteristic' of the *accident*-distribution which also, in the simplified circumstances assumed, is independent of the period of exposure to risk. Moreover, since the total number of accidents met with by the whole group at risk, our S_1, is, within the limits of fluctuations of sampling, directly proportional to time, the characteristic is also independent of S_1. If we express this characteristic in terms, not of M and σ, but of the two sums S_1 and S_2 and the whole number of persons at risk, say W, it becomes

$$\frac{S_2 - S_1}{S_1^2} W - 1. \tag{3.4}$$

W being constant for any one group, the expression

$$\frac{S_2 - S_1}{S_1^2} \tag{3.5}$$

must also be independent of time or of S_1.

3.14.   For the word-distribution the argument is precisely similar. If for a certain set of words the chance of being used (the 'liability' to be used) is exactly the same for each, we should expect the distribution (the complete distribution) to be of the Poisson type, though in this case only as a good approximation for the great majority of words, and not so very closely for words used with great frequency like *Deus* in the *Imitatio*. We should therefore expect the relation (3.2) to hold good, at least to a high degree of approximation. Now we do not know the complete distribution in any practical case, but a few lines of algebra show that if σ^2/M exceeds unity for the incomplete or decapitated distribution, the ratio must *à fortiori* exceed unity for the complete distribution; i.e. if we insert any arbitrary value for the leading frequency f_0 to complete the distribution, and work out σ^2 and M as before, we shall get a higher value of σ^2/M for the complete than for the decapitated distribution. If the reader makes the experiment on Table 2.1, inserting a value of $f_0 = 3832$, so as to make $S_0 = 5000$, he will find that the table so completed gives a ratio σ^2/M of 68·588 against the ratio 63·190 for the decapitated distribution. And as in fact we find that, in every case which we have, σ^2 exceeds M for the decapitated distribution, the same rule (3·3) must *à fortiori* hold for the unknown complete distributions. The following are the values of M and σ^2 for all the tables of the preceding chapter except 2.8 for which constants were not evaluated, but beyond all doubt the rule would hold in that instance also.

Table	M	σ^2	Table	M	σ^2
2·1	7·042	444·987	2·6	9·552	1060·217
2·2	5·834	257·298	2·7	7·015	259·052
2·3	4·673	120·118	2·9	10·432	357·320
2·4	3·928	74·395	2·10	6·368	220·532
2·5	1·841	8·952			

3.15.   The excess of σ^2 over M is, it will be noted, in most instances very much greater for these word-distributions than for the accident-distributions. The same hypothesis suggests itself to account for the facts, viz. that the 'liabilities' are not the same for all words, but widely different—a hypothesis that in this case seems almost to border on a truism. Following the same course of reasoning as in § 3.13, we come to the conclusion that if, as in § 3.10, we stage by stage increase the size of sample from the same work by some method that keeps the sample representative of the whole at each stage, the expression (3.5) for the complete (though unknown) distribution should remain constant. But the two sums S_1 and S_2 are precisely the same for the complete and for the decapitated distribution, since in forming these sums for the complete distribution f_0, the number of words not used, is multiplied by zero and it does not matter what value it takes. The expression (3.5) is therefore constant for the decapitated distribution: we have discovered the 'characteristic' the existence of which was conjectured in § 3.10. In actual examples it is found that, since S_1^2 greatly exceeds S_2, (3.5) gives a very small decimal. It is inconvenient working with small decimals, and for practice it is handier to multiply the expression by 10,000, taking as the 'characteristic',

$$K = 10,000 \frac{S_2 - S_1}{S_1^2}. \qquad (3.6)$$

3.16.   It may be noted that the assumption italicised in § 3.13, that all individuals retain their relative liabilities throughout the period of exposure to risk, is in general not valid for actual cases of accident statistics: increasing practice, increasing age, temporary illness or worry, and all kinds of extraneous factors may send the liability of one individual up or down compared with that of another (cf. ref. 3.3, the second paper by E. G. Chambers). In the successive distributions of Table 3.2, for example, v_λ^2 or the expression (3.4) does not keep constant but shows quite a definite trend, taking the values 0·334, 0·276, 0·250, 0·204, 0·208, the values for the individual years (data for which will be found in the original Report) dropping from 0·334 in the first year to as low as 0·073 in the fourth year and rising again to 0·195 in the fifth. But if, in drawing samples of successively increasing sizes from one and the same work, we use a method of strictly random sampling or carefully devised spread sampling, we have taken the precise precautions necessary to ensure that the relative liabilities of *words* shall be kept the same throughout the experiment, subject of course to the unavoidable fluctuations of sampling. The distributions of Table 3.2 show the sort of definite changes which we might expect in word-distributions if the first sample covered the first 50 pages of the work, the second covered the first 100 pages, the third the first 150 pages, and so on: if we worked like that, variations of matter and variations of style would affect the successive distributions, and we should not expect the 'characteristic' to remain the same. Illustrations of the point will be found in Chapter 9, §§ 9.9 and 9.12. With these explanations the non-mathematical reader may pass on to Chapter 4. I proceed to the more complete development of the preceding notions.

3.17.   Reverting for a moment to the theory of the accident-distribution, the argument that the distribution for a homogeneous group of persons, all with the same liability to accident, should be a Poisson distribution, was given by Greenwood and Yule (ref. 3.1, p. 257) as follows: 'For consider the matter thus. Let the N persons be exposed to risk during a small interval of time—an interval so small that the chance of any one person meeting with two accidents may be regarded as negligible. Let the chance of a person meeting with an accident during this small interval be p, and the chance of his not meeting with an accident be q. Then at the end of the interval the numbers with 0 and with 1 accident respectively will be given by $N(q+p)$. At the end of 2 intervals the numbers with 0, 1 and 2 accidents will be given by the expansion of $N(q+p)^2$, and so on. At the end of T intervals, therefore, the distribution will be given by the binomial expansion of $N(q+p)^T$. But here p is very small and q near unity, while T we must suppose very large in order to give us a finite number of accidents. Hence if λ is the ratio of the number of accidents n (i.e. pTN) to the number N of persons at risk the true distribution is given by the Poisson series

$$e^{-\lambda}\left(1+\lambda+\frac{\lambda^2}{2!}+\dots\right).$$

This, as it seems to us,...is the form to which "uncomplicated distributions" should be expected to be assignable.' This argument still seems to me sound: time can be broken up into infinitesimal intervals, and the Poisson series is the *strict* limit to the binomial.

3.18.   But the passage from binomial series to Poisson series does not seem to be so straightforward in the case of the word-distribution. We are in no way concerned with time. The scheme that gives rise to the word-distribution may be pictured somewhat as follows. Let us suppose all the words in the writer's treasure-chest to be written out on tickets, some—the words most rarely used—on only one ticket each, some on two tickets, some on three, and so on; some few, words very frequently employed, on several hundreds or even thousands of tickets each. We regard the process of writing (it does sound rather ridiculous put in this way) as bearing an analogy to the drawing of tickets out of this chest, each ticket being returned to the chest after drawing and noting, so as not to alter the make-up of the collection of tickets in the chest: the author's balance in his treasury of words, in happy contrast to what happens with his Bank, is not lessened by his drawing on it. The chance of drawing any particular word will be given by the ratio of the number of tickets bearing that word to the total number of tickets in the chest, say Z. Let us fix our attention on the m words each of which is written on r tickets, so that the value of the chance p is r/Z, the complementary chance being q, where $p+q=1$. If we make n drawings, the numbers of these words which may be expected to occur 0, 1, 2, 3, ... times are given by the successive terms of the binomial expansion of $m(q+p)^n$, or

$$m\left(q^n + nq^{n-1}p + \frac{n(n-1)}{1\cdot 2}q^{n-2}p^2 + ...\right). \tag{3.7}$$

Note that here the total number of cards drawn bearing words within the mr-group is $mnp = mnr/Z$, whence for *all* words the total number of cards drawn is

$$S(mnr/Z) = \frac{n}{Z}S(mr) = n,$$

as it must be, since we draw some card with some word at every drawing. Is it now in this instance legitimate to substitute a Poisson series for the binomial series? The answer depends solely on a question of fact: is the value of p sufficiently small to justify the approximation? Writing $np = \lambda$, the mean and the variance of the Poisson series are both λ: p must therefore be sufficiently small to make npq sensibly equal to np. If $p = 0\cdot001$, I think we may call the approximation quite close, for the variance of the Poisson series will only be in error as against the binomial by one part in a thousand. Now we may be fairly confident that for the great majority of the words in the treasure-chest p will be under this limit, often greatly under it, so things do not look bad. But we do not *know* the distribution of p's in the chest and can only speculate about it. Let us try to throw some further light on the subject by consideration of the problem not of authorship, but of sampling from a known and enumerable universe, a problem that is of equally fundamental importance for us.

3.19. Let us suppose we are drawing a random sample from all the words in the *De Imitatione Christi*. Particulars for nouns, adjectives and verbs are given in Tables 2.1, 2.6 and 2.7, the numbers of words (vocabulary, S_0) and of occurrences, S_1, being as follows.

	Vocabulary	Occurrences
Table 2.1, nouns	1,168	8,225
„ 2.6, adjectives	529	5,053
„ 2.7, verbs	1,157	8,116
Total	2,854	21,394

A count of 50 pages, chosen at random by Tippett's numbers by the method of §3.5 from Pohl's edition of the text (ref. 3.7), gave an estimate of the total length of the *Imitatio* of 42,000 words, with a standard error of 550. Nouns, adjectives and verbs therefore account for only about a half, probably rather more than a half, of all occurrences, the remainder being due to personal and possessive pronouns, relative adjectives and pronouns, adverbs, prepositions, conjunctions, interjections, the omitted verb *esse*, proper names and so forth. The proportion due to these 'other words' seemed high, but a count of half a dozen random pages gave a proportion of 47.6 per cent, which is quite confirmatory. If, then, we went through the whole text entering every word as it occurred on a ticket and throwing these tickets into a chest, we should end up with some 42,000 tickets in the chest. The chance p would not exceed our limit 0·001 for any word with not more than 42 tickets. Confining ourselves to nouns, adjectives and verbs we find from Tables 2.1, 2.6 and 2.7 that only $36 + 20 + 28 = 84$ of these words occur 43 times or more. But 84 on 2854 is only 2·94 or roundly 3 per cent, so that 97 per cent of these, the most important, words have a value of p less than 0·001, the value we have taken as critical for good approximation of the binomial to the Poisson series. If $p = 0·01$, npq differs from np by 1 per cent. One-hundredth of 42,000 is 420. One word amongst the nouns nearly but not quite reaches this limit—*Deus* with 418 occurrences—and one adjective exceeds it, *omnis* with 586 occurrences: no single verb nearly reaches it. For *omnis*, $p = 0·0140$, so npq would differ from np by less than $1\frac{1}{2}$ per cent, surely no very serious error. But what, it may be asked, about the words other than nouns, adjectives and verbs? My reply is, that while some of them may occur with greater frequency, possibly much greater frequency, than any word in our tables, really we are not interested. No one would dream of piling up his work and cluttering up his tables by tabulating every occurrence of *qui* (*quae, quod,* etc.), or of the verb *esse*; or, in dealing with a work in English, every occurrence of *a, the,* or *and.* No one would want to include such words as these in a concordance, and there is no reason for including them in our work. Some of the 'other words', it is true, adverbs possibly for example, are more *significant* words, as they have been termed, and might be included, but no one of them is likely to be particularly frequent. *Within the limitations of our work* then, as it seems to me, the Poisson approximation in this instance will hold very well: and we have taken rather an unfavourable test case, for the *Imitatio* tables give words occurring with much greater values of X than those based on any other work of sample of comparable size, cf. Tables 2.2, 2.3, 2.4.

3.20.   But this throws a good deal of light on the contents of the writer's treasure-chest. We know that it must contain more, far more, words than happen to have been used in the *Imitatio*. Of nouns alone, there are no less than 603 which occur in the sample from the other works of Thomas à Kempis on which Table 2.2 is based, but which do *not* occur in the *Imitatio*, and these as might be expected are all relatively rare or infrequent words: all but one occur only 9 times or less, the remaining one 15 times, and the value of p for every one of them would be well under the limit 0·001. Table 2.2 is only a small sample from Thomas's other works, but even if we had tabulated every single word that occurs in his writings, it must be emphasised that they would not cover all the words in his treasury, all the words that he might have used: the number of words used would only give a lower limit to the number that were 'at risk'. Thomas transcribed with his own hand a manuscript of the Vulgate, a task that occupied him for fifteen years, and almost any word from that most familiar of volumes might well have been used. Any such words additional to those in Table 2.1 would, like the 603 in Table 2.2, tend to be relatively infrequent words. Hence if, for practical purposes, we may regard the Poisson series as an adequate approximation to the binomial when we are sampling from the limited vocabulary of one single work, *à fortiori* we may so regard it for the sampling of the writer from his treasure-chest of words. The passage from binomial series to Poisson series remains, however, in this case a practical approximation: it is not, as in the case of accidents, a true theoretical passage to the limit.

3.21.   We will take it accordingly that if we write

$$rp = \lambda \quad \cdot \tag{3.8}$$

the distribution for a homogeneous set of m words will be given by the Poisson series

$$me^{-\lambda}\left(1+\lambda+\frac{\lambda^2}{2!}+\frac{\lambda^3}{3!}+\cdots\right). \tag{3.9}$$

The number of words not occurring in the sample is $me^{-\lambda}$, the number occurring once is $me^{-\lambda}\lambda$, the number occurring twice $\frac{1}{2}me^{-\lambda}\lambda^2$, and so on.

The mean of the series is λ and the variance also λ. Note that if we double n, the number of drawings or the total of occurrences for *all* words, we double λ: λ is directly proportional to the number of occurrences.

3.22. The entire distribution we suppose to be compounded of a number of such components as (3.9) with different values of λ. Let the mean of the λ-distribution be $\bar{\lambda}$ and its standard deviation σ_λ, and let the mean of the *complete* word-distribution be M_c and its standard deviation σ_c. We evidently have at once

$$M_c = \bar{\lambda}, \tag{3.10}$$

and since the total variance is the mean variance of the component distributions, which is $\bar{\lambda}$, plus the variance of the means, which is σ_λ^2,

$$\sigma_c^2 = \bar{\lambda} + \sigma_\lambda^2 = M_c + \sigma_\lambda^2. \tag{3.11}$$

Now since all λ's are directly proportional to the total number of occurrences, doubling say the number of occurrences will double $\bar{\lambda}$ and also double σ_λ. Hence the coefficient of variation of λ or

$$v_\lambda = \frac{\sigma_\lambda}{\bar{\lambda}} \tag{3.12}$$

is independent of the number of occurrences. But

$$v_\lambda^2 = \frac{\sigma_\lambda^2}{\bar{\lambda}^2} = \frac{\sigma_c^2 - M_c}{M_c^2}, \tag{3.13}$$

and hence the fraction on the right of this equation is independent of the number of occurrences, that is, of size of sample. It is a 'characteristic' of the *complete* distribution, independent of size of sample. So far this is all known theory.

3.23. Now if S_1 and S_2 denote the first and second moments of the distribution about zero, and k is the highest value of X that occurs,

$$\left. \begin{array}{l} S_1 = S_0^k(f_x X) = S_1^k(f_x X) \\ S_2 = S_0^k(f_x X^2) = S_1^k(f_x X^2) \end{array} \right\}. \tag{3.14}$$

That is to say, S_1 and S_2 are just the same for the complete and the incomplete distribution, since the coefficient of f_0 is zero. W being the whole number of words in the distribution, we therefore have

$$M_c = \frac{S_1}{W} \tag{3.15}$$

and

$$\sigma_c^2 = \frac{S_2}{W} - \frac{S_1^2}{W^2}. \tag{3.16}$$

Hence the quantity on the right of (3.13) which is independent of the number of occurrences may be written

$$\frac{W^2}{S_1^2}\left(\frac{S_2}{W}-\frac{S_1^2}{W^2}-\frac{S_1}{W}\right)=\frac{S_2-S_1}{S_1^2}W-1. \tag{3.17}$$

But W is independent of the number of occurrences. Hence, if the whole expression on the right is independent of the number of occurrences,

$$\frac{S_2-S_1}{S_1^2} \tag{3.18}$$

must be independent of the number of occurrences, and forms the 'characteristic' of the *incomplete* distribution we have been seeking. We could, if we liked, express it in terms of the number of words in the incomplete or decapitated distribution, say N, and its mean and standard deviation, say M_d and σ_d, for

$$\frac{S_2-S_1}{S_1^2}=\frac{\sigma_d^2+M_d^2-M_d}{NM_d^2}=\frac{1}{N}\left(\frac{\sigma_d^2-M_d}{M_d^2}+1\right), \tag{3.19}$$

and we might take

$$\frac{\sigma_d^2-M_d}{M_d^2} \tag{3.20}$$

as the characteristic. But, I think, the first form (3.18) is preferable: it is straightforward and simple, and the sums S_1 and S_2 can be run off very quickly on a calculating machine. Moreover, although means and standard deviations can be used for the comparison of distributions based on the same or approximately the same numbers of observations, they are of little use otherwise, and attention can be concentrated on the characteristic. As written in (3.18) the characteristic is a very small decimal, for S_1 is large compared with S_2: for practical purposes it is convenient to multiply it by a factor of 10,000, as already mentioned in § 3.15.

3.24.   Summarising then, if f_x is the number of words occurring X times and

$$S_1=S(f_xX), \quad S_2=S(f_xX^2), \tag{3.21}$$

the quantity

$$K=10,000\frac{S_2-S_1}{S_1^2} \tag{3.22}$$

is independent of the size of sample S_1 and may be expected to be the same, within the limits of fluctuations of sampling, for all sizes of sample. The factor 10,000 is introduced only to avoid the inconvenience of handling small decimals. This is the expression already given in equation (3.6) after a brief explanation of the method of its derivation. I have termed K the 'characteristic' of the distribution. It is a linear function of the square of the coefficient of variation of the quantities λ which measure the relative chances of different words being used, and for a constant value of the total number of words at risk W is the greater the greater v_λ. The relation between v_λ and K, cf. equations (3.13) and (3.17), is

$$v_\lambda^2 = 10^{-4} WK - 1. \tag{3.23}$$

It may be noted that, in the expression (3.22) for the characteristic, the term S_1 in the numerator tends to become of less and less importance as the size of sample is increased. Thus from Table 4.5 of the next chapter, in which data are given for a series of samples of increasing size from the same material, we see that for samples of about 2000 occurrences S_1 is some 15 per cent of S_2; for samples of some 4000 occurrences only a little over 8 per cent; for samples of about 6000 occurrences rather less than 6 per cent, and finally for a sample of some 8000 occurrences only some 4·4 per cent. Other material would of course have given other values for the ratio, but Tables 6.7 and 6.4, for samples of some 16,000 and 20,000 occurrences respectively, give ratios of only 1·2 and 2·4 per cent—lower values still. For large samples K tends to the limit $10{,}000\,S_2/S_1^2$.

3.25. In the case of an accident-distribution there are really *two* principal characteristics, (1) v_λ, (2) the value of $\bar{\lambda}$ per unit of time. In the case of our word-distributions the latter falls out, for there is no time scale. The expression (3.22) is accordingly, I submit, *the* characteristic, so long as we confine ourselves to moments no higher than the second. If the third and fourth moments, S_3 and S_4, were brought into account it is possible that similar 'characteristics', independent of size of sample, could be obtained. If μ_3 and μ_4 are the third and fourth moment coefficients (moments divided by S_0) of the λ-distribution, moments being taken about the mean, and

$$\beta_1 = \frac{\mu_3^2}{\mu_2^3}, \quad \beta_2 = \frac{\mu_4}{\mu_2^2},$$

both β_1 and β_2 must be independent of time or 'size of sample'. Accordingly, expressing these β's in terms of the moments of the complete accident-distribution, one would be given two 'characteristics' of higher order for that distribution, and it might prove possible in similar fashion to derive two characteristics of higher order for the incomplete or decapitated distribution. It may be doubted, however, how far they would be serviceable. In distributions of the present kind, with a tendency to rather wild outlying observations, even S_2 must be subject to very large fluctuations of sampling, and with S_3 or S_4 matters would be much worse.

3.26.   But if anyone were to ask me what is the standard error of even the mean of one of our word-distributions, let alone its standard deviation or its higher moments, I should have to confess myself beaten. As a matter of fact, as we have seen, samples on which word-distributions are based are not very likely to be random samples, so questions as to their standard errors can hardly arise: in judging the 'significance' of differences between them one will be thrown back on experience and common sense. But even if one were presented with a truly random sample one would, so it seems to me, still be in great difficulties. In any ordinary case it is S_0 in our notation which is assumed to be fixed, and the fluctuations of sampling in S_1, S_2 and the derived parameters which are to be determined or measured. But in our way of working with words, it is S_1 which is arbitrarily fixed and S_0 and S_2 which are subject to fluctuations of sampling. What, in these circumstances, is the standard error of the mean? or of the standard deviation? or of the characteristic? I must leave the problem to more competent hands.

3.27.   One further note for the attention of the statistician: Greenwood and Yule (ref. 3.1) showed that assuming the λ-distribution to be given by Pearson's binomial curve, the complete accident-distribution could be described by a binomial distribution with negative index, the two parameters of which could be simply expressed in terms of its mean and standard deviation. I made one or two attempts to see whether this expression could be made to describe a word-distribution with any accuracy, guessing at different values for W, but they were all complete failures. Pearson's binomial curve, I take it, will not give any adequate fit to a λ-distribution with a tail extended to such an outrageous length as must be the case. Zipf, to whose work reference was made at the end of the last chapter (§ 2.25, ref. 2.6), holds that his three distributions not only can be adequately described by a formula of the form

$$f_x = f_1 X^{-r},$$

where f_x is the frequency of words with X occurrences, but that in each case $r = 2$. I spent some time on a re-examination of his data and cannot agree with the claim that the formula holds to any satisfactory degree of precision even for his distributions: it certainly does not hold for any of my own that I have tested. Nor is it a likely sort of formula, since for values of r exceeding 1 but not exceeding 2 the mean of the theoretical distribution is infinite, and for values exceeding 2 but not 3 the standard deviation is infinite.

REFERENCES

A. STATISTICAL METHOD

The general notions of sampling have been treated very summarily and with special reference to our particular problem in §§ 3.1–3.9. The worker who has no experience of sampling is recommended to read Y & K, Chapter 18, 'Preliminary Notions on Sampling', which is of quite a general character and should present no difficulty. The standard error of the mean given in § 3.5, equation (3.1), will be found in § 20.30 (i.e. section 30 of Chapter 20, the same notation as in this volume). The Poisson distribution is dealt with in §§ 10.40 *et seq.* Theory of accidents or 'multiple happenings' is not treated in Y & K; (3.1) and (3.2) below are the two fundamental papers. Reference has only been made in the text to (3.1), but the theory was a good deal more completely developed in (3.2). The fact that v_λ, in the simple case, is independent of the period of exposure to risk—an obvious enough result—was first emphasised I think, in my note of (3.3), the publication of which was delayed by the outbreak of war.

(3.1) Greenwood, M. and Yule, G. U. (1920). 'An inquiry into the nature of frequency distributions representative of multiple happenings, etc.' *Jour. Roy. Stat. Soc.* 83, 255.

(3.2) Newbold, Ethel M. (1927). 'Practical applications of the statistics of repeated events, particularly to industrial accidents.' *Jour. Roy. Stat. Soc.* 90, 487. (Especially Appendix, pp. 518–35.)

(3.3) Chambers, E. G. and Yule, G. U. (1942). *Theory and Observation in the Investigation of Accident Causation.* I. *Introduction.* E.G.C. II. *Note on the Statistical Theory of Accidents with Special Reference to the Time Factor.* G.U.Y. III. *Application of Mr Yule's Suggestions to Accident Data.* E.G.C. Discussion by Dr J. O. Irwin and Professor M. Greenwood. Supplement to *Jour. Roy. Stat. Soc.* 7, p. 89, 1941 (but not published till year given above).

(3.4) Tippett, L. H. C. (1927). *Random Sampling Numbers.* Tracts for Computers, No. xv. Cambridge: University Press.

(3.5) Kendall, M. G. and Babington Smith, B. (1939). *Tables of Random Sampling Numbers.* Tracts for Computers, No. xxiv. Cambridge: University Press.

For the higher moments of frequency distributions referred to in § 3.25 see Y &·K, Chapter 9 generally, and for the β's § 9.8.

B. CITATIONS IN TEXT OR TABLES

(3.6) Onions, C. T. *et al.* (1933). *The Shorter Oxford English Dictionary.* 2 vols. Oxford: Clarendon Press.

(3.7) à Kempis, Th. (1902–22). *Opera Omnia,* voluminibus septem edidit Michael Josephus Pohl. Friburgi Brisigavorum: sumptibus Herder.

(3.8) Greenwood, M. and Woods, Hilda M. (1919). *The Incidence of Industrial Accidents upon Individuals with Special Reference to Multiple Accidents.* Industrial Fatigue Research Board, Report 4. London: H.M. Stationery Office.

(3.9) Farmer, E. and Chambers, E. G. (1939). *A Study of Accident Proneness among Motor Drivers.* Industrial Health Research Board, Report 84. London: H.M. Stationery Office.

Chapter 4

THE CHARACTERISTIC K: PRACTICAL PROBLEMS

4.1. It was shown in the last chapter that the quantity termed the characteristic,

$$K = 10,000 \frac{S_2 - S_1}{S_1^2},\qquad (4.1)$$

in which the factor 10,000 is introduced simply in order to give a number of convenient size and not a small decimal, is independent of the size of sample S_1, and consequently may be expected to be the same, within the limits of fluctuations of sampling, for all sizes of sample. This statement is of course subject to the provision that the samples are random samples, or are taken by a well thought out method of spread sampling, so that at every stage they are representative samples of one and the same work. But this is a purely theoretical conclusion, and the practical student will probably not be thoroughly convinced unless the characteristic stands the test of actual trial. Indeed I hardly felt entirely convinced myself, and decided to carry out such a test. But, before proceeding to describe this, it may be desirable to illustrate the sort of values that the characteristic can take. To the un-practised eye it is possible that all or most of the distributions given as illustrations in Chapter 2 look almost as like each other as the individual members of a flock of sheep look to a city clerk or a lecturer on statistics. So the inexperienced reader may perhaps be inclined to remark: 'You tell me that K is constant for all sizes of sample from the same work, but I want to know first whether very different values will be found for samples from different sources; most of your tables look to me much the same.' The question is readily answered by bringing together the values of K for the tables in question. Here they are:

	Table and subject	Characteristic K
Table 2.1.	Nouns: *De Imitatione Christi*	84·2
Table 2.2.	Nouns: à Kempis, *Miscellanea*	59·7
Table 2.3.	Nouns: Gerson's theological works	35·9
Table 2.4.	Nouns: Macaulay's essay on Bacon	27·2
Table 2.5.	Nouns: non-Vulgate, Gerson	69·3
Table 2.6.	Adjectives: *De Imitatione Christi*	236·6
Table 2.7.	Verbs: *De Imitatione Christi*	52·9
Table 2.9.	Nouns: St John's Gospel, Basic	141·5
Table 2.10.	Nouns: selected, St John's Gospel, A.V.	177·9
	Nouns: all, St John's Gospel, A.V.	161·5

I have added to the list the value obtained for St John's Gospel by including the thirty-four nouns omitted from the A.V. in order to obtain comparability with the Basic Version: this is the figure that would be comparable, e.g. with that for the *Imitatio*. There is clearly no doubt at all about the answer: the values of the characteristic show a very large, indeed almost an astonishing, range, from 27 to 237, a range of almost 9 to 1. And these tables were in no way selected; excepting the last, which was only compiled much later, they are a complete collection of all the distributions that had been compiled when the chapter was written. We need have no fear that the characteristic will fail to exhibit considerable differences from one case to another. Tables 2.1, 2.4 and the figure in the last line relate in each case to all nouns in a single work, and the range in the value of the characteristic is from 27 to 161.

4.2.   For a practical test, I thought I would like to base my smallest samples on some 2000 occurrences, so as to give at least a fairly substantial basis for the characteristic. If I formed four of such samples, say a, b, c and d, then by adding together the numbers of times a word occurred in any two of them, a and b, a and c, b and c, and so on, I could get a sample based on some 4000 occurrences. By adding together the numbers of times a word occurred in any three I could get a sample based on some 6000 occurrences. And finally by adding together the numbers of times a word occurred in all four I could get a sample based on some 8000 occurrences. In an old edition of Macaulay's *Essays* (ref. 4.2) the essay on Bacon, the longest of his essays, started a short way down page 349 and ended about half-way down page 418: omitting the first and last incomplete pages there were 68 complete pages on which to work. I decided to note nouns only, not other words, the previous work on Thomas à Kempis and Gerson having been done on nouns, and for simplicity to use the method of spread sampling. Samples taken from a few pages gave an average of 2·44 nouns to a full line, and this implied that a sample of 12 lines from each of the 68 pages would give something approximating to the 2000 occurrences desired for the smallest samples, since $2·44 \times 12 \times 68 = 1991$ to the nearest unit. As there were 56 lines to a page four samples could be taken from a page with a few lines to spare, and this was a necessary margin: incomplete lines may be cut out or paired with others and one has also to allow for the omission of verse or Latin quotations. These latter were so long on some pages as to cut samples rather short, and it was thought permissible slightly to extend samples on adjacent pages to make up the deficiency.

4.3.   The general scheme having been settled, the samples or sub-samples of 12 lines were marked off on each page. Though the position of the sample on the page hardly seemed likely to affect matters, the actual positions were varied, the samples being taken in the order *abcd* on one page, *dabc* on the next, *cdab* on the next, and so forth. All samples *a* were then read through and the nouns, in order as they occurred, written out on manuscript sheets. Never, to the best of my recollection, having been taught English grammar, I occasionally got into difficulties over the question 'What is a noun?' Verbal nouns in *-ing* present one such problem. Consider the two sets of words—

> the torturing of Peacham
> the propriety of torturing prisoners.

In the first instance 'torturing' is clearly a noun, as one might very well substitute 'torture'. In the second, it seems to be a gerund (vide S.O.E.D. sub *-ing*[1], 2) governing the object 'prisoners'. There are other troubles of a minor kind. 'Every thing', 'any thing', 'every body' and so on were so printed in the old-fashioned way: they have been counted as single words and as substantives. Hyphened words are a problem: in general it seems that they are on the way to become single words, and *steam-engine*, *water-wheel*, *brother-in-law*, etc. were so reckoned. But treatment was not always uniform. *Privy-councillor* was entered simply as *councillor*: *attorney* and *Attorney-General* were taken together. Simple titles, as *Lord*, *Lady*, *Earl*, were omitted when they occurred as titles only, as in *Lord Southampton*, *Lady Coke*, *the Earl of Essex*, but entered as nouns when they occurred separately. Homonyms, or distinct words spelt in the same way, were distinguished: e.g. *page* (boy) and *page* (of a book), *sap* (juice) and *sap* (military). Perhaps not quite logically I also distinguished *air* (atmosphere) from *air* (of music), though the words appear to be really the same. I do not recall whether *mere* spelling variants occurred in this work; my rule was not to distinguish them, though if different forms were associated with different meanings (e.g. *metal* and *mettle*, *travel* and *travail*) they *would* be distinguished as different words. But all these are minor troubles, and differences of treatment would make very little difference in the final results.

4.4. When the manuscript list for samples *a* had been completed, each word as it occurred was entered on a card and the occurrences booked up on to one line of that card by ticks or strokes (units), with a cross-stroke for every fifth to facilitate counting. The usual small cards, 5 in. × 3 in., were big enough, and a single line sufficed for the entries of even the most frequent word. When all the words had been booked on to the cards, the totals of the ticks were entered at the end of the lines. The cards were then sorted into packs by these totals, the packs counted and re-counted for checking, and the table compiled.

4.5.   Samples b were then treated in the same way, but after the completion of the entries not only the total for b had to be entered at the end of the line, but also on a lower line the total of the occurrences in a plus the occurrences in b. This total would most naturally be denoted by $a + b$, but for brevity, as in the tables that follow, I have denoted it by ab: thus ab means the sample obtained by adding together the occurrences for a and b, and similarly abc means the sample obtained by adding together the occurrences for a, b and c, and so on. The totals for b and for ab having been duly entered, the cards were then sorted twice, first to give the distribution for b and then to give the distribution for ab. The ab distribution was checked against the others by the sums S_1, for, denoting the distribution to which the summation applies by a prefix, we evidently must have

$$_{ab}S_1 = {}_aS_1 + {}_bS_1. \tag{4.2}$$

4.6.   The work was continued in precisely the same way, all the possible tables being booked up at each stage, and the work checked by the equations of the form (4.2). The completion of samples c gives four new tables, for c, ac, bc and abc. The completion of samples d gives no less than eight, viz. those for d, ad, bd, cd, abd, acd, bcd and $abcd$. In all there are fifteen distributions, four based on about 2000 occurrences each, six on about 4000 occurrences each, four on about 6000 occurrences each, and one on about 8000 occurrences.

4.7.   The distributions are shown in Tables 4.1 to 4.4. Table 4.1 gives the four distributions for the initial samples a, b, c and d of some 2000 occurrences each: the actual numbers of occurrences S_1 will be found collected in col. 3 of Table 4.5, and range from 1996 to 2041. Table 4.2 gives the six distributions based on all possible pairs of a, b, c and d, each distribution being therefore founded on some 4000 occurrences. Table 4.5 shows that the actual numbers of occurrences range from 3996 to 4049. Table 4.3 gives the four distributions based on all possible triplets of a, b, c and d, each distribution being therefore founded on some 6000 occurrences: referring again to col. 3 of Table 4.5 we see the actual numbers range from 6004 to 6049. Finally Table 4.4 (already entered as an illustration in Chapter 2 as Table 2.4) gives the distribution based on the number of times each word occurred in the four samples a, b, c and d taken together: it is founded on 8045 occurrences. These tables are worth a close inspection. A summary of the principal constants will be found in Table 4.5 and of numbers showing their proportional variation in Table 4.6.

4.8. Looking first at Table 4.1, it is obvious to the eye that the four samples are very fairly consistent with one another. They lead off with some 59 to 63 per cent of once-nouns, nouns occurring only once, cf. Table 4.5, col. 9, and the frequencies then tail away in the usual fashion: towards the foot of each column there is one word with an outstanding number of occurrences ranging from 53 to 75, as a matter of fact the word *man*. The means (Table 4.5, col. 5) range from 2·12 to 2·21 and the standard deviations from 2·89 to 3·17 (Table 4.5, col. 8). The frequencies in the four columns show

TABLE 4.1. Sampling Experiment. Table showing the number f_x of nouns occurring X times in four samples, each based on about 2000 occurrences of a noun, from Macaulay's essay on Bacon. For the actual number on which each sample was based $= S_1 = S(f_x X)$, and for other constants of the distributions, see Table 4.5. The following tables all relate to the same experiment

X	Number f_x of nouns occurring X times in samples				X	Number f_x of nouns occurring X times in samples			
	a	b	c	d		a	b	c	d
1	535	580	589	591	17	2	—	—	—
2	169	174	158	167	18	—	2	3	1
3	69	68	68	73	19	—	—	1	—
4	42	29	32	47	20	1	—	1	—
5	24	24	21	25	21	—	—	—	1
6	18	15	16	24	22	—	—	1	1
7	14	9	15	11	23	—	1	—	—
8	4	8	12	8	26	1	—	—	—
9	7	8	7	2	29	—	1	—	—
10	5	5	5	4	53	—	—	1	—
11	3	3	5	—	63	1	—	—	—
12	4	4	1	3	64	—	1	—	—
13	1	2	1	3	75	—	—	—	1
14	2	—	2	1					
15	—	2	—	—	Total	903	936	937	964
16	1	—	—	1					

few at all conspicuous divergences from one another. The degree of consistence of the four distributions with one another was tested by the χ^2 method (refs. A): the rows in Table 4.1 were grouped as follows: 1, 2, 3, 4, 5, 6, 7–8, 9–11, 12 and upwards, and the resulting table of four columns and nine rows treated as a contingency table. I found $\chi^2 = 19·66$: the degrees of freedom ν (number of rows less one multiplied by number of columns less one) are 24, and Pearson's n' for entering Table XII of *Tables for Statisticians and Biometricians* is 25. Entering that table accordingly, I made $P = 0·72$, that is to say, one would expect to get a worse agreement on *random* sampling some seven times out of ten. This is a high degree of consistence.

TABLE 4.2. Six samples, each based on about 4000 occurrences of a noun, given by combining the samples of Table 4.1 in pairs. See heading of that table

X	Number f_x of nouns occurring X times in samples					
	ab	ac	bc	ad	bd	cd
1	739	751	772	794	780	778
2	244	261	251	226	263	253
3	119	106	125	119	126	124
4	74	66	62	70	65	66
5	48	48	47	56	56	49
6	43	29	25	35	33	34
7	17	16	26	23	22	31
8	14	27	17	21	17	11
9	14	14	12	11	9	11
10	11	12	7	10	12	15
11	4	6	12	18	8	12
12	3	5	7	8	9	7
13	12	12	4	3	4	6
14	6	3	5	1	3	6
15	3	3	4	5	7	4
16	3	5	5	2	4	3
17	2	1	7	4	3	2
18	4	4	2	3	4	2
19	1	2	5	—	3	1
20	2	4	2	2	1	4
21	3	3	2	2	1	3
22	1	1	1	4	2	2
23	1	3	1	—	1	1
24	2	1	—	1	1	—
25	2	—	—	1	1	—
26	—	—	1	—	—	—
27	2	—	—	1	1	1
29	1	—	1	1	—	—
30	1	1	—	1	—	—
31	—	1	—	—	—	1
32	—	1	—	—	—	—
33	—	—	—	—	1	—
34	—	—	—	—	1	—
35	—	—	—	1	—	—
36	—	1	1	—	—	1
37	1	—	1	—	—	—
38	—	1	1	—	—	1
39	—	—	—	—	—	1
40	—	—	—	—	—	2
41	1	—	1	—	—	—
42	—	—	—	1	—	—
44	—	—	—	1	1	—
47	—	—	1	—	—	—
48	—	1	—	—	—	—
49	1	—	—	—	—	—
51	—	—	—	—	1	—
116	—	1	—	—	—	—
117	—	—	1	—	—	—
127	1	—	—	—	—	—
128	—	—	—	—	—	1
138	—	—	—	1	—	—
139	—	—	—	—	1	—
Total	1380	1390	1409	1426	1441	1432

TABLE 4.3. Four samples, each based on about 6000 occurrences of a noun, given by combining the samples of Table 4.1 in sets of three. See heading of that table

X	Number f_x of nouns occurring X times in samples				X	Number f_x of nouns occurring X times in samples			
	abc	abd	acd	bcd		abc	abd	acd	bcd
1	880	910	901	906	33	—	1	2	1
2	306	297	314	311	34	—	2	1	—
3	146	166	153	162	35	1	—	—	—
4	93	82	84	87	36	—	—	—	1
5	66	64	56	58	37	—	1	1	—
6	44	37	41	45	38	1	1	—	—
7	31	44	38	46	39	—	2	1	—
8	20	25	33	22	41	—	—	—	1
9	29	27	21	19	45	—	1	—	1
10	15	19	17	14	46	1	—	—	—
11	14	15	13	14	47	—	—	1	—
12	8	7	10	13	48	1	—	1	—
13	6	6	13	11	49	1	—	—	—
14	10	10	11	10	53	—	—	1	—
15	7	8	6	4	54	—	—	—	1
16	3	4	5	3	55	1	—	—	1
17	8	5	7	7	58	—	1	—	—
18	4	6	5	4	59	—	1	—	—
19	5	3	3	4	60	—	—	1	—
20	1	7	5	3	62	—	—	—	1
21	2	3	1	6	63	1	—	—	—
22	7	1	1	1	66	—	—	1	—
23	3	—	3	4	67	1	—	—	—
24	3	2	3	2	69	—	—	—	1
25	1	3	1	5	71	—	1	—	—
26	3	1	4	2	180	1	—	—	—
27	3	2	—	1	191	—	—	1	—
28	1	3	2	2	192	—	—	—	1
29	1	—	3	2	202	—	1	—	—
30	2	3	2	1					
31	3	—	1	1	Total	1736	1773	1768	1780
32	2	1	—	1					

TABLE 4.4. Sample based on about 8000 (8045) occurrences of a noun given by combining all four samples of Table 4.1. See heading of that table

X	f_x	X	f_x	X	f_x	X	f_x
1	990	14	10	27	3	40	1
2	367	15	13	28	4	41	1
3	173	16	3	29	1	45	2
4	112	17	10	30	3	48	1
5	72	18	7	31	2	57	1
6	47	19	6	32	1	58	1
7	41	20	5	33	1	65	1
8	31	21	1	34	1	76	1
9	34	22	4	35	1	81	1
10	17	23	7	36	1	89	1
11	24	24	2	37	1	255	1
12	19	25	1	38	2	Total	2048
13	10	26	5	39	4		

TABLE 4.5. Data for the preceding Tables 4.1–4.4. If f_x is the frequency of nouns occurring X times,

$$S_0 = N = S(f_x), \quad S_1 = S(f_x X), \quad S_2 = S(f_x X^2)$$

M in col. 5 is the mean S_1/S_0. Col. 6 gives the number of distinct nouns per 1000 occurrences of a noun $= 1000 S_0/S_1$: cols. 7 and 8 the variance and the standard deviation: col. 9 the percentage of nouns occurring only once and col. 10 the characteristic K, equation (4.1)

1	2	3	4	5	6	7	8	9	10
Sample	S_0	S_1	S_2	M	$1000 \times S_0/S_1$	σ^2	σ	% of 1's	K
a	903	2,000	13,140	2·21	451	9·550	3·09	59·2	27·85
b	936	1,996	13,434	2·13	469	9·805	3·13	62·0	28·71
c	937	2,008	12,152	2·14	467	8·377	2·89	62·9	25·16
d	964	2,041	14,035	2·12	472	10·077	3·17	61·3	28·79
Mean	—	—	—	2·15	465	9·452	3·07	61·3	27·63
ab	1,380	3,996	48,796	2·90	345	26·975	5·19	53·6	28·06
ac	1,390	4,008	46,174	2·88	347	24·904	4·99	54·0	26·25
bc	1,409	4,004	46,674	2·84	352	25·050	5·01	54·8	26·62
ad	1,426	4,041	49,967	2·83	353	27·010	5·20	55·7	28·12
bd	1,441	4,037	50,433	2·80	357	27·150	5·21	54·1	28·47
cd	1,432	4,049	47,441	2·83	354	25·134	5·01	54·3	26·47
Mean	—	—	—	2·85	351	26·037	5·10	54·4	27·33
abc	1,736	6,004	102,918	3·46	289	47·323	6·88	50·7	26·88
abd	1,773	6,037	108,587	3·40	294	49·651	7·05	51·3	28·14
acd	1,768	6,049	104,255	3·42	292	47·262	6·87	51·0	26·84
bcd	1,780	6,045	104,927	3·40	294	47·414	6·89	50·9	27·06
Mean	—	—	—	3·42	292	47·912	6·92	51·0	27·23
$abcd$	2,048	8,045	183,963	3·93	255	74·395	8·63	48·3	27·18

TABLE 4.6. The data of cols 5–10 of the preceding table, reduced by putting the mean of the four values for a, b, c and d in each table equal to 1000

1	2	3	4	5	6	7
Sample	M	S_0/S_1	σ^2	σ	% of 1's	K
a	1028	970	1010	1007	965	1008
b	991	1009	1037	1020	1011	1039
c	995	1005	886	941	1025	911
d	986	1016	1066	1033	999	1042
Mean	1000	1000	1000	1000	1000	1000
ab	1349	742	2854	1691	874	1016
ac	1340	747	2635	1625	880	950
bc	1321	757	2650	1632	893	964
ad	1316	760	2858	1694	908	1018
bd	1302	768	2872	1697	882	1030
cd	1316	762	2659	1632	885	958
Mean	1324	756	2755	1662	887	989
abc	1609	622	5007	2241	826	973
abd	1581	633	5253	2296	836	1019
acd	1591	628	5000	2238	831	971
bcd	1581	633	5016	2244	830	979
Mean	1591	629	5069	2255	831	986
$abcd$	1827	549	7871	2811	787	984

4.9.   Indeed the consistence seems to me specially remarkable from the standpoint of the use of words when it is remembered how our samples were taken. If they had been random samples from the whole work they might well, so to speak, have been all tangled up with one another, *a* having many words from the same sentences as *b*, and so on. But actually each of our samples was based on a separate and distinct set of passages, and in these

TABLE 4.7. Showing the 2048 words in the vocabulary of Table 4.4 classified according to the samples in which they occurred. A capital letter *A* signifies 'occurring in the corresponding sample', a Greek letter 'not occurring in the corresponding sample', e.g. A = occurring in sample *a*, α = not occurring in sample *a*. $A\beta\gamma\delta$ = occurring in *a*, but not *b*, *c* or *d*. $A\beta C\delta$ = occurring in *a* and *c*, but not in *b* or *d* and so on

	Class	Number of words		Class	Number of words
1	$A\beta\gamma\delta$	268	10	$\alpha\beta CD$	81
2	$\alpha B\gamma\delta$	280	11	$ABC\delta$	62
3	$\alpha\beta C\delta$	275	12	$AB\gamma D$	58
4	$\alpha\beta\gamma D$	312	13	$A\beta CD$	53
5	$AB\gamma\delta$	68	14	αBCD	64
6	$A\beta C\delta$	64	15	$ABCD$	271
7	$A\beta\gamma D$	59			
8	$\alpha BC\delta$	67		Total	2048
9	$\alpha B\gamma D$	66			

separate and distinct sets of passages the author remains self-consistent as regards his admixture of more and less frequently occurring words. The actual nouns (vocabulary of nouns) on which each several sample is based are also of course largely different from one sample to another: it is in fact an interesting question to ask ourselves what percentage of the nouns (vocabulary) in any one sample is found or not found in any other. The answer is that just about half the nouns in any one of the four samples will be found in any other, and just about half will not: the mean percentage of common nouns is actually 48·9 with a range from 45·7 to 50·8. These figures are by no means obvious, but they can be obtained from the totals at the foot of Tables 4.1 to 4.4, summarised in col. 2 of Table 4.5. The easiest way to proceed and to enable us to get comparable figures for other tables is to calculate at once, as in Table 4.7, the number of words occurring in each sample or specified set of samples *only*: the reader unfamiliar with the notation used would do well to read the text-book chapter cited in refs. A. From Table 4.5, col. 2, foot, we have for the totality of nouns 2048, of which 1780 occur in *b*, *c* or *d*. The difference $2048 - 1780 = 268$ is the number occurring in a only or $(A\beta\gamma\delta)$ in the notation of Table 4.7. The figures under 2, 3 and 4 in Table 4.7 are obtained similarly. Next, Table 4.5 shows S_0 for abc as 1736, for bc as 1409. The difference $1736 - 1409 = 327$. This must be the number of nouns in a but not in b, c or d, plus the nouns in a and d but not in b or c. But the first of these numbers $(A\beta\gamma\delta)$ we have found to be 268, therefore the second or $(A\beta\gamma D) = 327 - 268 = 59$. The remaining entries in Table 4.7 can be obtained step by step in the same way, and having completed that table we can readily answer any such question as that with which we started. Take sample a for example, and suppose we want to find out how many and what percentage of nouns it has in common with b, c or d. Sample a includes all the classes of Table 4.7 with an A in the class-symbol, eight in all, as below:

Sample a	Number of words	Of which are common to		
		Sample b	Sample c	Sample d
$A\beta\gamma\delta$	268	—	—	—
$AB\gamma\delta$	68	68	—	—
$A\beta C\delta$	64	—	64	—
$A\beta\gamma D$	59	—	—	59
$ABC\delta$	62	62	62	—
$AB\gamma D$	58	58	—	58
$A\beta CD$	53	—	53	53
$ABCD$	271	271	271	271
Total	903	459	450	441
Percentage common	—	50·8	49·8	48·8

Of the eight classes, the four with a B in the class-symbol contain words common to sample b, the four with a C in the symbol contain words common to sample c, and the four with a D in the symbol contain words common to sample d. The numbers in these classes are tabulated in the three columns to the right, and totalled. There are 459 words common to sample b, and 459 is 50·8 per cent of 903, and so on. All the corresponding percentages were calculated for samples b, c and d, and the mean of the twelve was 48·9 per cent as stated above. The high degree of consistency observed is therefore obtained in spite of the fact that a round half of the nouns in any one of the samples is different from that in any other. It is a statistical consistency for the mode in which the writer uses nouns in general.

4.10.   Turning now to Table 4.2, we see that the distributions have greatly extended. The outstanding *man* occurred 116 to 139 times, and there is quite a considerable number of nouns which occurred from 30 to 50 times. The distributions again look very fairly consistent, there being only a few rather conspicuous divergences, for example in lines 11 and 13. It should be noted that the only independent pairs of samples in this table are ab and *cd, ac* and *bd, bc* and *ad,* so it is better to look at these pairs when making comparisons. In all other pairs of samples in the table one of the basic samples is common to both members of the pair, *a* being common to *ab* and *ac,* and so on, so that the distributions for the two members of such a pair are bound to be more or less alike. Investigation by the method of § 4.9 shows that for the independent pairs the average percentage of nouns common to the two members of the pair is 55·1, with a range of 53·4 to 56·3; while for the overlapping pairs the average is 75·1, with a range of 72·4 to 76·7. Table 4.3 shows the distributions extending still further, *man* occurring 180 to 202 times. The distributions of this table look very consistent, but then they ought to be: of the three initial samples on which any one of them is based two are common to any other. There are no independent pairs. In Table 4.4 finally we have the distribution based on all four of the original samples. The total number of occurrences is here over 8000 and the distribution has reached its greatest extension. The most frequent nouns are *power* (65 occurrences), *time* (76), *mind* (81), *philosophy* (89) and *man* (255).

4.11.   Now let us see how the characteristic K has behaved. The value for each distribution is given in Table 4.5, col. 10. For the four initial samples *a, b, c* and *d* of some 2000 occurrences each the characteristics range from 25·16 to 28·79, a range of 3·63 units. Four observations are preposterously few on which to found an estimate of the standard error, but so far as they go (if we use 3 as the divisor for the sum of the squares of deviations (cf. refs. A), and not 4) they give an estimate of 1·70. The mean value for this first group is 27·63. For the second group of distributions, based on some 4000 occurrences, K ranges from 26·25 for *ac* to 28·47 for *bd.* All the values for this group fall therefore within the range of the values for the first group, and the mean 27·33 is only slightly lower than the mean for that group. For the third group, based on some 6000 occurrences for each distribution, the range is from 26·84 for *acd* to 28·14 for *abd.* All the values for the third group fall therefore within the range for the second group and *a fortiori* within the range for the first group. The mean is 27·23, very slightly lower again. Finally, for the total distribution based on the whole 8045 occurrences the value of K is 27·18, only 0·45 lower than the mean for the first group in which the distributions were based on the comparatively small total of some 2000 occurrences each. The slight fall in the mean value of K is continuous from the first group to the last, but no great importance can be attached to it, for so far as we are in a position to estimate them it seems clearly to lie well within the limits of fluctuations of sampling, the standard error being of the order $1·70/2 = 0·85$ for samples of 8000. If the fall be real, it may be due to slight heterogeneity of the samples, for which there is evidence (§ 7.8). The experiment could hardly have better illustrated the statistical constancy of the characteristic.

4.12.   Brief inspection shows how greatly this behaviour differs from that of the mean, variance, etc. The means are given in col. 5 of Table 4.5. For a, b, c and d they range from 2·12 to 2·21, with a general average of 2·15— the simple arithmetic mean was taken both in this and the following cases, not the weighted mean. For the second group the general average is 2·85, for the third 3·42, and for the final table the mean is 3·93. The absolute increase with size of sample is at first large, then smaller. For the *complete* distribution the mean would of course be directly proportional to S_1, since the divisor would be the constant number of words at risk W (cf. §§ 3.12 *et seq.*, and equation (3.15)): but in our case the divisor is S_0 (or the N of § 3.23), which increases with S_1. As will be seen from Table 4.6, col. 2, in which comparative figures are given, the total increase in the mean is over 80 per cent. In the next column, col. 6, of Table 4.5 I have given the ratio $1000 S_0/S_1$, the number of nouns in the vocabulary per 1000 occurrences of a noun. As this is a thousand times the reciprocal of the mean its behaviour is naturally precisely the reverse. The general average falls from 465 for the first group of samples to 351 for the second and 292 for the third and a figure of 255 for the final table, a drop of 45 per cent over the range (Table 4.6, col. 3). Col. 7 of Table 4.5 gives the variance or square of the standard deviation. Here the rate of increase with size of sample is enormously rapid, cf. Table 4.6, col. 4. The final variance is little less than eight times the variance of the initial samples. The standard deviation itself (Table 4.5, col. 8 and Table 4.6, col. 5) of course does not increase so rapidly, but we have an increase from a mean of 3·07 for the first group to a figure of 8·63 for the final table, an increase in the proportion of roundly 2·8 to 1. The percentage of once-nouns, $100 f_1/S_0$, is given in Table 4.5, col. 9. Here there is a steady and quite conspicuous drop as the size of sample is increased, from a mean of 61.3 for the first group to a figure of 48·3 for the final table, or in the proportion of 1000 to 787 (Table 4.6, col. 6), but this is not nearly so large a change as in most of the other cases. For all the preceding measures the figure for the final table, Table 4.4, lies wholly *outside* the range of values for the initial samples a, b, c and d. For the characteristic K, the value for the final table lies well *within* the range of values for a, b, c and d and only 1·6 per cent (Table 4.6, col. 7) below their mean. The contrast is complete. All the measures in Table 4.5 except the characteristic show systematic, and for the most part large, changes with size of sample. The characteristic alone appears to be constant within the limits of fluctuations of sampling. The result will, I hope, give some confidence in the use of the characteristic even to the non-mathematical reader.

4.13.   The characteristic was derived from the expression for v_λ^2, the square of the coefficient of variation of the liabilities of the words at risk, v_λ^2 and K being linear functions of each other. From (3.23) we have

$$v_\lambda^2 = 10^{-4} WK - 1. \tag{4.3}$$

Let us consider what sort of values of v_λ this is likely to imply and what we can further conjecture about the form of the λ-distribution, in order to throw a little more light on the meaning and implications of K.

4.14.   In order to estimate v_λ we have to estimate W, the number of words at risk, the total number of words in the author's 'treasure-chest'. This number is, I believe, likely to be much larger, even very much larger, than the estimates usually given for an author's vocabulary, but the conception is an entirely different one. It is not a question of the number of words the author has in fact used in the finite field of his writings, but of how many words he had at call for purposes of use (cf. §§ 3.19, 3.20), and the phrase 'had at call' should be understood in the widest possible sense. It is, I think, true that every word one has ever read is in some sense stored in the mind: if one says one cannot *remember* the word for this or the other, one usually means no more than that one cannot at the moment *recall* it. That there *was* a record in the memory is shown by the fact of 'recognition' when the word does turn up, as was pointed out by St Augustine over 1500 years ago (*Conf.* x. xix). Our language about the memory is indeed very deficient: there seems to be no term to express the simple existence of a record in the mind, as distinct from the capacity to call up that record at a given time. The two things are both important, but entirely distinct; and the second, as most of us know, varies greatly from time to time. Capacity to recall is subject not only to secular change, to that all too familiar deterioration with age which often renders it impossible to recall when wanted even a well-known name or word, but to fluctuation from day to day, hour to hour, and second to second. At one instant we may be quite unable to recall a word that is wanted; a moment or two later, for no assignable reason, it may suddenly toss up. In writing, for example, the sentence a few lines above, I could not for the life of me think of the word *deterioration*. Falling off..., worsening..., decrease..., these were clearly not the words I wanted. There was surely a better term. Leaving a blank, I went on: and shortly afterwards, as I was poking the fire, the wanted word suddenly flashed into view. No sharp line, I submit, can be drawn between such ill-trained dogs of words, which will not come when we whistle for them but soon appear from nowhere with a disarming smile, and those words which we fail to recall for some considerable period of time and then describe as 'completely forgotten'. Some casual, some exceptional stimulus may bring them back. So that, as I picture it, the writer's treasury really does contain all the words he has ever read, and for any man of wide reading they are bound to add up to a very impressive total.

4.15.   But, the sceptical reader may say, is this really so? Surely we *have* completely forgotten many words; they have gone entirely beyond recall? You yourself remarked that, before you took up again the study of Latin, you only had a very small vocabulary remaining from what you had learned in school (§ 2.21). True: but I was using ordinary terms in an ordinary sense: one had very few words, out of all those learned in school, which were still *readily at call*, or the meanings of which were still readily at call. What I submit is, that the chance of recall of a word once learnt is not strictly and mathematically zero though it may be indefinitely small, 10^{-10} (i.e. 0·000,000,000,1) if you please, or less than that. I knew very well an old lady who once, in her last years, when under morphia, suddenly started talking fluent Hindustani: she was heard, and what she was saying in part at least interpreted, by a younger brother. She had not spoken the language for well over forty years, and in normal circumstances this would have been an impossible feat. But the records of words and sentence structure were there, and somehow the drug had rendered them accessible. If morphia, why not some other stimulus or release?

4.16.   To use a metaphor somewhat different from that of § 3.18, perhaps a better analogy to the facts though it is not susceptible of the same numerical treatment, the writer's treasure-chest may be pictured as containing, beneath the top layers of words in daily and hourly use, lower layers of less frequently but still fairly frequently used words, words also fairly readily at call and in numbers greatly exceeding those in daily use. Below these again will be layers of words in still less frequent use, and more difficult of recall, but amounting in all to a still larger total. And right at the bottom of the chest there will be layer on dusty layer, but rarely disturbed, of words very infrequently used and very hard to recall. The λ's for words in the top layers will be relatively large: for words in the bottom layers microscopically small, but not zero.

4.17.   To get some first rough notion of the order of magnitude of the numbers in question, I made several sample counts of the numbers of nouns, adjectives and verbs in certain dictionaries by the method of §§ 3.4, 3.5. The results are given in brief in Table 4.8. My first count was that of nouns in Lewis and Short's *Latin Dictionary*, and was made on 200 random pages. This, I finally decided, was over-elaboration. Only a rough estimate is needed, and it is no use attempting greatly to reduce the standard error of sampling, since one worker may differ quite considerably from another in the words he includes under the term 'noun'. For the later counts in English dictionaries I therefore contented myself with the modest number of 50 pages. As will be seen from the table, counts were made in two different dictionaries, the original edition of the *Concise Oxford*, and the first issue of the *Shorter Oxford* (2 vols.), both of which happened to be on my shelves. The scope of the *Concise Oxford Dictionary* is more or less strictly limited to 'current' words, not including even all words used by Shakespeare or in the Authorised Version of the Bible: scientific and technical terms are included only in so far as they seem to have attained a certain limited currency amongst the general public. This proved rather a troublesome dictionary to count, with long lists of words in italics occasionally to be found under some main heading in heavy type. The *Shorter Oxford Dictionary* 'is designed to embrace not only the literary and colloquial English of the present day together with such technical and scientific terms as are most frequently met with or are likely to be the subject of inquiry, but also a considerable proportion of obsolete, archaic, and dialectal words and uses'. It proved a much easier dictionary to use: a look-out must of course be kept for words not given separate articles and included only at the end of some principal article, but these are clearly set in heavy type.

4.18.   Considering first the Latin vocabulary, it is obvious that Lewis and Short's dictionary includes a very large number of words which would be almost certainly unknown to either of our authors, Thomas à Kempis or Gerson. There are words, for example, known only from inscriptions, or from one passage in an out-of-the-way author, semi-technical words that can only be vaguely defined ('a disease of animals', an 'unknown kind of fish') or not defined at all ('a word of uncertain meaning found only in —'), and so forth. On the other hand, while the dictionary contains a fair number of late-Latin words and apparently most but not all of the nouns in the Vulgate, it is not a dictionary of mediaeval Latin and very many words of 'middling and infamous latinity' which are not included therein must have been known to the authors with whom we are concerned. The proportion of the nouns found in the vocabularies of Tables 2.1–2.3 but not in Lewis and Short is, however, less than might be expected. The three vocabularies include in all 2454 nouns: of these only 148 or 6·03 per cent are not in Lewis and Short. For the *Imitatio* the proportion is 38/1168 or only 3·25 per cent; for the sample from the miscellaneous works of Thomas à Kempis 38/1406 or 2·70 per cent; for the sample from Gerson's works 101/1754 or 5·76 per cent. All these nouns are, however, very infrequently used, 70 to 80 per cent of them in the respective vocabularies occurring only once. As a result, the

TABLE 4.8. Giving rough estimates of total numbers of nouns, adjectives and verbs in several dictionaries, Latin and English

	Pages sampled	Estimated total number of nouns, adjectives or verbs	Standard error
Latin: Lewis and Short, *Latin Dictionary*			
Nouns	200	17,000	760
Adjectives	200	9,700	600
Verbs	100	7,200	750
English: *Concise Oxford Dictionary*, 1911			
Nouns	50	24,600	1,100
Adjectives	50	13,000	1,500
Verbs	50	7,700	1,100
English: *Shorter Oxford English Dictionary*, 2 vols. 1933			
Nouns	50	58,000	3,000
Adjectives	50	27,000	2,600
Verbs	50	13,500	1,500

percentages in our small samples must seriously underestimate the percentages in the respective vocabularies of words at risk, which are likely to be a good deal higher, an important point that is dealt with in the next chapter (§§ 5.14 *et seq.*). This leaves us with the very indefinite conclusion that the total of nouns at risk is 17,000 less a heavy deduction for nouns unknown to the respective authors plus an addition of something a good deal more than 6 per cent and possibly three or four times that amount for late-Latin words. I see no practicable way of making a real estimate, but would put W for the nouns of Thomas à Kempis and Gerson as probably of the order of 10,000: 5000 would, in my opinion, be probably too low. It is a natural question whether we should not assign a higher value for Gerson, with his observed vocabulary of 1754 (Table 2.3), than for Thomas à Kempis, with his observed vocabulary of 1406 for the comparable sample from the miscellaneous writings (Table 2.2). This may well be, as Gerson was certainly much the more widely read, especially in the classics, which he quotes freely: but no such conclusion would be justified on the basis of the samples alone. As pointed out in the next chapter (§§ 5.1–5.13), deductions from the relative magnitudes of the vocabularies in small samples as to the relative magnitudes of W's may be entirely fallacious. I am not inclined therefore to hazard separate guesses for the values of W for nouns in Thomas à Kempis and in Gerson. Nor will I venture on guesses for adjectives or verbs, on which no work has been done.

4.19.   Turning to the English vocabulary and considering it with reference to Table 2.4 for Macaulay's essay on Bacon, I think we may omit the evidence of the *Concise Oxford Dictionary*: it is too much limited to current words, too poor in older and archaic words, to be an adequate guide to the vocabulary of any writer whose reading has been wide. It will be seen that the number of nouns in the *Shorter Oxford Dictionary* is enormous, somewhere about 58,000. Of these quite a large number are of a later date than Macaulay, and therefore cannot have formed part of his vocabulary. A number of obsolete words that are rare, and of technical terms, he may not have known. It occurred to me that it might be possible to make a rather better controlled estimate of W than in the last case by running through again the 50 pages that had been sampled, and omitting such nouns as could hardly have been known to Macaulay owing to their late date, or were unlikely to have been known to him owing to their technical character, or to their being both obsolete and rare—there is obviously a considerable margin for personal opinion as regards this last class especially. I made such a count accordingly, omitting (1) nouns of later date than Macaulay or with a date only in the last years of his life, (2) the rarer obsolete or archaic words, (3) technical terms he would, in my judgment, be unlikely to know. I was on the other hand generous with old law terms, with which as a lawyer he might well be acquainted, and as a very minor matter with Anglo-Indian nouns, with which his four years in India would have made him familiar. The result of the count was rather surprising even to my liberal notions: it gave an estimate in round numbers of no less than $32,000 \pm 1400$ nouns as possibly known to Macaulay. As a further control yet another count was made, with greater strictness on the rarer or more out-of-the-way words. The result was an estimate of $23,500 \pm 1000$ roundly. At a much later date it occurred to me that it might be a useful control to make a parallel count for someone with whom I was much better acquainted than I was with Macaulay, viz. myself. A count made on precisely similar lines for my own vocabulary of nouns gave a figure, $23,000 \pm 1000$, not significantly different from the last and more stringent count for Macaulay: I was lower in my count on a number of the pages, but quite appreciably higher on others, especially those with many scientific words. In view of these counts it seems hardly possible to put the total *W* of nouns at risk for Macaulay as less than some 20,000, with a possible estimate of something more like 30,000. I fully realise that such figures are likely to strike the reader as impossibly high, but let him recall the meaning of *W* and what was said in § 4.14. If he prefers to make another count himself the dictionaries are there.

4.20.   It may, of course, be said that we ought to proceed by making an estimate direct from Macaulay's works, but the trouble is that the task would be almost overwhelmingly formidable. We would have to proceed by applying to his works as a whole the method of sampling applied to the essay on Bacon. If we took a series of samples each spread over the whole of the works (as samples *a*, *b*, *c* and *d* were each spread over the whole of the essay) and representing respectively when combined say 1/10, 2/10, 3/10, ... 9/10 and the whole of the works, the resulting graph of vocabulary plotted against size of sample *might* enable us to extrapolate and find a fair estimate for the limit. How close an estimate would depend on the final slope of the graph obtained: if even the difference between the vocabularies for 9/10 of the works and the whole works was at all considerable, a close estimate of the limit would still remain impossible. Of course even the whole of an author's works does not show the whole of his vocabulary in the sense defined.

4.21.   This last remark raises another point as to such estimates. Surely, it may be argued, you are forgetting that in any practical case we are dealing with writings in a given field: the nature of that field will determine the words used, and will confine the author to (it may be) but a very small selection of all the words he knows. His entire vocabulary will not really be at risk for writings in that field. With both Thomas à Kempis and Gerson, for example, we are dealing with religious writings only: surely this completely excludes large numbers of words—the chance of their occurrence will be mathematically zero?

4.22.   Now certainly the nature of the field determines the λ's of the given vocabulary, tends to make certain words (such as *God*, *Lord*, *man*, *grace*, *faith*, *world*, etc. in religious writings) relatively frequent, and others infrequent or very rare. But can we say that it makes the chance of any word known to the author being used *strictly and mathematically* zero? Even in an extreme instance (e.g. vulgarly obscene words) it seems to me that it would probably be more exact to describe the chance as infinitesimally small rather than zero, but the point is hardly worth contesting, for the totality of such words is so minute a fraction of the entire vocabulary. But for words in ordinary use in any branch of literature it does not seem to me possible to regard as zero the chance of a particular word occurring in a writing on a given field, *merely because the word is foreign to that field*. The more closely attention is paid to the point, the more clear does it seem to me that almost any word *may* occur in a work on almost any subject. The field determines relative frequencies, it may make the chance of a given word so small that it is very unlikely to be found in a sample of specified size, but it does not make the chance absolutely zero: that at least is my view. Quotations and allusions, or half-jesting usages, may bring in the most rare and obsolete forms. Fables, parables, allegories, tales told by the way, and above all tropes, similes, metaphors, analogies of every kind, may introduce words quite remote from the subject with which the author is dealing. Sheep, lambs and sheepfold; goats, vine and vineyard; seed, tares, fig-tree, grapes and thorns, figs and thistles; the plough and the yoke—these are agricultural words, but biblical use has woven them into the very tissue of Christian religious thought. The *talent* is an ancient weight and hence a money of account: but the parable of the talents has rendered it more familiar as a term for mental endowments than in its original sense. In modern religious writings the most purely technical terms of physical science may occur. And at times one may meet with real oddities. In a reported sermon I found a reference to a certain reddish resin used in varnish manufacture. The preacher appeared to have been misled by the commercial name 'dragon's blood' into regarding its importation as an indication of the growth of superstition.

4.23.   Illustrations may be drawn in plenty from the works of Thomas à Kempis. How does he come to mention a shoemaker and his awl, a tiler and his tiles, a smith and his hammer, a tailor and his needle and thread, a barber and his razors? By giving a string of vigorous similes for the state of a cleric without religious books:

Nam clericus sine sacris libris quasi miles sine armis: equus sine frenis; navis sine remis: scriptor sine pennis; avis sine alis: ascensor sine scalis; sutor sine subulis: tector sine tegulis; faber sine malleis: sartor sine acu et filis; rasor sine cultris: sagittator sine iaculis; viator sine baculo: caecus sine ductore. (*Doctrinale Iuvenum*, Pohl, IV. 189.)

And a few lines lower down on the same page we find amongst other things a kitchen and its pots and pans making an appearance:

Similiter claustrum et congregatio clericorum sine sacris libris: quasi coquina sine ollis mensa sine cibis; puteus sine aquis: rivus sine piscibus; saccus sine vestibus: hortus sine floribus; bursa sine pecuniis: vinea sine botris; turris sine custodibus: domus sine utensilibus. (*Ibid.*)

He mentions the familiar windmill; for the heart revolves good thoughts and evil, sad thoughts and happy, like a mill driven by the wind:

Cor non potest diu quiescere nec lingua tacere: aut enim bona aut mala imaginatur; aut tristia pensat, aut laeta revolvit: sicut molendinum quod a vento movetur. (*Manuale Parvulorum*, Pohl, IV. 168.)

To conclude with an example from a very different field, we may well ask how Macaulay comes to mention, in an essay on Bacon, the substantive *abortive*, i.e. a drug causing abortion. Marry, because

We have no patience with a philosophy which, like those Roman matrons who swallowed abortives in order to preserve their shapes, takes pains to be barren for fear of being homely.

The nature of the field then, I submit, while it determines the λ-distribution, and therefore the words that tend to be most frequent and the vocabulary per 1000 occurrences in a given sample, cannot necessarily be held to affect W, the total vocabulary at risk.

4.24.   Some, however, may differ from these conclusions: in Table 4.9 I have therefore given the values of v_λ corresponding to the characteristics of Tables 2.1 to 2.4 for a wide range of values of W. It may be noted in the first place that since v_λ is not far from proportional to the square root of W, the values in the last column, for $W = 30{,}000$, are only some 2·5 times the values in the first column for $W = 5000$. For the first three tables based on Latin nouns I estimated (§ 4.18) that W was probably of the order 10,000, and on this estimate the range of v_λ is roundly from about 9 down to about 6. If the reader prefer an estimate of something more like 5000, in my opinion too low a figure, he can take the v_λ's of the preceding column, which range from 6·41 down to 4·12. In the case of Table 2.4, based on Macaulay's essay on Bacon, for the reasons given in § 4.19 I am hardly inclined to put W lower than 20,000, and this would bring its v_λ to 7·38, not far from the value of Table 2.2 on the assumption of $W = 10{,}000$. All these figures are obviously of the nature of rough guesses: the clear and important point is that on *any* reasonable assumption as to the value of W the values of v_λ are very high. Now it is evident from what has been said above (§§ 4.14–4.16 and the earlier discussion in §§ 3.18–3.20) that the λ-distributions are almost certainly of the same form as the word-distributions, although they are continuous and not discontinuous: the frequency is a maximum at zero, falls away rapidly at first and then more and more slowly, finally extending into a long tail with a few λ's greatly in excess of all others. From equation (3.13),

$$v_\lambda^2 = \frac{\sigma_c^2 - M_c}{M_c^2},$$ (4.4)

it appears that if, in the *complete* word-distribution, M_c is small compared with σ_c^2, as will be true for our distributions on any reasonable assumption as to W, v_λ will be very nearly the same as the coefficient of variation of the

TABLE 4.9. Showing the values of v_λ for Tables 2.1 to 2.4, for various assumed values of W

Table	K	Value of v_λ if W is taken as			
		5,000	10,000	20,000	30,000
2·1	84·2	6·41	9·12	12·94	15·86
2·2	59·7	5·37	7·66	10·93	13·34
2·3	35·9	4·12	5·91	8·47	10·33
2·4	27·2	3·69	5·12	7·38	8·98

word-distribution itself. Hence, if the student completes any word-distribution by assigning to W any value he pleases and inserting the value of f_0—the number of words which do not occur—he will have a rough sort of picture of the general form of the λ-distribution: only a rough picture, for the distribution is discontinuous and cannot represent very closely even a grouping of the λ-distribution, but it will have the right kind of form, and a coefficient of variation only slightly in excess of that required. If, for example, we assign to W the value 10,000, the coefficients of variation of the word-distributions 2.1–2.4 so completed work out at 9·19, 7·74, 6·01, 5·24, against the v_λ values of Table 4.9: 9·12, 7·66, 5·91, 5·12. The illustration may enable the student to attach a rather more concrete conception to the λ-distribution.

4.25.   Can we find any more direct and simple meaning for the characteristic than that given by its relation to v_λ? The fact may already have struck the reader that for the four tables 2.1–2.4 the order of the characteristics is the same as that of the means, or the reverse of that of the ratio S_0/S_1.

	Characteristic	Mean	$1000 S_0/S_1$
Table 2.1	84·2	7·04	142
Table 2.2	59·7	5·83	171
Table 2.3	35·9	4·67	214
Table 2.4	27·2	3·93	255

Is this by any possibility a general relation? At first I was inclined to think the answer might be yes, at least for distributions of the same or nearly the same W—and before the work of § 4.19 had been completed, with its counts of nouns that might have been known to Macaulay, I was rather playing with the notion that W might be of the order 10,000 for all of them. My thoughts ran somewhat as follows. If W has some fixed value and K is large, v_λ is consequently also relatively large: this will imply in turn a relatively large number of high values of λ, i.e. of words very frequently employed. That is to say, though the conclusion may seem paradoxical, the author's vocabulary will in use be highly *concentrated*, concentrated on to those words that are used over and over again. These words will account for a high proportion of all the occurrences, and consequently the ratio of vocabulary to occurrences for a given size of sample will tend to be relatively low. Conversely if, for the same value of W, K is comparatively small, v_λ will be comparatively small, the author's vocabulary will not be so greatly concentrated on to a few special words, and the ratio of vocabulary to occurrences for a given size of sample will tend to be relatively high. A pretty argument but, I fear, fallacious. In the first place the completed work of § 4.19 makes it fairly clear that W can hardly fail to be higher for Macaulay than for Thomas à Kempis or Gerson, so that the fundamental condition for the argument fails: the high proportion of vocabulary to occurrences for Table 2.4 is, as we have interpreted it, due more to a high W than a high v_λ. In the second place the argument tacitly implies a constant similarity of form in the distributions, an assumption which may by no means be true. As was pointed out in § 3.25, the characteristic is based only on the first and second moments S_1 and S_2, and two distributions with the same first two moments and consequently the same characteristic may nevertheless differ in their higher moments, i.e. they are not necessarily similar distributions. If not, the argument given above breaks down, even for constant W. The empirical relation noted for the four tables in question must therefore, I think, be in some degree a happy chance. There may of course be in fact some statistical *tendency* towards such a relation for samples of the same size—only a very much wider experience can show whether this is so or not—but it is no *necessary* relation, for K does not explicitly involve S_0. The matter may readily be illustrated on simple theoretical examples, which the non-mathematical reader may, if he please, omit.

4.26.   Let us consider the simplest possible type of compound Poisson distribution, a distribution with only two components. Let the total words at risk be W. Of these let us suppose qW to have liability λ, pW liability $b\lambda$, where b is not less than unity, q not less than 0·5, and $p+q = 1$. Then

$$\bar\lambda = (q+pb)\,\lambda, \tag{4.5}$$

$$\sigma_\lambda^2 = pq(b-1)^2\,\lambda^2, \tag{4.6}$$

and hence
$$v_\lambda^2 = \frac{pq(b-1)^2}{(q+pb)^2}. \tag{4.7}$$

For the word-distribution
$$\left. \begin{aligned} S_1 &= W(q+pb)\,\lambda \\ S_2 &= Wq(\lambda+\lambda^2) + Wp(b\lambda+b^2\lambda^2) \end{aligned} \right\}, \tag{4.8}$$

$$S_2 - S_1 = W(q+pb^2)\,\lambda^2, \tag{4.9}$$

and hence
$$K = \frac{10^4}{W}\frac{q+pb^2}{(q+pb)^2}. \tag{4.10}$$

This may be verified from (4.7), v_λ^2+1 reducing to the fraction on the right.

4.27.   Now consider how K varies with changes in b and in q. Differentiating with regard to b we find
$$\frac{dK}{db} = K\frac{2pq(b-1)}{(q+pb)\,(q+pb^2)}. \tag{4.11}$$

If q takes its maximum value unity, $p = 0$ and the differential coefficient becomes zero, K then taking the constant value $10^4/W$, as is evident from (4.10). Otherwise, since $(b-1)$ is positive, K increases with b for all values of q, for high values of b tending to the limit
$$\text{Limit } K = \frac{10^4}{W}\frac{1}{p}. \tag{4.12}$$

For the special case $q = p = 0{\cdot}5$,
$$K = \frac{10^4}{W}\frac{2(b^2+1)}{(1+b)^2}, \tag{4.13}$$

a value which only slowly increases from $10^4/W$ for $b = 1$ to twice that value for $b = \infty$.

4.28.   Again, differentiating with respect to q after replacing p by $1-q$, we have
$$\frac{dK}{dq} = K(b-1)^2\frac{b-q(b+1)}{(q+pb^2)\,(q+pb)}. \tag{4.14}$$

This is positive if the numerator of the fraction is positive or
$$q < \frac{b}{b+1}.$$

Hence, with increasing q, K increases up to a maximum for
$$q = \frac{b}{b+1}, \tag{4.15}$$

when it takes the value
$$K_{\max} = \frac{10^4}{W}\frac{(b+1)^2}{4b}, \tag{4.16}$$

and thereafter decreases again. For a given value of b there must then in general be a lower and higher value of q, on either side of the value (4.15), for which K takes identical values. In fact, equating the expression on the right of (4.10) to a value for K less than the maximum (4.16) but not less than the lowest possible value $10^4/W$, we shall have a quadratic for q with two real roots. The two resulting distributions with these respective values of q will have the same characteristic but will exhibit quite different vocabularies S_0 for any given size of sample S_1.

4.29.   Table 4.10 gives some arithmetical examples, in which W has been taken as 10,000 throughout. In the upper half of the table are shown

TABLE 4.10. Showing the vocabulary S_0 for a given size of sample S_1, in certain bi-compound Poisson distributions. Words at risk $W = 10,000$ for all tables: q = proportion of this total with smaller λ, b = ratio of larger to smaller λ K = the characteristic

Constants	1	2	3	4
q	0·99	0·99	0·99	0·99
b	51	101	401	901
K	12·00	25·75	64·36	81·19
S_1	Vocabulary S_0			
300	260	225	150	123
1,500	1042	815	393	247
9,000	4567	3687	1731	952
15,000	6358	5324	2666	1479
30,000	8560	7791	4567	2666
60,000	9819	9407	7018	4567
Constants	5	6	7	8
q	0·999385	0·997512	0·9108	0·999
b	401	401	101	101
K	64·34	100·75	9·26	9·26
S_1	Vocabulary S_0			
300	244	174	262	278
1,500	1140	747	835	1283
9,000	5147	3646	1682	5592
15,000	7001	5297	2170	7445
30,000	9100	7782	3269	9347
60,000	9919	9507	5026	9957

the data for four distributions for each of which $q = 0·99$, but with values of b increasing from 51 to 901. It will be seen that for every size of sample S_1 from 300 to 60,000, the vocabulary S_0 decreases with increasing K— exactly the relation noted for our four tables 2.1–2.4. But the proportionate decrease varies considerably with size of sample. For the sample of 300 the vocabulary drops from 260 in the first column to 123 in col. 4, a decrease of 53 per cent. For the sample of 9000, the drop is from 4567 to 952, a decrease of 79 per cent. For the largest sample of 60,000 the drop is from 9819 to 4567, a decrease of only 53 per cent again.

4.30. The distribution of col. 3, in the upper half of the table, is based on $q = 0.99$, $b = 401$. But from equation (4.15) the maximum value of K for this value of b will be given by making

$$q = \frac{b}{b+1} = \frac{401}{402} = 0.997512.$$

The value of q taken for col. 3 is lower than this: there must therefore be another value of q greater than 0.997512 which will also give $K = 64.36$. This was found by solving the quadratic to be, as near as may be, 0.999385, which actually makes $K = 64.34$; but for these very high values of q, K is very sensitive to minute errors in that constant. The vocabularies for this distribution are given in col. 5 in the lower half of Table 4.10, and it will be seen that the vocabulary of col. 5 is considerably greater than the corresponding vocabulary of col. 3 for every size of sample. Col. 6 gives the figures for the distribution having the maximum characteristic possible for the same assigned value of b. The vocabularies are throughout less than those of col. 5 but greater than those of col. 3. It thus appears that the distribution with the higher characteristic may yield vocabularies either higher or lower than those given by another with a lower characteristic.

4.31. For $b = 101$, as in col. 2 in the upper half of the table, the value of q that will make K a maximum is

$$q = \frac{101}{102} = 0.9902,$$

so that by chance this distribution corresponds very nearly to maximum K. The data for $q = 0.999$, $b = 101$, had as it happens already been worked out and are given in col. 8. The quadratic yielded $q = 0.9108$ as the lower value which should give the same characteristic as 0.999, viz. $K = 9.26$. The data for this are given in col. 7. The vocabularies of col. 2, the distribution corresponding to maximum K, are lower than those of col. 8 for every size of sample, though obviously the ratios vary greatly. But the comparison of col. 2 with col. 7 shows a very interesting result. For the smallest sample of 300, the vocabulary of col. 2 is some 14 per cent *less* than that of col. 7; for the next sample of 1500 it is only some 2.5 per cent less: but for the sample of 9000 the vocabulary of col. 2 is more than double that of col. 7, and a similar great excess rules for all the remaining samples right up to that of 60,000. It is quite clear from these illustrations that there is no *general* theoretical necessity, even for a set of distributions with the same total W of words at risk, for a higher K to correspond to a lower vocabulary in an assigned size of sample. Only in a very specialised and artificial case will we get a simple inverse relation between S_0 and K. Given a distribution with sums S_0, S_1, S_2 and characteristic K, let us multiply every frequency f_x by the same arbitrary factor p, so that the new frequencies are pf_1, pf_2, pf_3, etc. Then the sums for the new distribution are pS_0, pS_1, pS_2 and its characteristic consequently K/p. But this case is a highly special one. In general we can only say that the concentration implied by K is that measured approximately for large samples by the ratio S_2/S_1 (§ 3.24) and leave it at that. The reader may find a theorem given at the end of the book (§ 11.7) helpful in enabling him to get a practical grasp of the matter.

4.32.   A very important question concerning the characteristic remains to be answered, viz. what sort of range of variation is it likely to exhibit in different but similar works of the same author? This is obviously a question that can only be answered empirically, by actual trial: an account of two such trials will be found in Chapter 6. It is convenient before proceeding to this purely statistical investigation to deal with some difficulties and sources of fallacy which are met with in handling statistics of literary vocabulary.

REFERENCES

A. STATISTICAL METHOD

§ 4.8. For the method of testing goodness of fit, see Y & K, Chapter 22. Note especially § 22.8 and Example 22.5. The tables referred to are:

(4.1) Pearson, Karl (1924). *Tables for Statisticians and Biometricians*. 2nd edition. London: The Biometric Laboratory, University College.

§ 4.9 and Table 4.7. For the notation used, see Y & K, Chapter 1.

§ 4.11. For the estimation of the variance from small samples see Y & K, Chapter 23, §§ 23.4, 23.5, especially equation (23.3).

B. CITATIONS IN TEXT OR TABLES

(4.2) Macaulay, T. B. (1880). *Critical and Historical Essays*. London: Longmans, Green, Reader & Dyer.

(4.3) Lewis, C. T. and Short, C. (1927). *Latin Dictionary*. Oxford: Clarendon Press.

(4.4) Fowler, H. W. and Fowler, F. G. (1911). *The Concise Oxford Dictionary of Current English*. Oxford: Clarendon Press.

(4.5) Onions, C. T., *et al.* (1933). *The Shorter Oxford English Dictionary*. 2 vols. Oxford: Clarendon Press.

(4.6) à Kempis, Th. (1902–22). *Opera Omnia*, voluminibus septem edidit Michael Josephus Pohl. Friburgi Brisigavorum: sumptibus Herder.

Chapter 5

CERTAIN DIFFICULTIES AND SOURCES OF FALLACY

(1) RICHNESS OF VOCABULARY; VOCABULARY RATIOS

5.1.　In this chapter I propose to consider certain difficulties or possible sources of fallacy in the interpretation of statistics of literary vocabulary, and will first discuss the conception of the 'richness' of an author's vocabulary. The simple reading of some work will often give one quite a strong impression that the author has a remarkable wealth of words at his command, far greater than that of some other with whom we may mentally compare him; or possible *per contra* that his vocabulary is relatively poor and limited. The one author, we may say, on such an impressionist judgment, has a 'rich', the other a relatively 'poor' vocabulary. In this sense I formed an impressionist judgment that the vocabulary of Gerson was richer than that of Thomas à Kempis, and the judgment was borne out by the statistical data subsequently compiled. The sample from the miscellaneous works of Thomas à Kempis, Table 2.2, gave only 1406 nouns on 8203 occurrences; the sample from the theological works of Gerson, Table 2.3, 1754 nouns on 8196 occurrences. Everything seems quite simple and straightforward—a first judgment simply on impressions, support forthcoming from statistical data quite impersonally obtained. Yet, I suggest, the matter is or may be very much more complex than appears at first sight, and the greatest caution must be exercised in drawing conclusions. The basis of the impressionist judgment is obscure. The basis of the statistical judgment is clear—it is founded on a sample *of a particular stated size*. To transform the correct statement 'in a sample of n occurrences the vocabulary of author A is twice as great as that of author B' into the general statement 'the vocabulary of author A is twice as great as that of author B' may be an entirely fallacious proceeding. The careful reader of §§ 4.24–4.31 will realise why this is so, but the point is so important that repetition will do no harm and it deserves full illustration.

5.2.　Suppose we are comparing two authors whose words at risk (the total words in their treasure-chests) are respectively W_1 and W_2. The only definite meaning I find it possible to attach to such a phrase as 'the relative richness of the vocabulary of the second author compared with that of the first' is the ratio W_2/W_1. Now suppose we compare the ratios of the actual vocabularies of the two authors in random samples of gradually increasing size, using samples of the same size of course for each comparison. Let us start with very small samples indeed. In a sample say of five words the chance of any word being repeated is very small, and such a sample will consist in the great majority of instances of five distinct and separate words, however poor the author's vocabulary. Hence, as the size of sample approaches zero, the ratio of vocabularies for any two authors whatever tends to the limit unity, quite independently of the ratio W_2/W_1. On the other hand, as the size of sample is steadily increased, more and more of the words of each author will be brought in, and ultimately in the limit the ratio will approach indefinitely close to W_2/W_1. In fact in symbolic terms, if ρ denote the ratio of vocabularies, we have

$$\left. \begin{array}{ll} \lambda = 0, & \text{Limit } \rho = 1 \\ \lambda = \infty, & \text{Limit } \rho = W_2/W_1 \end{array} \right\}. \tag{5.1}$$

The argument is quite general and must hold in any case. We can, therefore, only be at all confident that the ratio of vocabularies approaches closely to the true limit W_2/W_1, the relative richness of the authors' treasure-chests, if the samples are 'indefinitely large'. But how large this means we cannot say *a priori*, we can only find out empirically. This would be a most laborious business, but it could be done by applying to both of the authors the procedure of sampling very briefly outlined in § 4.20. A limit to the size of sample obtainable will be given by the length of the works of the less voluminous of the two authors, say author A. Suppose this is 500,000 words. We may then proceed by a method of 'spread sampling' such as was used for the experiment with the essay on Bacon (§§ 4.2 *et seq.*, but which later work shows to be not wholly satisfactory, see § 7.8) to take samples from author A of perhaps a tenth of each page, giving a first sample of about 50,000 words. Trial will give the necessary size of sample from each page of B to give a total sample also of about 50,000 words from his works, and we shall then have a first value of ρ based on a pair of samples of 50,000. Repetition of the process will give a second value for a pair of samples of 100,000 occurrences, and so on. With good luck it might be that only a few repetitions would clearly suggest an approach to a limit in the value of ρ. With bad luck it might be that not even when we had reached a pair of samples of the largest size possible, 500,000 occurrences, was there any close indication of the limit. No one can say, for no one has yet tried any such experiment. But only by an experiment on *some* such lines—there would be obvious difficulties about details which we have not stopped to consider—would it at first sight seem possible to arrive at any definite conclusion. A different method is, however, suggested later which would present considerable advantages, but would remain very laborious (§ 7.23). The sort of comparison that can be based on concordances—A's vocabulary is so many thousand words and B's so many thousand words—without any regard to the lengths of their respective works—does not seem to me to carry any significance at all. If we attach significance to it, as indicating the relative richness of their respective vocabularies, we are tacitly assuming that *both* authors' published works practically exhaust their vocabularies; surely a rather rash assumption.

5.3. Let us consider how, in some simple theoretical examples, the value of ρ passes from the initial to the final limit of (5.1). To begin with, let us take the simplest possible theoretical case, which can hardly correspond to anything in practice but will serve as a first illustration of the difficulties. Let the first author have W_1 words at risk all with one and the same parameter λ, and the second W_2 words at risk all with one and the same but a different parameter $a\lambda$. Both word-distributions will then be given by simple Poisson series. For equality of size of sample we must have

$$W_1 \lambda = W_2 a\lambda$$

or
$$a = W_1/W_2, \tag{5.2}$$

and the ratio of vocabularies is

$$\rho = \frac{W_2(1-e^{-a\lambda})}{W_1(1-e^{-\lambda})} = \frac{1-e^{-a\lambda}}{a(1-e^{-\lambda})}. \tag{5.3}$$

Evidently if we put $\lambda = \infty$ in this equation ρ takes the value W_2/W_1 as required by the upper limit in (5.1). Putting $\lambda = 0$, the fraction takes the indeterminate form $0/0$, but expanding the exponentials in terms of powers of $a\lambda$ and of λ and ignoring powers beyond the first, we have at once

$$\lambda = 0, \quad \text{Limit}\,\rho = \frac{W_2 a}{W_1} = 1,$$

as required by the lower limit of (5.1). Further, to define the nature of the function let us determine the initial and final slopes of the graph. Differentiating (5.3), we have

$$\frac{1}{\rho}\frac{d\rho}{d\lambda} = \frac{ae^{-a\lambda}}{1-e^{-a\lambda}} - \frac{e^{-\lambda}}{1-e^{-\lambda}}. \tag{5.4}$$

This gives at once $\qquad \lambda = \infty, \quad \text{Limit}\,\dfrac{d\rho}{d\lambda} = 0. \tag{5.5}$

For $\lambda = 0$ (5.4) becomes indeterminate; but expanding the exponentials, we have

$$\frac{1}{\rho}\frac{d\rho}{d\lambda} = \frac{a(1-a\lambda)}{a\lambda - \frac{1}{2}a^2\lambda^2} - \frac{1-\lambda}{\lambda - \frac{1}{2}\lambda^2} = \frac{1}{2}\frac{1-a}{(1-\frac{1}{2}a\lambda)(1-\frac{1}{2}\lambda)},$$

or, since ρ becomes unity for $\lambda = 0$, we have

$$\lambda = 0, \quad \text{Limit}\frac{d\rho}{d\lambda} = \frac{1}{2}(1-a). \tag{5.6}$$

The graph giving the values of ρ for successive values of λ or of size of sample therefore rises, or falls, with finite slope from the value unity at the origin zero, and gradually asymptotes to the limiting value W_2/W_1 as size of sample increases.

5.4. Table 5.1 shows the vocabulary, for the sizes of sample specified in col. 1, for three Poisson distributions A, B and C; the words at risk W being taken as 10,000 for A, 20,000 for B, and 5000 for C. In cols. 5 and 6 are

TABLE 5.1. Showing the vocabulary S_0 in three simple Poisson distributions for successive sizes of sample S_1. For distribution A, $W = 10{,}000$; for B, $W = 20{,}000$; for C, $W = 5000$. The ratios of vocabularies, ρ, in the last two columns were calculated from data carried to more places than the figures in cols. A, B and C so as to be correct to within a unit in the last digit given

1	2	3	4	5	6
Size of sample S_1	Vocabulary in distribution			Ratio of vocabulary in	
	A	B	C	B on A	C on A
0	0	0	0	1·0000	1·0000
300	296	298	291	1·0075	0·9852
1,500	1,393	1,445	1,296	1·0375	0·9304
3,000	2,592	2,786	2,256	1·0749	0·8704
6,000	4,512	5,184	3,494	1·1489	0·7744
9,000	5,934	7,248	4,174	1·2213	0·7033
12,000	6,988	9,024	4,546	1·2913	0·6506
15,000	7,769	10,553	4,751	1·3584	0·6116
18,000	8,347	11,869	4,863	1·4219	0·5826
21,000	8,775	13,001	4,925	1·4815	0·5612
24,000	9,093	13,976	4,959	1·5371	0·5454
27,000	9,328	14,815	4,977	1·5883	0·5336
30,000	9,502	15,537	4,988	1·6351	0·5249
60,000	9,975	19,004	5,000	1·9051	0·5012
120,000	10,000	19,950	5,000	1·9951	0·5000

given the ratios ρ for B on A and C on A. Looking first at the ratios of col. 5 where $W_2/W_1 = 2$, we see that a small sample of 300 occurrences would only give a ratio of 1·0075, suggesting a vocabulary for B less than 1 per cent in excess of that of A. The ratio would only rise to roundly 1·15 for a sample of 6000 and 1·22 for a sample of 9000—the sort of sizes of sample with which we have been dealing. It is not until we get to samples of 60,000 occurrences or more that we begin to get from the sample a ratio somewhere near the true figure, viz. 2. Equation (5.6) for the initial slope of the graph may be approximately verified from the first two ratios in the table. A sample of 300 corresponds to a value of $\lambda = 300/10,000 = 0·03$. The first two values of ρ are 1·0000 and 1·0075, difference $+0·0075$, so that the slope over the first small interval is $+0·0075/0·03 = +0·25$. The parameter a, equation (5.2), is 0·5, so by (5.6) the slope of the initial tangent is $0·5 \times 0·5 = +0·25$, which checks.

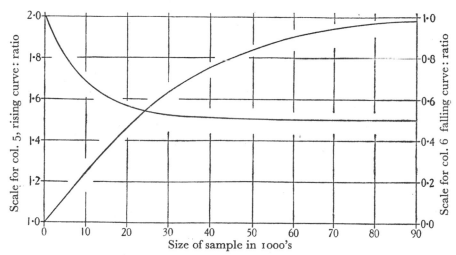

Fig. 5.1. Vocabulary ratios. Graphs for cols. 5 and 6 of Table 5.1: col. 5, rising curve and scale on left; col. 6, falling curve and scale on right. Both word-distributions are simple Poissons.

5.5.   The ratios for C on A in col. 6 follow a reciprocal course, but the approximation towards the limiting ratio $W_2/W_1 = 0·5$ is more rapid. The very small sample of 300 would only suggest that the vocabulary of C was some 1·5 per cent less than that of A, but a sample of 6000 would suggest 23 per cent less, and a sample of 9000 would suggest 30 per cent less. A sample of 25,000 or so would give a value of the ratio not very far from the truth. The slope over the initial interval is here $-0·0148/0·03 = -0·493$. The parameter a is 2, and the slope of the tangent at the origin by (5.6) is therefore $-0·5$. The two figures agree within the limits of approximation. Fig. 5.1 shows graphs of the ratios in cols. 5 and 6.

5.6. It may be noted that if we had taken the ratios of A on B, for which also $W_2/W_1 = 0.5$, instead of C on A, we should have got ratios converging less rapidly to the limit; for since W_1 (the denominator value of W) would then be 20,000, the value of λ corresponding to any assigned size of sample would be only half as large as before, or would correspond to the λ for half that size of sample in the C/A ratios. Thus for A/B we will find 0.9304 for a sample of 3000, 0.8704 for a sample of 6000, 0.7744 for a sample of 12,000, and so on. *Per contra*, if we had taken the ratios A/C, for which $W_2/W_1 = 2$, instead of B/A, we should have got ratios *more* rapidly convergent than those of col. 5: ρ would be 1.0749 for a sample of 1500, 1.1489 for a sample of 3000, 1.2913 for a sample of 6000, and so forth. The rapidity of convergence with increasing size of sample depends on the absolute values of W_1 and W_2, being less rapid for large values of W, more rapid for small values.

5.7. In the general case let us suppose that in the first distribution there are n_1 words with the parameter λ_1, n_2 with the parameter $a_2\lambda_1$, n_3 with the parameter $a_3\lambda_1$, and so on, where $n_1 + n_2 + n_3 + ... = W_1$: and in the second distribution m_1 words with parameter λ_2, m_2 with parameter $b_2\lambda_2$, m_3 with parameter $b_3\lambda_2$, and so on, where $m_1 + m_2 + m_3 + ... = W_2$. Then

$$\rho = \frac{m_1(1 - e^{-\lambda_2}) + m_2(1 - e^{-b_2\lambda_2}) + m_3(1 - e^{-b_3\lambda_2}) + ...}{n_1(1 - e^{-\lambda_1}) + n_2(1 - e^{-a_2\lambda_1}) + n_3(1 - e^{-a_3\lambda_1}) + ...}, \quad (5.7)$$

subject to the condition for equality of size of sample,

$$(n_1 + n_2 a_2 + n_3 a_3 + ...) \lambda_1 = (m_1 + m_2 b_2 + m_3 b_3 + ...) \lambda_2. \quad (5.8)$$

At the upper limit $\lambda = \infty$, ρ clearly takes the form

$$\rho = \frac{m_1 + m_2 + m_3 + ...}{n_1 + n_2 + n_3 + ...} = \frac{W_2}{W_1},$$

in agreement with the upper limit of (5.1). To obtain the lower limit, as before in §5.3 expand the exponentials, retaining only the first powers of the exponents, when we have

$$\rho = \frac{(m_1 + m_2 b_2 + m_3 b_3 + ...) \lambda_2}{(n_1 + n_2 a_2 + n_3 a_3 + ...) \lambda_1} = 1,$$

by (5.8), in agreement with the lower limit of (5.1). The limits (5.1) are therefore duly verified.

5.8. To give illustrations, corresponding to the more general case of the variation of the vocabulary-ratio ρ with increasing size of sample, we may use the compound Poisson distribution of two components, the theory of which was given in §§ 4.26–4.28. Table 5.2 gives some arithmetical examples. Since in these cases there is a very rapid initial variation of ρ with size of sample, the vocabulary has been shown for samples of 50, 100, 150, and so on up to a sample of 600, thenceforward proceeding by the same scale as in Table 5.1. In col. 2 the simple Poisson distribution A of

TABLE 5.2. Showing the vocabulary S_0 in three bi-compound Poisson distributions D, E, F for successive sizes of sample S_1, together with the same data for the simple Poisson distribution A of Table 5.1 in the greater detail of this table. For A, $W = 10,000$; for D, $W = 10,000$; for E, $W = 20,000$; for F, $W = 5000$. For D, E and F, $q = 0.99$, $b = 401$ (cf. § 4.26)

1	2	3	4	5
Size of sample S_1	Vocabulary in distribution			
	A	D	E	F
50	50	43	46	37
100	100	75	86	60
150	149	100	120	75
200	198	119	150	87
250	247	136	176	98
300	296	150	199	109
350	344	163	220	119
400	392	175	239	128
450	440	186	256	138
500	488	197	272	148
550	535	207	287	158
600	582	217	300	167
1,500	1,393	393	494	338
3,000	2,592	677	785	610
6,000	4,512	1,219	1,353	1,106
9,000	5,934	1,731	1,904	1,547
12,000	6,988	2,212	2,439	1,937
15,000	7,769	2,666	2,958	2,283
18,000	8,347	3,093	3,462	2,591
21,000	8,775	3,495	3,950	2,863
24,000	9,093	3,874	4,425	3,105
27,000	9,328	4,231	4,885	3,319
30,000	9,502	4,567	5,332	3,509
60,000	9,975	7,018	9,134	4,551
120,000	10,000	9,102	14,036	4,959

Table 5.1 has been repeated, on this more detailed scale, as a standard of comparison. In cols. 3, 4 and 5 are shown the vocabularies for three bi-compound distributions, D, E and F. For all three q, the proportion of words with the lower value of λ, has been taken as 0.99, and b, the ratio of the larger to the smaller λ, as 401, so that the three distributions are similar to each other in these respects. But for D the words at risk W have been taken as 10,000; for E as 20,000; and for F as 5000. Distribution D is in fact identical with the distribution used for col. 3 of Table 4.10. In Table 5.3

are given the vocabulary-ratios ρ for three pairs of these distributions, these ratios, as in Table 5.1, having been calculated from more detailed figures than those shown in the preceding table, so as to obtain a value of ρ true to within a unit in the last place of decimals. In col. 2 are given the values of

TABLE 5.3. Showing the ratios of vocabularies, ρ, for certain pairs of the distributions of Table 5.2. These ratios were calculated from data carried to more places than the figures of Table 5.2, so as to be correct to within a unit in the last digit given

1	2	3	4	5	6	7
Size of sample	Ratio of vocabulary in					
	D on A	A on D	E on D	D on F	D on E	F on D
0	1·0000	1·0000	1·0000	1·0000	1·0000	1·0000
50	0·8608	1·1618	1·0768	1·1458	0·9286	0·8728
100	0·7531	1·3278	1·1458	1·2551	0·8728	0·7967
150	0·6692	1·4944	1·2053	1·3265	0·8297	0·7539
200	0·6030	1·6583	1·2551	1·3659	0·7967	0·7321
250	0·5505	1·8166	1·2953	1·3820	0·7720	0·7236
300	0·5082	1·9676	1·3265	1·3826	0·7539	0·7233
350	0·4740	2·1098	1·3497	1·3741	0·7409	0·7277
400	0·4459	2·2427	1·3659	1·3607	0·7321	0·7349
450	0·4227	2·3658	1·3763	1·3452	0·7266	0·7434
500	0·4033	2·4795	1·3820	1·3290	0·7236	0·7524
550	0·3869	2·5847	1·3840	1·3129	0·7225	0·7617
600	0·3731	2·6803	1·3826	1·2981	0·7233	0·7704
1,500	0·2818	3·5480	1·2590	1·1606	0·7943	0·8616
3,000	0·2610	3·8310	1·1606	1·1095	0·8616	0·9013
6,000	0·2703	3·6998	1·1095	1·1024	0·9013	0·9071
9,000	0·2917	3·4286	1·1001	1·1192	0·9090	0·8935
12,000	0·3166	3·1586	1·1024	1·1422	0·9071	0·8755
15,000	0·3432	2·9141	1·1096	1·1675	0·9013	0·8565
18,000	0·3706	2·6987	1·1192	1·1939	0·8935	0·8376
21,000	0·3983	2·5107	1·1302	1·2208	0·8848	0·8191
24,000	0·4261	2·3471	1·1422	1·2478	0·8755	0·8014
27,000	0·4536	2·2048	1·1547	1·2747	0·8661	0·7845
30,000	0·4806	2·0807	1·1675	1·3014	0·8565	0·7684
60,000	0·7036	1·4213	1·3014	1·5421	0·7684	0·6485
120,000	0·9102	1·0987	1·5421	1·8353	0·6485	0·5449

the ratio for the vocabularies of distribution D on those of distribution A, the simple Poisson. For both these distributions W is 10,000, so that $W_2/W_1 = 1$. For exceedingly small samples of a size near zero the ratio starts with this value, as it must, but even for a sample of 50 has dropped to 0·86. It continues dropping, at first very rapidly and then more slowly, until it reaches a minimum of 0·26 or just over that value for a sample, as may be estimated by interpolation, in the neighbourhood of 3300. Thereafter it increases, but even for a sample of 30,000 has only attained 0·48.

It is not until we reach the largest sample shown, 120,000, that ρ has risen to a value anywhere near unity, viz. 0·91. The course of affairs is shown in the graph, Fig. 5.2. For all sizes of sample given in the table between 350 and 30,000 the values of ρ would suggest that the D-vocabulary is only a half to a quarter of the A-vocabulary, instead of the two vocabularies being equal as they are. Col. 3 gives the reciprocal ratios for A on D, the course

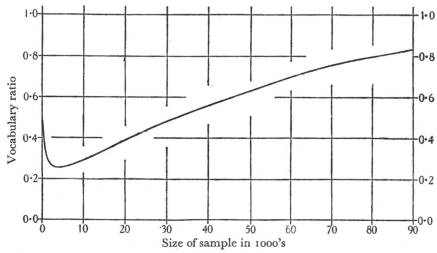

Fig. 5.2. Vocabulary ratios of Table 5.3, col. 2: ratio of total vocabularies, unity; numerator distribution, a bi-compound Poisson; denominator distribution a simple Poisson.

of which is naturally just the reverse of those in col. 2. The ratio rises from unity to a maximum of over 3·8 for a sample of 3300 or so and then falls off again, but remains over 2 even for a sample of 30,000.

5.9.   Col. 4 gives the ratios for E-vocabularies on D-vocabularies; for D the number of words at risk is 10,000, for E it is 20,000, so that $W_2/W_1 = 2$. Ratios here do not run to such extreme values as in cols. 2 or 3, but the run of the figures is even more remarkable. The ratio rises from the initial unity to a first maximum of over 1·38 for a sample in the neighbourhood of 550, which may be estimated as about 554, and then *falls off again* to attain a minimum which may be estimated at just about 1·10 for a sample near 9900. Thereafter it rises once more and finally tends to asymptote to the value 2, but even for a sample of 120,000 has attained no more than the value 1·5421. Fig. 5.3 shows the course of the ratios, somewhat diagrammatically, as it is impossible on such a scale to represent accurately the rapid rise to the first maximum or the very flat minimum. To compare with this course of affairs we have given in col. 5 the ratios for D on F: here

$W_2/W_1 = 2$ as in col. 4, but the W's are 10,000 and 5000 respectively, with the result that convergence towards the limit is more rapid, cf. § 5.6. The first maximum is reached earlier, for a sample between 250 and 300 that may be estimated as 277 or 278, and the following minimum also a good deal earlier, for a sample between 3000 and 6000 that may be estimated at about 5390. After the minimum the rise is more rapid at each point of the scale,

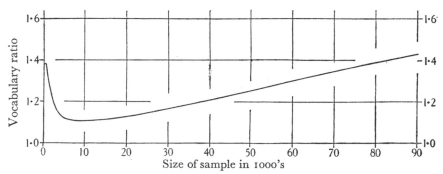

Fig. 5.3. Vocabulary ratios of Table 5.3, col. 4: ratio of total vocabularies, 2; both distributions, bi-compound Poissons. Note the temporary maximum of 1·38 for a sample of just over 550 and the very slow rise after the following minimum.

and for the largest sample of 120,000 ρ has attained a value of nearly 1·84—a value much more nearly suggestive of the W_2/W_1 ratio than the 1·54 of col. 4. Cols. 6 and 7 give respectively the reciprocals of the ratios of col. 4 and of col. 5: we have given them simply for the sake of completeness, as obviously either of the pair of distributions might have been used as the denominator, but need not spend further time on them.

5.10.   The reader may well find such results exceedingly puzzling. It may help him to understand matters a little better if he will study Table 5.4. The distribution D consists, it will be remembered, of two components. In one component, the lower component, there are 9900 words at risk, all with the same chance of being used measured by a parameter λ. In the other component there are only 100 words at risk, also all with the same chance of being used, but their parameter is 401λ, i.e. they are more than 400 times as likely to be used as the others. Table 5.4 in cols. 1, 2 and 3 shows how each sample is, on the average, made up out of occurrences of words in the lower and the upper component respectively. Thus a sample of 50 tends to be made up of roundly 10 occurrences of words from the lower component and 40 occurrences of words from the upper component. A sample of 1500 is on the average made up of 297 occurrences of words from the lower component and 1203 occurrences of words from the upper component, and so on. All these figures are in fact in the same proportion. There is a proportion of $q/(q+pb)$ or 0.198 of occurrences of words from the lower component, and a proportion of $pb/(q+pb)$ or 0.802 of occurrences of words from the upper component. Cols. 4, 5 and 6 show similarly how the *vocabulary* of each sample is on the average made up by contributions from the lower and the

TABLE 5.4. Giving an analysis of distribution D, Table 5.2, showing how much of each sample and of each vocabulary is contributed by the lower and by the upper component of the distribution respectively

1	2	3	4	5	6
Sample			Vocabulary		
Lower component	Upper component	Total	Lower component	Upper component	Total
9·9	40·1	50	9·9	33·0	43
19·8	80·2	100	19·8	55·2	75
29·7	120·3	150	29·7	70·0	100
39·6	160·4	200	39·5	79·9	119
49·5	200·5	250	49·4	86·5	136
59·4	240·6	300	59·2	91·0	150
69·3	280·7	350	69·1	94·0	163
79·2	320·8	400	78·9	96·0	175
89·1	360·9	450	88·7	97·3	186
99·0	401·0	500	98·5	98·2	197
108·9	441·1	550	108·3	98·8	207
118·8	481·2	600	118·1	99·2	217
297	1,203	1,500	292·6	100·0	393
594	2,406	3,000	576·5	100·0	677
1,188	4,812	6,000	1,119·5	100·0	1,219
1,782	7,218	9,000	1,630·8	100·0	1,731
2,376	9,624	12,000	2,112·4	100·0	2,212
2,970	12,030	15,000	2,565·9	100·0	2,666
3,564	14,436	18,000	2,993·0	100·0	3,093
4,158	16,842	21,000	3,395·2	100·0	3,495
4,752	19,248	24,000	3,774·0	100·0	3,874
5,346	21,654	27,000	4,130·8	100·0	4,231
5,940	24,060	30,000	4,466·8	100·0	4,567
11,880	48,120	60,000	6,918·2	100·0	7,018
23,760	96,240	120,000	9,001·9	100·0	9,102

upper component. Thus the sample of 50 occurrences, as in Table 5.2, col. 3, may be expected to show a vocabulary of roundly 43 words in all, and Table 5.4, cols. 4 and 5, tells us that this will probably be composed of some 10 words from the lower component and 33 from the upper. There being 9900 words in the lower component, the 10 occurrences from the lower component in col. 1 are almost bound to be occurrences of separate words; but the common words of the upper component are some of them repeated, so that the 33 words of col. 5 yield the 40 occurrences of col. 2.

If we pass on to a sample of 1500, we find (col. 5) that *all* the 100 words of the upper component are likely to have been drawn, and 293 words will probably have been drawn from the lower component. This time a few of the 293 will probably have occurred more than once, the lower component thus contributing not 293 but 297 occurrences to the sample (col. 1). But the 100 words of the upper component will probably have occurred some 12 times each, so that they contribute no less than 1203 occurrences to the sample (col. 2). So matters continue: when we reach the largest sample given, the sample of 120,000 occurrences, over 9000 of the 9900 words in the lower component will probably have occurred, and have occurred on an average some 2 or 3 times each, thus yielding 23,760 occurrences to the sample (col. 1). The 100 words of the upper component, on the other hand, will have been used on an average over 960 times each and have yielded 96,240 occurrences to the sample (col. 2). The figures of cols. 4 and 5 are, it will be seen, far from standing in a constant ratio to each other like those of cols. 1 and 2. The contribution of the lower component to the vocabulary is at first much less than that of the upper component, but ultimately far greater. In this particular instance the change-over of the lower component from less to greater importance occurs for a sample of slightly less than 500.

5.11. Now compare these vocabularies of distribution D with those of the simple non-compound Poisson, distribution A of col. 2, Table 5.2, and see how distribution D manages to make up the same size of sample with smaller vocabularies. For the sample of 50 the vocabulary of distribution A is also 50, i.e. all the words in the sample will probably be distinct words. For distribution D the vocabulary is only 43, because some of the 33 common words of the upper component are likely to have occurred more than once, thus contributing not 33 but 40 occurrences to the sample. Passing to the much larger sample of 1500 the state of affairs becomes more striking. Distribution A requires 1393 words to make up this sample, each word occurring on the average only 1500/1393 = 1·08 times. But distribution D makes up the same size of sample with only 393 words. Few of the 293 rare words of the lower component occur more than once, and they only contribute 297 occurrences to the sample. But the 100 common words of the upper component occur on an average some 12 times each, so that they contribute no less than 1203 occurrences. *The required sample is made up by frequent drawing on the small batch of common words*, and it is thus completed with a relatively small number of separate and distinct words. This explains why the general run of the ratios ρ over the central part of col. 2, Table 5.3.

is well below unity. But why do the ratios rise again towards unity near the end of the table? Simply because in both distributions these large samples are beginning to exhaust the entire stock of words. In the largest sample *all* the words will probably have occurred in the case of distribution A, and 9102 of the 10,000 in the case of distribution D. It may be noted that while, in the case of distributions D and F, a sample of 120,000 has exhausted the

TABLE 5.5. Giving an analysis, on similar lines to Table 5.4, of distribution F, Table 5.2

1	2	3	4	5	6
Sample			Vocabulary		
Lower component	Upper component	Total	Lower component	Upper component	Total
9·9	40·1	50	9·9	27·6	37
19·8	80·2	100	19·8	39·9	60
29·7	120·3	150	29·6	45·5	75
39·6	160·4	200	39·4	48·0	87
49·5	200·5	250	49·3	49·1	98
59·4	240·6	300	59·0	49·6	109
69·3	280·7	350	68·8	49·8	119
79·2	320·8	400	78·6	49·9	128
89·1	360·9	450	88·3	50·0	138
99·0	401·0	500	98·0	50·0	148
108·9	441·1	550	107·7	50·0	158
118·8	481·2	600	117·4	50·0	167
297	1,203	1,500	288·3	50·0	338
594	2,406	3,000	559·7	50·0	610
1,188	4,812	6,000	1,056·2	50·0	1,106
1,782	7,218	9,000	1,496·5	50·0	1,547
2,376	9,624	12,000	1,887·0	50·0	1,937
2,970	12,030	15,000	2,233·4	50·0	2,283
3,564	14,436	18,000	2,540·6	50·0	2,591
4,158	16,842	21,000	2,813·0	50·0	2,863
4,752	19,248	24,000	3,054·7	50·0	3,105
5,346	21,654	27,000	3,269·0	50·0	3,319
5,940	24,060	30,000	3,459·1	50·0	3,509
11,880	48,120	60,000	4,500·9	50·0	4,551
23,760	96,240	120,000	4,909·3	50·0	4,959

bulk of the stock of words, it is highly unlikely that such a size of sample would suffice so nearly to exhaust the stock in any *practical* case. For here we have only considered a range of λ's in the proportion of 1 to 401, and in any real instance the range must be vastly in excess of this. Note, for example, that in Table 2.8 for a sample from the Vulgate (a book of some 750,000 words or more) we still have as large a proportion of the nouns as 24 per cent occurring only once, and the most frequent words occur several thousand times. It must, in real examples, take a sample of very great magnitude nearly to exhaust the stock of rare words. Table 5.5 gives an analysis, similar to that of Table 5.4, for distribution F of Table 5.2. Since the constants q and b for this distribution are the same as for D, the figures for the *samples* (cols. 1, 2 and 3) are the same in Table 5.5 as in Table 5.4. But since W is 5000 instead of 10,000, there are only 50 words in the upper component and 4950 in the lower, and the figures for the *vocabulary* (cols. 4, 5 and 6) are consequently different. I leave the study of this table and comparison with Table 5.4 to the reader.

5.12.   Enough has been said, I think, fully to justify the statement in § 5.1 that this matter of judging relative richness of vocabulary 'is or may be very much more complex than appears at first sight, and the greatest caution must be used in drawing conclusions'. The *observed* ratio of vocabularies is a function in the first place of the size of sample, and for any assigned size of sample is dependent not only on the ratio W_2/W_1 but also on the absolute values of W_2 and W_1 and the forms of the respective λ-distributions. Two authors *cannot* give the same value of ρ for all sizes of sample save in the one special and exceptional case, namely when $W_1 = W_2$ and the λ-distributions for the two authors are identical. In that instance, and that instance only, ρ retains the value unity for all sizes of sample. If, for *any* one size of sample, ρ differs significantly from unity, it cannot retain the same value for all other sizes of sample. It is possible, of course, that practical examples may not give such *large* variations as are shown in Table 5.3, and that the simple bi-compound distributions assumed have introduced peculiar complexities that will not be found in comparisons between real vocabularies, but no one can say what will happen till the trial is made, and as already pointed out in § 5.2 the work for such a trial is likely to prove very laborious. Table 5.3 indicates clearly that the trial might have to be carried out in much greater detail than was suggested in § 5.2, i.e. with a very detailed scale for small samples as in Tables 5.2 *et seq.*: and moreover, in the case of the *very* small samples of 50 or 100 occurrences or so, it would also be necessary, if we proceeded by direct sampling, to take not one but several of such samples to get a valid average for the vocabulary. At a later stage of the work a much more hopeful method suggested itself (described in § 7.23) that was tested on a small scale, i.e. up to samples of 16,000 occurrences.

5.13.   But the results given justify the further statement in § 5.1 that the basis of such an impressionist judgment as was considered in that paragraph is obscure, and in fact raise a very interesting question as to its nature. It would appear that such a judgment must be in part determined by the 'virtual size of sample' on which the judgment is based. Even if two readers had read the same amount of the works in question, he who had the better memory would probably be basing his judgment on a larger 'virtual sample' than the other, and their respective judgments might honestly and rightly differ in consequence. In the case of an author whose works are very familiar it is possible that one judges from a sample that is virtually large: in the case of a writer whose work is new to one it seems likely enough that one may form an impression from a mere page or two. The real content of such judgments is by no means clear. And to look at the matter from the opposite standpoint, if we *define* the relative richness of the vocabularies of two authors as given by the ratio W_2/W_1, it is evident that this will not in general correspond with *any* impressionist judgment.

(2) PERCENTAGES OR RATIOS, FALLACIOUS AND OTHERWISE

5.14. We often desire, in studying a literary vocabulary, to note the proportion of some special class of words to the whole. The special class may consist, for example, of words characteristic, or possibly characteristic, of an earlier or a later phase of the author's writings; in my own work, of words not given in Lewis and Short's *Latin Dictionary*, or of words not occurring in the Vulgate; in Mersand's work on Chaucer (ref. 5.1), of Romance words. As has been specially emphasised by Mersand, such proportions may be measured in two entirely distinct ways. In his terminology we may state the proportion of such words either (1) in the dynamic vocabulary, or (2) in the static vocabulary (§ 2.24): or, as I would put it, we may state (1) the proportion amongst *occurrences*, i.e. the proportion of occurrences of words of the special class to all occurrences, or (2) the proportion in the *vocabulary*, i.e. the proportion of the number of words in the list of the special class to the total number of words in the vocabulary. The important point, which does not seem to have been remarked, is that while the first method gives a proportion or percentage that is independent of size of sample, the second method gives a proportion which is a function of size of sample and which may in consequence be misleading if percentages based on samples of different sizes are compared. This is really evident from elementary considerations. The proportion (1) based on occurrences must be constant (within the limits of fluctuations of sampling) for all sizes of sample, since words tend to occur simply in proportion to their respective λ's. As regards the proportion (2) based on vocabulary, in a very small (random) sample few or no words will occur more than once and the percentage based on vocabulary must therefore tend in the limit, as the sample approaches zero, to the same value as the percentage based on occurrences. In a very large sample, on the other hand, the complete stock of words approaches exhaustion, and the proportion based on vocabulary must therefore tend to its value in the lists of words at risk. In general these initial and final limits are obviously not identical. It is as well to consider the matter more fully from the standpoint of our general theory, but the non-mathematical reader may if he likes go on at once to the illustrations of §§ 5.17 *et seq.*

5.15.　　In the special class let there be m_1 words with parameter λ, m_2 with parameter $a_2\lambda$, m_3 with parameter $a_3\lambda$, and so on: in the rest let there be n_1 words with parameter $b_1\lambda$, n_2 with parameter $b_2\lambda$, and so on. Then the proportion of occurrences of words of the special class to occurrences of all words, or the *weighted* proportion as we may term it, each word being weighted by the number of times it occurs, will be

$$p_w = \frac{m_1 + m_2 a_2 + m_3 a_3 + \dots}{m_1 + m_2 a_2 + m_3 a_3 + \dots + n_1 b_1 + n_2 b_2 + n_3 b_3 + \dots} . \tag{5.9}$$

If
$$m_1 + m_2 + m_3 + \dots = w_1, \tag{5.10}$$

$$n_1 + n_2 + n_3 + \dots = w_2, \tag{5.11}$$

w_1 being the number of words at risk in the special class and w_2 the number at risk in the rest, and if $\bar{\lambda}_1, \bar{\lambda}_2$ are the mean values of the parameter for the special class and for the rest, we may also write this more briefly

$$p_w = \frac{w_1 \bar{\lambda}_1}{w_1 \bar{\lambda}_1 + w_2 \bar{\lambda}_2} . \tag{5.12}$$

Obviously neither (5.9) nor (5.12) is dependent on size of sample, it being remembered that $\bar{\lambda}_1 / \bar{\lambda}_2$ is constant for all sizes of sample. For the proportion, in the sample vocabulary, of words in the special class to words in the entire vocabulary we have on the other hand

$$p_v = \frac{m_1(1 - e^{-\lambda}) + m_2(1 - e^{-a_2\lambda}) + m_3(1 - e^{-a_3\lambda}) + \dots}{m_1(1 - e^{-\lambda}) + m_2(1 - e^{-a_2\lambda}) + \dots + n_1(1 - e^{-b_1\lambda}) + n_2(1 - e^{-b_2\lambda}) + \dots} . \tag{5.13}$$

Using the same method of approximation as before to find the lower limit, expanding exponentials and retaining only first powers of the exponents, we have

$$\lambda = 0$$

$$\left. \text{Limit } p_v = \frac{m_1 + m_2 a_2 + m_3 a_3 + \dots}{m_1 + m_2 a_2 + m_3 a_3 + \dots + n_1 b_1 + n_2 b_2 + n_3 b_3 + \dots} = p_w \right\} \tag{5.14}$$

and $\qquad \lambda = \infty$

$$\text{Limit}\, p_v = \frac{m_1 + m_2 + m_3 + \dots}{m_1 + m_2 + m_3 + \dots + n_1 + n_2 + n_3 + \dots} = \frac{w_1}{w_1 + w_2} \Bigg\} . \quad (5.15)$$

The limits suggested by elementary considerations are therefore duly verified.

5.16.   But it is an interesting question *how* p_v passes from the initial to the final limit. It will be noticed that the expression (5.13) for p_v is of the same sort of form as the expression (5.7) for the ratio ρ, and it may therefore be conjectured that, as in the case of ρ, the course of p_v from the initial to the final limit is not in general *monotonic*, i.e. it does not in general increase continuously or decrease continuously from the one limit to the other. In Tables 5.4 and 5.5, it is true, the proportion of the vocabulary drawn from the lower component, which may be regarded as a 'special class', increases continuously, but these are very simple instances. Table 5.6 gives a similar analysis of vocabulary for a slightly more complex example, a compound Poisson distribution of three components. The number of words at risk, W, has been taken as 10,000; the proportions of these words in the three components as $q_1 = 0.9$, $q_2 = 0.09$ and $q_3 = 0.01$; and the parameters as λ, 51λ and 451λ. Thus the value of λ for a given size of sample S_1 is given by

$$S_1 = 10,000[0.9 + 51(0.09) + 451(0.01)]\lambda = 100,000\lambda.$$

The contributions of the several components to the vocabulary of each sample are given in the columns headed A, B and C, with the total in the following column. In the next to last column is shown the percentage of the total vocabulary contributed by the middle component B. Here the initial limit is given by the proportion $(0.09 \times 51)/10 = 0.459$, or 45.9 per cent: the final limit is the value of q_2, viz. 0.09, that is, 9 per cent. The *general* trend of p_v, as given by the limiting values, is therefore a decrease. But, looking at the figures, we see that the course of the percentage is anything but monotonic. It *rises* sharply from the initial 45.9 to 67.3 for a sample of 1500, and only thenceforward exhibits a continuous and unbroken fall. If then the special class consist solely of words from the middle component, the percentage p_v for this special class will follow a precisely similar course. It would however be more natural to suppose that the special class consisted to a large extent of words belonging to the lower component: so long as we do not overweight the lower component the course of affairs will remain essentially the same. As an example I have supposed the special class to consist of 200 words from the lower component (1/45th of the whole) and 30 words from the middle component (1/30th of the whole). The percentage contributed by this special class to the total vocabulary of each sample is shown in the last column. Here the initial limit is $10[0 \cdot 9/45 + (0 \cdot 09 \times 51)/30]$ or $1 \cdot 73$ per cent, the final limit $100 \times 230/10,000$ or $2 \cdot 3$ per cent. The general trend, as between the limits, is therefore a rise. Actually we find the percentages rising rapidly from the initial $1 \cdot 73$ to a maximum of $2 \cdot 75$ for a sample of 3000, and from thence onwards *decreasing* continuously. Over a

TABLE 5.6. Giving an analysis of the vocabulary, for various sizes of sample, for a triply-compound Poisson distribution, showing how many words are contributed to the sample from the lower, middle and upper components respectively: the two last columns showing (1) the percentage of the vocabulary from the middle component on the total, (2) the percentage of the total contributed by a 'special class' consisting of 1/45th of the lower and 1/30th of the middle component

$$W = 10,000; \; q_1 = 0 \cdot 9, \; q_2 = 0 \cdot 09, \; q_3 = 0 \cdot 01; \; \lambda\text{'s in proportions } 1:51:451.$$

| Sample | Vocabulary | | | | B per-centage of total | A/45 + B/30 per-centage of total |
	Lower component A	Middle component B	Upper component C	Total		
0	—	—	—	—	45·9	1·73
200	18·0	87·3	59·4	164·7	53·0	2·01
400	35·9	166·1	83·5	285·5	58·2	2·22
600	53·8	237·3	93·3	384·4	61·7	2·37
1,500	134·0	481·2	99·9	715·1	67·3	2·66
3,000	266·0	705·1	100·0	1,071·1	65·8	2·75
6,000	524·1	857·8	100·0	1,481·9	57·9	2·72
9,000	774·6	890·9	100·0	1,765·5	50·5	2·66
12,000	1,017·7	898·0	100·0	2,015·7	44·6	2·61
15,000	1,253·6	899·6	100·0	2,253·2	39·9	2·57
18,000	1,482·6	899·9	100·0	2,482·5	36·3	2·54
21,000	1,704·7	900·0	100·0	2,704·7	33·3	2·51
24,000	1,920·4	900·0	100·0	2,920·4	30·8	2·49
27,000	2,129·6	900·0	100·0	3,129·6	28·8	2·47
30,000	2,332·6	900·0	100·0	3,332·6	27·0	2·46
60,000	4,060·7	900·0	100·0	5,060·7	17·8	2·38
120,000	6,289·3	900·0	100·0	7,289·3	12·3	2·33
∞	9,000·0	900·0	100·0	10,000·0	9·0	2·30

range of sizes of sample with which we should very likely be dealing in practice p_v *falls* with increasing size of sample, notwithstanding that the general trend is a rise. It is important to note the possibility of this sort of behaviour. As a general rule the 'special class' we are considering is a class of relatively rare words, i.e. of words each of which is relatively infrequently used. Thus in Mersand's case it is more natural to state the percentage of Romance words rather than the complementary percentage of Germanic words. In my own case it is more natural to state the percentage of words *not* in the standard dictionary or *not* in the Vulgate rather than the complementary percentage of ordinary words that are in the dictionary or are in the Vulgate. Provided that the special class is such a class of relatively rare words, the initial limit of p_v will be less than the final limit, and the *general* trend will therefore be a rise. But the preceding work warns us that over any limited range with which we may be concerned we cannot be sure whether the trend is a rise or a fall. Some evidence, however, may possibly be given us by comparison of the values of p_w and p_v, if they are both known. If for some moderately large sample p_v *greatly* exceed its lower limit p_w, it seems probable that this may indicate so rapid an upward trend that in spite of minor fluctuations it is likely to remain monotonic. The conclusion is rather conjectural, but it will be noticed that in each of the three following illustrations p_v does greatly exceed p_w and there is no indication of the trend being anything but monotonic.

5.17.   *Illustration* 5.1. We may first give a brief illustration from figures incidentally cited in § 4.18, which may have puzzled the careful reader. In the *De Imitatione Christi*, for which the complete noun-distribution was given in Table 2.1, 32·5 per thousand of the nouns in the vocabulary were not found in Lewis and Short's *Latin Dictionary*, see Table 5.7 below. In the sample from the miscellaneous works of Thomas à Kempis other than the *Imitatio*, on which Table 2.2 was based, the proportion was 27·0 per thousand. In the sample from the theological works of Gerson, on which Table 2.3 was based, the proportion was 57·6 per thousand. But in the total vocabulary for the *Imitatio* and the two samples together the proportion was 60·3 per thousand, i.e. a higher proportion than for any one of the three constituents of the mixture. At first sight at all events the result looks most paradoxical, but it is simply an example of p_v tending to be the larger the larger the sample. Perhaps the following way of looking at the matter may be helpful. The nouns not in the given dictionary in the respective samples numbered 38, 38 and 101. The sum of these figures is 177; but of course some few of the words in the three samples are identical, and actually the total number of separate nouns not in the dictionary is only 148, roundly 84 per cent of 177. But the *total* vocabularies of the respective samples (cf. figures at the foot of Tables 2.1, 2.2 and 2.3 or Table 9.2) are 1168, 1406 and 1754, the sum of which is 4328, and so many of these words are identical that the actual total of separate nouns proves to be only 2454, roundly 57 per cent of 4328. On pooling the three samples together, the words of the special class (being relatively rare words) overlap much less than the words of the 'rest'—which are more largely common words—so that their proportion to the whole is increased. When we take the proportions p_w on *occurrences*, as in the last column of Table 5.7, there is no such odd result. Occurrences, whether of nouns in the special class or of all nouns, simply

TABLE 5.7. Showing the proportion per 1000 of words not in Lewis and Short's *Latin Dictionary* (1) on vocabulary, (2) on occurrences, for the *De Imitatione Christi* and for samples from the miscellaneous works of Thomas à Kempis and the theological works of Gerson (cf. Tables 2.1, 2.2, 2.3, or Tables 9.1 and 9.2, and Table 9.4)

Work or works	Proportion per 1000 of nouns not in Lewis and Short in	
	Vocabulary, p_v	Occurrences, p_w
De Imitatione Christi	32·5	7·17
Thomas à Kempis, *Miscellanea*: sample	27·0	7·07
Gerson, theological works: sample	57·6	19·77
The three together	60·3	11·33

add together, so that if s_1, s_1', s_1'' are the numbers of occurrences in the special class, S_1, S_1', S_1'' the numbers of total occurrences, the proportion in the pool is

$$\frac{s_1 + s_1' + s_1''}{S_1 + S_1' + S_1''},$$

which may be written

$$\frac{1}{S_1 + S_1' + S_1''}\left\{\left(\frac{s_1}{S_1}\right)S_1 + \left(\frac{s_1'}{S_1'}\right)S_1' + \left(\frac{s_1''}{S_1''}\right)S_1''\right\}.$$

That is to say, p_w for the pool is simply the weighted mean of the p_w's for the constituents, using as weights the total numbers of occurrences. In our own case this is practically identical with the simple arithmetic mean of the p_w's of the constituents, as may readily be verified from the data of the table, since the three samples are very nearly of the same size. It will be noted from Table 5.7 that, in each instance, the weighted mean p_w is much less than the vocabulary mean p_v. This is a clear indication that the special class is a class of relatively rare, i.e. very infrequently used, words. The main advantage of stating both p_v and p_w seems to me in fact to be that it does show quite clearly (if the sample is reasonably large) how far the words of the special class are at all commonly used, or how far they occur but rarely.

5.18.   *Illustration 5.2.* The data accumulated in the sampling experiment on Macaulay's essay on Bacon can be utilised for an illustration, if we pick out some appropriate set of words for a 'special class'. I decided to select a very simply defined set, viz. the 990 nouns (Table 4.4) that occurred only once in the whole experiment. Of these 238 occurred in the initial sample *a* of about 2000 occurrences, 247 in sample *b*, 237 in sample *c* and 268 in

TABLE 5.8. Taking the 990 once-nouns of Table 4.4 and showing the number s_0 occurring in each sample of the sampling experiment on Macaulay's essay on Bacon, together with the total vocabulary of each sample S_0 (from Table 4.5, col. 2) and the percentage of s_0 on S_0

Sample	s_0	S_0	$100 s_0/S_0$
Samples of about 2000 occurrences			
a	238	903	26·36
b	247	936	26·39
c	237	937	25·29
d	268	964	27·80
Total	990	3740	26·47
Samples of about 4000 occurrences			
ab	485	1380	35·14
ac	475	1390	34·17
bc	484	1409	34·35
ad	506	1426	35·48
bd	515	1441	35·74
cd	505	1432	35·27
Total	2970	8478	35·03
Samples of about 6000 occurrences			
abc	722	1736	41·59
abd	753	1773	42·47
acd	743	1768	42·02
bcd	752	1780	42·25
Total	2970	7057	42·09
Total of 8045 occurrences			
abcd	990	2048	48·34

sample *d*, as shown in the column headed s_0 in Table 5.8. The values of s_0 for the samples of about 4000 and 6000 occurrences will be given by simply adding the numbers for the initial samples: thus for the sample *ab* the number will be $238 + 247 = 485$, for *ac* $238 + 237 = 475$, for *abc* $238 + 247 + 237 = 722$, and so forth. In the following column of the table are given the total vocabularies of the same samples, taken from col. 2 of Table 4.5, and finally in the last column the percentages $100 s_0/S_0$. It will be seen that for the initial samples of about 2000 occurrences p_v ranges from 25·29 to 27·80 per cent with a mean, based on the totals given, of 26·47 per cent. For the double samples of about 4000 occurrences it ranges from 34·17 to 35·74 per cent, with a mean of 35·03. For the triple samples of about 6000 occurrences it ranges from 41·59 to 42·47 per cent with a mean of 42·09, and finally in the total distribution it takes the highest value, 48·34 per cent. Evidently the rate of rise in the percentage, at first rapid, subsequently slackens off. I have not given all the corresponding values of p_w. As the words of the special class only occur once, the numbers of the s_0 column may be read as 'occurrences' as well as 'vocabulary'. The total number of occurrences (Table 4.5, col. 3) being 8045, the mean value of p_w for samples of each size, if obtained from the totals like the mean values of p_v given in the table, must remain constant at $990/8045 = 12\cdot31$ per cent. If the reader so desire, he can work out the percentages for the separate samples from the numbers of occurrences given in Table 4.5: they range from 11·80 to 13·13 in the samples of about 2000; from 11·85 to 12·76 in the samples of about 4000; and from 12·03 to 12·47 in the samples of about 6000. As we have seen from equation (5.14), for very small samples p_v tends to approach p_w, in this case 12·31 per cent. As an illustration, I took out at random, by Tippett's numbers, 50 of the initial sub-samples based on twelve lines of the text (§ 4.2) and counted the number of special nouns and the total number of distinct nouns (vocabulary) in the first 20 occurrences of each. These 50 samples of 20 occurrences yielded a mean number of 2·44 nouns of the special class, and a mean total vocabulary of 17·94 nouns, percentage 13·60—slightly in excess, as one might expect, of the limiting value 12·31 for a sample of zero size.

5.19. *Illustration* 5.3. The various writings of an author may be regarded as samples, though of course not random samples, from his works. If these writings differ greatly in length from one another, and we rank them in order of length and set down against each the value of p_v for some special class, we may be able to note, superposed on the irregularities due to individual characteristics of the different works, the trend of p_v due to increasing size of sample. Usually, as already remarked, the *general* trend to be expected will be an increase, the words of the special class being in general relatively rare (infrequently used) words, though over any given limited range the general rule may not hold, the trend not being monotonic. Mersand, in his study of the Romance vocabulary of Chaucer (ref. 5.1) to which reference has already been made more than once, gives in a table on pp. 75–7 of his book some data that seem admirably fitted to afford a test of this notion. Data are given for each of sixty-one works or parts of works by Chaucer, *inter alia*, as to its total length in words—practically all significant words were counted except proper names, see p. 41 for rules—and

Table 5.9. Showing the percentages of Romance words on vocabulary and on occurrences in the works of Chaucer, the works being arranged in order of length (total words). Data from Mersand (ref. 5.1): the percentages re-calculated (see text)

Work	Total words	Percentage of Romance words		Work	Total words	Percentage of Romance words	
		Vocabulary p_v	Occurrences p_w			Vocabulary p_v	Occurrences p_w
1 *Prov.*	44	8·57	6·82	31 B. *Ship.*	3,474	32·47	12·06
2 *Adam.*	51	7·89	5·88	32 C. *Pard.*	3,721	35·31	12·31
3 *Gentil.*	157	31·94	23·57	33 G. *SN.*	4,069	33·13	11·06
4 *Wom.Unc.*	173	19·10	10·98	34 *L.G.W.* A.	4,209	30·47*	11·29
5 *Bal.Comp.*	173	32·14	17·92	35 *L.G.W.* B.	4,230	23·91*	7·52*
6 *Rosem.*	183	30·43	16·39	36 *Host*	4,251	31·00*	9·22*
7 *Lak.St.*	195	31·37	16·41	37 D. *Sum.*	4,571	36·67	12·84
8 *Purs.*	205	23·23	11·71	38 B. *NP.*	4,821	35·26	10·58
9 *Truth*	218	17·24	11·47	39 A. *Mil.*	5,140	26·67	8·52
10 *Wom.Nob.*	225	41·59	24·00	40 F. *Squire*	5,181	37·49	11·33
11 *Bukton*	264	15·45	7·20	41 *PF.*	5,376	34·42	12·00
12 *Merc.B.*	308	26·32	16·88	42 B. *Monk*	5,889	37·50	12·16
13 *Scog.*	393	25·82	12·98	43 G. *CT.*	5,952	33·33	10·84
14 A. *Ck.*	451	24·35	15·30	44 D. *WB.Prol.*	6,631	37·21	10·24
15 *Form.A.*	473	31·72	16·28	45 A. *Prol.*	6,683	39·06	12·00
16 *Fort.*	576	39·04	19·79	46 F. *Frank.*	6,878	37·58	10·96
17 *Venus*	592	37·61*	19·09	47 B. *ML.*	7,852	37·84	11·98
18 *Am.Comp.*	744	20·33	8·74	48 *BD.*	8,590	28·79	7·15
19 *Comp.Pite*	911	28·57	15·92	49 E. *Clerk.*	8,994	40·29	12·74
20 *Comp.L.*	1,018	17·76	6·97	50 E. *Mch.*	9,112	38·58	11·02
21 B. *Thop.*	1,156	27·82	12·89	51 *R.R.* A.	10,583	37·84*	11·91
22 *A.B.C.*	1,411	35·06	16·09	52 *R.R.* C.	11,787	44·52	12·02
23 B. *Prior.*	1,824	28·94	11·84	53 *HF.*	12,969	37·24	10·70
24 H. *Manc.*	1,976	30·86	10·43	54 *Astr.*	14,779	45·25	20·45
25 C. *Phis.*	2,179	35·59	13·49	55 B. *Mel.*	16,826	46·47	13·52
26 *Mars.*	2,283	32·85	13·93	56 A. *Kn.*	17,149	40·41	11·87
27 *Anel.*	2,696	29·63	10·61	57 *L.G.W.*	21,238	36·92*	7·17*
28 D. *Friar*	2,832	31·96	11·58	58 *R.R.* B.	21,613	45·96	14·63*
29 D. *WB.*	3,210	35·19	10·78	59 I. *Pars.*	29,672	51·27	14·95
30 A. *Rv.*	3,308	21·71	7·22	60 *Boeth.*	51,187	49·85	15·28
				61 *T.C.*	64,908	43·47	8·50

* In these cases my figure differs from Mersand's by more than one unit per cent (see text). Mersand's figures are as follows: p_v (on vocabulary) 17, 38·97; 34, 45·77; 35, 36·92; 36, 45·91; 51, 38·87; 57, 38·33; p_w (on occurrences) 35, 11·57; 36, 10·85; 57, 8·26; 58, 12·34.

its total vocabulary, the Romance vocabulary and Romance occurrences, the percentage of Romance on total vocabulary p_v, and the percentage of Romance on total occurrences p_w. As the lengths of the works exhibit a great range, from the little *Proverbe of Chaucer* of 44 words and *Chaucers wordes unto Adam, his owne scriveyn* of 51, up to the *Boethius* of over 51,000 and the *Troilus and Criseyde* of nearly 65,000,'there is ample scope for exhibiting any trend in the value of p_v with 'size of sample' or length of the work. Unfortunately, however, I met with some serious trouble. After having already done the work on the percentages printed in the table, I noticed that one of them was clearly quite inconsistent with the absolute figures given. This led me to re-calculate *all* the percentages, with the result that I found a number of small differences of little importance, but several quite large divergences implying that either the percentages or the figures for the absolute numbers of words were more or less seriously in error owing to misprints, or mis-calculations, or that most horrid and disturbing source of error, the author inadvertently picking up the wrong figure from his working sheets. There were eleven cases in which the difference between us exceeded one unit in the percentage, and in some instances it was very substantial; cf. the percentages to which an asterisk is attached in Table 5.9, which are my revised figures, and Mersand's values given in the footnote. One of my puzzles does not appear in the table: the value for p_w for the *Boethius*, line 60, is 15·28; on the numbers of words as printed in the book, 7823/31,187, it works out at 25·08 per cent. On communicating with the author, he informed me that this discrepancy was accounted for, as I had conjectured, by the fact that the 'total words' should read 51,187, as in Table 5.9, not 31,187. With one of my other emendations, 31·00 for 45·91 in line 36, p_v column he agreed. For the rest he was unable to help, as all his papers had been long since destroyed. This left it rather difficult to decide what was best to be done, but finally I decided to retain the revised percentages of my own calculation, and it is these that are given in Table 5.9.

5.20.   Table 5.9 gives first the abbreviation of the title of the work as in Mersand's table, next the total number of words (occurrences), next the percentage of Romance vocabulary on total vocabulary of the work p_v, and finally the percentage of Romance occurrences on total occurrences (words) of the work p_w. The works have been re-arranged in order of length, i.e. total words or occurrences. A mere glance down the column for p_v shows how clear is the trend. In the first group of 15 works, nine values of p_v are under 30 per cent and only one is over 40 per cent. In the final group of 16 works, only one value of p_v is under 30 per cent and nine are over 40 per cent. Summarising by the four groups of 15, 15, 15 and 16 works, marked off by the blank lines in the table, we have the following averages: the figures given are the simple arithmetic means, each poem or other work being regarded as one experimental sample, whatever its length:

Group	Mean length (words)	Mean p_v	Mean p_w
1–15	234	24·48	14·25
16–30	1,781	30·19	12·62
31–45	4,947	33·59	10·93
46–61	19,634	41·39	12·18
All	—	32·56	12·49

When we average over these groups of 15 or 16 works, irregularities due to genuine differences between them are, to a great extent at least, eliminated, and the mean p_v rises without a break from each group to the next, the group of longest works yielding no less than 41·39 per cent of Romance words in the vocabulary against only 24·48 per cent for the group of shortest works. To complete the picture, it may be added that if we take a larger sample than any given here, viz. the entire works of Chaucer together, the proportion of Romance words in the vocabulary is 4189/8072 (ref. 5.1, pp. 40–43) or 51·9 per cent, a higher figure than for any single work, even the *Parson's Tale* (Table 5.9, line 59). It seems odd that so apparently paradoxical a result should not have received comment. In the column for p_w differences are much smaller and there is no continuous trend: the mean falls from the first to the third group and then rises again. These results cannot be affected to any important extent by the possible errors in some of the individual percentages. The most doubtful group is the third in which three of my values of p_v differ seriously from those printed by Mersand. If we replace my figures by Mersand's, the mean value for p_v for this group is raised from 33·59 to 36·47: if we simply omit lines 34, 35 and 36, the mean of the remaining 12 values of p_v is 34·88. Both figures lie between that for the second group and that for the fourth group. In the p_w column for the third group there are two doubtful values: if Mersand's figures are substituted for mine the mean is raised to 11·31; if the two doubtful figures are simply omitted, the mean of the remaining 13 is 12·27, and both these alternatives would make the means of p_w run *more* uniformly than they do on my own figures.

5.21. We may complete the trial by applying tests for statistical significance. For the standard deviation of p_v I find the value 8·929: hence the standard error for the mean of 15 observations is 2·306, and for the mean of 16 is 2·232. Writing down the deviations of the group means of p_v from the general mean 32·56, dividing by the standard error and squaring, we have:

Group	Deviation of mean p_v	Ratio to standard error	Square of ratio
1–15	−8·08	3·50	12·25
16–30	−2·37	1·03	1·06
31–45	+1·03	0·45	0·20
46–61	+8·83	3·98	15·84
			29·35

Here χ^2 is 29·35, the degrees of freedom ν are 3 or the n' for Table XII in *Tables for Statisticians* is 4, and entering the table accordingly we find that P lies between 0·000002 and 0·000001, i.e. the chances are only something between 1 and 2 in a million of our getting such a set of deviations (without respect to their order) by simple random sampling.

5.22.   When we apply the same process to the group means for p_w results are very different. For the standard deviation of p_w I find 3·855, making the standard error for the mean of 15 observations 0·9955 and that for the mean of 16 observations 0·9639. We have accordingly:

Group	Deviation of mean p_w	Ratio to standard error	Square of ratio
1–15	+1·76	1·77	3·13
16–30	+0·13	0·13	0·02
31–45	−1·56	1·57	2·46
46–61	−0·31	0·32	0·10
			5·71

χ^2 is now only 5·71, n' is 4 as before, and interpolating in Table XII of *Tables for Statisticians* we find $P = 0·129$. That is to say we might, on random sampling, expect such a set of deviations rather more often than once in eight trials. The deviations are of no statistical significance.

5.23.   It is clear from these illustrations that p_v, the percentage of words of a special class in the vocabulary, is a quantity that must be used with the greatest caution. In such a case as that of Chaucer's works, if we find that a shorter work A gives a lower value for the percentage p_v of Romance words than a longer work B, we cannot be sure that this is not due solely to the difference in size of sample, not implying any real or essential difference between A and B. Only if the *longer* work exhibit the *lower* percentage must the difference be due to some definite peculiarity in one or other work: indeed the real difference between the two works may have been largely masked by the effect of the difference between their lengths. With p_w, the proportion based on occurrences (dynamic vocabulary, uses in text), there is no such source of possible fallacy. A passage in Mersand that seems to imply the contrary (ref. 5.1, Chapter VIII, Section C: Percentages of Romance uses, p. 83) is mistaken—or possibly I misapprehend his meaning. It is really rather remarkable how clearly the trend of p_v stands out in Table 5.9. With a shorter list of works and a shorter range of lengths. individual real differences might much more largely, or even wholly, mask the trend.

5.24.   In the previous paragraphs of this section, §§ 5.14–5.23, we have discussed two only of the possible ratios between the four quantities *special vocabulary*, *special occurrences*, *total vocabulary* and *total occurrences*, namely

special vocabulary/total vocabulary

and   special occurrences/total occurrences,

which measure the proportionate frequency of words of some defined special class in the vocabulary and in the text, respectively, of the given sample. The first, as we have shown, is liable to lead to fallacious conclusions owing to its being a function of the size of the sample. Of the two other possible ratios,

special vocabulary/total occurrences

and   special occurrences/total vocabulary,

the second seems devoid of useful meaning. The first, however, indicating the proportion of words of the special class (vocabulary) to the size of the sample, has been used not perhaps directly in the simple form given but with a transformation which certainly does not improve it. If two poems are in identical metre, or two prose works are set in the same type with the same length of line, the *numbers of lines* in the two will be closely proportionate to the total occurrences (total words as ordinarily counted), and we may substitute *number of lines* for *total occurrences* without seriously altering the ratio between the proportions for the two works of the pair. Number of *pages* might similarly be substituted for number of occurrences if all the pages were set solid, or if each partly filled page was measured up at its true proportion of a page. Thus Mersand does not give, in his table of pp. 75–7, the percentage of Romance vocabulary on total occurrences for each work, but he does give Romance vocabulary per line, and judging from his citations a number of other workers have used the method: he also gives Romance occurrences per line, which seems redundant when the percentage of Romance occurrences on total occurrences has been given (cf. Table 5.9). But clearly this 'per line' method should only be used— I feel apologies are necessary for emphasising anything so obvious—when the condition stated above is fulfilled, i.e. when the unit of measurement, the line, carries the same meaning from one work to another: poems compared must be identical in metre, prose works compared must be printed in the same type with the same length of line; and prose works and poems cannot properly be compared at all. Now the poems of Chaucer are of course not all in the same metre. The short ballad-metre lines of *Sir Thopas* (21 of Table 5.9) average only 5.58 words to a line; the metre of four accents in rhymed couplets of *The Book of the Duchesse* (48) 6·44 words; the couplets of *The Shipmannes Tale* (31) 8·00 words. The quantities treated as 'lines' in the four prose works *Boethius* (60), *the Astrolabe* (54), *The Tale of Melibeus* (55) and *The Parson's Tale* (59) are almost of a different order of magnitude. *The Parson's Tale* has 29 words to a 'line', *The Tale of Melibeus* 18, *Boethius* about 26, the *Astrolabe* about 38! In the case of the two *Tales* one may say for certain that the so-called 'lines' are no more *lines* than the 'verses' in the Bible, but *clauses* arbitrarily marked off for convenience of reference, *vide* the Oxford Chaucer (ref. 5.2, vol. v, pp. 203 and 447). What Mersand's figures taken for the numbers of lines of *Boethius* and the *Astrolabe* represent I do not know, as in the Oxford edition the actual lines of these two texts are simply numbered as printed, giving actual lines of 10 or 12 words, not 26 or 38, figures which I have simply estimated from Mersand's ratios; I can but suppose that they too represent clauses, not lines. To me it seems clear that ratios on such a shifting basis can only serve to mislead, and are best ignored.

5.25.   Rather than use them, I accordingly calculated from Mersand's data the actual percentages of Romance vocabulary on total occurrences and give these figures in Table 5.10, retaining the order of the works by total occurrences as in Table 5.9. Now consider how this ratio may be expected to vary with size of sample. For very small samples 'vocabulary' tends to approximate more and more close to 'occurrences' as the size of sample is decreased, and consequently the ratio of Romance *vocabulary* to total occurrences becomes more and more nearly equal to the ratio of Romance *occurrences* to total occurrences, i.e. approximately 12·5 per cent (cf. the averages in § 5.20). As regards very large samples, on the other hand, 'total occurrences' may increase without limit but 'Romance vocabulary' can only increase up to the total of Romance words at risk. Hence for very large samples the ratio tends to the limit zero. This cross-ratio, say p_c, tends therefore in every case to *decrease* with size of sample. The limits given may readily be verified for the compound Poisson distribution. Using the notation of §§ 5.15, 5.16,

$$p_c = \frac{m_1(1-e^{-\lambda}) + m_2(1-e^{-a_2\lambda}) + m_3(1-e^{-a_3\lambda}) + \cdots}{(m_1 + m_2 a_2 + \ldots + n_1 b_1 + n_2 b_2 + \ldots)\lambda}, \qquad (5.16)$$

and hence, expanding exponentials,

$$\lambda = 0$$

$$\left. \text{Limit} \, p_c = \frac{m_1 + m_2 a_2 + m_3 a_3 + \dots}{m_1 + m_2 a_2 + \dots + n_1 b_1 + n_2 b_2 + \dots} = p_w \right\}, \qquad (5.17)$$

and evidently, $\qquad \lambda = \infty, \quad \text{Limit} \, p_c = 0.$ $\qquad\qquad$ (5.18)

Between these limits the variation is necessarily monotonic. For the expression (5.16) may, omitting constants, be broken up into fractions of the form, say,

$$y = \frac{1 - e^{-\lambda}}{\lambda}$$

and

$$\frac{1}{\lambda} \frac{dy}{d\lambda} = \frac{e^{-\lambda}}{1 - e^{-\lambda}} - \frac{1}{\lambda}.$$

This is negative if

$$\frac{e^{-\lambda}}{1 - e^{-\lambda}} < \frac{1}{\lambda} \quad \text{or} \quad e^{\lambda} - 1 > \lambda \quad \text{or} \quad \lambda + \frac{\lambda^2}{2!} + \frac{\lambda^3}{3!} + \dots > \lambda,$$

which, as λ is positive, is necessarily true. This is then an unusually straightforward case.

5.26.   Inspection of Table 5.10 shows how clear is the downward trend. Of the fifteen percentages in the first group nine are over 10 per cent, in the next group only three, in the last two groups none. In the first group no percentage is under 5, in the second only one, in the third two, in the last ten, and the two final figures (lines 60, 61) are the lowest of the whole table. The averages of the four groups (simple arithmetic means) are as follows:

Group	Mean p_c	Group	Mean p_c
1–15	11·91	31–45	6·41
16–30	8·96	46–61	4·42

The first mean is as it should be rather lower than the limit of 12·5 per cent for a zero sample, and the trend is conspicuously and continuously downward: it seems hardly worth while applying a test for significance. This percentage also, like p_v, may therefore easily mislead, and must be used with equal caution. The reader may find it instructive as a further illustration to calculate from Table 5·6 the percentages of the Middle Component Vocabulary B on size of sample, and compare them with the given percentages on total vocabulary.

5.27.   Our conclusions as to these percentages seem to be applicable in a wider field than the statistics of vocabulary pure and simple. We may note in an author's writings other characteristics besides words—particular constructions, for example; idioms; instances of anacoluthon; similes and metaphors; unusual forms of the cases of a noun or the parts of a verb; peculiarities of word order, and so forth. To use perfectly general terms let us say that we list various *peculiarities* of different *types*. Then the particular

TABLE 5.10. Showing the percentages of Romance vocabulary on total occurrences in the works of Chaucer, the works being arranged in order of length (total words). Percentages calculated from the data of Mersand (ref. 5.1). Cf. Table 5.9

	Work	Percentage of Romance vocabulary on total occurrences		Work	Percentage of Romance vocabulary on total occurrences
1	Prov.	6·82	31	B. Ship.	6·51
2	Adam.	5·88	32	C. Pard.	8·01
3	Gentil.	14·65	33	G. SN,	6·73
4	Wom.Unc.	9·83	34	L.G.W. A.	3·54
5	Bal.Comp.	15·61	35	L.G.W. B.	3·64
6	Rosem.	15·30	36	Host.	6·05
7	Lak.St.	16·41	37	D. Sum.	7·70
8	Purs.	11·22	38	B. NP.	7·20
9	Truth	9·17	39	A. Mil.	5·27
10	Wom.Nob.	20·89	40	F. Squire	7·08
11	Bukton	7·20	41	PF.	7·05
12	Merc.B.	8·12	42	B. Monk	6·78
13	Scog.	11·96	43	G. CY.	5·90
14	A. Ck.	10·42	44	D. WB.Prol.	6·23
15	Form.A.	15·22	45	A. Prol.	8·47
16	Fort.	17·01	46	F. Frank.	5·79
17	Venus	14·86	47	B. ML.	5·99
18	Am.Comp.	6·72	48	BD.	3·86
19	Comp.Pite	9·44	49	E. Clerk	5·51
20	Comp.L.	5·30	50	E. Mch.	5·65
21	B. Thop.	9·60	51	R.R. A.	5·69
22	A.B.C.	11·06	52	R.R. C.	6·03
23	B. Prior.	7·95	53	HF.	4·75
24	H. Manc.	8·00	54	Astr.	2·71
25	C. Phis.	9·18	55	B. Mel.	3·71
26	Mars.	8·89	56	A. Kn.	4·85
27	Anel.	7·42	57	L.G.W.	2·91
28	D. Friar	7·13	58	R.R. B.	4·82
29	D. WB.	6·88	59	I. Pars.	3·80
30	A. Rv.	4·99	60	Boeth.	2·63
			61	T.C.	2·03

type of peculiarity (such and such a construction and so forth) corresponds to the particular *word* of the special class in our previous work; the number of different *types* considered corresponds to the number of *words* at risk in the special class; the number of different *types* noted in any one work corresponds to the number of words (vocabulary) of the special class noted in the work, and the number of *occurrences* of all peculiarities to the number of occurrences of words of the special class. Length of the work (size of sample) would, I think, in this case too be best measured by total words: with some loss of precision, that would with reasonable care be only slight, by lines or by pages. Then instead of p_w we would have the number of *occurrences* of peculiarities per 100 words, or per page, and instead of p_c the number of *types of peculiarity* per 100 words or per page. The first would be independent of size of sample, the second would tend to decrease with size of sample, as before.

5.28. Thus Lutoslawski (ref. 5.3), from whom I have borrowed the term, lists 500 'peculiarities' of the later style of Plato drawn from the work of Lewis Campbell and others. Unfortunately, however, he gives no straightforward percentages but awards 'marks' on a complex and somewhat fantastic scheme of his own. The full rules, for which I must refer to the original, are complicated and detailed. Each type of peculiarity in the work is awarded 1, 2, 3 or 4 marks according to the class into which it falls, and the total of marks for the work is termed the number of 'units of affinity'. Such a process is not readily tractable by theory, and for myself I would hardly venture a guess how either total units of affinity or units of affinity per page might be expected to vary with size of sample, it being remembered that the points of division between classes II and III, and III and IV, are raised with increasing length of the work. The author himself says (ref. 5.3, p. 143, § 3):

Nobody has hitherto observed that only exactly equal amounts of text should be compared in order to give precise conclusions. Dialogues of different size were compared, instead of taking as a standard measure a certain amount of text of each dialogue.... We are unable to introduce the required completeness into our calculations, but we shall make due allowance for the size of the compared dialogues, admitting as a rule that the stylistic comparisons are inconclusive unless the presumed later work is equal or smaller in size. A greater number of later peculiarities in a longer work can lead to valid conclusions only under exceptional circumstances.

This passage is remarkable as showing that the author was apparently quite alive to the possible dangers of varying sizes of sample, and if we may equate 'number of later peculiarities' with 'units of affinity' we may take it that in his view the total units of affinity tend to increase with size of sample, 'a greater number of peculiarities in a longer work' being possibly merely due to its length. But do total units of affinity tend to increase *in direct proportion* to size of sample? The answer is given most briefly in the marginal summary of the last paragraph on p. 184: 'The increase of the equivalent of affinity is not proportional to the size of the sample of text investigated.' This seems perfectly clear: the total 'units of affinity' do not increase in direct próportion to size of sample but more slowly. That which seems clear in the marginal summary ceases, however, to be so clear when the whole of the paragraph is read:

We are warned also against the error of supposing the opportunities for the occurrence of a greater number of peculiarities to be proportional to volume. In this respect the subdivision of each part of the *Republic* into several samples of text is very instructive. Even those who believe the *Republic* to have been written during many years cannot deny that BB. III–IV are the immediate continuation of B. II, and with it form one whole. The style of equal samples of text in these books is also very uniform. But the influence of the size becomes evident if we compare a small sample with a larger one. Part b_1 (357A–367E) of $7\frac{1}{2}$ pp. (ed. Didot) contains only an equivalent of 21 units of affinity, while the following $29\frac{1}{2}$ pp., being four times larger, have seven times more peculiarities. In another case two succeeding samples of text differ much less, namely, c_2 (471C–541B), being nearly thrice as long as c_1 (449A–471B), has less than twice as many peculiarities of later style. The whole of the *Republic*, being ten times larger than the tenth book, contains only a little more than thrice as many peculiarities of later style. From these examples, which might be indefinitely multiplied, it becomes evident that only equal amounts of text should be compared. Future enquirers should base their calculations on an amount of text equal for each dialogue, or divide each dialogue into such equal samples of text, for instance, of ten thousand words each.

Three examples are given. In the first the larger sample has *more* peculiarities per page than the smaller. In the second and third the larger sample has *fewer* peculiarities per page than the smaller. The examples flatly contradict one another. As the *Republic* is very heterogeneous, the third example is really not very informative, for we are not told how B. x stands relatively to other books or sections of the *Republic*: as a matter of fact it has the highest number of units per page of the five sections given, and the dialogue as a whole might well be expected to give a lower figure. The example would have been better put thus, taking the necessary data from the table on pp. 162 *et seq.* of ref. 5.3. Of the five sections into which the books of the *Republic* have been divided, viz. I, II–IV, V–VII, VIII–IX, X, B. I exhibits the lowest number of units of affinity per page, viz. 2·39, against 2·50, 4·34, 5·46 and 6·84 for the others. The *Republic* as a whole (194 pp., 407 units) gives only 2·10 units per page, lower even than B. I. We may add a second example from the data of the same table. The *Gorgias, Symposium, Cratylus* and *Phaedo* show respectively 1·44, 2·49, 2·70 and 3·13 units of affinity per page. If the four dialogues are taken as one whole the group gives only 1·26 units per page, again a lower figure than that of the lowest member of the group. These examples quite definitely suggest a tendency of units per page to fall with increasing size of sample. If the conclusion is true, what becomes of the first example? I can only conclude that either there is some error in the figures or, in spite of what is said as to uniformity of style, the sub-section of the *Republic* which Lutoslawski denotes by b_1 (from B. II) does in fact differ substantially in style from the following longer sub-section b_2 (from BB. II–III) and the inclusion of this comparison was a slip. Notwithstanding the slight confusion, we must give Lutoslawski credit for remarking on the importance of size of sample.

5.29. A few words may be said in conclusion on a point that may be puzzling the reader. It is natural to ask why in these statistics we are troubled by the fact that several forms of percentage or ratio—those based in whole or in part on *Vocabulary*—are functions of size of sample, a difficulty which we do not meet in any other branch of statistics. The answer is that, as was pointed out in § 1.8 and emphasised in § 3.12, we are using the term 'size of sample' in a sense quite different from the normal. If we are dealing with distributions of personal accidents we apply the term in its proper sense, *the number of persons exposed to risk*: *that* is our sample, and the equivalent in statistics of words is the number of words at risk W. The total number of occurrences, S_1, which we have been terming 'size of sample' is equivalent to the *total number of accidents* that have happend to the persons at risk or, since (within the limits of fluctuations of sampling) total accidents are proportional to time, we may say S_1 is equivalent to *time of exposure to risk*. That is an entirely different matter. But the transfer of the term is almost unavoidable. We *are* dealing with samples of *text* and it may be noted that Lutoslawski uses the term in the quotation above: we might speak, in the accident case, of our dealing with samples of *time*, only we don't. Moreover, nobody has ever thought of stating for personal accidents parallels to our theorems for words, for the simple reason that nobody has ever been particularly interested in the composition of the 'accidented population', as one might term the aggregate of all those who have met with accidents. The statement

If a mixed population of men and women is exposed to risk and their mean liabilities are different, the proportion of women in the accidented population will be a function of the time.

8-2

is a precise parallel to our statement about p_v. But alas! who cares? The aggregate 'words-that-have-been-used' on the other hand, the 'accidented population' of words, is precisely that in which we are interested.

5.30.   The paper by G. H. Thomson and J. R. Thompson mentioned in ref. 5.4 is of considerable interest as an early attempt to deal with vocabulary very much from the statistical standpoint here adopted. The vocabulary was determined for a series of samples, ranging in length from 200 to 4000 occurrences, taken from a single chapter of Dickens's *David Copperfield*, and the graph drawn showing vocabulary as a function of size of sample. Rather remarkably it was found possible to fit this graph with considerable precision to a formula based on the assumption that the word-distribution sampled was a compound Poisson distribution of three components only. The simplicity of the result is perhaps partly due to the fact that the samples are taken from a single chapter and largely overlap, thus tending to give a rapid approximation to the limit. The authors hoped at the time to publish further work on the subject, but I learn from Professor Godfrey Thomson that the war of 1914–18 put an end to that intention. I regret that this paper did not come to my notice until the draft of the present book was already in the publishers' hands.

REFERENCES

A. Statistical Method

§§ 5.21, 5.22. For references on the method of testing goodness of fit, see Chapter 4, refs. A.

B. Citations in Text or Tables

(5.1) Mersand, Joseph (1937). *Chaucer's Romance Vocabulary*. Brooklyn, New York: The Comet Press Inc.

(5.2) Chaucer, Geoffrey (1894–97). *The Complete Works*, ed. by the Rev. Walter W. Skeat. Oxford, Clarendon Press.

(5.3) Lutoslawski, W. (1897). *The Origin and Growth of Plato's Logic, with an Account of Plato's Style and of the Chronology of his Writings*. London: Longmans, Green & Co.

(5.4) Thomson, Godfrey H. and Thompson, J. Ridley (1915). 'Outlines of a method for the quantitative analysis of writing vocabularies.' *Brit. Jour. Psych.* 8, 52.

Chapter 6

WORD-DISTRIBUTIONS FROM DIFFERENT WORKS OF THE SAME AUTHOR: MACAULAY AND BUNYAN

6.1.   To return now to the question of the characteristic, the sampling experiment described in §§ 4.2 *et seq.* shows that distinct samples from the same work, if each of them is well spread over that work, will yield closely similar results and values of the characteristic in good agreement with one another. But there is another question of fact which is of interest: What sort of variation may one expect in the characteristic, or more generally in the form of the frequency distribution, in samples taken in the same way from *different* works of the same general character by the same author? In works of very diverse character such as may come from the pen of a versatile writer—a theological treatise and a light-hearted novel—a book of travels written for the many and a report on the scientific results of the same expedition compiled for the specialist—the nature of the work rather than the nature of the author will probably take control, and such comparisons will not be illuminating. We want to know rather how much the author is likely to vary when working on the same kind of material in the same kind of way, it may be over a period of years. Two trials have been made to test the point.

(A)   MACAULAY'S *ESSAYS*

6.2.   Macaulay's *Essays* seemed to me very well adapted for one trial of this kind. They are a reasonably homogeneous set of works of the same species, all written for the same periodical, the *Edinburgh Review*. The output covers a period of seventeen years, from 1825 to 1842. Individual essays are for the most part far too brief to give a sample of anything like 8000 occurrences, and indeed work on that scale with a number of samples would be almost overwhelming: but the sampling experiment showed that samples of about 4000 occurrences would serve moderately well, and I decided to aim at that for my scale of operations. The three following essays were selected for the trial:

A. Milton. August 1825,   B. John Hampden. December 1831,
C. Frederic the Great. April 1842,

making four altogether with the essay on Bacon of July 1837, which we may denote by D. The essay on Milton is the first of the collection; that on Frederic the Great the last. The edition used was the same as before (ref. 6.1).

6.3.   The essay on Milton fails to give as many as 4000 occurrences of a noun, though not far short of that number, so there is no question of taking a sample. The essay on Hampden, on the other hand, yields rather over 4000 occurrences, but the whole essay was again included: this was, I am

TABLE 6.1. Showing the number f_x of nouns occurring X times in samples of about 4000 occurrences each (cf. Table 6.2, col. 3) from Macaulay's *Essays*: A, on Milton; B, on Hampden; C, on Frederic the Great. Comparative data for D, the essay on Bacon, will be found in Table 4.2

X	Number f_x of nouns occurring X times in essay			X	Number f_x of nouns occurring X times in essay		
	A	B	C		A	B	C
1	851	721	865	25	—	1	—
2	305	233	260	26	1	1	1
3	128	117	150	27	1	1	1
4	73	77	75	28	—	1	1
5	38	34	50	29	—	3	1
6	36	25	35	30	2	—	—
7	20	19	19	31	1	2	—
8	13	20	19	33	—	—	2
9	10	12	16	34	—	—	1
10	6	15	13	36	—	1	—
11	9	5	4	37	1	—	—
12	12	7	6	39	—	2	1
13	4	6	3	44	—	—	1
14	1	4	4	47	—	1	—
15	5	3	6	56	—	1	—
16	3	3	3	63	—	—	1
17	5	1	1	64	—	1	—
18	3	4	2	68	1	—	—
19	3	2	—	73	—	1	—
20	2	1	2	83	—	1	—
21	—	2	—	87	—	—	1
22	1	2	1	93	—	1	—
23	1	—	—				
24	1	2	—	Total	1537	1333	1545

sorry to say, actually owing to a blunder. The essay had been quite correctly estimated as giving rather too large a sample and two lines on each page had been omitted, as well as the first and last part-pages. But a slip of 100 was made in adding the words on the manuscript sheets, it was thought the total was coming out below estimate, and the omitted lines were brought in, the mistake in addition not being discovered till the work had been done and the distribution compiled. The excess over 4000 is not, however, very material for purposes of rough comparison. The essay on Frederic the Great is much lengthier, covering pp. 791–834 of the edition used. Omitting the first and last incomplete pages, it was estimated by samples that a sample based on the first 40 complete lines of each page (56 lines) would give about 4000 nouns. Actually when the work was nearly done it was found that this would give a rather excessive sample, and the sampling was therefore stopped on p. 831, omitting the 40-line samples from pp. 832 and 833. The sample

TABLE 6.2. Data for the samples from the three essays A, B, C, of Table 6.1 and for the samples from D, the essay on Bacon taken from Table 4.5

1	2	3	4	5	6	7	8	9	10
Essay or sample	S_0	S_1	S_2	M	$1000 \times$ S_0/S_1	σ^2	σ	% of 1's	K
A	1,537	3,923	31,489	2·55	392	13·973	3·74	55·4	17·91
B	1,333	4,149	62,839	3·11	321	37·453	6·12	54·1	34·09
C	1,545	4,061	40,045	2·63	380	19·010	4·36	56·0	21·82
mean of 6 samples	1,413	4,022	48,247	2·85	351	26·037	5·10	54·4	27·33
D ab	1,380	3,996	48,796	2·90	345	26·975	5·19	53·6	28·06
ac	1,390	4,008	46,174	2·88	347	24·904	4·99	54·0	26·25
bc	1,409	4,004	46,674	2·84	352	25·050	5·01	54·8	26·62
ad	1,426	4,041	49,967	2·83	353	27·010	5·20	55·7	28·12
bd	1,441	4,037	50,433	2·80	357	27·150	5·21	54·1	28·47
cd	1,432	4,049	47,441	2·83	354	25·134	5·01	54·3	26·47

covers roundly two-thirds of the whole essay. The three resulting distributions for these essays A, B and C are given in Table 6.1. For D, the essay on Bacon, it will be remembered, the four basic samples a, b, c and d were of about 2000 occurrences each: the distributions of the six samples of about 4000 occurrences obtained by combining these in all possible pairs were given in Table 4.2, to which the reader is referred. The values of the three sums S_0, S_1 and S_2, as well as of the mean, the vocabulary per 1000 occurrences, variance, standard deviation, percentage of once-words and characteristic for A, B, C and the six samples of D, are given in Table 6.2, the means of the values for the six samples being added to give a rough general figure for D appropriate to a sample of about 4000.

6.4.   Let us look first at the values of the characteristic K, given in col. 10 of Table 6.2. It will be seen that A and B, as it happens, give the extreme values for the four essays, 17·91 and 34·09: the six samples of D, which follows B in order of date, give a mean of 27·33, and the last essay C on Frederic the Great a characteristic 21·82. The essay on Milton gives the lowest value for the characteristic yet obtained. It would be of interest to know whether, if we got the values of the characteristic for all the twenty-

seven essays of the collection, or all of sufficient length, this first and early
essay would prove to be exceptional in the very low value found. Macaulay
only took his B.A. degree in 1822 and was elected a Fellow of Trinity College
in 1824, the year before the publication of the essay. He writes in the preface
to the volume of the essays: 'No attempt has been made to remodel any of
the pieces which are contained in this volume. Even the criticism on Milton,
which was written when the author was fresh from college, and which contains scarcely a paragraph such as his matured judgment approves, still
remains overloaded with gaudy and ungraceful ornament.' It is, I think,
this alone which accounts for the low characteristic and high vocabulary.
In C, the essay on Frederic the Great, which has the next lowest characteristic and a not materially different vocabulary (col. 2), I would attribute the
results rather to the great variety of scene and subject. It will be noted that
in these four essays the empirical relation on which comment is made in
§ 4.25 again holds good, the characteristics standing in the same order as
the means, or the reverse order from the vocabulary per 1000 occurrences:

Essay	M	K	Essay	M	K
A	2·55	17·91	D	2·85	27·33
C	2·63	21·82	B	3·11	34·09

In order of date of the essays the characteristics run A, 17·91; B, 34·09;
D, 27·33; C, 21·82. There is no evidence of any *continuous* trend in the value
of the characteristic with time so far as these few figures go. The range in
variation of K may seem large, but actually all four characteristics are low
compared with the others so far determined for distributions based on nouns,
and stand together in a group as the lowest values in the list:

Macaulay	Table 6.1, A	17·9
,,	,, 6.1, C	21·8
,,	,, 4.2, D	27·3
,,	,, 6.1, B	34·1
Gerson	,, 2.3	35·9
Thomas à Kempis	,, 2.2	59·7
Imitatio	,, 2.1	84·2
St John: Basic	,, 2.9	141·5
St John: A.V., all	—	161·5
St John: A.V., selected	,, 2.10	177·9

It may be noted that the figures for Gerson and Thomas à Kempis are not
quite properly comparable with the others, for they are based on samples
spread over the authors' whole works. Such a sample tends to give for K a
value lower than the mean value for the individual works, see below, §§ 6.7
and 6.14. Four values are absurdly few on which to found an estimate of
either mean or standard deviation, but so far as they go the mean of the
four characteristics is 25·29 and the estimated standard deviation 7·0,

using 3 as the divisor of the sum of squares of deviations and not 4; the standard deviation is roundly 28 per cent of the mean. I should guess this estimate of the standard deviation to be probably on the high side.

6.5.   Glancing briefly at the other data of Table 6.2, we see that the vocabulary ranges from 1333 for B (in spite of a sample well over 4000), through 1413 for the mean of D, to 1537 and 1545 for A and C respectively: the general average of these four figures is 1457. Table 2.1 for the *Imitatio* gave only 1168 for a sample of over double the size, 8225 occurrences. Table 2.2 for a sample of 8203 occurrences spread over the miscellaneous works of Thomas à Kempis shows a vocabulary of only 1406: a rough count made some half-way through the work for this table gave a vocabulary of only 1005 for a sample of 4373 occurrences. Table 2.3 for a sample of 8196 occurrences spread over the theological works of Gerson gives a vocabulary of 1754, but a rough count made some half-way through the work gave a vocabulary of only 1196 for a sample of 4000 occurrences. The Macaulay vocabularies are consistently high for the given size of sample. It may be mentioned that the three essays A, B and C, the nouns of which were entered on to the same set of cards, yielded together a total vocabulary of 2832. The cards for the sampling experiment on D were collated with these and gave 711 nouns that did not occur in A, B or C, making a total vocabulary for the four essays of 3543 nouns on a sample of 20,178 occurrences, i.e. $3923 + 4149 + 4061 + 8045$, the first three figures being taken from col. 3 of Table 6.2 and the last from col. 3 of Table 4.5. A detailed statistical analysis of the distribution of the vocabulary between the several essays is given in Chapter 7. The means are all low, ranging from 2·55 for A to 3·11 for B, and the figures for the vocabulary per 1000 occurrences correspondingly high. The standard deviations are all low, but rather erratic, A and B again exhibiting the extreme values 3·74 and 6·12. The percentage of once-nouns does not vary greatly, fluctuating round a general average of about 55 per cent.

6.6.   The reader may find of interest the lists given in Table 6.3 of most frequent nouns, those occurring 20 times or more in the samples from the three essays A, B, C. The essay on Milton is naturally for the most part literary in character, but touches also on the politics of the poet and the politics of his time. There is only one word really outstanding in frequency and that is the commonly frequent noun *man*. *Poet* and *poetry* occur 37 and 30 times respectively: *work*, 26 times, and *feeling*, 20 times, may also be associated with the literary side of the essay. The political words *king*, *power*, *liberty*, *people*, with 20 to 24 occurrences, stand at the bottom of the short list. As already stated, it is I think the overloading of this essay with ornament which mainly accounts for the high vocabulary and the comparative lack of concentration on to any particular word or group of words from which the low variance and low characteristic result; but the duplicity of subject—poetry and politics—must also exert an influence in the same direction. The essay on Hampden shows a great contrast. There are 25

TABLE 6.3. Words occurring 20 times or more in the samples from the three essays of Macaulay, A, B and C

A. Milton		B. Hampden		C. Frederic	
X	Words	X	Words	X	Words
20	feeling: king	20	country	20	country: troop
22	power	21	act: nation	22	life
23	liberty	22	court: opposition	26	battle
24	people	24	part: power	27	day
26	work	25	government	28	power
27	time	26	day ♦	29	part
30	mind: poetry	27	liberty	33	prince: year
31	character	28	place	34	time
37	poet	29	law: person: war	39	war
68	man	31	army: party	44	army
		36	year	63	man
		39	member: people	87	king
		47	commons		
		56	time		
		64	house		
		73	man		
		83	parliament		
		93	king		

words in the list as against 12, and 6 of these occur more than 40 times against only a single one in the Milton list. The essay is intensely concentrated on the struggle between the king and parliament. *Man* is still a frequent word, but *king* and *parliament* head the list, and *commons*, and *house* (mainly though not always associated with the *house* of commons), both occur more than 40 times. Lower in the list we may associate *court* with *king*, and *act, opposition, party, member* with *parliament*. *Country, nation, power, government, law, war* and *army* are words all obviously relevant to the great struggle. This intense concentration, in terms of our fundamental hypothesis, tends to throw on to a relatively small group of words very high values of λ and so to raise v_λ and the characteristic: compare the very high values of the characteristic for such intensely concentrated works as the *Imitatio* (84·2) and St John's Gospel, A.V. (161·5). Finally in the essay on Frederic the Great we have a list of 14 words, of which 3 occur more than 40 times, *king, man* and *army.* Of parliament we naturally hear nothing, but such words as *army, war, battle, troop* clearly enough indicate the important part played in the essay by the wars of the king. But the concentration on war is not nearly so intense as the concentration on the political struggle in the essay on Hampden. As already remarked, scene and subject are much more varied: the youth and education of the prince, Frederic's literary essays

TABLE 6.4. Showing the number f_x of nouns occurring X times in the samples from four of Macaulay's essays taken together; Milton, Hampden, Bacon and Frederic the Great

X	f_x	X	f_x	X	f_x	X	f_x
1	1460	22	11	44	2	74	2
2	605	23	5	46	1	82	2
3	315	24	7	47	3	86	1
4	212	25	4	48	2	88	2
5	159	26	4	49	3	90	1
6	122	27	6	50	2	94	1
7	84	28	5	51	4	95	1
8	68	29	9	52	3	100	1
9	58	30	6	54	3	104	1
10	46	31	7	55	3	106	1
11	40	32	1	56	2	128	1
12	25	33	5	57	2	134	1
13	30	34	5	58	1	139	1
14	24	35	2	59	2	141	1
15	23	36	7	60	4	143	1
16	19	37	5	62	1	193	1
17	24	38	4	64	3	239	1
18	25	39	5	65	1	459	1
19	11	40	3	68	1		
20	9	42	3	72	1	Total	3543
21	12	43	2	73	1		

$S_0 = 3543$; $S_1 = 20,178$; $S_2 = 838,468$; $M = 5\cdot695$; $\sigma^2 = 204\cdot220$; $\sigma = 14\cdot291$; $v = 2\cdot51$; Percentage of once-nouns $= 41\cdot2$; Vocabulary per 1000 occurrences $= 176$; $K = 20\cdot1$.

and ambitions and the antics of the men of letters whom he gathered into his household, all come into the picture, and Voltaire plays a part secondary only to that of Frederic himself. The essay is far more variegated than that on Hampden, and it is this that, in my judgment, leads to the lowering of the characteristic. As an author wanders from one part of his field into another, first one group of words will be mainly wanted, then a different group: the consequence will be a general tendency to level up the values of λ and so reduce v_λ and the characteristic.

6.7.   The truth of this general conception may readily be put to the test. Suppose we enter on each of the 3543 cards for words included in one or more of the four essays (§ 6.5) the total number of times the word occurred in the four essays together, we can then sort the cards by these totals and form the word-distribution for the four essays taken as a whole. If our argument is right, this distribution should give a characteristic lower than the average for the four separate essays, as the pooling of works on somewhat diverse subjects will have tended to reduce v_λ. The work was done accordingly—it took a good deal longer to do than to describe—and it had to be done with care for any slip would at once be discovered by the sum S_1 for the new distribution failing to agree with the sum of S_1's for the several essays. The distribution is shown in Table 6.4, and as stated at the foot we find $K = 20\cdot1$. The characteristics of the four essays are $17\cdot91$, $34\cdot09$, $21\cdot82$ (Table 6.2) and $27\cdot18$ (Table 4.5), total $101\cdot00$, mean $25\cdot25$. The value for Table 6.4 lies between the lowest and next to lowest of the values for the four component essays, well below the mean, and our argument is completely confirmed. This result is important, and should be borne in mind in comparing the characteristic for a single short work, as for Table 2.1 based on the *Imitatio*, with characteristics derived from samples spread over the whole of an author's miscellaneous works, as in the case of Tables 2.2 and 2.3 for Thomas à Kempis and Gerson. It is possible that the same effect is seen in the slow fall of the mean value of the characteristic in Table 4.5 for the experiment on sampling (see below, § 7.8, where this conclusion is confirmed). For the four basic samples the mean is $27\cdot63$; for the samples pooled in pairs, $27\cdot33$; for the samples pooled in triplets, $27\cdot23$; and for all four pooled together, $27\cdot18$. If the four basic samples are in fact slightly diverse this is the effect to be expected.

(B)   BUNYAN'S WORKS

6.8.   A second trial I decided to carry out on samples from four of Bunyan's works, which might be expected to give a good contrast with Macaulay's *Essays*. The works chosen were the four tales:

A. *The Pilgrim's Progress*, Part I. 1678,
B. *The Pilgrim's Progress*, Part II. 1684,
C. *The Life and Death of Mr Badman*. 1680,
D. *The Holy War*. 1682.

Samples of approximately 4000 occurrences of a noun were taken from each of these works. The editions used, refs. 6.2–6.4, were modern cheap editions, offering the great advantage that one could use them as working copies and pencil-mark them freely to note the passages sampled. The method of sampling was varied slightly from that used for Macaulay's essays, so as to arrive at the size of sample desired by a method of successive approximation, and was a distinct improvement. A first rough estimate of the number of lines per page required was made by counting the nouns on some 20 to 25 pages spaced evenly throughout the work: suppose this estimate was 15 lines. A number smaller than this, sufficiently smaller (taking into account the magnitude of the standard error) almost certainly to give *too small* a number of occurrences, was then arbitrarily chosen, say 12 lines, and the nouns on the first 12 lines of each page entered up on manuscript sheets and counted. This gave a second estimate on a much firmer foundation for the total number of lines per page needed: if the estimate were say 2·54 lines more, the nouns could be listed and counted from an additional 2 lines, and so a third estimate obtained. If this third estimate confirmed the second and showed about half a line per page more to be needed, one could take another line from every second page— obviously one can hardly deal with fractions of a line. With a little ingenuity an approximation to any desired fraction of a line can usually be obtained without much difficulty; the equivalent of three-quarters of a line per page, for example, can be got by taking one line from each page, omitting those with numbers divisible by 4, and so forth; or if a very small fraction of a line is wanted the required number of whole lines can be got by determining pages from which single lines are to be taken by random numbers. It seems hardly necessary to give the full details of the actual work; the same principle was applied in each case. In the *Pilgrim's Progress*, as every reader will remember, there is a good deal of verse, which was included in the samples; on pages with verse the same depth of page, instead of number of lines, was taken as for the pages in prose. Texts quoted from the Bible were also included; the only omissions, affecting the *Pilgrim's Progress* alone, were the marginal headings or comments. The sample from A covers just over 50 per cent of the whole work; that from B some 57 per cent; that from C about 37 per cent, and that from D about 26 per cent.

6.9.   The troubles with which one meets in deciding what to include in the lists of nouns were dealt with in connection with the sampling experiment on Macaulay's essay on Bacon, § 4.3, and similar troubles of course occur with every author. As in Macaulay, hyphened nouns could hardly be treated quite consistently; familiar and accepted instances were entered as single nouns—who would divide the familiar *wicket-gate*?—but compound words made up for the nonce, like *heart-holiness, family-holiness, conversation-holiness*, were divided. Again, as in Macaulay, titles in connection with a name were omitted, and only entered if they occurred separately. Verbal nouns in *-ing* are very frequent in Bunyan (see below, §§ 6.16–6.17) and also a source of some trouble. But a special difficulty occurs in Bunyan, notably in the *Pilgrim's Progress*, from his liberal use of substantives as names for persons, places and even things. All such names, or the substantival portions of them, were omitted; one would certainly not include names as nouns in any ordinary case and there seemed no reason for including them here; inclusion might indeed prove misleading, for there is such a crowd of them —*Christian* himself to begin with, and *Evangelist*, *Mr Legality*, *Passion* and *Patience*, *Sloth*, *Discretion*, *Piety*, *Charity*, *Giant Despair*, the *Lord Old Man*, the *Lord Lechery* (with all the rest of our nobility), *Mr Two-tongues* (who, as *Mr By-ends* informed Christian, was his mother's own brother by father's side, a relationship which always puzzled me as a child), *Mercy* (a pretty lass, Mr Brisk thought her, but troubled with ill conditions)—there is no end to the vivid procession. For place-names we have similarly the *Slough of Despond*, the *City of Destruction*, the *Valley of Humiliation*, the *Valley of the Shadow of Death*, the *Hill* called *Lucre*, *Doubting Castle*, the *Country of Conceit*, *Vanity Fair*, and for other matters 'the large upper chamber, whose window opened toward the sun-rising', the name of which was *Peace*, and the key called *Promise* which opened the door of the dungeon in Doubting Castle; the list might be indefinitely extended. None of these, or the substantives which form part of them (except of course when they occurred separately) were entered in the lists of nouns. But the *Interpreter* pleaded for admission on the ground that this was his office not his name and was duly entered, as was also the *Recorder* in the *Holy War* on similar grounds.

6.10.   All my statistical tables have hitherto been bare figures, only illustrated by some few citations of the actual words. For this work on Bunyan, whose vocabulary is relatively modest, I have given complete word lists in Appendices 1 to 4. Following these appendices notes on some nouns give a brief indication of meaning, in the main to distinguish homonyms, i.e. distinct words of the same spelling, e.g. *rush*, quick movement, not the plant; *miss*, young woman (mistress), not the noun corresponding to the verb 'to miss'; in some instances for the sake of brevity the Latin may be given, e.g. *cock*, gallus, not hay-cock, cock of the hat, etc.; *tear*, lacrima, not a rent in cloth, etc. I fear the necessary explanation may have been omitted in some cases, for it is easy to forget the existence of a homonym. Where two homonyms both occur in the samples they are distinguished by numbers, cf. *boot*, *fat*, *host*, *pole*, *post*, *rest*, *stick*, *yard*. In some instances an indication of meaning may be given simply as a matter of interest for a word used in an archaic sense, e.g. *haunt* used in the sense of habit as well as place of resort, *noble* used in the sense of the coin, not a peer of the realm, or to show the particular sense or senses in which a word of very diverse meanings has been used, e.g. *general* occurs in the singular or plural in the sense of the military officer of that rank, in the plural also as *generals*, the opposite of *particulars*. Appendix 1 gives the nouns of sample A arranged according to the frequency distribution, first the nouns occurring once only in that sample—a long list of five hundred—then the list of those occurring twice in the sample, and so on, until towards the end one can hardly speak of 'lists', for there are only one or two words of each number of occurrences; *hand* and *pilgrim* are the only nouns occurring 34 times, *world* the only noun occurring 35 times, *gate* the only noun occurring 36 times, and so on up to *man* with 197 occurrences. Appendices 3, 4 and 5 gives the lists for samples B, C and D in similar form. I do not propose to comment here on these lists, but the reader may find it of interest to glance through them before (or after) studying the numerical tables. The careful reader may note that some mere spelling variants have been separately listed, e.g. *aught* and *ought*, *veil* and *vail* (once in A.V.) and perhaps *owlet* and *howlet*, though possibly the latter (if I rightly understand the *Shorter Oxford English Dictionary*) may be a distinct word. This is really a breach of my own rule and must have been done by inadvertence.

6.11.   The four distributions are shown together in Table 6.5, and the sums S_0, S_1 and S_2, together with means, standard deviations and characteristics, are given in Table 6.6. A glance at Table 6.5 and the similar tables for Macaulay's essays, Tables 6.1 and 4.2, shows that the Bunyan distributions are very different, with much more extensive 'tails' and much lower vocabularies. The Macaulay vocabularies (Table 6.2, col. 2) range from 1333 to 1545, the Bunyan vocabularies (Table 6.6, col. 2) from 996 to 1030, or on the average only some 70 per cent of the former: the greatest numbers of occurrences in the Macaulay distributions range only from 68 to 139, the greatest numbers of occurrences in the samples from Bunyan from 133 to 246. The means in Bunyan (Table 6.6, col. 5) are closely consistent, ranging from 3·88 to 4·03 round a general average of nearly 4·0: for the Macaulay means, less closely consistent, the general average is roundly 2·8. The vocabulary per 1000 occurrences is correspondingly lower for Bunyan than for Macaulay, 248 to 258 against 321 to 392. As we might have guessed from the look of the distributions, the standard deviations for Bunyan (Table 6.6, col. 8) are very considerably greater than those for Macaulay, 8·82 to 11·37 against 3·74 to 6·12, this measure of dispersion exhibiting in both cases a good deal more variation from sample to sample than is shown by the means.

The percentages of once-nouns do not show any great contrast, but, as we might expect from the greater dispersion, are rather lower for Bunyan than for Macaulay, averaging about 51·7 per cent for the former against some 55 per cent for the latter.

TABLE 6.5. Showing the numbers f_x of nouns occurring X times in samples of about 4000 occurrences each (cf. Table 6.6, col. 3) from four of Bunyan's works: A. *Pilgrim's Progress*, Part I; B. *Pilgrim's Progress*, Part II; C. *Mr Badman*; D. *Holy War*

X	Number f_x of nouns occurring X times in sample				X	Number f_x of nouns occurring X times in sample			
	A	B	C	D		A	B	C	D
1	500	519	558	517	36	1	1	—	2
2	179	179	160	159	37	—	1	1	1
3	87	87	88	84	38	1	1	—	1
4	54	52	49	54	39	—	1	1	1
5	29	42	31	34	40	—	1	2	—
6	27	19	27	22	41	1	—	—	—
7	21	18	15	26	42	—	—	1	—
8	13	17	12	15	43	1	1	1	1
9	10	10	6	11	45	—	1	—	—
10	6	9	16	12	46	—	1	—	—
11	8	3	10	4	47	—	—	1	—
12	7	5	5	6	48	—	—	—	1
13	4	5	6	6	50	1	—	—	—
14	5	5	5	5	55	—	—	1	—
15	5	3	3	—	57	—	1	1	—
16	5	3	1	6	59	1	—	—	—
17	3	5	4	3	61	—	1	—	1
18	4	2	2	1	62	—	1	—	—
19	5	3	1	1	67	—	—	1	—
20	2	3	1	2	68	—	1	—	—
21	—	1	—	2	86	—	—	1	—
22	4	1	2	2	96	—	1	—	—
23	4	2	—	2	99	1	1	—	—
24	2	2	2	3	102	—	—	—	1
25	—	1	1	—	104	—	—	—	1
26	1	1	2	1	105	—	—	—	2
27	1	—	3	—	131	1	—	—	—
28	1	2	2	—	133	—	1	—	—
29	—	—	1	1	178	—	—	1	—
30	1	—	—	1	197	1	—	—	—
31	1	1	2	1	206	—	—	1	—
32	2	—	1	—	246	—	—	—	1
33	2	2	—	1					
34	2	1	1	1	Total	1005	1020	1030	996
35	1	2	—	—					

6.12.   Turning now to the characteristics given in col. 10 of Table 6.6 we see that they run much higher than those for Macaulay, ranging from 56·48 to 87·96, against 17·91 to 34·09. There is again no evidence of any continuous trend in the value of the characteristic with time: rearranged in order of date the characteristics run:

A	1678	66·94	D	1682	87·96
C	1680	80·65	B	1684	56·48

The empirical relation noted for Macaulay, and in other instances, that the characteristics run in the same order as the means, does not hold good for

TABLE 6.6. Data for the four samples from Bunyan's works of Table 6.5. A. *Pilgrim's Progress*, Part I; B. *Pilgrim's Progress*, Part II; C. *Mr Badman*; D. *Holy War*

1	2	3	4	5	6	7	8	9	10
nplc	S_0	S_1	S_2	M	$1000 \times S_0/S_1$	σ^2	σ	% of 1's	K
A	1,005	4,047	113,675	4·03	248	96·894	9·84	49·8	66·94
B	1,020	4,016	95,104	3·94	254	77·737	8·82	50·9	56·48
C	1,030	3,992	132,516	3·88	258	113·635	10·66	54·2	80·65
D	996	4,001	144,815	4·02	249	129·260	11·37	51·9	87·96

these four samples from Bunyan, but the range in the values of the means is very small. Adding the Bunyan characteristics to the little table in § 6.4 this will now stand as follows:

Macaulay	Table 6.1, A	17·9
,,	,, 6.1, C	21·8
,,	,, 4.2, D	27·3
,,	,, 6.1, B	34·1
Gerson	,, 2.3	35·9
Bunyan	,, 6.5, B	56·5
Thomas à Kempis	,, 2.2	59·7
Bunyan	,, 6.5, A	66·9
,,	,, 6.5, C	80·6
Imitatio	,, 2.1	84·2
Bunyan	,, 6.5, D	88·0
St John: Basic	,, 2.9	141·5
St John: A.V., all	—	161·5
St John: A.V., selected	,, 2.10	177·9

The Bunyan characteristics stand in a series broken by the figures for the miscellaneous works of Thomas à Kempis and the *Imitatio*; notwithstanding the considerable range of variation they form a fairly definite group rather below the middle of the range: how they stand in relation to the characteristics for Macaulay can be seen very clearly from the chart of characteristics just before the Appendices facing p. 284. The mean value of the four is 73·01; the estimated value of the standard deviation, using 3 as the divisor of the sum of squares of deviations, is 14 or 19 per cent of the mean. The corresponding figure for the four Macaulay essays (§ 6.4) is 28 per cent of the mean, which in my personal opinion is probably an overestimate, rather unduly affected by the very low characteristic for the essay on Milton. Quite roughly, indeed rather conjecturally considering the paucity of the data, it looks as if we might in general expect the standard deviation of the characteristic for a set of similar works of the same author to be some 20 to 25 per cent of the mean. However rough, it is a useful estimate to have, pending investigation on a more extended scale, and is confirmed by the set of four samples from Thomas à Kempis below, § 10.22.

6.13. Even before starting the work on Part I of the *Pilgrim's Progress* I had expected to find a high value of the characteristic, comparable with though lower than that found for the *Imitatio*, for notwithstanding its wealth of detail the story impresses one in the same sort of way as a work of intense concentration—that concentration on one central idea which is likely to lead to a corresponding concentration of vocabulary on certain nouns; *way* and *man* in this case (see Appendix 1, end). The actual value found, 66·9, proved somewhat lower than I had looked for, but was fairly in accordance with this judgment. For Part II of the *Pilgrim's Progress* I had similarly expected to find a lower characteristic than for Part I, and this expectation was also realised, the characteristic being only 56·5 against 66·9. The tale stands lower, I believe, in the estimation of every critic. There are notable touches of the same genius, as in the meeting with the fiend during the passage through the Valley of the Shadow of Death:

Thus they went on, till they came to about the middle of the Valley, and then Christiana said, Methinks I see something yonder upon the road before us, a thing of such a shape such as I have not seen. Then said Joseph, Mother, what is it? An ugly thing, child; an ugly thing, said she. But, mother, what is it like? said he. It is like I cannot tell what, said she. And now it was but a little way off; then said she, It is nigh.

But taken as a whole the allegory has lost something of its grip, and the pilgrimage has become a conducted tour—for numerical evidence, cf. Appendices 1 and 2, where it will be found that the word *guide* occurs 37 times in sample B against once only in sample A, and the word *conductor*, which does not occur in sample A at all, 12 times. Oddly enough the words *pilgrim* and *pilgrimage* are also much more frequent in sample B than in sample A (99 : 34 and 35 : 9), but this rather suggests an attempt to make up for lack of truth in the picture by mere use of the words, as with a novelist who *tells* you his hero is clever but fails to convince by his portraiture. What I had not expected was the high value of the characteristic for *Mr Badman* (80·6) and for the *Holy War* (88·0); but this was due to a fallacious judgment based on my lower opinion of the works. The *Holy War*, like the *Pilgrim's Progress*, is an allegorical tale but not so good a tale, the allegory over-strained and the story rather long drawn out. The *Life and Death of Mr Badman* is a moral, rather than allegorical, tale of the life of a very bad man indeed (the name possibly suggested by that of one John Wildman, who gave a good deal of trouble to the Church at Bedford) told in a conversation between Mr Wiseman and Mr Attentive. There are many pleasing touches of the life of the time and pithy, probably local, sayings; but also many wholly incredible moral stories. A number of these are taken from that amazing anthology, *A Mirrour or Looking-Glasse both for Saints and Sinners*, of Samuel Clark or Clarke (the name is spelt both ways even on his own title-pages), a nonconformist divine and voluminous writer, of which the first edition was issued in 1646 and several greatly expanded further editions at later dates (ref. 6.5). Here is one of the stories quoted by Bunyan:

Also at Oster, in the duchy of Magalapole, saith Mr Clark, a wicked woman used in her cursing to give herself body and soul to the devil, and being reproved for it, still continued the same; till, being at a wedding-feast, the devil came in person, and carried her up into the air, with most horrible outcries and roarings; and in that sort carried her round about the town, that the inhabitants were ready to die for fear. And by and by he tore her in four pieces, leaving her four quarters in four several highways; and then brought her bowels to the marriage-feast, and threw them upon the table before the mayor of the town, saying, Behold these dishes of meat belong to thee, whom the like destruction waiteth for if thou dost not amend thy wicked life.

It seems incredible now that anyone could have believed such a lurid story, a story the end of which bears on its face the marks of careless imaginative invention: for what was the devil doing, playing the part of guardian angel and warning the mayor against the consequences of his naughty life? The *Pilgrim's Progress* is a tale for all time; *Mr Badman* a tale for a time long past. For different reasons then I had placed both the *Holy War* and *Mr Badman* a good deal lower than the *Pilgrim's Progress* and, not logically but thought-lessly, expected correspondingly lower characteristics. For the fallacy that led to my mistaken expectation is obvious; the concentration that leads to a high characteristic may be a quality that marks the great work, but it is only *one*; if the work in other ways is faulty, it still falls short of perfection. No one who reads *Mr Badman* or the *Holy War* will deny their concentration. Lack of concentration at least is not the fault of either, though the concentration falls on different words. In *Mr Badman*, as in both parts of the *Pilgrim's Progress*, the most frequently occurring noun is *man*; in the *Holy*

War it is town. The story centres round 'the town of Mansoul', which is nearly always mentioned in those words and not simply as 'Mansoul', so that *town* becomes by far the most frequently used noun, cf. Appendix 4, end.

6.14.   In § 6.6 it was suggested that the relatively low value of the characteristic K found for Macaulay's essay on Frederic the Great was due to the varied subject-matter of the essay, the effect of this variety being to bring into use first one set of words, then another, and so reduce v_λ and K.

TABLE 6.7. Showing the number f_x of nouns occurring X times in the four samples from Bunyan's works (*Pilgrim's Progress*, Part I; *Pilgrim's Progress*, Part II; *Mr Badman*; *Holy War*) taken together

X	f_x	X	f_x	X	f_x	X	f_x
1	931	24	5	48	2	112	1
2	370	25	4	49	5	116	1
3	195	26	10	51	1	117	1
4	128	27	1	52	1	119	1
5	91	28	5	53	1	124	1
6	79	29	3	54	1	131	1
7	47	30	1	55	1	133	1
8	39	31	5	56	1	134	1
9	35	33	3	57	1	135	1
10	25	34	3	58	2	139	1
11	30	35	5	60	1	160	1
12	20	36	6	63	2	168	1
13	23	37	2	64	1	189	1
14	13	38	2	68	2	216	1
15	15	39	2	69	1	261	1
16	15	40	2	76	1	292	1
17	9	41	3	87	1	297	1
18	13	42	5	90	1	305	1
19	6	43	2	94	1	638	1
20	9	44	3	96	1		
21	15	45	1	102	1		
22	7	46	1	109	1	Total	2246
23	6	47	1	111	1		

$S_0 = 2246$; $S_1 = 16056$; $S_2 = 1339592$; $M = 7 \cdot 149$; $\sigma^2 = 545 \cdot 331$; $\sigma = 23 \cdot 352$; $v = 3 \cdot 27$; Percentage of once-nouns = 41·5; Vocabulary per 1000 occurrences = 140; $K = 51 \cdot 34$.

The notion was confirmed in § 6.7 by forming the frequency distribution of numbers of occurrences of nouns in the samples from the four essays taken together, which gave a characteristic well below the mean for the four components. A similar test was applied to the four samples from Bunyan. The total number of occurrences of each noun was entered on its card, the cards sorted by these totals, and the frequency distribution drawn up. It is given in Table 6.7. As before S_1 must be given by the sum of the S_1's for the four component distributions, $4047 + 4016 + 3992 + 4001 = 16,056$; but it may be pointed out that this agreement is only a *check* on the work, not a *criterion* of its correctness, since—as I know from maddening experience—it is perfectly possible for a pair of compensating errors to occur which leaves the S_1-test fulfilled. The value found for K is $51 \cdot 34$; the values found for the four component samples are in order of magnitude:

$$87 \cdot 96 \qquad 80 \cdot 65 \qquad 66 \cdot 94 \qquad 56 \cdot 48$$

This result is even more striking than that for the Macaulay work, since the characteristic for the total distribution is not merely much lower than the mean of those for the four components ($73 \cdot 01$) but lower than that of any single component. The greater magnitude of the reduction is presumably due to the even more diversified character of these four works of Bunyan as compared with the four essays of Macaulay. This diversity is illustrated by the very different numbers of occurrences in the different samples of some of the nouns, for example such words as the following, the numbers following the noun giving the occurrences in samples A, B, C and D:

Army: 1, 1, 0, 26. Boy: 0, 39, 6, 2. Brother: 22, 7, 6, 1. Captain: 2, 0, 2, 105. Castle: 6, 5, 0, 38. Child: 12, 57, 39, 4. Conductor: 0, 12, 0, 0. Country: 22, 13, 1, 7. Death: 24, 16, 40, 10. Faith: 30, 9, 7, 3. Father: 7, 26, 25, 36. Gentleman: 10, 8, 1, 24. Hell: 7, 6, 28, 4. Hill: 32, 16, 0, 1. Interpreter: 18, 17, 0, 0. Journey: 10, 19, 1, 1. Judgment: 14, 3, 42, 9. King: 16, 25, 0, 61. Lord: 41, 45, 26, 104. Master: 4, 13, 43, 16. Mayor: 0, 0, 0, 24. Mother: 3, 24, 14, 0. Neighbour: 12, 11, 31, 2. Petition: 0, 0, 0, 21. Pilgrim: 34, 99, 0, 0. Pilgrimage: 9, 35, 0, 0. Prince: 11, 8, 0, 105. Recorder: 0, 0, 0, 20. Righteousness: 13, 24, 1, 1. Shepherd: 15, 13, 0, 0. Sin: 28, 12, 86, 13. Town: 19, 21, 6, 246. Valley: 16, 14, 0, 1. War: 0, 2, 0, 34. Wife: 15, 14, 37, 3. Woman: 3, 40, 13, 2. Work: 23, 5, 10, 13.

The important results of this paragraph and § 6.7 should be borne in mind when we compare the characteristic of a general sample from an author's works with the characteristics of samples from individual works.

C. ON CERTAIN CLASSES OF NOUNS IN MACAULAY AND IN BUNYAN

6.15. These investigations on Macaulay and Bunyan were actually undertaken for the sole purpose of throwing light on the degree of consistence that might be expected between distributions based on different but similar works of the same author. They raised, however, some purely statistical problems not envisaged at the start, consideration of which is postponed to the next chapter, and also led me, to satisfy my own curiosity, to make some enquiry into the relative frequency in the two authors of certain classes of nouns, viz. verbal nouns in -*ing*, monosyllabic nouns and (with more especial reference to Bunyan) nouns that occur in the Bible. All three classes are relatively more frequent in Bunyan than in Macaulay, and the reader may perhaps find the results of interest.

6.16.   *Verbal Nouns in -ing.* There is a certain difficulty of classification here. The original function of the suffix, to quote the *Shorter Oxford English Dictionary*, was to form a noun of action; but, originally abstract, these substantives even in Old English came to express a completed action, a process, habit, or art, as *learning, tidings,* or sometimes became concrete as *bedding*. It seemed to me impossible to draw any clear line between pure nouns of

TABLE 6.8. Showing the numbers f_x of verbal nouns in -*ing* occurring X times in the samples from Macaulay and from Bunyan respectively

1	2	3	1	2	3	1	2	3
X	Macaulay f_x	Bunyan f_x	X	Macaulay f_x	Bunyan f_x	X	Macaulay f_x	Bunyan f_x
1	67	115	8	1	2	17	1	—
2	12	36	9	—	1	21	1	—
3	9	11	10	1	1	24	—	1
4	1	4	11	1	2	27	2	—
5	1	7	12	—	2	52	1	—
6	1	1	14	—	2	Total	102	190
7	3	3	16	—	2			

Macaulay: $S_0 = 102$; $S_1 = 327$; $M = 3\cdot21$.   Bunyan: $S_0 = 190$; $S_1 = 463$; $M = 2\cdot44$.

action and nouns that have come commonly to express a completed action, or process, or to be used in a concrete sense, for so many nouns have merely added the newer meaning while still retaining the older; *learning* is a case in point. I therefore included all nouns which appeared to be by origin verbal nouns in -*ing*, whatever the present usual meaning; some words that the ordinary reader might not expect, such as *lightning*, would therefore be found in my lists. Table 6.8 shows the two distributions, which it will be seen are very limited in extent, no such noun occurring any very large number of times in either author. Moreover, as might perhaps be expected, the nouns of this class that show the largest numbers of occurrences are precisely those which have come to be used very largely in senses other than that of the simple noun of action. The two nouns occurring 27 times in Macaulay are *learning* and *writing*, the noun occurring 52 times is *feeling*. In Bunyan the noun occurring 24 times is *beginning*, which is frequently used in such senses as the time at which something begins, the origin, the initial stage, as well as in the sense of the noun of action. The mean number of occurrences is for Macaulay 3·21, against 5·70 for all nouns (Table 6.4); for Bunyan 2·44, against 7·15 for all nouns (Table 6.7). As regard the proportions of the nouns in the vocabulary (p_v of §§ 5.14 *et seq.*) and amongst occurrences (p_w, *ibid.*), we have

		Nouns in -*ing*	All nouns	Percentage of nouns in -*ing*
Macaulay.	S_0: vocabulary	102	3,543	p_v 2·88
	S_1: occurrences	327	20,178	p_w 1·62
Bunyan.	S_0: vocabulary	190	2,246	p_v 8·46
	S_1: occurrences	463	16,056	p_w 2·88

The percentage of these nouns in the vocabulary p_v, is nearly three times as great in Bunyan (8·46) as in Macaulay (2·88), and even so this is not quite a fair comparison. For the sample from Macaulay is some 20,000 occurrences, that from Bunyan only some 16,000; p_v is a function of size of sample (§§ 5.14 *et seq.*) and its general trend in this case will be upward with increasing size of sample. It is true that this trend may not be monotonic, but the 2·88 for Macaulay is considerably greater than the lower limit for small samples 1·62 (§§ 5.14–5.16), and we may perhaps reasonably expect the trend to be upward even over this part of the range. If so, the percentage for Macaulay for a sample of 16,000 occurrences, to compare with Bunyan, will be lower than 2·88, and the Bunyan percentage may well be *more* than three times that for Macaulay. The percentage based on occurrences, p_w, is not a function of size of sample (§§ 5.14 *et seq.*), so we may make a comparison without risk of fallacy. The difference here is not so great, for the Bunyan nouns are less frequently repeated than those in Macaulay. The percentage of nouns in -*ing* amongst occurrences or in the text is 2·88 for Bunyan against 1·62 for Macaulay, the former being 1·78 times the latter. It may be added that, while inspection of the Macaulay list of nouns in -*ing* suggested that some 50 per cent had acquired in modern usage senses other than that of the simple noun of action—the classification is often not easy—the Bunyan list gave only some 25 per cent.

6.17. This difference between the vocabularies of the two authors appears to be due to the frequent use by Bunyan of idioms that are now old-fashioned or almost obsolete. Consider, for example, such passages as the following:

1. I could direct thee to the obtaining of what thou desirest. (*Pilgrim's Progress*, I.)

2. Thou must hate his setting of thy feet in the way that leadeth to the ministration of death. (*Ibid.*)

3. Both by awakening of them, counselling of them, and.... (*Ibid.*)

4. He has also now an opportunity of getting of it. (*Ibid.*)

5. By altering of some of his principles. (*Ibid.*)

6. Things must be managed here to the supporting of the weak, as well as to the warning of the unruly. (*Pilgrim's Progress*, II.)

7. He made three most fierce assaults...upon Ear-gate, to the shaking of the posts thereof. (*Holy War.*)

8. Until he should again have opportunity to do the town of Mansoul a mischief for their thus handling of him as they did. (*Ibid.*)

9. It is for your life and the lengthening of your days. (*Ibid.*)

10. Even let so many of our friends as are willing to venture themselves for the promoting of their Prince's cause.... (*Ibid.*)

11. A day of humiliation should be kept...to the justifying of their Prince, the abasing of themselves before him.... (*Ibid.*)

Such phrases, using a noun in -*ing* derived from a transitive verb followed by *of*, have an archaic ring. A modern author would surely have written differently, employing either the gerund construction, in which case the words in -*ing* would not have been reckoned amongst the nouns, or nouns of a different form; or he would have resorted to an entirely different construction. In the first example he might possibly have written simply 'to obtaining what', but more probably would have used the different construction 'how to obtain what'. In the second, third, fourth and fifth he might have used the gerund construction, omitting 'of', or perhaps in the last instance have written 'by the alteration of'. In the sixth example he might have either used different forms of noun, 'for the support of the weak, as well as the caution of the unruly', or a different construction, 'so as to support the weak, as well as to warn the unruly'; and so forth. Even apart from this '*of* construction', in such phrases as the following I think it would be the tendency in modern usage to avoid the noun in -*ing*:

12. The people of the fair made a great gazing upon them. (*Pilgrim's Progress*, I.)

13. They fell to devising about the next thing propounded. (*Holy War.*)

14. Things of my father's providing and mine. (*Ibid.*)

'Stood and stared at them', 'started discussing the next question', 'things that my father and I have provided' would sound more familiar at the present day. One naturally associates Bunyan's writings with the Bible, but I do not think his idiom in these respects is specially biblical. The idiom of citations 1–11 is hardly *characteristic* of the A.V., though of course it occurs; two texts that come to my mind are:

> The getting of treasures by a lying tongue is a vanity.... (Prov. 21. 6);
> Love is the fulfilling of the law (Rom. 13. 10);

and other instances could be given. So far as it goes it supports the view of the obsolete character of such diction that Moffatt in his modern translation (ref. 6.6) evades both nouns in *-ing* in the two texts cited:

A man making money by fraud chases a bubble....
Love is the fulfilment of the law.

6.18.   Both the general use of nouns in *-ing* and the idiom with 'of' would I think be found to be very frequent in Chaucer. In Skeat's *Student's Chaucer* (ref. 6.7) the first two lines in the book rhyme with nouns in *-inge* (*Romaunt of the Rose*, A),

Many men seyn that in sweveninges
Ther nis but fables and lesinges.

In the Glossarial Index to the volume the first noun in *-inge* is *abregginge* and the first reference for this took me to *Boethius*, Book v, Prose 1; the sample, or example, thus pitched on was therefore a chance sample except for the fact that it had to contain one noun in *-inge*. I read through this short Prose, with some 150 occurrences of a noun in all, and found no less than ten nouns in *-inge* with thirteen occurrences:

amonestinge, bitydinge (3), moevinge, knettinge, dwellinge, beinge, werkinge, tilyinge, abregginge (2), bindinge;

and there were the three following instances of the 'of' construction:

by cause of tilyinge of the feeld,
the causes of the abregginge of fortuit hap,
the which abregginge of fortuit hap.

It may be merely 'fortuit hap' that led one to a Prose quite so full of examples, but nevertheless I conjecture an investigation would confirm a high frequency of nouns in *-inge*. The evidence, I think, justifies the tentative conclusion that the frequency of nouns in *-ing* in Bunyan's works is due to his fairly frequent use of a form of phraseology now practically obsolete, and probably even in his own day obsolescent. Is it possible that such idioms still survived in common popular use in the Bedfordshire dialect of his time?

6.19.   *Monosyllabic Nouns.* There are very few cases of doubtful classification here: in fact *seer* seems to be the only really doubtful instance as it may be pronounced disyllabically when used in the simple sense of 'one who sees', but it has been reckoned as a monosyllable. *Mayor* seems to be definitely a monosyllable, identical in pronunciation with *mare*, in spite of the look of the word and its derivation. Table 6.9 gives the two distributions —distributions very different from those of Table 6.8 and covering the whole range of the distributions for all nouns, Tables 6.4 and 6.7. The numbers of these nouns are 730 in the samples from Bunyan and 779 in the samples from Macaulay. A comparison of the two lists, somewhat hasty and

TABLE 6.9. Showing the numbers f_x of monosyllabic nouns occurring X times in the samples from Bunyan and from Macaulay respectively

1	2	3	1	2	3	1	2	3
	Bunyan	Macaulay		Bunyan	Macaulay		Bunyan	Macaulay
X	f_x	f_x	X	f_x	f_x	X	f_x	f_x
1	242	275	36	1	2	95	—	1
2	112	122	37	—	1	96	1	—
3	70	81	38	2	1	100	—	1
4	49	41	39	—	2	102	1	—
5	24	31	40	2	—	106	—	1
6	32	30	41	2	—	111	1	—
7	10	18	42	3	1	112	1	—
8	20	15	43	—	1	116	1	—
9	15	14	44	—	1	117	1	—
10	8	11	45	1	—	119	1	—
11	6	12	46	1	—	124	1	—
12	8	8	47	1	1	128	—	1
13	11	5	48	2	2	131	1	—
14	7	12	49	4	—	134	1	—
15	5	5	50	—	1	135	1	—
16	7	4	51	1	2	139	1	—
17	5	9	53	1	—	141	—	1
18	7	8	54	1	1	143	—	1
19	5	4	55	—	2	160	1	—
20	5	4	56	—	1	168	1	—
21	5	4	57	1	1	189	1	—
22	6	1	58	1	—	193	—	1
23	3	2	59	—	1	216	1	—
24	3	3	60	—	2	239	—	1
25	2	2	62	—	1	261	1	—
26	4	2	63	1	—	292	1	—
27	1	—	64	—	2	297	1	—
28	1	3	68	1	1	305	1	—
29	2	2	69	1	—	459	—	1
30	—	3	74	—	2	638	1	—
31	2	2	82	—	1			
33	—	3	86	—	1			
34	—	2	87	1	—	Total	730	779
35	3	—	90	1	1			

Bunyan: $S_0 = 730$; $S_1 = 8879$; $M = 12 \cdot 16$.
Macaulay: $S_0 = 779$, $S_1 = 6956$, $M = 8 \cdot 93$.

not checked, gave a total of 455 words common to the two, so there were considerably over 1000 monosyllabic nouns in all recorded from the two authors, a figure which well illustrates the amazing richness of the English language in monosyllables. The mean number of occurrences for monosyllabic nouns in the samples from Bunyan is 12·16, against only 7·15 (Table 6.7) for all nouns or 4·73 for nouns of more than one syllable. In the samples from Macaulay, the mean for monosyllabic nouns is 8·93, against only 5·70 for all nouns (Table 6.4) or 4·78 for nouns of more than one syllable. In both authors monosyllabic nouns recur more frequently than the general run of nouns: they are the nouns in commoner use. The following statement shows the numbers and percentages of such nouns in the vocabularies of the two authors and amongst the occurrences:

		Monosyllabic nouns	All nouns	Percentage of monosyllabic nouns
Bunyan.	S_0: vocabulary	730	2,246	p_v 32·5
	S_1: occurrences	8,879	16,056	p_w 55·3
Macaulay.	S_0: vocabulary	779	3,543	p_v 22·0
	S_1: occurrences	6,956	20,178	p_w 34·5

The percentage of monosyllabic nouns in the vocabulary is only 22·0 for Macaulay against 32·5 for Bunyan. But the limiting value of p_v for very small samples in Macaulay (§§ 5.14 *et seq.*) is 34·5: in so far then as we may assume the change of p_v with size of sample to be monotonic, reduction of the Macaulay sample from 20,000 to 16,000 would probably mean an *increase* in the percentage of monosyllabic nouns to something more than 22·0. Turning to the more satisfactory and more important comparison of proportions amongst occurrences, the percentage is only 34·5 for Macaulay against 55·3 for Bunyan. Some five nouns out of nine, as they occur in the text of Bunyan's works, are monosyllabic.

6.20.   Tables 6.10 and 6.11 give a summary comparison of the two distributions of Table 6.9 with the respective distributions for all nouns, condensed from Tables 6.7 and 6.4, and serve further to emphasise the contrast between the two authors. As Table 6.10 shows, of all the nouns that occur only once in Bunyan no more than 26·0 per cent are monosyllabic; but as we proceed to nouns of more frequent occurrence the percentage rises (after a slight break in the middle) to 43·1 per cent for nouns occurring 11 to 20 times and 47·3 per cent for nouns occurring 21 to 100 times, and finally to 90·9 per cent for the 22 nouns that occur 101 times or more. The following is the list of these nouns, *captain* (mainly in the *Holy War*) and *pilgrim* (only in the *Pilgrim's Progress*) being the two exceptions which are disyllabic:

102.	King.	109.	*Captain.*	111.	House.	112.	Child.	116.	Word.
117.	Gate.	119.	Name.	124.	Prince.	131.	Hand.	133.	*Pilgrim.*
134.	Day.	135.	Life.	139.	Sin.	160.	Heart.	168.	Place.
189.	Time.	216.	Lord.	261.	Thing.	292.	Town.	297.	Way.
305.	God.	638.	Man.						

For Macaulay, Table 6.11, only 18·8 per cent of the once-nouns are mono-syllabic and this figure rises, again after a break in the centre of the table, to no more than 33·1 per cent for nouns with 21 to 59 occurrences and 60·6 per cent for nouns with 60 occurrences or more. I am puzzled by the

TABLE 6.10. Bunyan: summary comparison of the distribution for mono-syllabic nouns (Table 6.9) with that for all nouns (Table 6.7)

X	All nouns	Monosyllabic nouns	Percentage monosyllabic
1	931	242	26·0
2	370	112	30·3
3	195	70	35·9
4– 10	444	158	35·6
11– 20	153	66	43·1
21–100	131	62	47·3
101 up	22	20	90·9
Total	2246	730	32·50

considerable irregularity of the figures. In both authors, a graph of the data, if the percentages are evaluated for a larger number of overlapping intervals of the range, suggests a flat 'shelf' in the curve, if not an actual drop in the percentage, covering the sort of range from 4 to 40 or 45 for Bunyan, and a rather shorter range say from 11 to 45 for Macaulay. Thus we have the following percentages for the values or ranges of X stated:

For Bunyan		For Macaulay	
X	Percentage monosyllabic	X	Percentage monosyllabic
3	35·9	11–20	30·9
4–10	35·6	16–25	32·3
11–20	43·1	21–30	31·9
21–30	47·4	26–35	34·0
25–40	37·0	31–40	29·5
31–40	33·3	36–45	29·0
31–45	36·4		

Puzzling irregularities of the same kind are noted also in the tables of similar form in a later chapter, Tables 8.19, 8.20, 8.23 and 8.24, cf. §§ 8.22 and 8.25.

6.21.   More than one writer has emphasised the biblical character of Bunyan's diction, but I do not know of any study of the share that biblical words actually take in his vocabulary: it seemed to me accordingly that it would be of interest to obtain data on the subject. Let it be noted that by 'biblical' words one means no more, in this connection, than words which occur in the Authorised Version (1611) of the Bible: one does not mean words which at once suggest a biblical origin, still less words that were certainly or almost certainly acquired by the author from the Bible. What a word suggests to a reader depends on the reader's knowledge and the contents of his mind; to one reader the word *treatise*, say, may merely suggest a ponderous tome on some subject of mathematics or of science; to another it may

TABLE 6.11. Macaulay: summary comparison of the distribution for monosyllabic nouns (Table 6.9) with that for all nouns (Table 6.4)

X	All nouns	Monosyllabic nouns	Percentage monosyllabic
1	1460	275	18·8
2	605	122	20·2
3	315	81	25·7
4–10	749	160	21·4
11–20	230	71	30·9
21–59	151	50	33·1
60 up	33	20	60·6
Total	3543	779	21·99

invariably call up the name of Theophilus and the first verse of Acts. Very few readers, I suspect, regard *ink* or *string* as biblical words and still fewer statisticians associate *variance* with the New Testament. As to the second point, we can obviously never know save in exceptional instances from what source a writer *acquired* a particular word: when Bunyan mentions an *ephah* or a *hin* we may be confident (even if he is not quoting a specific text) that he got those words from the Bible; but when he writes of *man* or of *wheat* one may well doubt it, as one may also doubt whether he first acquired the word *fair* from the half-dozen references to the fairs of Tyre in Ezek. 27. In my particular case the definition of biblical words has been limited to words occurring in the canonical books, *excluding the Apocrypha*. This is not, in my opinion, a desirable limitation, but it was done for convenience; in Cruden's *Concordance* a separate concordance is given for the Apocrypha, and it would have meant a good deal more labour to look for many words twice over. All the 2246 cards for the nouns occurring in the four samples from Bunyan's works were, then, run through and marked with B or a β according as each noun was or was not traced in Cruden's *Concordance* to the canonical books. The work was rather troublesome. In the old edition of Cruden that was used (ref. 6.8), since it was the one on my own shelves, words are quite often entered seriously out of their alphabetical order; and to add to the trouble i's and j's are confounded, both in the middle of words and as initial letters, and u's and v's confounded in the middle of words though distinguished as initials. Further, a substantive is sometimes misplaced under the adjective or the verb of the same form or, even worse, two entirely distinct words confounded together. Thus Bunyan in the *Holy War* uses the substantive *former*, in the sense of *maker*, with reference to the deity, and this noun occurs in our sample. It is actually biblical, Bunyan's phrase 'the former of all things' occurring twice in Jer. 10. 16 and 51. 19, but these references are given in the middle of Cruden's list of uses of the adjective *former*, i.e. earlier: this error has been carried on into quite modern concordances. I felt some doubt as to how to treat verbal nouns in -*ing*: if they are entered as substantives or found used as substantives in some of the references cited, there is no difficulty; but it seemed to me that if the verb were used at all in the Bible they ought to be entered as biblical, and this was done. A smaller point of doubt is the treatment of nouns occurring only in the alternative readings of the margin, which are distinguished in Cruden by an obelus: it seemed to me they ought to be included. This is the safer course, as the obelus is easily overlooked.

6.22.   The results of the little investigation are given in Table 6.12, which shows the total distribution of nouns in the four samples from Bunyan, Table 6.7, analysed into the two components for nouns occurring in the canonical books of the Bible, B, and nouns not so occurring, β. The two components are sharply contrasted. The distribution of biblical words covers the whole range. The distribution of non-biblical words on the contrary is greatly truncated. In the second half of Table 6.12, col. 7, there are only two non-biblical nouns, one occurring 24 times, viz. *mayor*, frequent in the *Holy War* but absent from our other samples, and the other occurring 43 times, viz. *gentleman*, which is present in all our samples though in that from *Mr Badman* it is only found once. All the nouns occurring 44 times or more are biblical. In the vocabulary 672/2246 or 29·9 per cent of the nouns are non-biblical, 70·1 per cent biblical. But, as the non-biblical nouns are so largely nouns of infrequent occurrence, the proportions amongst occurrences are widely different: 1485/16,056 or 9·2 per cent only of the occurrences are non-biblical, 90·8 per cent biblical. Of the two streams that contribute to Bunyan's vocabulary, the main stream of biblical words and the tributary of his native dialect, it is remarkable how much the latter, in spite of its far smaller bulk, contributes to the colour and flavour of the text.

6.23.   But fully to bring out the significance of the figures given we require some comparative data for secular writings; the Bible is such a vast reservoir of words that even a secular writer may well show a very substantial proportion of words that are biblical in our sense. One would have preferred a secular writer contemporary with Bunyan, but the only writer immediately available to us is Macaulay. The biblical or non-biblical character of Macaulay's vocabulary did not seem to me, however, a subject

TABLE 6.12. Showing the number f_x of nouns occurring X times in the four samples from Bunyan's works, distinguishing nouns that occur in the canonical books of the Authorised Version of the Bible, B, and nouns that do not occur, β. The total distribution will be found in Table 6.7

1	2	3	4	5	6	7	8
X	B	β	Total	X	B	β	Total
1	519	412	931	23	6	—	6
2	265	105	370	24	4	1	5
3	136	59	195	25	4	—	4
4	97	31	128	26	10	—	10
5	73	18	91	27	1	—	1
6	66	13	79	28	5	—	5
7	39	8	47	29	3	—	3
8	33	6	39	30	1	—	1
9	32	3	35	31	5	—	5
10	24	1	25	33	3	—	3
11	27	3	30	34	3	—	3
12	16	4	20	35	5	—	5
13	21	2	23	36	6	—	6
14	12	1	13	37	2	—	2
15	13	2	15	38	2	—	2
16	14	1	15	39	2	—	2
17	9	—	9	40	2	—	2
18	13	—	13	41	3	—	3
19	5	1	6	42	5	—	5
20	9	—	9	43	1	1	2
21	15	—	15	44 up	56	—	56
22	7	—	7				
				Total	1574	672	2246

For the β-distribution, $S_0 = 672$, $S_1 = 1485$.
For the total distribution, $S_0 = 2246$, $S_1 = 16,056$.

of any interest in itself, and I did not feel at all inclined to make a complete investigation on the same lines as for Bunyan, but decided to proceed by way of sample. I had prepared a manuscript list of his complete vocabulary, combining the two separate card catalogues for samples A, B, C and for D, and went through this marking every tenth noun from the first onward, i.e. nouns 1, 11, 21, 31, etc. This gave a sample, or rather sub-sample, of 355 nouns, which one might hope would be an effectively unbiased sample. These nouns were then looked up in Cruden and sorted into biblical and non-biblical, the numbers of occurrences in Macaulay being also noted. The totals found were:

	Biblical, B	Non-biblical, β	Total
Vocabulary	155	200	355
Occurrences	1721	690	2411

In the vocabulary 43·7 per cent of the nouns are biblical, 56·3 per cent non-biblical, against Bunyan's 70·1 per cent, 29·9 per cent. For occurrences the percentages are: biblical 71·4 per cent, non-biblical 28·6 per cent, against Bunyan's 90·8 per cent, 9·2 per cent. Even for Macaulay, then, the proportion of biblical nouns as they occur in the text is, judging by the sample, some 70 per cent, though this estimate may be on the high side, cf. § 6.24. It is indeed rather remarkable that for the samples from Macaulay as for those from Bunyan the biblical words are preponderantly those with the larger numbers of occurrences, and are indeed overweighted amongst occurrences as compared with vocabulary to an extent quite comparable with, though rather less than, that for the religious writer. The mean numbers of occurrences for biblical and non-biblical nouns in the two authors work out at

	Biblical	Non-biblical
Bunyan	9·26	2·21
Macaulay	11·10	3·45

But because words are biblical they are by no means necessarily religious. The following are the 15 'biblical' nouns with 20 occurrences or more in Macaulay that were caught by our sample of one in ten:

Army, Child, Crown, Day, Face, Feeling, Love, Man, Measure, Opinion, Point, Proceeding, Queen, Title, Wisdom.

The verbal noun *proceeding* is classified as biblical only because the verb is biblical. It will be noticed that not one of these words is definitely religious in character. Of course words of a definitely religious character, or which one associates for the most part with religion, do occur in Macaulay, but either with far smaller frequencies of occurrence than in Bunyan or in secular senses other than those of his usage. The following list of nouns, ranked by their frequency of occurrences in Bunyan, illustrates the point:

Noun	Number of occurrences in Bunyan	Number of occurrences in Macaulay	Noun	Number of occurrences in Bunyan	Number of occurrences in Macaulay
Religion	36	18	Grace	49	10
Devil	37	6	Heaven	52	9
Righteousness	39	0	Soul	68	10
Spirit	39	54	Pilgrim	133	0
Pilgrimage	44	0	Sin	139	3
Hell	45	5	Lord	216	55
Faith	49	17	God	305	30

In reading these figures it must be remembered that the sample for Macaulay is roundly one of 20,000 occurrences against only 16,000 occurrences for Bunyan. *Spirit* is actually more frequent in Macaulay than in Bunyan, but mainly in such senses as the following: 'he does not sacrifice sense and spirit to pedantic refinements', 'the spirit of the age', 'in form as well as in spirit', 'a spirit far more daring and inventive than his own'. *Faith* and *grace* may often of course occur in purely non-religious senses. *Lord* is wholly or almost wholly (I can only write from memory) used by Macaulay as the secular title, by Bunyan mainly in the religious sense. *God* occurs in Macaulay (again, if my memory serves me rightly) a number of times in the sort of senses for which one would write *god* or *gods* without the capital.

6.24.   Our sub-sample from Macaulay is not a large one, but seems adequate to indicate the difference between the biblical character of Bunyan's vocabulary and his. The standard error of the percentage of biblical or non-biblical nouns based on this sub-sample is the square root of $56\cdot3 \times 43\cdot7/355$ or $2\cdot63$, so that these percentages are known within reasonable limits of precision. It must be remembered, however, that the Macaulay sample is larger than the Bunyan sample and these values of p_v are therefore not properly comparable. As p_v approaches p_w for small samples, it is probable, though not certain, that reduction of the Macaulay sample to 16,000 would slightly raise the percentage of biblical nouns. For the percentage of biblical nouns amongst occurrences we cannot give a simple standard error, but it is rather the question of possible bias in the sample that first arises since the high figure obtained for total occurrences, 2411, catches the eye at once. Since the sample is one in ten this should obviously be nearer 2000, or more precisely $20,178 \times 355/3543 = 2022$. The excess of observation over expectation may fairly safely be ascribed to the fact that our sub-sample happens to have caught amongst the biblical nouns the most frequent noun in Macaulay, viz. *man* with 459 occurrences. The mean given by the sub-sample is $2411/355$ or $6\cdot792$: the mean of the universe from which we are drawing (Table 6.4) is $5\cdot695$, difference $+1\cdot097$. The standard deviation in the universe is $14\cdot291$, giving as the standard error for means of samples of 355 the value $0\cdot757$. The difference is therefore $1\cdot45$ times the standard error. This is well within the limits of fluctuations of sampling. Even on the assumption of normal distribution of the means we would have $P = 0\cdot15$; but in point of fact the distribution can hardly be normal, but rather skew with a longer tail towards positive values, so that the true value of P would be higher than this. Our mean is not properly speaking biased, but merely errs on the large side owing to the chances of sampling. It may be conjectured that in consequence the sample percentage of biblical occurrences, 71·4, is rather too great. The excess of observed over expected occurrences is 389: if we deduct this figure from the biblical occurrences, 1721, we get 1332, and 1332/2022 is only 66 per cent. It looks as if the observed sample percentage might be too high by as much as some 5 points.

6.25.   This concludes, for the present, my short studies of different types of noun—verbal nouns in -*ing*, monosyllabic nouns and biblical nouns, in Bunyan and Macaulay. In all studies of the kind that I have seen—a very limited number—it is usual to give nothing more in the way of statistics than totals and percentages. The preceding paragraphs sufficiently show, I think, how much more illuminating it is to base the whole work on frequency distributions. The reader will find in Chapter 8 (see especially §§ 8.20 *et seq*.) an additional statistical analysis of the distributions into two etymological groups: (1) Old English-Teutonic, (2) Latin-Romance.

6.26.   Critics and eulogists innumerable, writing mainly on the *Pilgrim's Progress*, have commented on Bunyan's vocabulary, though so far as I am aware it has never received the full and detailed study which so interesting a vocabulary seems to deserve. Here it is natural to end with the words of the later author on the earlier, of Macaulay on Bunyan; I cite from the close of his essay on Southey's edition of the *Pilgrim's Progress*.

The style of Bunyan is delightful to every reader, and invaluable as a study to every person who wishes to obtain a wide command over the English language. The vocabulary is the vocabulary of the common people. There is not an expression, if we except a few technical terms of theology, which would puzzle the rudest peasant. We have observed several pages which do not contain a single word of more than two syllables. Yet no writer has said more exactly what he meant to say. For magnificence, for pathos, for vehement exhortation, for subtle disquisition, for every purpose of the poet, the orator, and the divine, this homely dialect, the dialect of plain working men, was perfectly sufficient. There is no book in our literature on which we would so readily stake the fame of the old unpolluted English language, no book which shows so well how rich that language is in its own proper wealth, and how little it has been improved by all that it has borrowed.

That is a generous tribute from the man of many words to the man who had but few.

REFERENCES

A. STATISTICAL METHOD

§§ 6.4 and 6.12. For the method of estimation of variance from small samples, previously used in § 4.11, see Y & K, Chapter 23, §§ 23.4, 23.5, especially equation (23.3). § 6.24. Standard error of a percentage, Y & K, p. 351; of the mean, pp. 386–7.

B. CITATIONS IN TEXT OR TABLES

(6.1) Macaulay, T. B. (1880). *Critical and Historical Essays.* London: Longmans, Green, Reader & Dyer.

(6.2) Bunyan, John (1937). *The Pilgrim's Progress.* Everyman's Library, No. 204. London: J. M. Dent.

(6.3) Bunyan, John (1928). *Grace Abounding* and *Mr Badman.* Everyman's Library, No. 815. London: J. M. Dent.

(6.4) Bunyan, John (1902). *The Pilgrim's Progress, The Holy War* and *Grace Abounding.* London, Edinburgh and New York: Thomas Nelson. (Used only for *The Holy War.*)

(6.5) Clark (or Clarke), Samuel (1657). *A Mirrour or Looking-Glasse both for Saints and Sinners Held forth in some thousands of Examples....* By Sa. Clark, Pastor in Bennet Fink, London. The third edition very much enlarged. London, Printed by T. R. and E. M. for Tho. Newbery, and are to be sold at his shop at the three Golden Lyons, in Corn-hill near Royall-Exchange. (This, in the library of St John's College, is the only edition that I have seen.)

(6.6) Moffatt, James (1935). *A New Translation of the Bible.* London: Hodder and Stoughton.

(6.7) Skeat, W. W. (1895). *The Student's Chaucer.* Oxford: Clarendon Press.

(6.8) Cruden, Alexander (1842). *A complete Concordance to the Old and New Testament, etc.* The 10th edition. London: printed for Longman & Co. and others.

Chapter 7

THE DISTRIBUTION OF THE VOCABULARY OVER SAMPLES FROM SEVERAL WORKS OF THE SAME AUTHOR: VOCABULARY RATIOS OF BUNYAN TO MACAULAY

7.1. In the sampling experiment of §§ 4.2 *et seq.* we have data for four sub-samples. In the investigation based on Macaulay (§§ 6.2 *et seq.*) we have data for samples from four of his essays. In the investigation based on Bunyan (§§ 6.8 *et seq.*) we have data for samples from four of his works. The vocabulary of the sampling experiment has already been classified, in Table 4.7, to show how many of the words (nouns) occurred in one only of the four samples, *a* or *b* or *c* or *d*, how many occurred in any specified two samples, and so forth. These class frequencies are repeated in col. 3 of Table 7.1, but the order of the classes has been re-arranged. In that instance it was possible to calculate the required class frequencies from data in preceding tables without the trouble of re-sorting the cards. The total vocabulary for the four essays of Macaulay was classified in similar fashion, but the classification had to be effected by sorting the cards, and this sorting was troublesome, as the cards for essays A, B and C had to be collated with the entirely separate set of cards for D, the essay on Bacon used for the sampling experiment. It must be remembered that in this instance the sample for D was roundly twice the size of the other samples, some 8000 occurrences against 4000. The class frequencies are given in col. 4 of Table 7.1. The cards for the four works of Bunyan were similarly sorted, but with no trouble since all the data were on the one set of cards, and the frequencies found are given in col. 5 of the same table. Before proceeding with this chapter, the reader who is not already thoroughly familiar with the notation used and the treatment of such data as those with which we are dealing— statistics of attributes as they are termed—should study the text-book chapters to which he is directed in refs. A. To summarise briefly, the capital A (positive symbol) denotes a noun 'occurring in sample A', the corresponding Greek letter α (negative symbol) 'not occurring in sample A', and so on. A class symbol like $ABCD$ denotes 'occurring in all four samples A, B, C and D', $ABC\delta$ 'occurring in A, B and C but not in D', $A\beta C\delta$ 'occurring in A and C but not in B or D' and so forth. There are four letters in each class-symbol of Table 7.1 (*classes of the fourth order*) and each letter may be either a capital or a Greek letter, so there must be in all 2^4 or 16 classes. In our particular case, however, since we are only considering nouns falling into at least one of the four samples, the frequency of the class $\alpha\beta\gamma\delta$ is zero,

TABLE 7.1. Table showing the distribution of the total vocabulary over the four samples of the experiment in sampling (§§ 4.2 *et seq.* and Table 4.7), the four essays of Macaulay (§§ 6.2 *et seq.*), and the four works of Bunyan. (§§ 6.8 *et seq.*) $AB\gamma D$ means 'in samples A, B and D but not C': $\alpha B\gamma D$, 'in samples B and D but not A or C,' and so on

1	2	3	4	5
	Class	Four samples of experiment in sampling	Four essays of Macaulay	Four works of Bunyan
1	$ABCD$	271	402	259
2	$ABC\delta$	62	55	82
3	$AB\gamma D$	58	132	92
4	$A\beta CD$	53	144	66
5	αBCD	64	140	51
6	$AB\gamma\delta$	68	79	111
7	$A\beta C\delta$	64	100	83
8	$A\beta\gamma D$	59	178	50
9	$\alpha BC\delta$	67	74	63
10	$\alpha B\gamma D$	66	168	65
11	$\alpha\beta CD$	81	173	74
12	$A\beta\gamma\delta$	268	447	262
13	$\alpha B\gamma\delta$	280	283	297
14	$\alpha\beta C\delta$	275	457	352
15	$\alpha\beta\gamma D$	312	711	339
16	$\alpha\beta\gamma\delta$	—	—	—

but it has been inserted to remind the reader of its existence and of this fact. A class frequency is denoted by putting the class symbol in brackets: in this notation

$$(\alpha\beta\gamma\delta) = 0.$$

There are simple equations relating frequencies of lower order to those of the fourth order. Thus the number of words occurring in A, B or C (whether they occur in D or no) is obviously given by

$$(ABC) = (ABCD) + (ABC\delta) = 271 + 62 = 333$$

for the data of the sampling experiment (Table 7.1, col. 3). Similarly

$$(AB) = (ABCD) + (ABC\delta) + (AB\gamma D) + (AB\gamma\delta)$$
$$= 271 + 62 + 58 + 68 = 459$$

and so on, and the whole number of words, usually denoted by N in data of this kind (the S_0 of our frequency distributions), is given by the sum-total for all the sixteen classes, 2048 for col. 3. A tabulation of *all* the class frequencies for each case would occupy a great deal of space, as there are 81 of them, but Table 7.1 gives all that is necessary since all other frequencies can be determined from those there given by simple addition. It is sometimes convenient, however, to have before one, instead of or in addition to the set of sixteen frequencies of Table 7.1, a different set of sixteen, viz. the frequencies of the *positive* classes, i.e. the classes denoted by capitals only. These are given in Table 7.2. Their convenience is obvious; we are given at once the number of words occurring in all four samples (line 1), the numbers

TABLE 7.2. The frequencies of the positive classes
calculated from the data of Table 7.1

1	2	3	4	5
	Class	Four samples of experiment in sampling	Four essays of Macaulay	Four works of Bunyan
1	ABCD	271	402	259
2	ABC	333	457	341
3	ABD	329	534	351
4	ACD	324	546	325
5	BCD	335	542	310
6	AB	459	668	544
7	AC	450	701	490
8	AD	441	856	467
9	BC	464	671	455
10	BD	459	842	467
11	CD	469	859	450
12	A	903	1537	1005
13	B	936	1333	1020
14	C	937	1545	1030
15	D	964	2048	996
16	N	2048	3543	2246

occurring in any specified three (lines 2–5), the numbers occurring in any specified two (lines 6–11), the numbers occurring in any one (lines 12–15), and finally at the bottom the total number of words or total vocabulary. The unpractised reader might as an exercise check some of the figures in Table 7.2 from Table 7.1, and then try the reverse operation, deriving some of the figures of Table 7.1 from those of Table 7.2.

7.2.   A careful inspection of Table 7.1 shows a remarkable similarity in the run of the frequencies of cols. 3, 4 and 5. Col. 3 is by far the most regular, as is natural since the four samples are all distributed over the same essay. It leads off with the large frequency 271 for nouns occurring in all four samples; the frequency of nouns occurring in three of the samples but not in the fourth (2–5) ranges from 53 to 64; of nouns occurring in two of the samples only (6–11) from 59 to 81, but that of nouns occurring in one sample only (12–15) from 268 to 312. The classes with high frequencies are therefore (1) the leading class $ABCD$, of nouns common to all four samples, (2) the four $A\beta\gamma\delta$, etc. of nouns peculiar to a single sample. The figures of cols. 4 and 5 are much more irregular, partly because the four samples are drawn from different works, partly in col. 4 because D was a sample of roundly 8000 occurrences, not 4000, with the result that the frequency of every class with a D in the symbol is larger than that of any other class of the same group with a δ; in lines 2 to 5, for example, the frequencies $(A\beta\gamma D)$, $(A\beta CD)$ and (αBCD) are all much larger than $(ABC\delta)$. Notwithstanding these irregularities the same principal characteristic is clearly exhibited, the leading frequency of line 1 and the four of lines 12 to 15 being notably the largest.

TABLE 7.3. Giving (in addition to line 1) the averages of lines 2–5, 6–11, and 12–15 of Table 7.1, i.e. mean frequencies of classes of words common to four, three or two of the samples or special to one only

1	2	3	4	5
Lines of Table 7.1	Words common to number of classes below	Four samples of experiment in sampling	Four essays of Macaulay	Four works of Bunyan
1	4	271·00	402·00	259·00
2– 5	3	59·25	117·75	72·75
6–11	2	67·50	128·67	74·33
12–15	1	283·75	474·50	312·50

To eliminate the irregularities, we may average the three groups, lines 2–5, 6–11, 12–15; these averages are given in Table 7.3, which brings out the similarity of the three distributions very clearly. Not only are the first and last frequencies by far the largest, but we note also two minor uniformities: (1) in each column the mean frequency of classes 6–11 (words common to two samples) is slightly greater than the mean frequency of classes 2–5 (words common to three samples); (2) the mean frequency of classes 12–15 (words peculiar to one sample) is greater than the frequency of words common to all four samples. These two minor uniformities are, however, only average results; the principal uniformity, the outstanding magnitude of the frequencies $(ABCD)$ on the one hand and $(A\beta\gamma\delta)$ etc. on the other, is clearly the most important.

7.3. As a consequence, if we pick out from Table 7.1 the eight classes of the fourth order which together made up any one class of the first order, say A, we shall find that the frequencies $(ABCD)$ and $(A\beta\gamma\delta)$ taken together contribute one half or more of the total (A). That is to say, one-half or more. of the nouns in any one sample is contributed by (1) nouns common to all four samples, together with (2) nouns special or peculiar to that sample,

TABLE 7.4. Compiled from Table 7.1 and showing the composition of the first order classes A, B, C and D in terms of the fourth-order classes

1	2	3	4	5
Line in Table 7.1	Class	Four samples of experiment in sampling	Four essays of Macaulay	Four works of Bunyan
1	$ABCD$	271	402	259
2	$ABC\delta$	62	55	82
3	$AB\gamma D$	58	132	92
4	$A\beta CD$	53	144	66
6	$AB\gamma\delta$	68	79	111
7	$A\beta C\delta$	64	100	83
8	$A\beta\gamma D$	59	178	50
12	$A\beta\gamma\delta$	268	447	262
Total	A	903	1537	1005
1	$ABCD$	271	402	259
2	$ABC\delta$	62	55	82
3	$AB\gamma D$	58	132	92
5	αBCD	64	140	51
6	$AB\gamma\delta$	68	79	111
9	$\alpha BC\delta$	67	74	63
10	$\alpha B\gamma D$	66	168	65
13	$\alpha B\gamma\delta$	280	283	297
Total	B	936	1333	1020
1	$ABCD$	271	402	259
2	$ABC\delta$	62	55	82
4	$A\beta CD$	53	144	66
5	αBCD	64	140	51
7	$A\beta C\delta$	64	100	83
9	$\alpha BC\delta$	67	74	63
11	$\alpha\beta CD$	81	173	74
14	$\alpha\beta C\delta$	275	457	352
Total	C	937	1545	1030
1	$ABCD$	271	402	259
3	$AB\gamma D$	58	132	92
4	$A\beta CD$	53	144	66
5	αBCD	64	140	51
8	$A\beta\gamma D$	59	178	50
10	$\alpha B\gamma D$	66	168	65
11	$\alpha\beta CD$	81	173	74
15	$\alpha\beta\gamma D$	312	711	339
Total	D	964	2048	996

the second being usually though not always the larger contribution of the two; the remaining six classes only contribute rather less than a half. Table 7.4 shows this analysis for all the four samples A, B, C and D in the three sets of data, and Table 7.5 the percentages of the form

$$100 \frac{(ABCD) + (A\beta\gamma\delta)}{(A)}.$$

For example, in the first section of Table 7.4, col. 3, we have $(271 + 268)/903 = 59.7$ per cent, in col. 4 $(402 + 447)/1537 = 55.2$ per cent. and so on. The figures range roundly from 50 to 60 per cent, and only in two instances of the twelve (Table 7.4, A, col. 3 and B, col. 4) is the contribution from nouns special to the class less than that of nouns common to the four classes.

TABLE 7.5. Giving the percentages of words common to the four samples, together with words special to each sample, on the total for each of the samples A, B, C and D of Table 7.4

1	2	3	4
Class	Four samples of experiment in sampling	Four essays of Macaulay	Four works of Bunyan
A	59·7	55·2	51·8
B	58·9	51·4	54·5
C	58·3	55·6	59·3
D	60·5	54·3	60·0

7.4.   The uniformity is so striking that it looks as if we ought to be able to account for the broad outlines by some purely statistical reasoning, the sampling experiment giving the simplest case and larger or smaller divergences remaining to be ascribed, in the Macaulay and Bunyan data, to essential differences between the works sampled or of course to mere fluctuations of sampling. If, as is approximately the case with the sampling experiment, the four samples may be regarded as taken at random from one and the same work, we might expect the figures of Table 7.1, col. 3, to be more or less closely reproduced by some such sampling process as the following. Let us write out all the nouns of the total frequency distribution Table 4.4 on counters, giving each noun that occurs x times x counters, so that there are 8045 counters altogether, and then deal them at random into four trays labelled A, B, C and D. To ensure approximate randomness we might, for example, toss the counters into a spinning circular tray with four equal quadrants A, B, C and D. Sorting the counters in each quadrant by nouns, and listing and counting the *nouns* in each—not the number of counters—we shall then have data like those of Table 7.1; $(ABCD) =$ number of nouns appearing in all four quadrants, $(ABC\delta) =$ number of nouns appearing in quadrants A, B and C but not in D, and so forth. The process described would not be a process of simple random sampling as described and defined in § 3.3, for it step by step exhausts the 'universe' from which we are drawing: it might be termed 'random partitioning'.

7.5.   Given then the frequency distribution showing the number f_x of words occurring x times each, and supposing the process of random partitioning carried out as described, we have to determine the expected numbers falling into the classes $ABCD$, $ABC\delta$, etc. We need not, however, find *directly* expressions for the set of fourth-order frequencies: we may if we prefer it choose the set of frequencies of the positive classes of Table 7.2, or any other fundamental set of sixteen algebraically independent frequencies. The most convenient set for our purpose is in fact that given by the total vocabulary N and the frequencies of the *negative* classes, those the symbols for which consist entirely of Greek letters. We may state the simple result quite generally, supposing our circular tray divided not into four quadrants merely but into r equal sectors, representing r samples $ABCD...R$ compounded into our total frequency distribution like Table 4.4. The chance of a word entered on x counters *not* falling into any one of k named sectors is

$$\left(\frac{r-k}{r}\right)^x.$$

If there are f_x of such words, the expected number of them not falling into any one of the k named sectors is therefore

$$f_x\left(\frac{r-k}{r}\right)^x,$$

and the entire number of counters not falling into any one of the k named sectors is the sum of such expressions for all values of x from unity to the maximum value in the frequency distribution. That is to say,

$$\text{Frequency of negative class of the } k\text{th order} = S\left\{f_x\left(\frac{r-k}{r}\right)^x\right\}. \qquad (7.1)$$

The arithmetic is most briefly and simply carried out directly as indicated by this equation. With $r = 4$, we evaluate the three frequencies

$$.(\alpha) = S\{f_x(\tfrac{3}{4})^x\}, \quad (\alpha\beta) = S\{f_x(\tfrac{1}{2})^x\}, \quad (\alpha\beta\gamma) = S\{f_x(\tfrac{1}{4})^x\}, \qquad (7.2)$$

which actually give us fourteen frequencies since $(\alpha) = (\beta) = (\gamma) = (\delta)$, and so forth. We know the value of N (the S_0 of the frequency distribution) and are also given $(\alpha\beta\gamma\delta) = 0$, and can then calculate the complete set of fourth-order frequencies, or the frequencies of the positive classes or any other set we like. But simply for the sake of more clearly exhibiting how $(ABCD)$, $(ABC\delta)$, $(AB\gamma\delta)$ and $(A\beta\gamma\delta)$ are built up—and we need only concern ourselves with these four since obviously $(ABC\delta) = (AB\gamma D) = (A\beta CD) = (\alpha BCD)$, and so on—I have preferred to calculate these fourth-order frequencies *direct* from the frequency distribution. The equations, derived from equations (7.2), are

$$
\begin{aligned}
(ABCD) &= S\{f_x[1 - 4(\tfrac{3}{4})^x + 6(\tfrac{1}{2})^x - 4(\tfrac{1}{4})^x]\} \\
(ABC\delta) &= S\{f_x[(\tfrac{3}{4})^x - 3(\tfrac{1}{2})^x + 3(\tfrac{1}{4})^x]\} \\
(AB\gamma\delta) &= S\{f_x[(\tfrac{1}{2})^x - 2(\tfrac{1}{4})^x]\} \\
(A\beta\gamma\delta) &= S\{f_x(\tfrac{1}{4})^x\}
\end{aligned}
\right\} \qquad (7.3)
$$

The numerical coefficients were first tabulated up to sufficiently high values of x, and then multiplied by the successive values of f_x in Table 4.4.

7.6. Table 7.6 gives the results, the figures of each line in cols. 2–5 giving to two places of decimals the products of f_x (Table 4.4) by the numerical coefficients of equations (7.3). To check each step of the work the 'check total' of col. 6 was run out, viz. (fig. in col. 2) + 4 (col. 3) + 6(col. 4) + 4(col. 5), which should reproduce the value of f_x from Table 4.4 within the limits of errors of rounding-off. Summing the columns, we have for the expected frequencies on random partitioning:

$$(ABCD) = 277 \cdot 51, \qquad (AB\gamma\delta) = 71 \cdot 58,$$
$$(ABC\delta) = 61 \cdot 60, \qquad (A\beta\gamma\delta) = 273 \cdot 66.$$

Clearly in these totals the second place of decimals cannot be trusted as precise. Now note how they are made up. In col. 2, since nouns with only one, two or three occurrences obviously cannot occur in all four samples, they contribute nothing to the total. For $x = 4$ the numerical coefficient of the $(ABCD)$ formula is only 0·094, but as f_x is large (112) we get the substantial contribution of 10·50. The numerical coefficient then rises rapidly to a value of 0·781 at 10, 0·947 at 15, 0·987 at 20, 0·997 at 25 and 0·9993 at 30. The rise in the coefficient is so rapid at first that it more than overtakes the fall in the frequencies, and contributions to $(ABCD)$ actually increase. As the frequencies continue to fall away the contributions must finally do so, but words occurring 20 to 25 times or more must, with random partitioning, practically all fall into the class $ABCD$. Roughly, in this particular instance, the class is constituted to the extent of rather more than one-half (143·08) of nouns occurring 4 to 11 times—a range over which the frequencies are moderately high but the numerical coefficients low—the remainder (134·43) coming from words occurring 12 times or more, where the frequencies are rapidly tailing away but the coefficients rapidly approaching unity. Col. 3 for $(ABC\delta)$ is a great contrast. Nouns occurring

TABLE 7.6. Calculation of the expected class frequencies $(ABCD)$, $(ABC\delta)$, $(AB\gamma\delta)$, $(A\beta\gamma\delta)$ by random partitioning from the data of the Experiment on Sampling, Table 4.4. Col. 6 gives the check total which should reproduce f_x within the limits of errors of rounding off. In cols. 2–5 a dash signifies zero, and ·00 'less than 0·005'

1	2	3	4	5	6
X	$(ABCD)$	$(ABC\delta)$	$(AB\gamma\delta)$	$(A\beta\gamma\delta)$	Check total cf. § 7.6
1	—	—	—	247·50	990·00
2	—	—	45·87	22·94	366·98
3	—	16·22	16·22	2·70	173·00
4	10·50	15·75	6·13	·44	112·04
5	16·87	10·55	2·11	·07	72·01
6	17·90	6·20	·71	·01	47·00
7	21·02	4·52	·32	·00	41·02
8	19·31	2·74	·12	·00	30·99
9	24·19	2·35	·07	·00	34·01
10	13·27	·91	·02	·00	17·03
11	20·02	·98	·01	·00	24·00
12	16·62	·59	·00	·00	18·98
13	9·06	·23	·00	·00	9·98
14	·9·29	·18	·00	·00	10·01
15	12·31	·17	·00	·00	12·99
16	2·88	·03	·00	·00	3·00
17	9·70	·07	·00	·00	9·98
18	6·84	·04	·00	·00	7·00
19	5·90	·03	·00	·00	6·02
20	4·94	·02	·00	·00	5·02
21	0·99	·00	·00	·00	0·99
22	3·97	·01	·00	·00	4·01
23	6·97	·01	·00	·00	7·01
24	1·99	·00	·00	·00	1·99
25	1·00	·00	·00	·00	1·00
26	4·99	·00	·00	·00	4·99
27	2·99	·00	·00	·00	2·99
28	3·99	·00	·00	·00	3·99
29	1·00	·00	·00	·00	1·00
30 up	29·00	·00	·00	·00	29·00
Total	277·51	61·60	71·58	273·66	2048·03

only once or twice cannot be found in three of the samples, and the coefficient leads off with the value 0·094 for $X = 3$, reaches a maximum of no more than 0·146 at $X = 5$, and then quickly diminishes again. The bulk of the contributions to $(ABC\delta)$, 95 per cent, comes from nouns occurring 3 to 9 times;

69 per cent from the short range of nouns occurring 3 to 5 times. For $(AB\gamma\delta)$, col. 4, the initial numerical coefficient for $X = 2$ is $0 \cdot 125$, a maximum from which it quickly falls away to $0 \cdot 001$ at $X = 10$. The bulk of the contributions to this class, 98 per cent, comes from nouns occurring 2 to 5 times, but owing to the rapid decrease in f_x actually 64 per cent of the total frequency is contributed solely by nouns occurring twice. Finally, for $(A\beta\gamma\delta)$ the coefficients are the rapidly converging series $1/4$, $1/16$, $1/64$, etc., and just over 90 per cent of the total frequency is contributed by the once-nouns alone. The frequency of this class is so high simply because the frequency of once-nouns is so high compared with all the following values of f_x. The table brings out very clearly how the distribution of frequency over the fourth-order classes, by this method of random partitioning, is dependent on the form of the frequency distribution for the numbers of occurrences of the words. $(ABCD)$ is high because it includes a considerable proportion of words with even a very moderate number of occurrences and nearly all the words with, say, some 20 occurrences or more, and these come to a large total in the long tail of the frequency distribution. $(A\beta\gamma\delta)$ is high because it is mainly dependent on the number of once-nouns, the highest frequency of the whole distribution.

7.7. For the four samples from Bunyan the work was carried out in precisely the same fashion. It hardly seems necessary to give the full work in the form of Table 7.6 as it is precisely similar in general appearance, but the longer tail of the distribution throws a much larger proportion of the observations into the class $(ABCD)$. We have seen that the great bulk of nouns occurring 20 times or more falls into this class. In the sampling experiment, Table 4.4, they number only 62 out of 2048: in the Bunyan distribution, Table 6.7, 162 out of 2246. The totals found were, to two places of decimals,

$$
\begin{aligned}
(ABCD) &= 449 \cdot 17, & (AB\gamma\delta) &= 76 \cdot 02, \\
(ABC\delta) &= 75 \cdot 64, & (A\beta\gamma\delta) &= 259 \cdot 53.
\end{aligned}
$$

The 'expected' frequencies for the Macaulay data cannot be calculated in precisely the same way, owing to the troublesome fact that A, B and C are samples of roundly 4000 occurrences, while D is a sample of roundly 8000 occurrences. But the difficulty can be readily surmounted. The problem was treated, to use our mechanical analogy, as one of dealing the counters into a tray with *five* equal sectors instead of four, A, B, C, D and E, the expected frequencies were calculated for the fifth-order classes, and then D and E combined. Putting $r = 5$ in equation (7.1) and k successively 1, 2, 3 and 4, and working directly as indicated by that equation, the frequencies were found from Table 6.4

$$(\alpha) = 1939{\cdot}95, \quad (\alpha\beta) = 1212{\cdot}01, \quad (\alpha\beta\gamma) = 708{\cdot}72, \quad (\alpha\beta\gamma\delta) = 319{\cdot}12.$$

From these and the known $N = 3543$, $(\alpha\beta\gamma\delta\epsilon) = 0$, the table of fifth-order frequencies could be drawn up, of which the key values are

$$(ABCDE) = 471{\cdot}75, \quad (ABC\delta\epsilon) = 43{\cdot}21, \quad (A\beta\gamma\delta\epsilon) = 319{\cdot}12,$$
$$(ABCD\epsilon) = 67{\cdot}75, \quad (AB\gamma\delta\epsilon) = 70{\cdot}48, \quad (\alpha\beta\gamma\delta\epsilon) = 0{\cdot}00.$$

These were then reduced to the required fourth-order frequencies for a set of sectors in which D is double the size of any of the others by reckoning a DE, $D\epsilon$, or δE as a D and only $\delta\epsilon$ as a δ. Thus

$$(ABCD) = (ABCDE) + (ABCD\epsilon) + (ABC\delta E)$$
$$= 471{\cdot}75 + 67{\cdot}75 + 67{\cdot}75 = 607{\cdot}25$$
$$(ABC\delta) = (ABC\delta\epsilon) = 43{\cdot}21,$$

and so forth. It will be noted that we are treating the samples as if they were exactly and not merely approximately samples of 4000 (or 8000) occurrences, but this is sufficient precision for our purpose.

7.8. The fourth-order frequencies, expected and observed, for the three sets of data are brought together in Table 7.7. Let us consider them in turn. Taking first the sampling experiment, at first sight the agreement between observation and expectation looks fairly good; the general features in the run of the observed frequencies are clearly reproduced and no divergence is very large except that for $(\alpha\beta\gamma D) : d$, it may be remembered, is the largest of the four sub-samples (Table 4.5), but its small excess in size is quite insufficient to account for this excess in the number of nouns peculiar to the sample. Of the three uniformities brought out by Tables 7.3, 7.4 and 7.5 (§7.2) two are accounted for. To take the most important first, the proportion in Table 7.7, col. 3,

$$\{(ABCD) + (A\beta\gamma\delta)\}/(A) = (277{\cdot}51 + 273{\cdot}66)/950{\cdot}71$$
$$= 551{\cdot}17/950{\cdot}71 = 58{\cdot}1 \text{ per cent,}$$

which is only just lower than the lowest of the four corresponding percentages in col. 2 of Table 7.5, viz. 58·3, and only little lower than the mean of the four, 59·35. Again, in col. 3 of Table 7.7 the frequencies of the classes 2–5, with three positive symbols, are slightly less than those of classes 6–11 with two positive symbols, as with the means of the observed frequencies, Table 7.3, col. 3:

Classes	Table 7.7	Table 7.3 (means)
2– 5	61·60	59·25
6–11	71·58	67·50

Both these uniformities can then be explained by random partitioning of the vocabulary. But the third cannot be so explained. The expected frequency of words peculiar to one sample, classes 12–15 of Table 7.7, col. 3, is slightly less and not greater than the expected frequency of words common

TABLE 7.7. Comparing the observed class frequencies of the fourth order of Table 7.1 with those expected on the basis of random partitioning (§ 7.5)

1	2	3	4	5	6	7	8
	Class	Sampling experiment		Macaulay		Bunyan	
		Expected	Observed	Expected	Observed	Expected	Observed
1	$ABCD$	277·51	271	607·25	402	449·17	259
2	$ABC\delta$	61·60	62	43·21	55	75·64	82
3	$AB\gamma D$	61·60	58	154·17	132	75·64	92
4	$A\beta CD$	61·60	53	154·17	144	75·64	66
5	αBCD	61·60	64	154·17	140	75·64	51
6	$AB\gamma\delta$	71·58	68	70·48	79	76·02	111
7	$A\beta C\delta$	71·58	64	70·48	100	76·02	83
8	$A\beta\gamma D$	71·58	59	184·17	178	76·02	50
9	$\alpha BC\delta$	71·58	67	70·48	74	76·02	63
10	$\alpha B\gamma D$	71·58	66	184·17	168	76·02	65
11	$\alpha\beta CD$	71·58	81	184·17	173	76·02	74
12	$A\beta\gamma\delta$	273·66	268	319·12	447	259·53	262
13	$\alpha B\gamma\delta$	273·66	280	319·12	283	259·53	297
14	$\alpha\beta C\delta$	273·66	275	319·12	457	259·53	352
15	$\alpha\beta\gamma D$	273·66	312	708·72	711	259·53	339
16	$\alpha\beta\gamma\delta$	—	—	—	—	—	—
Total	—	2048·03	2048	3543·00	3543	2245·97	2246

to all four samples, 273·66 against 277·51. The general consensus between observation and expectation, however, as already stated, looks at first sight quite fair. But a closer examination suggests that deviations between the two, though small, may be systematic, and a reconstruction of the data to compare the frequencies of the positive classes instead of those of the classes of the fourth order leaves no doubt on the matter at all. This comparison is made in cols. 3 and 4 of Table 7.8. The result is astonishingly uniform; every observed frequency (N excluded of course) is lower than expectation with the single exception of (D), though the average deficiency is not large, being only of the order of 2·5 per cent. What is the source of this almost uniform divergence? Tentatively, I think, it may be ascribed to some heterogeneity of the four samples: indeed, there seems little doubt that this is the explanation when we come to note below the similar but considerably larger divergences in the Macaulay and Bunyan data. Such a heterogeneity would obviously result in a reduction of the numbers of nouns common to any four, three or two of the samples, owing to the slight differences between them, and the tendency of words to occur in pairs or triplets would in effect contribute to such heterogeneity. The number of nouns in the vocabulary of any one sample, (A) or (B), etc., would also tend to be reduced, for it has selected a more or less specialised group. The small reduction in the characteristic with increasing size of sample noted in the sampling experiment (§ 4.11) may then, as already suggested, be real and due to this slight heterogeneity: compare the much larger reductions found on pooling several distinct works in §§ 6.7 and 6.14.

TABLE 7.8. Giving the frequencies of the positive classes, derived from the figures of Table 7.7

1	2	3	4	5	6	7	8
	Class	Sampling experiment		Macaulay		Bunyan	
		Expected	Observed	Expected	Observed	Expected	Observed
1	ABCD	277·51	271	607·25	402	449·17	259
2	ABC	339·11	333	650·46	457	524·81	341
3	ABD	339·11	329	761·42	534	524·81	351
4	ACD	339·11	324	761·42	546	524·81	325
5	BCD	339·11	335	761·42	542	524·81	310
6	AB	472·29	459	875·11	668	676·47	544
7	AC	472·29	450	875·11	701	676·47	490
8	AD	472·29	441	1099·76	856	676·47	467
9	BC	472·29	464	875·11	671	676·47	455
10	BD	472·29	459	1099·76	842	676·47	467
11	CD	472·29	469	1099·76	859	676·47	450
12	A	950·71	903	1603·05	1537	1163·68	1005
13	B	950·71	936	1603·05	1333	1163·68	1020
14	C	950·71	937	1603·05	1545	1163·68	1030
15	D	950·71	964	2330·99	2048	1163·68	996
16	N	2048·03	2048	3543·00	3543	2245·97	2246

7.9. Turning now to the Macaulay data, Table 7.7, cols. 5 and 6, we note again the general similarity of observation and expectation, but divergences are much larger, and notably the number of nouns common to all four samples is only some two-thirds of expectation, 402 against 607·25. The frequencies 2–5 are on the average slightly in defect and the frequencies 6–11 very slightly in excess of expectation, but the frequencies 12–15 are on the average considerably in excess notwithstanding the defect for $(\alpha B\gamma\delta)$. The expected proportion of A's, B's or C's contributed by nouns common to all four samples and nouns special to the sample taken together is

$$(607\cdot25 + 319\cdot12)/1603\cdot05 = 57\cdot8 \text{ per cent,}$$

compared with a mean of 54·1 for the first three lines in Table 7.5, col. 3: for the D's the corresponding proportion is

$$(607·25 + 708·72)/2330·99 = 56·5 \text{ per cent,}$$

against 54·3. But this degree of agreement with observation in spite of the heavy deficiency of $ABCD$'s is attained largely by a reduction in the denominator of the ratios, (A), (B), (C) and (D) being all considerably in defect of expectation, as will be seen from Table 7.8. The excess of observation for the second term in the numerator, in classes 12 and 14, Table 7.7, is also a partial compensation for the defect of $ABCD$'s. The fact of observation that the frequency of classes 2–5, Table 7.7, is less than that of corresponding classes in the group 6–11 is in accordance with expectation. The relative proportions of frequencies 12–15 to $(ABCD)$ are, it must be noted, widely different in observation and expectation, owing to the heavy reduction in the latter. Turning now to Table 7.8, cols. 5 and 6, we see that there is in this case not a single exception to the rule that the observed frequency of a positive class is less than expectation. The deficiencies are also very much more considerable, roundly 34 per cent for $(ABCD)$, some 30 per cent on the average for classes 2–5, some 22 per cent for classes 6–11 and some 10 per cent for classes 12–15.

·7.10. In the Bunyan data, Table 7.7, cols. 7 and 8, we are not troubled by the irregularities due to the larger size of sample D in the Macaulay data, so the comparison of observation with expectation is more simply made. It brings out just the same general features. There is broad agreement between the runs of expected and observed frequencies, but an even heavier proportional deficiency in $(ABCD)$. Both the observed sets of frequencies 2–5 and 6–11 are in this case, on the average, slightly in defect and 12–15 uniformly in excess of expectation, the average excess amounting to as much as some 20 per cent. The expected proportion

$$\{(ABCD) + (A\beta\gamma\delta)\}/(A) = (449·17 + 259·53)/1163·68$$
$$= 708·70/1163·68 = 60·9 \text{ per cent,}$$

against a mean of 56·4 per cent for Table 7.5, col. 4. As before, this degree of agreement is brought about, in spite of the heavy deficiency in $(ABCD)$ only partially compensated by the much smaller excess in $(A\beta\gamma\delta)$, by the reduction in the denominator (A), cf. Table 7.8. The fact of observation that the frequency of classes 2–5 is on the average less than that of classes 6–11 is again in accordance with expectation on random partitioning. But the observed excess of frequencies 12–15 over $(ABCD)$ is contrary to expectation: this is a consequence of heterogeneity—of 'heterogeneous partitioning'—not of random partitioning. Turning now to Table 7.8, cols. 7 and 8, we see that there is once more not a single exception to the rule that the observed frequency of a positive class is less than that expected on random partitioning. The proportional deficiencies are roundly some 42 per cent for $(ABCD)$, 37 per cent on the average for classes 2–5, 29 per cent for classes 6–11 and 13 per cent for classes 12–15.

7.11.   It looks as if one ought to be able to devise some measure or index of homogeneity (or heterogeneity) from these differences or ratios between the observed and expected frequencies, but I have not seen my

TABLE 7.9. Giving the ratio of observation to expectation for $(ABCD)$ and for the means of the following groups of positive classes of Table 7.8, together with fitted geometric series of ratios

Classes	Sampling experiment		Macaulay		Bunyan	
	Observa- tion	Geometric series	Observa- tion	Geometric series	Observa- tion	Geometric series
1	0·977	0·961	0·662	0·642	0·577	0·550
2– 5	0·974	0·970	0·708	0·717	0·632	0·638
6–11	0·968	0·980	0·776	0·801	0·708	0·741
12–15	0·983	0·990	0·906	0·895	0·870	0·861
16	1·000	1·000	1·000	1·000	1·000	1·000

way to any satisfactory solution of the problem. Table 7.8 seemed at first to present a more hopeful basis than Table 7.7, and in Table 7.9 I have tabulated for the three sets of data the ratios of observation to expectation for $(ABCD)$ and for the *means* of the frequencies of classes 2–5, 6–11, and 12–15: for N the ratio is necessarily unity. The use of means for the Macaulay data is perhaps hardly quite fair, owing to that large sample D, but it was only desired to get a rough notion of the general run of the figures. For the sampling experiment the figures are too irregular, owing to fluctuations of sampling, to give a definite guide to the general trend. But the Macaulay and Bunyan data are fairly concordant, both forming a series descending steadily from unity for N to the lowest value for $(ABCD)$. We might of course take the value of the ratio for $(ABCD)$ alone as a measure of homo-geneity (homogeneity with respect to vocabulary) on the ground of its being the most sensitive of the four ratios: our measure would then be 0·977 for the sampling experiment, 0·662 for Macaulay and 0·577 for Bunyan. If we preferred a measure of heterogeneity we could use the complements of these figures, 0·023, 0·338 and 0·423. But this procedure would utilise only a single one of the data, and would not give a figure comparable with another case in which we had five or three samples instead of four. If we assume that the observed series approaches a geometric series $1, r, r^2, r^3, r^4$, the product of the ratios is r^{10}, and hence we can determine r by adding together the logarithms of the observed ratios and dividing by 10. Determining r in this way I found the values: sampling experiment, 0·990; Macaulay, 0·895; Bunyan, 0·861. These give the fitted geometric series shown in Table 7.9. Here the respective values of r, values each determined from all the data available, form the natural measures of homogeneity, or their complements 0·010, 0·105, 0·139, measures of heterogeneity. If the series really were a geometric series we could in the same way determine comparable figures for other cases with three, five or more samples. There is, however, no theoretical justification for assuming a geometric series. In fact the data rather suggest a graph that flattens out more quickly, the observed minimum ratios both for Macaulay and Bunyan being higher than the figures given by the fitted series. It might after all be better to try and found some measure on Table 7.7 rather than Table 7.8. This is in a sense a problem of measuring 'goodness of fit', but we do not want a measure indicating the probability of the given system of deviations in terms of fluctuations of sampling. We want a simple measure of *actual* goodness of fit, independent of the total number of observations. The contingency coefficient is not satisfactory for cases like those of Table 7.7 and would not yield comparable values if the number of samples were altered. I worked out one measure, viz. the ratio of the standard deviation of the differences between observation and expectation in Table 7.7 to the mean frequency $N/15$, expressed as a percentage. The values found for these coefficients of variation were: sampling experiment, 8·56 per cent; Macaulay, 31·13 per cent; Bunyan, 40·70 per cent. It will be remarked that our diverse measures all place the four samples from Bunyan as more heterogeneous (with regard to vocabulary of nouns) than the four essays of Macaulay, a conclusion which is certainly in accordance with my personal judgement. The problem of a satisfactory measure of heterogeneity is interesting, but I have not reached a definite conclusion.

7.12.　To summarise this rather long discussion:

It is the form of the frequency distribution for numbers of words with X occurrences which largely conditions the distribution of vocabulary over the samples and all the possible combinations of them which are shown in Table 7.1.

If the words are partitioned at random over, for example, four equal samples, the frequency $(ABCD)$ of words common to all four samples and the four frequencies of the type $(A\beta\gamma\delta)$ of words peculiar to each sample are outstanding in magnitude. The four of the type $(ABC\delta)$ and the six of the type $(AB\gamma\delta)$ are much smaller, but the latter slightly the greater of the two. While we have only shown these statements to be true in the particular instances investigated, the general similarity of all the word-distributions observed (cf. Chapter 2) warrants the expectation that they will be true in general. Similar statements may also be expected to hold for a number of equal samples other than four.

The most striking effect of heterogeneity between the samples, as when samples are combined from several different works of the same author, is to reduce the frequencies of all the positive classes below the expectation on random partitioning: the reduction is least for classes of the first order, greater for classes of the second order, and so on successively, the reduction steadily increasing with the order of the class. In less technical terms, the vocabulary of every sample is reduced, the vocabulary common to any pair of samples is reduced even more largely, the vocabulary common to any three samples is reduced more largely again, and so on.

ASSOCIATIONS

7.13.   Let us now turn to another problem arising from these same data, one concerning the frequencies of the second order. A little preliminary explanation may first be given for the reader unfamiliar with statistical

TABLE 7.10. Schematic association table

Attribute	Attribute		Total
	B	β	
A α	(AB) (αB)	$(A\beta)$ $(\alpha\beta)$	(A) (α)
Total	(B)	(β)	N

methods: for a fuller exposition he is referred to the text-book chapter cited in refs. A. Given any set of four second-order frequencies like (AB), $(A\beta)$, (αB), $(\alpha\beta)$, together with the corresponding frequencies of the first order, we may arrange them in a little table on the plan of Table 7.10. The rows add up to (A) and (α), the columns to (B) and (β), and in the bottom right-hand corner we have the grand total N. Such a table is called an *association table*. If there is no relation of any kind whatever between the attributes A

and B, we expect to find the same proportion of A's amongst the B's as amongst the non-B's, or in our notation

$$\frac{(AB)}{(B)} = \frac{(A\beta)}{(\beta)}. \tag{7.4}$$

This equates the ratios in the two columns of the table, but it is easy to show that if (7.4) holds for the columns the similar equation

$$\frac{(AB)}{(A)} = \frac{(\alpha B)}{(\alpha)}$$

must hold for the rows. Further, we have from (7.4),

$$\frac{(AB)}{(B)} = \frac{(AB)+(A\beta)}{(B)+(\beta)} = \frac{(A)}{N}$$

or

$$(AB) = \frac{(A)(B)}{N}. \tag{7.5}$$

This may be termed the *independence value* of (AB). Again, if (7.5) holds for (AB), it is easy to show that the similar equations

$$(A\beta) = \frac{(A)(\beta)}{N}, \quad (\alpha B) = \frac{(\alpha)(B)}{N}, \quad (\alpha\beta) = \frac{(\alpha)(\beta)}{N}$$

must hold for the three remaining frequencies of the second order. If $(AB)/(B)$ is not equal to but exceeds $(A\beta)/(\beta)$, in which case (AB) must also exceed its independence value, the two attributes are said to be *positively associated* or briefly *associated*. If on the contrary $(AB)/(B)$ is less than $(A\beta)/(\beta)$, or (AB) less than its independence value, the two attributes are said to be *negatively associated*. On the basis of these equations and definitions we may test for association either by comparing proportions as suggested by equation (7.4), or by comparing (AB) with its independence value as suggested by equation (7.5). But it is sometimes convenient to summarise the whole matter into a single numerical measure or 'coefficient' which will take the value zero if the attributes are independent, positive values if the association is positive and negative values if the association is negative. The simplest of such coefficients, which will very well serve our purpose, is the *association coefficient*

$$Q = \frac{(AB)(\alpha\beta)-(A\beta)(\alpha B)}{(AB)(\alpha\beta)+(A\beta)(\alpha B)}. \tag{7.6}$$

By the equations of the form (7.5) this takes the value zero, as required, when the attributes are independent. It takes positive values if the association is positive, and these values can range up to $+1$ if $(A\beta) = 0$ (all A's are B) or

$(\alpha B) = 0$ (all B's are A) or both. On the contrary it takes negative values if the association is negative, and these values can range down to -1, if $(AB) = 0$ (all B's are α) or $(\alpha\beta) = 0$ (all β's are A) or both. The coefficient can only range therefore from -1 through zero to $+1$.

TABLE 7.11. Showing the association between A, the occurrence of a noun in the sample from Part I of the *Pilgrim's Progress*, and B, its occurrence in Part II, for the total vocabulary from the four samples: data from Table 7.2

Attribute	Attribute		Total
	B	β	
A	544	461	1005
α	476	765	1241
Total	1020	1226	2246

7.14.   To take a numerical example, we have for the Bunyan data relating to Parts I and II of the *Pilgrim's Progress* in col. 5 of Table 7.2, $(AB) = 544$, $(A) = 1005$, $(B) = 1020$, $N = 2246$. If the reader draws a skeleton like that for Table 7.10, he can fill in these four numbers in the appropriate spaces and then get the frequencies for the five remaining spaces by simple subtraction: $1020 - 544 = 476 = (\alpha B)$, and so on. He will then have the association table, Table 7.11. Here

$$(AB)/(B) = 544/1020 = 0.533, \quad (A\beta)/(\beta) = 461/1226 = 0.376,$$

so that there is a clearly marked association between the presence of a noun in the vocabulary of Part I of the *Pilgrim's Progress* and its presence in Part II. Of the nouns in the sample from Part II, 53·3 per cent occur also in Part I, of the nouns not in Part II only 37·6 per cent, the total vocabulary with which we are concerned—or to use the technical term the 'universe' —being the entire vocabulary contributed by all four samples from Bunyan's works. We might, if we pleased, have tested the association by comparing the similar proportions for rows, which in this case are not very different:

$$(AB)/(A) = 544/1005 = 0.541, \quad (\alpha B)/(\alpha) = 476/1241 = 0.384,$$

that is, 54·1 per cent of the nouns present in the vocabulary of the sample from Part I occur also in the vocabulary of the sample from Part II, but only 38·4 per cent of the nouns not in the vocabulary of Part I. Or again, we might simply have compared the observed value of (AB), viz. 544, with its independence value $1020 \times 1005/2246 = 456\cdot4$; the excess is roundly 88 nouns. Finally, to get Q, we have

$$(AB)(\alpha\beta) = 416,160$$
$$(A\beta)(\alpha B) = 219,436$$

Difference $= + 196,724$

Sum $\quad = \quad 635,596$

$$Q = + 196724/635596 = +0\cdot310,$$

and this puts the matter in a nutshell. Within the given field, there is a positive but only moderate association between the presence of a noun in the vocabulary of Part I and its presence in the vocabulary of Part II. It may be emphasised that the field or universe with which we are dealing must always be borne in mind. If our universe were not merely the vocabulary for the four samples of Bunyan, but the entire vocabulary contributed by the work on Macaulay as well, the association would be largely increased. For (AB), $(A\beta)$ and (αB) would remain unaltered—they represent together the total vocabulary of nouns in the two parts of the *Pilgrim's Progress*— but $(\alpha\beta)$ would be raised by all the numerous nouns used by Macaulay but not by Bunyan. If our universe were some enormous general vocabulary of English nouns based on dictionaries, the association would be still further increased.

7.15.   In Table 7.12 are given all the coefficients of association arising from the data of Table 7.2, six for each of our sets of four samples: it seems unnecessary to give in full all the corresponding tables, which can readily

TABLE 7.12. Giving the association coefficient Q derived from the three sets of data of Table 7.2

Pair of attributes	Association coefficient Q		
	Sampling experiment	Macaulay	Bunyan
AB	$+0\cdot183$	$+0\cdot216$	$+0\cdot310$
AC	$+0\cdot146$	$+0\cdot072$	$+0\cdot105$
AD	$+0\cdot063$	$-0\cdot076$	$+0\cdot078$
BC	$+0\cdot141$	$+0\cdot215$	$-0\cdot046$
BD	$+0\cdot073$	$+0\cdot176$	$+0\cdot053$
CD	$+0\cdot110$	$-0\cdot080$	$-0\cdot025$
Mean	$+0\cdot119$	$+0\cdot087$*	$+0\cdot079$

* Mean of the three associations not involving D, $+0\cdot168$: of the three involving D, $+0\cdot007$.

be drafted by the reader on the lines of Table 7.11 if he so desires. These coefficients were a considerable surprise to me: they were so unexpectedly small. The association coefficient for Table 7.11 is actually the largest of the lot; that was indeed the reason why it was chosen for an illustration. The mean value of Q for the sampling experiment is $+0.119$, for Macaulay only $+0.087$, for Bunyan only $+0.079$. Two of the coefficients both for Macaulay and for Bunyan are actually slightly negative. Arguing in my mind that the common nouns, those with large numbers of occurrences, would in a process of sampling tend to occur in both samples of a pair and so throw up (AB) well above its independence value, I had expected much more substantial associations, say of the order of 0.5 or so. What was wrong with this argument? The first question that naturally arises is, how do these observed associations compare with the expectation on random partitioning? The required 'expected' association tables and thence their values of Q can be readily obtained from cols. 3, 5 and 7 of Table 7.8. They are as follows:

Sampling experiment $\qquad\qquad Q = +0.122$,
Macaulay: pairs AB, AC, $BC \qquad Q = +0.334$,
$\qquad\qquad$ pairs AD, BD, $CD \qquad Q = +0.114$,
Bunyan $\qquad\qquad\qquad\qquad Q = +0.258$.

The expected value of Q for the sampling experiment is in close agreement with the mean of the observed values. For Macaulay, where I have separated the associations that involve D from the others, the observed means $+0.168$ and $+0.007$ (see footnote to Table 7.12) are below expectation, as is that for Bunyan, $+0.079$. The effect of heterogeneity in so far as it implies dissimilarity is to reduce the association below expectation, only if it leads to an exceptionally similar pair the association may be increased: the value of Q for the two parts of the *Pilgrim's Progress*, $+0.310$, is above the expected value of $+0.258$. But even the expected associations, though larger than those observed, remain below the sort of values for which I had looked.

7.16.   Let us examine the matter a little further. We have taken the figures for our expected association tables from Table 7.8. Let us now see, by work on the lines of Table 7.6, how they are built up. By equation (7.2) we have the expected frequencies

$$(\alpha) = S\{f_x(\tfrac{3}{4})^x\}, \quad (\alpha\beta) = S\{f_x(\tfrac{1}{2})^x\}. \tag{7.7}$$

Hence also
$$\left.\begin{array}{l}(AB) = S\{f_x[1 - 2(\tfrac{3}{4})^x + (\tfrac{1}{2})^x]\}\\ (A\beta) = (\alpha B) = S\{f_x[(\tfrac{3}{4})^x - (\tfrac{1}{2})^x]\}\end{array}\right\}. \tag{7.8}$$

The numerical factors for (AB), $(A\beta)$ or (αB), and $(\alpha\beta)$ were duly calculated and multiplied by the successive values of f_x in the total distribution of the sampling experiment, Table 4.4, as with Table 7.6: the products are listed in Table 7.13 in the same form as the earlier table, the check total in col. 5 being the figure in col. 1 + 2 (col. 3) + col. 4. The totals at the foot of the columns must of course agree with the figures derived from Table 7.7 or 7.8. Those tables give $(AB) = 472 \cdot 29$, $(A\beta) = (\alpha B) = 478 \cdot 42$, $(\alpha\beta) = 618 \cdot 90$: Table 7.13 shows $(AB) = 472 \cdot 27$, $(A\beta) = (\alpha B) = 478 \cdot 43$, $(\alpha\beta) = 618 \cdot 89$,

TABLE 7.13. Direct calculation (on the lines of Table 7.6) of the expected class-frequencies (AB), $(A\beta)$, (αB), $(\alpha\beta)$, by random partitioning from the data of the experiment on sampling, Table 4.4

1	2	3	4	5
X	(AB)	$(A\beta)$, (αB)	$(\alpha\beta)$	Check total cf. § 7.16
1	—	247·50	495·00	990·00
2	45·87	114·69	91·75	367·00
3	48·66	51·36	21·62	173·00
4	48·13	28·44	7·00	112·01
5	40·08	14·84	2·25	72·01
6	31·00	7·63	·73	46·99
7	30·37	5·15	·32	40·99
8	24·91	2·98	·12	30·99
9	28·96	2·49	·07	34·01
10	15·10	0·94	·02	17·00
11	21·98	1·00	·01	23·99
12	17·80	·60	·00	19·00
13	9·53	·24	·00	10·01
14	9·64	·18	·00	10·00
15	12·65	·17	·00	12·99
16	2·94	·03	·00	3·00
17	9·85	·08	·00	10·01
18	6·92	·04	·00	7·00
19	5·95	·03	·00	6·01
20	4·97	·02	·00	5·01
21	1·00	·00	·00	1·00
22	3·99	·01	·00	4·01
23	6·98	·01	·00	7·00
24	2·00	·00	·00	2·00
25	1·00	·00	·00	1·00
26	4·99	·00	·00	4·99
27	3·00	·00	·00	3·00
28	4·00	·00	·00	4·00
29 up	30·00	·00	·00	30·00
Total	472·27	478·43	618·89	2048·02

values which agree within the accuracy of the arithmetic. Now look at the details, taking each row by itself: we may regard the figures of each such row as the frequencies of a component association table, these components being superposed and added up to give the resultant association table of the totals at the foot. In the first line, $X = 1$, $(AB) = 0$, and the value of Q for this component table is therefore -1. For the following lines Q takes the values:

$X = 2$,	$Q = -0{\cdot}515$	$X = 5$,	$Q = -0{\cdot}419$	$X = 8$,	$Q = -0{\cdot}493$
3,	$-0{\cdot}430$	6,	$-0{\cdot}440$	9,	$-0{\cdot}525$
4,	$-0{\cdot}412$	7,	$-0{\cdot}464$	10,	$-0{\cdot}559$

It is hardly necessary to continue further: indeed the precision to which the frequencies have been tabulated rapidly becomes insufficient to give the coefficients with any accuracy; for the last three coefficients above more extended figures were used. It is clear that all the component associations are *negative*, and on consideration it is evident that random partitioning must lead to such a result. For, returning to our mechanical analogy, suppose a word occurs four times and is consequently written on four of our counters. If the first counter falls into quadrant A, there are only three left which have a chance of falling into B. But if it has not fallen into A it may itself have fallen into B, and anyway there are still the three others left that have a chance of doing so. Hence the proportion of A's that are B will tend to be less than the proportion of non-A's that are B. Starting from the value -1 for $X = 1$, we see that the numerical value of Q first decreases and then begins to increase again: in fact it may be shown that with increasing X the value of Q tends again to -1 in the limit. It is only in the pool of these elementary or component tables, given by the totals at the foot, that the association becomes positive—a well-known effect of pooling (refs. A) that may often lead to fallacy. Evidently if the association had been zero for each row instead of negative, the association for the row of totals would have been considerably higher.

7.17. But this remark at once suggested the source of my difficulty. In the argument of §7.15, that nouns of frequent occurrence would tend to be present in both samples and so throw up (AB) above its independence value, I had unconsciously been thinking (as one always tends to think) in terms of the familiar simple random sampling, not random partitioning; and this fundamentally alters the whole matter, for with simple random sampling every elementary table for a single value of X must be an independence table. If, instead of 'partitioning' such a distribution as that of Table 4.4 into four equal samples, we wanted to draw from it four equal samples by simple random sampling, we might take all our counters with the words written on them and mix them up in a bag. Then we should draw a counter, note the word, *return the counter to the bag* and stir it up: draw another counter, note the word, and again return the counter, and so on until we had accumulated a sample of the required size. Then we should proceed to form another sample in precisely the same way, and so on. Since, for words with a given number of tickets or occurrences x, the drawing of words for one sample has nothing whatever to do with the drawing of words for any other, they must tend to be quite independent drawings, and therefore to give elementary tables with $Q = 0$. On this method of procedure, if the total number of occurrences is S_1, the chance of a word with x occurrences being drawn at any one drawing is x/S_1, and the chance of its not being drawn in, say s_1 drawings, is

$$q_x = \left(1 - \frac{x}{S_1}\right)^{s_1} = e^{-x(s_1/S_1)}, \qquad (7.9)$$

using the exponential approximation; or for the special case of a sample one-fourth the size of the original,

$$q_x = e^{-x/4}. \qquad (7.10)$$

If $p_x = 1 - q_x$, we then have

$$\left. \begin{array}{c} (AB) = S(f_x p_x^2) \\ (A\beta) = (\alpha B) = S(f_x p_x q_x) \\ (\alpha\beta) = S(f_x q_x^2) \end{array} \right\}. \qquad (7.11)$$

The values of q_x were calculated by equation (7.10), thence p_x^2, $p_x q_x$ and q_x^2, and the products by f_x were found and tabulated as in Table 7.14, in the same form as in Table 7.13. The first point that may strike the reader on comparing the two tables is that col. 2 of Table 7.14 leads off, not with a blank, but with a substantial contribution to (AB); how, he may ask himself, can a word that only occurs once come into both samples? The answer is of course that this may happen because every counter is always returned to the bag after drawing and noting; the second sample is drawn from a bag the contents of which are precisely the same as for the first, so that the word may well be drawn for both samples or indeed may be drawn twice or more in the same sample. Turning to the foot of Table 7.14, (AB) is increased by roundly 40 as compared with the figure in Table 7.13, $(A\beta)$ and (αB) reduced by 111, and $(\alpha\beta)$ increased by 181. In consequence (A) and (B) are reduced roundly by 71 (from 950·70 to 880·18) and the association very considerably increased as compared with the figure for random partitioning. For the totals of Table 7.14, $Q = +0.503$, just the sort of association I had expected to find for the presence of a word in two samples of the same author, as against the value of only $+0.122$ (§ 7.15) for the results of Table 7.13.

TABLE 7.14. Direct calculation of the expected class frequencies (AB), $(A\beta)$, (αB), $(\alpha\beta)$ by simple random sampling (not random partitioning) from the data of the experiment in sampling, Table 4.4

1	2	3	4	5
X	(AB)	$(A\beta)$, (αB)	$(\alpha\beta)$	Check total cf. § 7.16
1	48·44	170·55	600·46	990·00
2	56·82	87·60	134·99	367·01
3	48·16	43·11	38·61	172·99
4	44·76	26·04	15·16	112·00
5	36·66	14·72	5·91	72·01
6	28·36	8·15	2·34	47·00
7	27·99	5·89	1·24	41·01
8	23·18	3·63	·56	31·00
9	27·21	3·21	·38	34·01
10	14·32	1·28	·12	17·00
11	21·03	1·44	·10	24·01
12	17·16	·90	·05	19·01
13	9·24	·37	·02	10·00
14	9·40	·29	·01	9·99
15	12·40	·30	·01	13·01
16	2·89	·05	·00	2·99
17	9·72	·14	·00	10·00
18	6·85	·08	·00	7·01
19	5·90	·05	·00	6·00
20	4·93	·03	·00	4·99
21	0·99	·01	·00	1·01
22	3·97	·02	·00	4·01
23	6·96	·02	·00	7·00
24	1·99	·00	·00	1·99
25	1·00	·00	·00	1·00
26	4·98	·01	·00	5·00
27	2·99	·00	·00	2·99
28	3·99	·00	·00	3·99
29 up	30·00	·00	·00	30·00
Total	512·29	367·89	799·96	2048·03

7.18. Summarising briefly the results of §§ 7.13 *et seq.*, we found from our data that all associations for the presence of a word in two samples of the same author, the field of observation or 'universe' being the total vocabulary given by four samples, were quite small. For very similar samples, each spread over the same work, as in the sampling experiment, they averaged only + 0·119, for the Macaulay data + 0·087, for Bunyan + 0·079. Trial showed that the first value was in good accord with the expectation on random partitioning, while the second and third were in defect, heterogeneity tending on the whole to reduce the associations and even giving some of them small negative values. Only when the heterogeneous data happen to provide an exceptionally similar pair of samples, like those from Parts I and II of the *Pilgrim's Progress*, is the association possibly thrown up above the expected value. The basis for general conclusions is very limited, but we have at least no reason to expect that similar sets of samples taken from authors other than Macaulay and Bunyan would yield very different results. Hence if, for a set of samples generally similar in subject, we *do* get a very different result, we may have reason to suspect that our samples differ in some essential respect from those of the Bunyan and Macaulay work. If there were any reason to doubt the authenticity or authorship of any of the samples, a possible explanation might be that they were not in fact all by the same hand.

VOCABULARY RATIOS OF BUNYAN TO MACAULAY

7.19.   In §§ 5.1–5.13 it was emphasised that the ratio of the vocabulary of one author to that of another for a given size of sample is a function of the size of that sample. The limiting value of the ratio for very small samples is necessarily unity, and the limiting value for very large samples W_2/W_1, where the W's are the respective unknown total vocabularies at risk. Between these limits it was shown that in simple theoretical cases the course of the ratio might take the oddest forms. But these were *theoretical* cases, the frequency distributions for the respective authors being assumed to be, for example, compound Poisson distributions of only two components, and the odd features noticed may have been due only to the very simplicity of this assumption. Actual word-distributions, so far as we know them at least, do not present such obvious and discrete compoundedness. Our data for Macaulay and Bunyan are very modest, the sample for the latter amounting to no more than some 16,000 occurrences roundly; but can we not make some use of these data to get a notion of the course of the vocabulary ratios for the two authors up to this limit?

7.20.   If for each of two authors we have four samples A, B, C and D of 4000 occurrences each, it is evident that we can form four vocabulary ratios for samples of 4000, 8000, 12,000 and 16,000 by taking first the ratio for A, then the ratio for A and B together, then the ratio for A, B and C together, and finally the ratio for the entire aggregate of A, B, C and D. To do this we must have classified the words of the entire vocabulary as in Table 7.1 or 7.2; indeed it will be very convenient to have written out in full the frequencies for all classes of all orders. The number of words in sample A of one of the authors will then be (A). The additional number of words contributed by bringing in B will be (αB), the number of words in B but not in A. The further additional words introduced by bringing in C will be $(\alpha\beta C)$, the number of words in C but neither in A nor B. Finally, the additional words introduced by bringing in D will be $(\alpha\beta\gamma D)$, the number of words in D but not in A nor B nor C. This last addition is really only desirable as a check on our arithmetic (it is quite easy to make the slip of picking up a wrong frequency by mistake) since we obviously must thus arrive at the known total vocabulary for the author, N, or S_0 in our former notation: we have in fact

$$N = (A) + (\alpha B) + (\alpha\beta C) + (\alpha\beta\gamma D).$$

This is easily seen to be true on expanding the first three frequencies in terms of frequencies of the fourth order, when we arrive back at the complete list of Table 7.1 with the exception of $(\alpha\beta\gamma\delta)$, which is zero: generally, we have

$$(A) + (\alpha B) = N - (\alpha\beta),$$
$$(A) + (\alpha B) + (\alpha\beta C) = N - (\alpha\beta\gamma),$$
$$(A) + (\alpha B) + (\alpha\beta C) + (\alpha\beta\gamma D) = N - (\alpha\beta\gamma\delta) = N.$$

Determining the vocabularies for successive sizes of sample in this way for both authors we can then work out the ratios.

7.21. But the four vocabulary ratios at which we shall arrive in this way will be an arbitrary set, given by taking the four samples for each author in the particular order A, B, C, D. If the samples had been truly random samples this would have been of no essential importance, for the four from either author could only differ from one another by quantities of the order of fluctuations of sampling. But if, as in our case, the samples are taken from different works, on taking them in a different order we are quite likely to arrive at a more or less substantially different set of ratios. It occurred to me that it might be possible to eliminate such arbitrariness by taking the samples for each author in every possible order and averaging the results. As a matter of fact the effects of heterogeneity of samples cannot be wholly eliminated in this way (see below §§ 7.23, 7.24) but this was not realised at the time since the work of §§ 7.1 to 7.12 had not been completed; the reader *is* in a position to appreciate the difficulty if he likes to think it out for himself. Notwithstanding this, it may be of interest to present the work as it was done. For Macaulay we are once again given trouble by the fact that while A, B, and C are samples of 4000 occurrences roundly, D is a sample of 8000. Table 7.15 shows the work for this author. There are 24 possible orders in which the samples can be taken, as listed in col. 2. The first order is that already considered, ABCD. The first vocabulary, for a sample of 4000, is

(A), which is 1537 from Table 7.2. Bringing in B, we have to add (αB): this is (B) − (AB), or from Table 7.2 1333 − 668 = 665, and 1537 + 665 = 2202, the vocabulary for a sample of 8000. Bringing in ($\alpha\beta C$), which may most

TABLE 7.15. Estimation of size of vocabulary (nouns) for various sizes of sample from Macaulay's four essays, by taking the four samples A, B, C and D in all possible orders. D being a sample of 8000 occurrences does not properly occur in col. 3, but the mean vocabulary for a sample of 4000 from D has been taken from the data of Table 4.5 and an alternative mean for the column entered if this be included

1	2	3	4	5	6
	Samples taken in the order	Vocabulary for approximate size of sample			
		4000	8000	12,000	16,000
1	ABCD	1537	2202	2832	—
2	ABDC	,,	2202	—	3086
3	ACBD	,,	2381	2832	—
4	ACDB	,,	2381	—	3260
5	ADBC	,,	—	2729	3086
6	ADCB	,,	—	2729	3260
7	BACD	1333	2202	2832	—
8	BADC	,,	2202	—	3086
9	BCAD	,,	2207	2832	—
10	BCDA	,,	2207	—	3096
11	BDAC	,,	—	2539	3086
12	BDCA	,,	—	2539	3096
13	CABD	1545	2381	2832	—
14	CADB	,,	2381	—	3260
15	CBAD	,,	2207	2832	—
16	CBDA	,,	2207	—	3096
17	CDAB	,,	—	2734	3260
18	CDBA	,,	—	2734	3096
19	DABC	(1413)	2048	2729	3086
20	DACB	,,	2048	2729	3260
21	DBAC	,,	2048	2539	3086
22	DBCA	,,	2048	2539	3096
23	DCAB	,,	2048	2734	3260
24	DCBA	,,	2048	2734	3096
—	Mean	1472 (1457)	2192	2722	3147

readily be got from Table 7.1 as ($\alpha\beta CD$) + ($\alpha\beta C\delta$) = 173 + 457 = 630, the vocabulary for a sample of 12,000 is 2832. Since D is a sample of 8000 (as before, samples have been treated throughout as having these round values) we do not, with this order of taking the samples, get any value of the vocabulary for a sample of 16,000: but adding ($\alpha\beta\gamma D$), which from Table 7.1 is 711, we have 2832 + 711 = 3543, which agrees with the value of N and checks our work. The final control column for the sample of 20,000 has been omitted, as we do not want the figure, there being no sample greater than 16,000 for Bunyan. The work is continued in just the same way. For line 2 the order is *ABDC*: the first vocabulary will be (*A*) again; then (*αB*) will be added as before; then (*αβD*), which will give the vocabulary for a sample of 16,000, not 12,000, and finally (*αβCδ*) to check the work. When we come

TABLE 7.16. Estimation of size of vocabulary (nouns) for various sizes of samples from the four works of Bunyan, by taking the samples A, B, C and D in all possible orders

1	2	3	4	5	6
	Samples taken in the order	Vocabulary for approximate size of sample			
		4000	8000	12,000	16,000
1	ABCD	1005	1481	1907	2246
2	ABDC	,,	1481	1894	,,
3	ACBD	,,	1545	1907	,,
4	ACDB	,,	1545	1949	,,
5	ADBC	,,	1534	1894	,,
6	ADCB	,,	1534	1949	,,
7	BACD	1020	1481	1907	,,
8	BADC	,,	1481	1894	,,
9	BCAD	,,	1595	1907	,,
10	BCDA	,,	1595	1984	,,
11	BDAC	,,	1549	1894	,,
12	BDCA	,,	1549	1984	,,
13	CABD	1030	1545	1907	,,
14	CADB	,,	1545	1949	,,
15	CBAD	,,	1595	1907	,,
16	CBDA	,,	1595	1984	,,
17	CDAB	,,	1576	1949	,,
18	CDBA	,,	1576	1984	,,
19	DABC	996	1534	1894	,,
20	DACB	,,	1534	1949	,,
21	DBAC	,,	1549	1894	,,
22	DBCA	,,	1549	1984	,,
23	DCAB	,,	1576	1949	,,
24	DCBA	,,	1576	1984	,,
—	Mean	1013	1547	1933	2246

to lines 19–24 the leading sample is D. But D being a sample of 8000 we only start in col. 4 of the table. It seems so obviously unfair that D (the essay on Bacon) should not contribute its quota to col. 3 that I have entered (in brackets) the figure for the mean vocabulary of samples of about 4000 from that essay, i.e. the mean of the six values of S_0 for the samples *ab*, *ac*, etc. in col. 2 of Table 4.5, and have given an alternative mean for the column based on this figure in addition to the other three. Actually its inclusion makes no great difference. In every column of the table it will be noticed that the figures are largely repeated: this is inevitable, for in col. 4, for example, it can obviously make no difference whether we have introduced A and B in the order AB or the order BA, so the figure 2202 occurs four times. The same thing happens with the four orders starting with A and C, and the four starting with B and C, and at the foot of the column (D) is repeated six times. Similar repetitions occur in cols. 5 and 6. The table could have been very much condensed from such considerations, but it was thought better to keep it in the primitive form exhibiting clearly what was being done. The exceptional size of sample D is most troublesome, for it evidently results in uneven weighting of the different samples in the different columns, and it seems impossible to do anything to mitigate this unevenness except in the case of col. 3. The mean vocabulary, rounded off to the nearest unit, is given at the foot of each column, with the alternative mean in brackets for col. 3. Corresponding data for Bunyan are given in Table 7.16. Here everything is quite straightforward, and the four samples enter with equal weights into the columns for each size of sample.

7.22.   The mean vocabularies thus obtained are assembled in lines 8–11, cols. 3 and 4 of Table 7.17, and the ratios of the Bunyan vocabulary to the Macaulay vocabulary are entered in col. 5. These ratios run surprisingly smoothly and show a small but continuous *increase* from the sample of 4000 to the sample of 16,000. If this increase were real and not illusory it would be rather remarkable, for the vocabulary ratio must start from the value unity for indefinitely small samples, and must accordingly have dropped to a minimum for a sample of something under 4000 before rising again over the subsequent range. With a view to the possible determination of some earlier points on the graph, perhaps even checking the value of the ratio for samples of 4000, I started an investigation by way of random sampling. In my manuscript lists of nouns, the nouns on each page had been counted and the number entered at the foot together with the current total from the start, so that a noun with any number in the list (e.g. the 206th or the 3457th) could fairly readily be found. Lists of random numbers between the limits 0001 and 4000 were compiled to determine the words to be taken from the manuscript sheets. To determine which *sample* of Bunyan should be taken, lists of random digits between 1 and 4 were drawn up. As regards Macaulay, sub-samples *a* and *b* together of sample D were taken as one sample of 4000, and sub-samples *c* and *d* together as another, thus making five samples of 4000 in all: lists of random digits from 1 to 5 determined which of these should be taken. The work was done without difficulty on these lines, but proved very laborious and I had had quite enough of it when four samples of 100 had been compiled for each author. These gave the following vocabularies and ratios for samples of 100 occurrences:

Macaulay vocabulary	Bunyan vocabulary	Ratio
90	80	0·889
93	77	0·828
96	83	0·865
91	83	0·912
Mean 92·5	80·75	0·873

TABLE 7.17. Showing the observed and expected vocabularies of Macaulay and Bunyan for various sizes of sample, together with the ratios of Bunyan vocabulary to Macaulay vocabulary. Observed vocabularies for samples of 100 and 400 occurrences obtained from random samples (§ 7.22): for samples of 4000 to 16,000 from Tables 7.15, 7.16, numbers rounded to nearest unit. Expected vocabularies calculated from the frequency distributions of Tables 6.4 and 6.7. Chart in fig. 7.1

1	2	3	4	5	6	7	8
	Size of sample	Observation			Expectation		
		Macaulay	Bunyan	Ratio	Macaulay	Bunyan	Ratio
1	0	—	—	1·000	—	—	1·000
2	100	92·5	80·75	0·873	94·3	84·1	0·892
3	400	305	246	0·807	316·3	261·3	0·826
4	500	—	—	—	380	309	0·813
5	1,000	—	—	—	648	504	0·778
6	2,000	—	—	—	1046	785	0·750
7	3,000	—	—	—	1351	994	0·736
8	4,000 {	1472 (1457)	1013 —	0·688 (0·695)	1603 —	1164 —	0·726 —
9	8,000	2192	1547	0·706	2331	1651	0·708
10	12,000	2722	1933	0·710	2834	1986	0·701
11	16,000	3147	2246	0·714	3224	2246	0·697

It is obvious that fluctuations of sampling are large, as they must be for such small samples, and we cannot trust even the mean of the four as having any great precision. The result may however suffice further to convince the reader that for such small samples we must find a ratio much nearer unity than the 0·7 or so of the larger samples. The words having been noted on card catalogues, the four samples for each author could be pooled into one sample of 400; the vocabularies then were

Macaulay 305,   Bunyan 246,   Ratio 0·807.

These data have been brought together into lines 2 and 3, cols. 3–5 of Table 7.17. It is perhaps as well that I had not the energy to carry this method of sampling further so as to fill the gap up to samples of 4000. For strictly, as now seems clear, the samples should have been obtained by random partitioning, not random sampling: for these very small samples it does not seem likely that the two methods would lead to appreciably different results.

7.23.   We return now to the question whether the apparent rise in the ratio over the range from 4000 to 16,000 can be trusted. When the work was first done I saw no way of answering this question except by some method of taking out random samples of 4000 so as to control the first low value of the ratio obtained by the rather questionable method of Tables 7.15, 7.16,

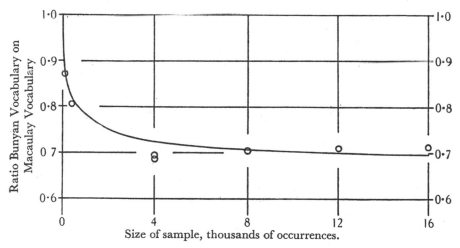

Fig. 7.1. Graph of the expected vocabulary ratios for Bunyan to Macaulay, and values of the ratios observed: from Table 7.17.

and this had proved far too slow and laborious to be practicable. But now, with the first part of the present chapter before us, there is no difficulty. By means of equation (7.1) we can obtain from Tables 6.4 and 6.7, giving the total noun-distributions for Macaulay and for Bunyan, the vocabularies to be expected for any size of sample desired, partitioned at random out of the total aggregate, and thence the ratio to be expected. This work was carried out for all the sizes of sample shown in col. 2 of Table 7.17, samples of 500, 1000, 2000 and 3000 having been included in order better to define the theoretical graph over the portion of rather rapid curvature. As throughout the work, the totals were regarded as roundly 20,000 for Macaulay, and 16,000 for Bunyan, so that e.g. for a sample of 1000 the fraction $(r-k)/r$ of equation (7.1) would be 19/20 for Macaulay and 15/16 for Bunyan.

Calculating the sum of equation (7.1) for this size of sample, for Macaulay it came to 2895·479, giving for the vocabulary 3543 − 2895·479 = 647·521, or roundly 648 as in Table 7.17, col. 6. For Bunyan the sum came to 1741·588, giving as the vocabulary 2246 − 1741·588 = 504·412, or roundly 504, as in Table 7.17, col. 7. Thence we have the ratio 0·778 as in col. 8 of the same table. The chart, fig. 7.1, shows the graph of the expected ratios and the points given by the observed ratios. Glancing first at the figures for the small random samples, we see that the mean vocabularies for the samples of 100 are very close to expectation but both slightly below it: the deficiency is a little more for Bunyan than for Macaulay, and the ratio consequently a little below expectation, 0·873 against 0·892. For the single sample of 400 the vocabularies are rather more below expectation, the respective deficiencies being 11·3 and 15·3: but if we may take the standard errors for these small samples as being approximately the square roots of the expectations, that is 17·8 and 16·2, both differences are well within the limits of fluctuations of sampling. It is difficult to see indeed how, with the method of sampling adopted, any bias could arise. Now turning to the lower part of the table or looking at the chart, we see that the expected ratios *do not show any rise*, but fall rapidly at first, slowly but continuously later, over the whole course of the table. Our question then is answered. The method of Tables 7.15, 7.16 has given results that are slightly but definitely misleading. The rise in the ratios that the method suggests is illusory.

7.24. What is the source of the error? If we examine in more detail the lower part of Table 7.17, we see that the mean vocabularies arrived at by the method of Tables 7.15, 7.16 are in every case well below the expected values—with naturally the exception of the last vocabulary for Bunyan, which is not an estimated expectation but the actual vocabulary observed. For the samples of 4000 the proportionate deficiency of the Bunyan vocabulary from expectation is considerably greater than that for Macaulay, with the result that the observed ratio is depressed. But this at once brings to mind the divergences noted in Table 7.8 (§7.8) where the observed frequencies (*A*), (*B*), (*C*) and (*D*) are all below expectation, and where also (cf. Table 7.9) the relative deficiency is on the average greater for Bunyan than for Macaulay. The matter may be pursued a little further. If from Tables 7.7 and 7.8 we work out the mean *expected* vocabularies corresponding to Table 7.15 and Table 7.16, col. 4, for Macaulay and for Bunyan, we find for Macaulay the ratio of observation to expectation to be 0·940, for Bunyan 0·937. These two differ but slightly, and correspondingly for samples of 8000 the vocabulary ratio observed in Table 7.17 is very little below expectation. If we go on and work out the mean values of the expected vocabularies corresponding to Table 7.15 and Table 7.16, col. 5, we find for Macaulay the ratio of observation to expectation to be 0·960, but for Bunyan the *higher* value 0·972. In this case, therefore, for samples of 12,000, we find in Table 7.17 an observed vocabulary ratio slightly *above* expectation. The final observed ratio, for samples of 16,000, is bound to be above expectation, since the vocabulary for Bunyan in col. 7 is an observed figure, the vocabulary for Macaulay in col. 6 an expected figure as usual somewhat in excess of that observed. There is in fact a fundamental fallacy involved in the method of Tables 7.15, 7.16. The samples are heterogeneous: this heterogeneity affects the values of all the class frequencies, as indicated by our previous discussion, and no method of averaging by taking the samples in all possible orders can eliminate the bias thus introduced. The method cannot yield accurate results. But it seemed worth discussing, as it might easily have occurred to somebody else and the source of fallacy is perhaps not very obvious. It may be emphasised that the graph only gives the course of the vocabulary ratio for various sizes of sample taken by random partitioning *from the given data*, limited to our given samples, from the four essays of Macaulay and the four works of Bunyan. The graph of fig. 7.1 would obviously not necessarily be identical with the first part of a graph based on much more extensive data from the two authors.

7.25. It was pointed out in §§ 5.2 and 5.12 how very laborious would be the work of determining the course of the vocabulary ratios for the complete works of any pair of authors by the direct process of taking samples, even if such samples were taken by a process of 'spread sampling', which the results of § 7.8 have shown might not be entirely satisfactory. The work of the last few paragraphs suggests an entirely different but indirect method, the method which in fact we have applied on a small scale to our very limited samples from Macaulay and Bunyan. Supposing we desired to form a graph of the vocabulary ratios based on the complete works of these two authors, we should have to form the complete word-distribution for each, and could then proceed to calculate vocabulary ratios exactly as in § 7.8. This sounds, and certainly would be, a big undertaking, but it would be far less troublesome and less laborious than any method of sampling, and the results more trustworthy. The work would be simple and straightforward: each author's works could be read straight through, and the occurrences of words (or nouns, if we limited ourselves to nouns) booked up on cards as they occurred. There would be no troublesome and finicking breaking up of each page into sub-samples, or annoying little practical difficulties such as the problem of what to do with half-filled pages. This method would give with ease and accuracy the first sharply curved portion of the graph: the magnitude of fluctuations of sampling for small samples would make many repetitions necessary to get anything like precise ratios by the direct method. For Table 7.17 I took four samples of 100 and averaged the results. One hundred samples of 100 would have been more like a satisfactory basis. I had only a single sample of 400, and this is clearly a very inadequate basis for determining the ratio with anything like precision.

REFERENCES

A. STATISTICAL METHOD

For the chapter generally see Y & K, Chapter 1, 'Theory of Attributes—Notation and Terminology'; for §§ 7.13–7.18, Chapter 3, 'Association of Attributes'.

§ 7.16. Effect of pooling on association: see Y & K, § 4.14.

§ 7.23. Standard error taken as the square root of the expectation: see Y & K, §§ 10.40–10.47, especially equation (10.27) and the example in § 10.47.

Chapter 8

THE ALPHABETICAL DISTRIBUTION OF ENGLISH VOCABULARY: ETYMOLOGICAL ANALYSIS OF THE BUNYAN AND MACAULAY DATA

8.1.   From an early stage of this work it had been my practice to count the number of cards (i.e. words or nouns) under each letter of the alphabet in the card catalogue for any sample, since the record of such a count is of great convenience for checking. Little attention, however, was paid to the alphabetical distribution of vocabulary obtained in this way until quite a late stage had been reached. When the work on Bunyan had been finished, I happened on one occasion to have open before me at the same time the first drawer of the Bunyan cards and the first drawer of the cards for the three essays of Macaulay, A, B and C. One can obviously form a rough judgment of the numbers of nouns falling under each initial letter from the distances between the guide cards—for my cards 1 inch = 100 cards packed close—and to my surprise it was evident at sight that the distributions of the two authors were quite substantially different. The first and most conspicuous difference simply hit one in the eye, for while in Macaulay the A's were very much more numerous than the B's, in Bunyan the B's were more numerous than the A's. Further inspection showed other points of difference. Relatively to the vocabulary of Macaulay, E's and I's seemed clearly deficient in Bunyan and W's obviously in excess, since they occupied little less space than the T's instead of only about half the space. On the other hand, when one compared the look of the card drawers for the three essays A, B and C of Macaulay with that of the separate card drawers for essay D, the experiment on sampling, the two distributions looked very much the same. The facts seemed so odd, that they called for further investigation.

8.2.   The contrast between Bunyan and Macaulay as regards alphabetical distribution of vocabulary is clearly brought out by Table 8.1. Col. 2 gives the number of nouns in the four samples from Bunyan falling under each letter of the alphabet and col. 3 gives the corresponding number of nouns for the four samples from Macaulay, A, B, C and D pooled together. In cols. 4 and 5 these absolute figures are reduced for comparability to proportions per 10,000. Looking at these last columns, we see that Macaulay as compared with Bunyan shows a heavy relative excess of A's, E's and I's,

and a heavy or moderately heavy deficiency of B's, F's, H's and W's. These
are the most conspicuous differences.

8.3.   In Table 8.2 the differences between the two authors are brought
out in another way, by first *ranking* the initial letters according to their
frequencies and then attaching to each letter the number of its rank. Cols.

TABLE 8.1. Showing the alphabetical distribution of the nouns in the vocabularies of the total samples from Bunyan and Macaulay. Cols. 2 and 3 give the
actual numbers of nouns with each initial letter, cols. 4 and 5 the distributions
per 10,000 nouns

1	2	3	4	5
Initial letter of noun	Number of nouns		Per 10,000	
	Bunyan	Macaulay	Bunyan	Macaulay
A	111	249	494	703
B	147	169	654	477
C	210	391	935	1104
D	153	237	681	669
E	69	162	307	457
F	112	150	499	423
G	72	107	321	302
H	110	112	490	316
I	72	172	321	485
J	22	27	98	76
K	18	22	80	62
L	84	122	374	344
M	124	209	552	590
N	40	52	178	147
O	41	73	183	206
P	188	338	837	954
Q	7	14	31	40
R	133	191	592	539
S	256	380	1140	1073
T	112	179	499	505
U	16	22	71	62
V	43	64	191	181
W	100	89	445	251
X	—	—	—	—
Y	5	8	22	23
Z	1	4	4	11
Total	2246	3543	9999	10,000

2 and 3 show the ranking of the alphabet for Bunyan, cols. 4 and 5 the
ranking for Macaulay: two letters with the same frequency have simply
been left in their alphabetical order. Cols. 7 and 8 give the rank of each
letter in the samples from Bunyan and Macaulay respectively. Where two
letters have the same frequency, each has been assigned the mean of the

two ranks concerned: thus F and T in Bunyan, of ranks 8 and 9, have each been assigned rank 8.5, while G and I have each been assigned rank 14·5. It will be noticed that ranks have been numbered as one would number an

TABLE 8.2. In cols. 2–5 the data of cols. 1–3 of Table 8.1 are re-arranged by ranking the initial letters in order of their frequency. Cols. 6–8 give the rank of each initial letter in the respective authors. Where frequencies are equal, ranks are averaged: e.g. F and T in Bunyan are each assigned the rank 8.5. Col. 9 gives the differences between the ranks of the letters in the two authors: thus A, which stands only tenth in frequency in Bunyan, stands fourth in Macaulay, a difference of 6 points

1	2	3	4	5	6	7	8	9
	Bunyan		Macaulay			Rank in		
Rank	Initial	Fre-quency	Initial	Fre-quency	Initial	Bunyan	Macaulay	Difference of ranks
1	S	256	C	391	A	10	4	−6
2	C	210	S	380	B	5	10	+5
3	P	188	P	338	C	2	1	−1
4	D	153	A	249	D	4	5	+1
5	B	147	D	237	E	16	11	−5
6	R	133	M	209	F	8·5	12	+3·5
7	M	124	R	191	G	14·5	15	+0·5
8	F	112⎫	T	179	H	11	14	+3
9	T	112⎭	I	172	I	14·5	9	−5·5
10	A	111	B	169	J	20	20	—
11	H	110	E	162	K	21	21·5	+0·5
12	W	100	F	150	L	13	13	—
13	L	84	L	122	M	7	6	−1
14	G	72⎫	H	112	N	19	19	—
15	I	72⎭	G	107	O	18	17	−1
16	E	69	W	89	P	3	3	—
17	V	43	O	73	Q	23	23	—
18	O	41	V	64	R	6	7	+1
19	N	40	N	52	S	1	2	+1
20	J	22	J	27	T	8·5	8	−0·5
21	K	18	K	22⎫	U	22	21·5	−0·5
22	U	16	U	22⎭	V	17	18	+1
23	Q	7	Q	14	W	12	16	+4
24	Y	5	Y	8	X	26	26	—
25	Z	1	Z	4	Y	24	24	—
26	X	—	X	—	Z	25	25	—

order of merit: 1, 2, 3, ... are the most frequent initial letters, ... 24, 25, 26 the least frequent. In col. 9 have been added the differences of the ranks in cols. 7 and 8, a positive sign meaning that the letter stands lower in the Macaulay list, a negative sign that it stands higher. The most conspicuous differences in this column are as follows, affecting the seven letters already mentioned in § 8.2:

A, 6 points nearer top in Macaulay than in Bunyan
B, 5   ,,   bottom   ,,   ,,
E, 5   ,,   top   ,,   ,,
F, 3·5 ,,   bottom   ,,   ,,
H, 3   ,,   bottom   ,,   ,,
I, 5·5 ,,   top   ,,   ,,
W, 4   ,,   bottom   ,,   ,,

There are 11 other differences of only a single unit or less, and for the remaining eight letters the ranks are identical in the two authors. From this it is evident that, in spite of conspicuous differences for a few letters, in the bulk the two distributions are not greatly dissimilar. In both S, C and P stand at the top (with only the slight interchange of order for C and S), while N, J, K, U, Q, Y, Z and X tail off at the bottom. The impression given is that of a general similarity broken by some source of disturbance affecting in the main a few letters only. For the moment let us leave it at that, just bearing in mind as a rough indication of the magnitude of the disturbance the figures given above: there are 7 differences in rank of 3 units or more, and of these 4 are differences of 5 units or more.

8.4.   The next point for investigation clearly is this: do we find any very much closer degree of consistence between samples from different works *of the same author*, or not? If not, if the vocabulary of one and the same author may exhibit wide variations in its alphabetical distribution as he passes

TABLE 8.3. Showing the alphabetical distributions of the nouns for the four separate samples from Bunyan's works

1	2	3	4	5	1	2	3	4	5
Initial letter of noun	Frequency in sample from Bunyan				Initial letter of noun	Frequency in sample from Bunyan			
	A	B	C	D		A	B	C	D
A	44	40	60	53	O	15	21	17	26
B	61	72	64	61	P	80	89	80	77
C	95	93	105	88	Q	2	4	4	2
D	74	61	71	65	R	62	57	53	54
E	27	29	33	37	S	121	117	109	106
F	52	53	49	57	T	58	47	44	59
G	36	40	39	36	U	3	3	8	9
H	47	57	55	42	V	15	17	12	20
I	24	27	30	25	W	54	48	53	45
J	10	9	11	10	X	—	—	—	—
K	11	13	7	9	Y	4	2	3	2
L	37	43	39	38	Z	—	—	—	1
M	51	58	64	53	Total	1005	1020	1030	996
N	22	20	20	21					

from one portion of his field to another, further enquiry seems hardly to be called for, for the distribution would then appear to be a function of subject rather than author. Tables 8.3–8.6 help to answer this question. Table 8.3 gives the alphabetical distributions for the four samples from Bunyan's works, and Table 8.4 the resulting ranking of the alphabet for each sample,

TABLE 8.4. Giving the ranks of the initial letters for the four distributions of Table 8.3, together with the ranking for the total distributions, in col. 6, from Table 8.2, col. 7

1	2	3	4	5	6
Initial letter of noun	Rank in sample from Bunyan				Total
	A	B	C	D	
A	12	13·5	7	9·5	10
B	6	4	5·5	5	5
C	2	2	2	2	2
D	4	5	4	4	4
E	15	15	15	14	16
F	9	9	11	7	8·5
G	14	13·5	13·5	15	14·5
H	11	7·5	8	12	11
I	16	16	16	17	14·5
J	21	21	20	20·5	20
K	20	20	22	20·5	21
L	13	12	13·5	13	13
M	10	6	5·5	9·5	7
N	17	18	17	18	19
O	18·5	17	18	16	18
P	3	3	3	3	3
Q	24	22	23	23·5	23
R	5	7·5	9·5	8	6
S	1	1	1	1	1
T	7	11	12	6	8·5
U	23	23	21	22	22
V	18·5	19	19	19	17
W	8	10	9·5	11	12
X	25·5	25·5	25·5	26	26
Y	22	24	24	23·5	24
Z	25·5	25·5	25·5	25	25

with the corresponding ranking for the total vocabulary from Table 8.2 for comparison in the last column. Tables 8.5 and 8.6 are similar tables for the four samples from Macaulay's *Essays*: in the case of Table 8.5 it must be remembered that sample D was based on some 8000 occurrences, not about 4000 as for A, B and C. Now take Table 8.4 and note the differences of rank of 3 units or more for every possible pair of the four samples. Thus taking the pair A and B, we find for H a difference of 3·5, for M a difference of 4, and for T a difference of 4. Proceeding in this way, we find the following differences:

Pair of samples	Differences of rank of 3 units or more	Pair of samples	Differences of rank of 3 units or more
AB	3·5, 4, 4	BC	6·5
AC	5, 3, 4·5, 4·5, 5	BD	4, 4·5, 3·5, 5
AD	3, 3	CD	4, 4, 4, 6

In all there are 19 differences of rank of 3 units or more, of which 5 are differences of 5 units or more, distributed over the six pairs of samples. The average for a single pair of samples is therefore 3·17 differences of 3 units or more of which 0·83 are of 5 units or more, as against the corresponding

TABLE 8.5. Showing the alphabetical distributions of the nouns for the four separate samples from Macaulay's *Essays*. It must be remembered that A, B and C were samples of roundly 4000 occurrences, D a sample of roundly 8000

1	2	3	4	5	1	2	3	4	5
Initial letter of noun	Frequency in sample from Macaulay				Initial letter of noun	Frequency in sample from Macaulay			
	A	B	C	D		A	B	C	D
A	101	88	101	158	O	31	32	32	43
B	62	56	60	91	P	152	134	157	199
C	156	159	163	209	Q	6	6	8	8
D	105	82	110	136	R	86	69	82	105
E	74	66	73	93	S	184	142	159	214
F	76	54	73	85	T	71	65	78	107
G	46	31	49	62	U	9	7	8	16
H	60	39	60	67	V	31	26	24	37
I	69	68	62	101	W	38	37	43	57
J	9	8	11	14	X	—	—	—	—
K	10	11	12	13	Y	1	6	4	4
L	50	45	51	73	Z	3	2	2	2
M	84	77	98	122					
N	23	23	25	32	Total	1537	1333	1545	2048

figures of 7 and 4 for the comparison of Bunyan with Macaulay. The Bunyan samples are very much more consistent with each other than is the distribution of Bunyan with that for Macaulay. Turning now to Table 8.6 for Macaulay and taking out the differences of 3 or more in the same way, we get an almost startling result:

Pair of samples	Differences of rank of 3 units or more	Pair of samples	Differences of rank of 3 units or more
AB	4, 3	BC	3
AC	None	BD	3
AD	4, 3	CD	None

In all there are only 6 differences in rank of 3 units or more and no single one of these is as much as 5 units: the average for a single pair of samples is

1 difference of 3 units or more, but none as great as 5. Bringing our figures together we have therefore:

	Differences of rank of	
Comparison	3 or more	5 or more
Bunyan and Macaulay, totals	7	4
Two Bunyan samples, mean	3·17	0·83
Two Macaulay samples, mean	1	0

Our question is therefore answered very clearly. Samples from one and the same author do show a degree of consistence notably greater than samples from different authors; so the distribution appears to be definitely

TABLE 8.6. Giving the ranks of the initial letters for the four distributions of Table 8.5, together with the ranking for the total distribution, in col. 6, from Table 8.2, col. 8

1	2	3	4	5	6
Initial letter of noun	Rank in sample from Macaulay				Total
	A	B	C	D	
A	5	4	5	4	4
B	12	11	12·5	11	10
C	2	1	1	2	1
D	4	5	4	5	5
E	9	9	9·5	10	11
F	8	12	9·5	12	12
G	15	17	15	15	15
H	13	14	12·5	14	14
I	11	8	11	9	9
J	21·5	21	21	21	20
K	20	20	20	22	21·5
L	14	13	14	13	13
M	7	6	6	6	6
N	19	19	18	19	19
O	17·5	16	17	17	17
P	3	3	3	3	3
Q	23	23·5	22·5	23	23
R	6	7	7	8	7
S	1	2	2	1	2
T	10	10	8	7	8
U	21·5	22	22·5	20	21·5
V	17·5	18	19	18	18
W	16	15	16	16	16
X	26	26	26	26	26
Y	25	23·5	24	24	24
Z	24	25	25	25	25

characteristic of the *author*. The fact that the Macaulay samples show a greater self-consistence than those from Bunyan is in accordance with our previous conclusion (§ 7.11) that the Bunyan samples are the more heterogeneous group of the two.

8.5. We may, however, look at these tables from a slightly different standpoint and ask ourselves another question. Given only the distribution for a single one of the samples from Bunyan or Macaulay, knowing that it came from one or other of the two authors and being given the total alphabetical distributions for comparison, would we have any doubt as to the author to which it should be assigned? Let us again apply quite a simple test. As we saw in § 8.2, it is the letters A, B, E, F, H, I, W which show the greatest differences of rank in the two authors. Let us then confine ourselves to these seven as test-letters, and compare the ranking of each of the component samples in turn with the ranking in the two total distributions. Taking Bunyan sample A as an illustration, the work is as follows:

1	2	3	4	5	6
				Difference of rank in Bunyan A from	
	Rank in total		Bunyan	Total	Total
Letter	Bunyan	Macaulay	A	Bunyan	Macaulay
A	10	4	12	2	8
B	5	10	6	1	4
E	16	11	15	1	4
F	8·5	12	9	0·5	3
H	11	14	11	0	3
I	14·5	9	16	1·5	7
W	12	16	8	4	8
			Totals disregarding sign	10	37

Cols. 2, 3 and 4 give the data: in col. 5 we write down the differences of the ranks in Bunyan sample A (col. 4) from the ranks in the total Bunyan vocabulary (col. 2), paying no attention to sign; the sum at the foot is a rough measure of the badness of agreement between the sample ranking and that for the total Bunyan vocabulary. In exactly the same way we enter in col. 6 the differences between the sample A ranking and the ranking for the total Macaulay vocabulary, and enter the sum, without regard to sign, at the foot. These respective sums are 10 and 37: we have found that the ranking of the given sample differs much less from that of the Bunyan vocabulary than from that of the Macaulay vocabulary, and are left in practically no doubt that the given sample (if we did not know from which author it had come) should be assigned to Bunyan. Going through the same process for all the samples we have the following results. For the Bunyan samples the sums of differences are

Bunyan sample	Sum of differences from total ranking for	
	Bunyan	Macaulay
A	10	37
B	13	42
C	14	32
D	8·5	33·5

For the Macaulay samples we have

Macaulay sample	Sum of differences from total ranking for	
	Bunyan	Macaulay
A	29	12
B	35	5
C	29	11
D	34	2

Not in a single instance could there be any doubt to which of the authors the given sample should be assigned. All the Bunyan samples are clearly assignable to Bunyan, the Macaulay samples to Macaulay. The peculiarities of the respective alphabetical distributions are, once more, clearly a function of author rather than material or subject.

8.6.   The methods of comparison used in the preceding paragraphs, though serving well to bring out the points required, are of a very elementary kind and the statistically minded reader may desire to see the results given by more general methods. For this purpose I have used either the ordinary product-sum coefficient of correlation r between the frequency series to be compared, e.g. cols. 2 and 3 of Table 8.1, or the product-sum correlation between ranks

$$\rho = 1 - \frac{6S(d^2)}{n(n^2-1)}, \tag{8.1}$$

where n is the number of ranks (26 in our case) and the d's are the differences of rank of corresponding members of the two series, e.g. as given in col. 9, Table 8.2. Giving n the value 26, (8.1) becomes

$$\rho = 1 - \frac{S(d^2)}{2925}. \tag{8.2}$$

I have followed the usual, but inexact, practice of using this formula even when some of the ranks have been averaged. A special problem is presented by Tables 8.3–8.6. For Tables 8.3 and 8.5 it seemed to me the best summary measure of self-consistence to use would be the value of r for all possible pairs of samples after these had been reduced to the same totals. The calculation is simpler than it sounds. (1) Reduce the four columns A, B, C, D to the same totals: instead of taking the usual 1000 or 10,000 I thought it convenient to take 2600 so as to make the mean the integral number 100. (2) Add up the four columns row by row, thus forming on the right a fifth column giving the totals for nouns under A, B, C, D, E, etc. Then evidently the sum of squares of deviations from the mean for this summation column, less the sum of squares of deviations from the mean for the four original columns, will give twice the required sum of deviation products for all possible pairs of the columns. For the rank correlation of Tables 8.4 and 8.6 a precisely similar process is applicable, but the work is greatly simplified. The columns already have identical means, so there is no necessity for reduction. Further, as for equation (8.1), the sum of squares of deviations for the original columns is given by the aid of the formula for the sum of the squares of the first n natural numbers. All the calculation that is necessary is to add up the ranks in each row of the four columns and find the sum of squares of deviations for the resulting summation column. Let this be $S(d_s^2)$. Then generally if m be the number of columns and n the number of ranks as before, the correlation ρ_{mn} for all possible pairs of columns is given by

$$\rho_{mn} = \frac{12S(d_s^2)}{m(m-1)\,n(n^2-1)} - \frac{1}{m-1},\tag{8.3}$$

or putting $m = 4$, $n = 26$,

$$\rho_{mn} = \frac{S(d_s^2)}{17550} - \frac{1}{3}.\tag{8.4}$$

For Tables 8.3 and 8.5, in addition to the correlation for all possible pairs of columns, I have also given the correlation between the columns A, B, C, D, reduced to the same totals, and the total distribution for the same author as given in col. 2 or col. 3 of Table 8.1. The following are the results. Since all the correlations are high and the scale of correlation consequently very contracted, I have given the values of $1 - r^2$ for the product-sum correlations as well as the values of r: these form a measure of *lack* of correlation and correspond more directly to the elementary measures or indices used in the preceding paragraphs. In calculating the values of $1 - r^2$, 6-figure values of r were used.

PRODUCT-SUM CORRELATIONS

1. Table 8.1, cols. 2 and 3, Bunyan and Macaulay total distributions. $r = 0.9502$. $1 - r^2 = 0.0972$.
2. Table 8.3, Bunyan four samples, intercorrelation of all possible pairs reduced to the same totals. $r = 0.9779$. $1 - r^2 = 0.0437$.
3. Table 8.5, Macaulay four samples, intercorrelation of all possible pairs reduced to the same totals. $r = 0.9880$. $1 - r^2 = 0.0239$.
4. Table 8.3, Bunyan four samples (reduced) and Table 8.1, col. 2, Bunyan total. $r = 0.9884$. $1 - r^2 = 0.0230$.
5. Table 8.5, Macaulay four samples (reduced) and Table 8.1, col. 3, Macaulay total. $r = 0.9934$. $1 - r^2 = 0.0132$.

RANK CORRELATIONS

6. Table 8.2, Bunyan and Macaulay totals. $\rho = 0\cdot945$.
7. Table 8.4, Bunyan four samples, intercorrelation of all possible pairs. $\rho = 0\cdot969$.
8. Table 8.6, Macaulay four samples, intercorrelation of all possible pairs. $\rho = 0\cdot987$.

8.7.   I do not think these correlations require much comment: they completely bear out the conclusions reached by elementary methods. Comparison of the second and third with the first confirms the conclusion that separate samples from the same author resemble each other much more closely, in respect to alphabetical distribution, than samples from the two distinct authors. The rank correlations 6, 7 and 8 are parallel to and merely confirm the product-sum correlations 1, 2 and 3. Correlations 4 and 5 confirm the close similarity between the distribution for any one sample from the author and the distribution of the total vocabulary given by a number of such samples, a very satisfying and perhaps it may seem to the reader a very natural conclusion. But is it not on the contrary rather a puzzle? Very little consideration shows that the alphabetical distribution, like most other characteristics of vocabulary, must be a function of size of sample, yet Table 8.3 gives a correlation of $0\cdot9884$ between the distribution for a sample of some 4000 occurrences and the distribution for a sample of some 16,000 occurrences.

8.8.   Let us look into the matter rather more closely. In Table 8.3 are given the alphabetical distributions for the four samples from Bunyan's works. This table was cross-added row by row to give the *average* distribution for a sample based on some 4000 occurrences, which was then reduced to a total of 10,000: this is given in Table 8.7, col. 2. To compare with this we have repeated in col. 3 of the same table the alphabetical distribution for the total Bunyan vocabulary, based on some 16,000 occurrences, from Table 8.1, col. 4. The two distributions certainly are on the whole surprisingly concordant: they may differ *significantly* in the technical sense, but do not differ at all materially. The effect of size of sample within the given range is evidently not great. But we may carry the investigation further. By the methods of the last chapter (§ 7.5) we can readily calculate from the word-distribution, as we saw, the vocabulary to be expected in a sample one-fourth the size of the original taken out of it by 'random partitioning'. If, in the word-distribution, there are f_x words occurring x times each,

$$S\{f_x(\tfrac{3}{4})^x\}$$

gives the expected number of words *not* occurring in the vocabulary of the sample, or if S_0 is the total vocabulary,

$$S_0 - S\{f_x(\tfrac{3}{4})^x\}$$

gives the expected number of words occurring in the sample. For the Bunyan data we found that this expected vocabulary for the sample (Table 7.8, col. 7, (A) etc.) is 1163·68, a value appreciably higher than the observed

TABLE 8.7. Bunyan data: showing the alphabetical distribution of nouns per 10,000 (1) in the average sample of some 4000 occurrences, based on the totals of rows in Table 8.3; (2) in the total vocabulary of some 16,000 occurrences, taken from Table 8.1, col. 4

1	2	3	1	2	3
Initial letter of noun	Nouns per 10,000		Initial letter of noun	Nouns per 10,000	
	Average sample	Total vocabulary		Average sample	Total vocabulary
A	486	494	O	195	183
B	637	654	P	805	837
C	941	935	Q	30	31
D	669	681	R	558	592
E	311	307	S	1118	1140
F	521	499	T	513	499
G	373	321	U	57	71
H	496	490	V	158	191
I	262	321	W	494	445
J	99	98	X	—	—
K	99	80	Y	27	22
L	388	374	Z	2	4
M	558	552			
N	205	178	Total	10002	9999

average $4051/4 = 1012·75$. By the same method, if we tabulate out the component word-distributions for nouns beginning with each separate letter, we can calculate the expected vocabulary *for each letter* and thus if necessary draw up a complete 'expected alphabetical distribution' for the sample. Comparison of this with the total distribution of Table 8.7, col. 3 would at once enable us to judge how far the differences between cols. 2 and 3 of that table represent the bias due to different sizes of sample or merely casual fluctuations. The labour involved in such a complete comparison was, however, more than I felt inclined to undertake and it was carried out for a few selected letters only. I began with A, but then it occurred to me that it would be better to choose letters which in Table 8.7 showed some of the larger differences between the two columns. Just

TABLE 8.8. Bunyan data, total vocabulary: showing the numbers of nouns with X occurrences under a few initial letters

X	Numbers of nouns with X occurrences under initial						
	A	G	I	N	R	V	W
1	49	22	43	17	59	19	39
2	17	12	11	4	24	10	11
3	7	9	7	5	13	1	5
4	11	3	2	1	6	2	10
5	5	—	1	—	6	1	7
6	2	7	2	—	5	2	4
7	3	2	2	—	3	3	3
8	3	3	1	1	1	1	1
9	1	—	1	1	2	1	4
10	3	—	—	1	2	—	1
11	2	3	—	1	1	1	—
12	1	—	1	—	1	—	1
13	1	—	—	1	1	—	1
14	3	1	—	1	—	—	—
15	—	—	—	—	—	—	1
16	—	—	—	—	1	1	—
18	1	—	—	1	1	—	—
19	—	—	—	1	—	—	—
20	—	—	—	—	1	—	—
21	—	1	—	—	—	—	1
22	—	—	—	—	1	—	—
24	—	—	—	—	—	—	1
25	—	—	—	1	—	—	—
26	—	1	—	—	1	—	—
28	1	1	—	—	—	—	—
29	—	—	—	—	—	—	1
31	1	—	—	1	—	1	—
33	—	—	—	—	—	—	1
35	—	—	1	—	1	—	1
36	—	—	—	—	1	—	1
38	—	1	—	—	—	—	—
39	—	—	—	—	1	—	—
42	—	2	—	—	—	—	—
43	—	1	—	—	—	—	—
49	—	1	—	—	—	—	—
51	—	—	—	—	—	—	1
55	—	—	—	—	1	—	—
56	—	—	—	1	—	—	—
58	—	—	—	—	—	—	1
60	—	—	—	1	—	—	—
69	—	—	—	—	—	—	1
96	—	—	—	—	—	—	1
116	—	—	—	—	—	—	1
117	—	1	—	—	—	—	—
119	—	—	—	1	—	—	—
297	—	—	—	—	—	—	1
305	—	1	—	—	—	—	—
Total	111	72	72	40	133	43	100

glancing through the table I picked out, in addition to A, the initials G, I, N, R, V and W. The cards for nouns under these seven letters were sorted and gave the distributions shown in Table 8.8. From these were then calculated the expected sample vocabularies. Thus for A I found

$$S\{f_x(\tfrac{3}{4})^x\} = 55\cdot4328,$$

or 55·43 to retain only two decimal places, so that $111 - 55\cdot43 = 55\cdot57$ is the expected vocabulary. The complete list for the letters chosen is as follows:

Letter	Expected vocabulary	Letter	Expected vocabulary
A	55·57	V	20·85
G	42·04	W	55·99
I	28·91		
N	22·25	Total vocabulary	
R	64·67	(whole alphabet)	1163·68

In Table 8.9, col. 4 the above figures are reduced to proportions per 10,000 of the total, the corresponding observed proportions in the total vocabulary and in the average sample being given in cols. 2 and 3. In cols. 5 and 6 are

TABLE 8.9. Bunyan data: showing for a few initial letters the proportions of nouns in the total vocabulary (col. 2) and in the average sample based on some 4000 occurrences (col. 3), both these figures being taken from Table 8.7, together with the calculated proportion in a sample of one-fourth partitioned out of the total (col. 4). Cols. 5 and 6 give the differences between the figures of cols. 3 and 4 and col. 2, and show the consilience between the divergences of cols. 3 and 4

1	2	3	4	5	6
Initial letter of noun	Nouns per 10,000			Differences	
	Total vocabulary	Average sample	Calculated sample	3 − 2	4 − 2
A	494	486	478	− 8	− 16
G	321	373	361	+ 52	+ 40
I	321	262	248	− 59	− 73
N	178	205	191	+ 27	+ 13
R	592	558	556	− 34	− 36
V	191	158	179	− 33	− 12
W	445	494	481	+ 49	+ 36

given the differences, col. 3 − col. 2 and col. 4 − col. 2. It will be seen that on every line the signs of these differences agree: if the proportion in the average sample is greater than that in the total vocabulary, then the proportion in the calculated sample is greater than that in the total vocabulary, and vice versa. There is also a fair degree of consilience between the magnitudes of corresponding differences: those for I are the largest in their respective columns; those for G come next, and those for W and R follow. The correlation between the two columns is $+0.959$. It is clear then that the differences observed between the two columns of Table 8.7, though not large, are in the main definitely significant and attributable to the difference between the sizes of sample on which the respective columns are based. We have not been greatly troubled by these effects of size of sample simply because they are relatively small within the range of size considered.

8.9. One further point remains to be mentioned before returning to our main investigation. The reader may have been wondering why I have not applied to such tables as 8.1, 8.3 and 8.5 the χ^2 method of testing goodness of fit. As a matter of fact I did at first use the method and the results it gave were very striking—but, unfortunately, so striking as at once to suggest that something must be wrong. Tables 8.3 and 8.5 were tested by adding to each a column of totals on the right, pooling the initials J, K, Q, U, X, Y, Z which have small frequencies, and then treating the table as a contingency table of 4 columns and 20 rows. Table 8.3 for Bunyan gave $\chi^2 = 31.18$, $P = 0.9969$. Table 8.5 for Macaulay gave $\chi^2 = 25.31$, $P = 0.9998$. The first value of P states that we should only get a better fit than that observed between the Bunyan samples, on random sampling, about three times in a thousand trials: the second that we should only get a better fit than that observed between the Macaulay samples about once in some 5000 trials. To have obtained *two* such high values of P makes one ask at once whether the method is properly applicable; and the answer must be, No. The proof of the χ^2 formula assumes, to use the scheme of § 3.18, that every word in the writer's treasure-chest is written on the same number of tickets, so that the chance of drawing any one word is the same as the chance of drawing any other. This is the very reverse of the truth; actually the chance of drawing some words is ten, or a hundred or a thousand or more times that of drawing others, and the result of this is greatly to reduce the standard deviation of sampling (cf. refs. A). One consequence of the great range of chances is indeed fairly obvious: for quite a large number of words the chances of being drawn are so high that they are almost bound to occur in every one of the four samples. We know in fact that 259 words are common to all four of the Bunyan samples and 402 common to all four of the Macaulay samples, cf. Table 7.1, cols. 5 and 4, top row, and this gives a solid basis of actual identity between the samples. The process of sampling on the scheme which more or less closely represents the author's process (§ 3.18) leads in fact to much more stable results than the χ^2 process of simple sampling and hence tends to give values of P which are much too high. Treating cols. 2 and 3 of Table 8.1 in the same way as a contingency table of two columns and twenty rows I found $\chi^2 = 72 \cdot 39$, which gives $P < 0 \cdot 0000005$. If our conclusion that *this* is too high rather than too low holds good, we need at least have no doubt that the alphabetical distributions for Bunyan and Macaulay differ significantly.

8.10.   To return then to our investigation of the alphabetical distribution of vocabulary, we have shown that (1) the distributions for Bunyan and Macaulay exhibit several striking points of difference, (2) the distributions for different works of *the same* author, either Bunyan or Macaulay, are quite closely consistent with one another. The respective distributions appear to be definitely characteristic of the *authors*, not of their subject matters, since if matter had been important the sub-samples from different works could not have been so self-consistent. How has this result come about? It would, I suppose, be a possible hypothesis that the author had some strong, purely personal, preferences for certain initial sounds and dislike of others: that Bunyan, for example, rather liked the explosive B as a start for a word and was repelled by the soft vowel sounds of A, E and I, and that the difference between his alphabetical distribution and that of Macaulay was due entirely to such idiosyncrasies. The hypothesis, as *sole* explanation at least, would not seem to be a very probable one, and in any case, so far as I can see, it would be impossible to prove. There is a more material factor which suggests itself, and is quite open to investigation. In reading Bunyan and Macaulay, still more in handling card catalogues of their respective vocabularies, it is impossible to avoid being struck by the larger proportion of words of Latin or Romance origin in the latter. Now Latin prefixes fall mainly under certain initial letters. Under A we have *a* or *ab*, *ad* (*ac-*, *af-*, *al-*, *ap-*, etc.) and *ante*: under C, *cum* (*co-*, *col-*, *com-*, *con-*, *cor-*), *circum* and *contra*: under D, *de* and *dis-* (*dif-*, *di-*): under E, *e* or *ex* (*ef-*) and *extra*: under I, *in* adverb or preposition (*il-*, *im-*, *ir-*) and *in* privative, *infra*, *inter*, *intra* and *intro*, and so forth; it is hardly necessary to go through the whole alphabet. If one author uses more words of Latin derivation than another, this will tend therefore to increase the vocabulary under certain letters of the alphabet more than that under others. This is obviously not the whole story, but we evidently have here quite a possible source of differentiation between the alphabetical distributions of Bunyan and Macaulay, and an etymological analysis of the two vocabularies will show at once whether it is the effective source or no: a glance at the card drawers for the work on Thomas à Kempis and Gerson suggested the conjecture was right, for in the Latin nouns A's were more frequent than B's as with Macaulay. Recognising my lack of qualifications for the task, I hesitated to embark on such an analysis; but intense dislike of leaving a problem unsolved induced me finally to try my hand at it. At least it taught me a great deal and if any philologist is sufficiently interested, I hope he will do the work again and do it better.

8.11. The *Shorter Oxford English Dictionary* was used as the authority on etymology, and nouns were classified under two broad heads only: I. Old English-Teutonic, II. Latin-Romance, with of course a residue of nouns not classed. In more detail the classes may be described as follows: Class I. Nouns from OE. (of whatever ultimate origin, including consequently some taken into OE., direct from Latin, or adopted from Romance languages, or taken through Latin from Greek): nouns from other Teutonic languages: some nouns introduced into ME. or later which it seems legitimate to take as of purely English origin, e.g. echoic words or words probably echoic such as *bump* or *rap*.

Class II. Nouns from Latin or Romance languages of later introduction than OE. The basis of the classification being the language from which the noun migrated into English, this class includes a certain number of words not of Latin or Romance *origin*, just as Class I includes some not of Teutonic *origin*. For example, it may include words introduced from Greek through Latin, from Arabic through French (e.g. *magazine*) or from Magyar through French (e.g. *coach*), or words like *wage* from the old French *g(u)age*, which itself derives ultimately from a Teutonic root.

Words not classed include (1) words of unknown or wholly doubtful derivation, (2) words introduced directly from Greek, Oriental languages or in general other languages not covered by Classes I and II, (3) compound words, whether hyphened or not, of which one component falls to Class I and the other to Class II (e.g. *breastplate, vineyard, waistcoat*).

A fundamental objection may be taken to my principle of classification on the ground that it is ambiguous since, as pointed out, it leaves some nouns of Latin or non-Teutonic *origin* in Class I and some of other than Latin or Romance *origin* in Class II. My reasons for deciding to classify simply by the language from which the word migrated directly into English were in brief: (1) This method is by far the simplest, and the data required for it are the most trustworthy and most frequently available. (2) If one attempts to go farther back into the history of the word there is no logical stopping point. It seemed best to adopt the simple rule, recognising of course that any grouping of the bulk of English words, with their extraordinarily varied origins, into only a couple of classes must leave the contents of those classes heterogeneous. Very broadly it is a division of the language into the older elements and the younger.

8.12. All the cards for Bunyan and for Macaulay were gone through with the *Shorter Oxford English Dictionary* and marked with a I or a II according to the classification of the noun,* or with a Δ if the noun could

TABLE 8.10. Bunyan: etymological analysis of the alphabetical distribution

1	2	3	4	5
Initial letter of noun	Number of nouns			
	I. OE.-Teutonic	II. Latin-Romance	Total	Not classed
A	19	92	111	—
B	105	34	139	8
C	52	156	208	2
D	49	102	151	2
E	19	49	68	1
F	62	47	109	3
G	40	28	68	4
H	76	28	104	6
I	6	65	71	1
J	2	19	21	1
K	18	—	18	—
L	56	27	83	1
M	50	73	123	1
N	22	16	38	2
O	12	28	40	1
P	33	150	183	5
Q	1	6	7	—
R	36	94	130	3
S	141	109	250	6
T	54	55	109	3
U	8	4	12	4
V	2	40	42	1
W	94	4	98	2
X	—	—	—	—
Y	5	—	5	—
Z	—	1	1	—
Total	962	1227	2189	57

not be classed. There are cases of difficulty, numerous altogether but not a large proportion of the whole, and I have no doubt that an expert linguist would object to some of my classifications and possibly prefer, with greater

* This symbolism is not happy for card-marking, since the symbol does not suggest the class; a few errors were found which looked as if a I had been written for a II, or vice versa, by a pure slip, and more than once I only just stopped myself in time from writing the wrong number. It would have been better to use L or R for the Latin-Romance class and T or G for the Teutonic or Germanic group.

caution, to leave a larger percentage of the nouns not classed: but I do not think it likely that my general results could be very substantially altered.

8.13.   Table 8.10 gives the etymological analysis of the alphabetical distribution for Bunyan, and Table 8.11 that for Macaulay. Leaving aside the nouns not classed, of the Bunyan nouns 962/2189 = 43·9 per cent fall

TABLE 8.11. Macaulay: etymological analysis of the alphabetical distribution

1	2	3	4	5
Initial letter of noun	Number of nouns			
	I. OE.-Teutonic	II. Latin-Romance	Total	Not classed
A	13	232	245	4
B	89	67	156	13
C	51	326	377	14
D	42	193	235	2
E	20	142	162	—
F	53	92	145	5
G	39	61	100	7
H	63	44	107	5
I	12	157	169	3
J	—	23	23	4
K	19	—	19	3
L	56	61	117	5
M	52	153	205	4
N	18	32	50	2
O	18	52	70	3
P	34	295	329	9
Q	4	10	14	—
R	34	154	188	3
S	141	231	372	8
T	62	110	172	7
U	7	14	21	1
V	1	62	63	1
W	79	7	86	3
X	—	—	—	—
Y	8	—	8	—
Z	1	3	4	—
Total	916	2521	3437	106

into Class I, the Teutonic group, of the Macaulay nouns only 916/3437 = 26·7 per cent. From both tables it will be seen at a glance that the alphabetical distributions of Class I nouns and Class II nouns are very different from one another. To facilitate comparison, in Table 8.12 the distributions have been reduced to totals of 10,000, the two Class I distributions have been placed next each other in cols. 2 and 3 and the two Class II distributions next each other in cols. 4 and 5. That he may not attach too much importance to small differences the reader should remember that the columns of this table are founded on vocabularies of no more than some 900 to 2500 nouns, so that a single word, according to the column, may be represented by 4 to 11 units: he may find it safer mentally to insert a decimal point before the last two digits and read the figures as percentages. The two

TABLE 8.12. Bunyan and Macaulay: alphabetical distributions per 10,000 for the two etymological groups

1	2	3	4	5
Initial letter of noun	I. OE.-Teutonic		II. Latin-Romance	
	Bunyan	Macaulay	Bunyan	Macaulay
A	198	142	750	920
B	1091	972	277	266
C	541	557	1271	1293
D	509	459	831	766
E	198	218	399	563
F	644	579	383	365
G	416	426	228	242
H	790	688	228	175
I	62	131	530	623
J	21	—	155	91
K	187	207	—	—
L	582	611	220	242
M	520	568	595	607
N	229	197	130	127
O	125	197	228	206
P	343	371	1222	1170
Q	10	44	49	40
R	374	371	766	611
S	1466	1539	888	916
T	561	677	448	436
U	83	76	33	56
V	21	11	326	246
W	977	862	33	28
X	—	—	—	—
Y	52	87	—	—
Z	—	11	8	12
Total	10000	10001	9998	10001

distributions for Class I nouns are, I think it will be agreed, rather remarkably consistent with one another. The two Class II distributions do not look in quite such good agreement. In particular there is the rather puzzling feature that the three vowels A, E and I, which are so much more frequent in Class II than in Class I, are in Class II itself much more frequent in Macaulay than in Bunyan. But on the whole the two Class I distributions are concordant and the two Class II distributions are concordant, but the

Class I distributions differ considerably from the Class II distributions. As before, I worked out the correlations between these distributions as measures of similarity. The following are the values of r and of $1 - r^2$:

Correlation between distributions		r	$1 - r^2$
Bunyan I	Macaulay I	0·9882	0·0236
Bunyan II	Macaulay II	0·9842	0·0314
Bunyan I	Bunyan II	0·3257	0·8939
Macaulay I	Macaulay II	0·3479	0·8790
Bunyan I	Macaulay II	0·3083	0·9050
Bunyan II	Macaulay I	0·3623	0·8687

The two direct correlations (between the alphabetical distributions for nouns of the same class) are 0·9882 and 0·9842, which I think we may call very fair agreement. Comparing them with the correlations given in § 8.6, it will be seen that the lower, 0·9842 for Class II, lies between the inter-correlation for the four Bunyan samples and the inter-correlation for the four Macaulay samples: the higher, 0·9882 for Class I, is just above the latter. The four possible cross-correlations, between a Class I distribution and a Class II distribution, are also positive but range between the much smaller values 0·31 to 0·36.

8.14.   With these facts before us we may ask ourselves the direct question: can we account for the difference between the Bunyan and the Macaulay alphabetical distributions, in the main at least, simply by the different proportions of words in the two etymological groups? Virtually we have already answered this question by the preceding analysis, but I attempted to obtain a clear and direct answer by the following procedure. Referring to Table 8.10, the Bunyan totals are Class I 962, Class II 1227, while from Table 8.11 the corresponding Macaulay totals are Class I 916, Class II 2521. Let us then multiply every figure in col. 2 of Table 8.10 by 916/962, every figure in col. 3 of the same table by 2521/1227, and add the products together row by row to form a new 'Total' column instead of col. 4. This will give us an estimated or 'expected' alphabetical distribution for Macaulay on the basis of the Bunyan distribution: in so far as this 'expected' distribution agrees with the actual distribution for Macaulay we have evidently shown that there is no difference between the two authors except as regards the proportions of their vocabularies taken from Class I and Class II. Table 8.13 shows the results of the calculation, col. 2 giving the 'expected' vocabulary and col. 3 that observed, taken from Table 8.11, col. 4. With the exception of a few letters, notably again the vowels A, E and I, for all of which the actual substantially exceeds the expected figure, the consilience of observation with expectation is obviously close: rounding off the expected figures to the nearest unit, I make the correlation between expectation and observation $r = 0\cdot9863$, $1 - r^2 = 0\cdot0273$. The correlation lies just half-way between the two first correlations given in the last section. We *have* accounted, in the main, for the difference between the Bunyan and the Macaulay vocabularies simply in terms of the respective proportions

TABLE 8.13. Macaulay: (1) the vocabulary 'expected' on the basis of the Bunyan distributions, Table 8.10, cols. 2 and 3 and (2) the observed distribution, from Table 8.11, col. 4

1	2	3	1	2	3
Initial letter of noun	Expected vocabulary	Observed vocabulary	Initial letter of noun	Expected vocabulary	Observed vocabulary
A	207·1	245	O	69·0	70
B	169·8	156	P	339·6	329
C	370·0	377	Q	13·3	14
D	256·2	235	R	227·4	188
E	118·8	162	S	358·2	372
F	155·6	145	T	164·4	172
G	95·6	100	U	15·8	21
H	129·9	107	V	84·1	63
I	139·3	169	W	97·7	86
J	40·9	23	X	—	—
K	17·1	19	Y	4·8	8
L	108·8	117	Z	2·1	4
M	197·6	205			
N	53·8	50	Total	3436·9	3437

of OE.-Teutonic and Latin-Romance words. By simply varying the proportions in the Bunyan vocabulary, as we see from the value of $1 - r^2$, we can account for more than 97 per cent of the variance of the Macaulay distribution. It is an interesting fact that, owing to the existence of these two great separate streams in our language, even the alphabetical distribution of an author's vocabulary may be distinctive and characteristic.

8.15. It may be as well then to note the principal differentiating characters between the alphabetical distributions of nouns in Class I and nouns in Class II. Class I, the Teutonic group, as we see from Table 8.12, is characterised by a relatively high proportion of B's, about 10 per cent of the total, and a relatively high proportion of W's, about 9 per cent; while Class II shows less than 3 per cent of B's and very few W's indeed. On the other hand Class I shows a relatively small proportion of the three vowels A, E and I, only some 4·5 to 5 per cent altogether, and hardly any V's; while Class II yields some 17 to 21 per cent of nouns under the three vowels (the proportions differ rather widely, as has already been noticed, for Bunyan and Macaulay) and some 2·5 to 3 per cent or more of V's. The V's are, however, too small a group to form a very good index, and as the K's are still fewer I have excluded them, though otherwise the fact that (in our data) they are all in the Teutonic group without exception would have made them quite useful. High B's and W's, low A's, E's and I's for the Teutonic group, and the reverse for the Latin-Romance group, is a sufficient short selection of differentiating characteristics without attempting to burden the memory with more.

8.16.   Table 8.14 exhibits the facts in another way by ranking the initial letters according to frequency in each of the two classes. In col. 4 I have given a mean ranking for Class I based on the sum of the figures in cols. 2 of Tables 8.10 and 8.11—the summation of the figures obviously having no

TABLE 8.14. Bunyan and Macaulay: ranking of initial letters in the two etymological groups, for Bunyan and Macaulay, with a mean based on the sum of the frequencies in the two authors. Bracketed letters are of equal rank

1	2	3	4	5	6	7
Rank	I. OE.-Teutonic			II. Latin-Romance		
	Bunyan	Macaulay	Mean	Bunyan	Macaulay	Mean
1	S	S	S	C	C	C
2	B	B	B	P	P	P
3	W	W	W	S	A	S
4	H	H	H	D	S	A
5	F	T	T	R	D	D
6	L	L	F	A	I	R
7	T	F	L	M	R	M
8	C	M	C	I	M	I
9	M	C	M	T	E	E
10	D	D	D	E	T	T
11	G	G	G	F	F	F
12	R	P⎱	R	V	B	V
13	P	R⎰	P	B	V	B
14	N	E	N	G⎱	G⎱	G
15	A⎱	K	E	H⎰	L⎰	L
16	E⎰	N⎱	K	O⎰	O	O
17	K	O⎰	A	L	H	H
18	O	A	O	J	N	N
19	U	I	I	N	J	J
20	I	Y	U	Q	U	U
21	Y	U	Y	U	Q	Q
22	J⎱	Q	Q	W	W	W
23	V⎰	V⎱	V	Z	Z	Z
24	Q	Z⎰	J	K⎱	K⎱	K⎱
25	X⎱	J⎱	Z	X⎰	X⎰	X⎰
26	Z⎰	X⎰	X	Y⎰	Y⎰	Y⎰

meaning except as a process of averaging—and in col. 7 a similar mean ranking for Class II. I do not attach much importance to these mean rankings, but it is convenient to have a single ranking for each class to which to refer. Both in Bunyan and in Macaulay the ten most frequent initials in the respective classes, though varied slightly in order, are as follows:

Class I: S B W H T F L C M D.

Class II: C P S A D R M I E T.

These two lists contain only fifteen different letters between them, which may be grouped as follows:

Common to lists for I and II   S T C M D

In Class I list, not II   B W H F L

In Class II list, not I   P A R I E

Comparing with these lists the top ten letters by rank in any vocabulary of nouns, we may be enabled, very roughly, to place that vocabulary on the scale for Teutonic character. Thus for Bunyan, Table 8.2, col. 2, the top ten letters are   S C P D B R M F T A.

Cutting out the five letters common to I and II, we are left with

B F   in list I,   P A R   in list II.

Two out of five of the test letters fall to Class I: of the vocabulary 44 per cent actually is Class I. Again, for Macaulay the top ten letters, Table 8.2, col. 4, are   C S P A D M R T I B,

and cutting out the letters common to lists for I and II we are left with

B   in list I,   P A R I   in list II.

Only one out of five test letters falls into Class I, and the actual proportion of Class I nouns in the vocabulary is 27 per cent.

8.17.   The only other English data that I have at the time of writing are those for St John's Gospel, Basic Version and A.V. (selected nouns), Tables 2.9 and 2.10. The first gave a vocabulary of only 296 nouns, the second a vocabulary of only 353, both far too limited a foundation for a satisfactory alphabetical distribution. I give the distribution for the A.V. however, for the sake of illustration, in Table 8.15, col. 2 showing the number of nouns under each initial, and col. 4 the ranking of the initials. The first ten letters are

S C W P B M F L D T,

and eliminating the five common letters we are left with

W B F L in list I, P in list II.

This would suggest a very high proportion of nouns in the Teutonic group, but actual analysis gave 196 in Class I, 154 in Class II, with 3 not classed, or 56 per cent (of the nouns classed) in Class I. This is a much higher proportion than in Bunyan, but nothing like the overwhelming proportion

TABLE 8.15. Alphabetical distribution of nouns in St John's Gospel (A.V., select nouns) (Table 2.10 and §§ 2.18, 2.19), and ranking of the initial letters. In col. 4 bracketed letters are of equal rank and have been placed simply in alphabetical order

1	2	3	4	1	2	3	4
Initial letter of noun	Number of nouns	Rank	Initial	Initial letter of noun	Number of nouns	Rank	Initial
A	13	1	S	O	5	15	N
B	25	2	C	P	27	16	E
C	30	3	W	Q	1	17	O⎫
D	18	4	P	R	11	18	V⎭
E	7	5	B	S	49	19	I⎫
F	23	6	M	T	18	20	J⎭
G	13	7	F	U	1	21	K
H	16	8	L	V	5	22	Q⎫
I	3	9	D⎫	W	28	23	U⎬
J	3	10	T⎭	X	—	24	Y⎭
K	2	11	H	Y	1	25	Z
L	19	12	A⎫	Z	1	26	X
M	24	13	G⎭				
N	10	14	R	Total	353	—	—

suggested by the test letters. With so small a sample we have no right to expect good agreement, and in any case we obviously want far more data before attaching much weight to empirical rules at present based on two authors only. The sample is clearly far too small to be worth detailed etymological analysis on the lines of Tables 8.10 and 8.11, and it should be noted that, owing to the special limitations put on the nouns included (§ 2.18, end), the data are not strictly comparable with those for nouns in Bunyan and Macaulay.

8.18. The question may possibly have arisen in the reader's mind, how far do the Class II distributions of Bunyan and Macaulay agree with a distribution for actual Latin nouns? Table 8.16 is given to answer this question. Col. 2, repeated from col. 7 of Table 8.14, gives the mean Bunyan-Macaulay ranking of the alphabet for nouns of Class II; col. 3, based on

Table 10.12, col. 5, the ranking for mediaeval Latin nouns (2454 in all) from the *De Imitatione Christi* together with samples from the miscellaneous works of Thomas à Kempis and the theological writings of Gerson. There is evidently *broad* general agreement between the two, but some fairly considerable differences of rank. The first ten letters for the Latin list differ

TABLE 8.16. Comparison of the ranking of initials (1) in nouns of Class II, Latin-Romance, Bunyan and Macaulay, col. 2, (2) in Latin nouns occurring in the samples from the *Imitatio*, à Kempis and Gerson, col. 3 (based on col. 5, Table 10.12)

1	2	3	1	2	3
Rank	Bunyan and Macaulay Class II Table 8.14 col. 7	à Kempis and Gerson Mediaeval Latin Table 10.12 col. 5	Rank	Bunyan and Macaulay Class II Table 8.14 col. 7	à Kempis and Gerson Mediaeval Latin Table 10.12 col. 5
1	C	C	14	G	O
2	P	P	15	L	N
3	S	S	16	O	H
4	A	A	17	H	G
5	D	I	18	N	B
6	R	D	19	J	J
7	M	M	20	U	U
8	I	F	21	Q	Q
9	E	R	22	W	Z
10	T	T	23	Z	K ⎫
11	F	L	24	K ⎫	W ⎬
12	V	V	25	X ⎬	X ⎭
13	B	E	26	Y ⎭	Y

from those for Class II by the omission of E, which has dropped from rank 9 to rank 13, and the inclusion of F, raised from 11 to 8. R has dropped from 6 to 9, B from 13 to 18, and G from 14 to 17. On the other hand I has been raised from 8 to 5, L from 15 to 11, and N from 18 to 15. The rank-correlation between the two columns is 0·960, while the corresponding rank-correlation between the Class II rankings for Bunyan and Macaulay, Table 8.14, cols. 5 and 6, is 0·986, an appreciably higher value. It seems clear that we must regard the two rankings as significantly differentiated.

8.19.   While it was the incidence of Latin prefixes on certain letters of the alphabet which suggested that the proportion of Latin nouns would affect the alphabetical distribution, our tables would make it clear (were such evidence necessary) that this is not the whole story. The fact that nearly all V's fall to Class II (it would be *all* the V's but for the fact that, under our rule, *verse* and *viper* having been adopted from Latin into OE. must be allotted to Class I) has obviously nothing to do with prefixes. All the K's fall to Class I since English, unlike German, retained the later Latin *c* as representing the *k* sound. The great majority of W's fall to Class I, since Latin nouns with initial *u*, i.e. the *w* sound, are spelt with initial *v* in English: initial W represents mainly OE. or Old Norse together with a certain number of words received through Old French before the replacement of the initial *w* by the later *g(u)*. These last account in the main for the few exceptional W's allotted to Class II, though we must not forget the delightful *wig*, which occurs in Macaulay, with its pedigree of *perruque—periwig—wig*. These are all matters affecting only the initial letter of the words, but in marking the cards for etymological class one could not help noticing how *patchily* class was often distributed over the alphabetical order even within one and the same initial letter. Thus take the nouns beginning with S that occur in the samples from Bunyan: there are 256 of these of which 250 were classed, and of those classed 141 or some 56 per cent (Table 8.10) fell to Class I. But of words beginning with Sh- there are 28; or omitting *shekel* (as Hebrew) and *shelving* (of uncertain etymology), which were not classed, 26. Of these 26 only a single one, viz. *shock* 'apparently adoption of French *choquer*', falls to Class II. All the rest fall to the Teutonic Group, Class I. Turning to the end of the S's, all the seven words beginning with Sw- fall to Class I. Again, of Bunyan's nouns beginning with T, 54 out of 109 (Table 8.10) or practically 50 per cent were assigned to Class I. But of 19 nouns beginning with Th- 17 fall to Class I: only two, *theme* and *throne*, are assigned to Class II and in Middle English they would not have been found in this position since, following the Old French originals, they were spelt without an *h*. In a more learned writer like Macaulay one might expect a larger number of nouns where the Th- represents the Greek θ, but it must be remembered that late introductions direct from the Greek would not be classed. In fact we find in the Macaulay lists *theologian, theology, theorist* and *theory*: *theism* also occurs, but as it is a seventeenth-century introduction direct from the Greek it was not classed. Contrast with the *th*- list in Bunyan the long list of nouns beginning with *tr*-: in this list only 8 out of 36 fall to Class I, 28 to Class II. To this great excess of nouns in the Latin-Romance class nouns in *trans*- make only a comparatively small contribution: if to *transformation, transgression, transgressor* we add *trespass* and *trespassing*, in which the first syllable represents the *trans*- of *transpassare*, we have only five in all.

ETYMOLOGICAL ANALYSIS OF THE
WORD-DISTRIBUTIONS

8.20. The analysis of the vocabulary into two etymological classes was made in the first instance solely in order to throw light on the queer problem of the alphabetical distribution of vocabulary. But, since it had been obtained, further use was naturally made of the data. Table 8.17 gives the complete analysis of the total word-distribution for the four Bunyan samples (Table 6.7) into distributions for Class I nouns and Class II nouns, together with the small residuum of nouns not classed. This residuum is not taken into consideration in what follows, but the values of the sums S_0 and S_1 for the residuum as well as for Class I and Class II are given at the foot of the table, since they are required as a check. If the work has been done correctly the sum of the S_0's for the three components must be equal to the S_0 for Table 6.7, and the sum of the S_1's for the three components must be equal to the S_1 for Table 6.7. It will be seen that this check duly holds, the S_0's adding to 2246 and the S_1's to 16,056. Table 8.18 for Macaulay gives an analysis of the total distribution for the Macaulay samples (Table 6.4) in precisely the same form, and the two tables may be considered together.

8.21. In Table 8.17 for Bunyan the difference between the two distributions for nouns of Class I and of Class II is very conspicuous. In spite of the fact that the Class II vocabulary is considerably the greater, nouns of this class, the Latin-Romance class, have largely dropped out of the second half of the table: amongst the 52 nouns with 46 or more occurrences there are 42 in the OE.-Teutonic class but only 10 in the Latin-Romance group. As a consequence of this great preponderance of Class I nouns in the 'tail' of the distribution, the mean number of occurrences for Class I nouns is nearly 10, while the mean number of occurrences for nouns of Class II is little more than 5 (see foot of the table). The number of occurrences of nouns in Class I is 9585, of nouns in Class II only 6321: in spite of the smaller *vocabulary* it is the Teutonic group which predominates in the *text*. For Macaulay, Table 8.18, the distributions for Class I and Class II are not nearly so sharply contrasted. The mean for the former is just under 7 (as against 10), the mean for the latter rather over 5, just slightly larger than the value for Bunyan. The Romance, Class II, *vocabulary* is more than 2·5 times the Teutonic, the Romance *occurrences* more than twice the Teutonic. In Macaulay it is the Latin-Romance vocabulary which predominates in and colours the text, just as in Bunyan it is the OE.-Teutonic vocabulary.

TABLE 8.17. Bunyan data: etymological analysis of the total word-distribution of Table 6.7. Class I, OE.-Teutonic. Class II, Latin-Romance. (For condensed comparison see Table 8.19)

1	2	3	4	5
	Number of nouns f_x			
X	Class I	Class II	Total classed	Not classed
1	371	521	892	39
2	156	207	363	7
3	88	105	193	2
4	55	70	125	3
5	43	46	89	2
6	34	45	79	—
7	17	28	45	2
8	16	23	39	—
9	14	21	35	—
10	5	20	25	—
11	11	19	30	—
12	9	10	19	1
13	10	13	23	—
14	7	6	13	—
15	7	8	15	—
16	9	6	15	—
17	5	4	9	—
18	5	8	13	—
19	4	2	6	—
20	5	4	9	—
21	8	7	15	—
22	5	2	7	—
23	2	4	6	—
24	2	3	5	—
25	3	1	4	—
26	4	6	10	—
27	—	1	1	—
28	1	4	5	—
29	1	2	3	—
30	1	—	1	—
31	3	2	5	—
33	1	2	3	—
34	1	2	3	—
35	2	3	5	—
36	3	3	6	—
37	1	1	2	—
38	1	1	2	—
39	1	1	2	—
40	2	—	2	—
41	2	1	3	—
42	3	2	5	—
43	—	1	1	1
44	1	2	3	—
45	1	—	1	—
Total	—	—	—	57

1	2	3	4
	Number of nouns f_x		
X	Class I	Class II	Total classed
46	1	—	1
47	1	—	1
48	2	—	2
49	3	2	5
51	1	—	1
52	1	—	1
53	1	—	1
54	1	—	1
55	—	1	1
56	1	—	1
57	1	—	1
58	2	—	2
60	1	—	1
63	1	1	2
64	—	1	1
68	1	1	2
69	1	—	1
76	1	—	1
87	1	—	1
90	1	—	1
94	1	—	1
96	1	—	1
102	1	—	1
109	—	1	1
111	1	—	1
112	1	—	1
116	1	—	1
117	1	—	1
119	1	—	1
124	—	1	1
131	1	—	1
133	—	1	1
134	1	—	1
135	1	—	1
139	1	—	1
160	1	—	1
168	—	1	1
189	1	—	1
216	1	—	1
261	1	—	1
292	1	—	1
297	1	—	1
305	1	—	1
638	1	—	1
Total	962	1227	2189

Class I: $S_0 = 962$, $S_1 = 9585$, $M = 9.964$.
Class II: $S_0 = 1227$, $S_1 = 6321$, $M = 5.152$.
Not classed: $S_0 = 57$, $S_1 = 150$, —

TABLE 8.18. Macaulay data: etymological analysis of the total word-distribution of Table 6.4. Class I, OE.-Teutonic. Class II, Latin-Romance. (For condensed comparison see Table 8.20)

1	2	3	4	5	1	2	3	4
	Number of nouns f_x					Number of nouns f_x		
X	Class I	Class II	Total classed	Not classed	X	Class I	Class II	Total classed
1	399	986	1385	75	43	1	1	2
2	159	431	590	15	44	—	2	2
3	88	224	312	3	46	1	—	1
4	39	168	207	5	47	1	2	3
5	31	125	156	3	48	1	1	2
6	25	97	122	—	49	—	3	3
7	15	67	82	2	50	1	1	2
8	17	51	68	—	51	1	3	4
9	17	40	57	1	52	1	2	3
10	9	37	46	—	54	—	3	3
11	10	30	40	—	55	2	1	3
12	3	22	25	—	56	—	2	2
13	8	22	30	—	57	1	1	2
14	8	16	24	—	58	—	1	1
15	7	16	23	—	59	—	2	2
16	8	11	19	—	60	1	3	4
17	5	19	24	—	62	1	—	1
18	2	23	25	—	64	2	1	3
19	4	7	11	—	65	—	1	1
20	—	8	8	1	68	1	—	1
21	2	9	11	1	72	1	—	1
22	—	11	11	—	73	—	1	1
23	3	2	5	—	74	1	1	2
24	4	3	7	—	82	1	1	2
25	3	1	4	—	86	1	—	1
26	1	3	4	—	88	—	2	2
27	3	3	6	—	90	1	—	1
28	1	4	5	—	94	—	1	1
29	1	8	9	—	95	1	—	1
30	5	1	6	—	100	—	1	1
31	2	5	7	—	104	—	1	1
32	—	1	1	—	106	—	1	1
33	2	3	5	—	128	1	—	1
34	—	5	5	—	134	—	1	1
35	—	2	2	—	139	—	1	1
36	1	6	7	—	141	1	—	1
37	1	4	5	—	143	1	—	1
38	3	1	4	—	193	1	—	1
39	2	3	5	—	239	1	—	1
40	—	3	3	—	459	1	—	1
42	1	2	3	—				
Total	—	—	—	106	Total	916	2521	3437

Class I: $S_0 = 916$, $S_1 = 6373$, $M = 6\cdot957$.
Class II: $S_0 = 2521$, $S_1 = 13592$, $M = 5\cdot392$.
Not classed: $S_0 = 106$, $S_1 = 213$,   —

For the actual proportions of nouns of Class I in the vocabulary (p_v, cf. §§ 5.14 *et seq.*) and amongst occurrences (p_w, *ibid.*) we have

		Class I nouns	All classed nouns	Percentage of Class I
Bunyan:	S_0: vocabulary	962	2,189	p_v 43·9
	S_1: occurrences	9,585	15,906	p_w 60·3
Macaulay:	S_0: vocabulary	916	3,437	p_v 26·7
	S_1: occurrences	6,373	19,965	p_w 31·9

For Macaulay the percentage of Class I nouns in the classed vocabulary, p_v, is 26·7 per cent, but the limiting value of p_v for very small samples is p_w (§§ 5.14–5.16) or 31·9 per cent. Hence if the size of the Macaulay sample were reduced from nearly 20,000 to some 16,000 occurrences for comparison with Bunyan it is probable (though not certain) that a slightly higher value than 26·7 per cent would be obtained for p_v. Even as the figures stand p_v for Bunyan is a good deal less than double that for Macaulay. But p_v gives little or no guide as to how the text would strike the reader. The percentage for *occurrences* in Bunyan, p_w, is practically double that for Macaulay, 60 per cent against 30 per cent. In other words, while in Bunyan, so far as his nouns are concerned, 60 per cent of his text is Teutonic—'Saxon' in the popular sense—in Macaulay on the other hand (again so far as his nouns are concerned) 70 per cent of his text is Latin-Romance. The two authors could hardly be better contrasted. It is, however, of interest to note that the later and more learned author, with a much larger Latin-Romance vocabulary and a much larger total vocabulary than the earlier but a rather smaller Teutonic vocabulary, nevertheless continued like his predecessor to give each of his Teutonic nouns (on the average) more use than his Latin-Romance nouns, in a proportion not far from 7 to 5 (6·957 to 5·392). The five nouns used most often by him (in our samples), as against the seven used most often by Bunyan, are all nouns of the Teutonic class, Class I. The actual words in question are

Bunyan: Time, lord, thing, town, way, God, man.
Macaulay: Mind, year, time, king, man.

Time and *man* are common to both lists, and it will be noticed that all these nouns are monosyllabic as well as Teutonic. *Man* is the most frequently used in both authors, but *God* is hardly a characteristic substantive in Macaulay's *Essays*.

8.22. Tables 8.19 and 8.20 are condensed groupings of Tables 8.17 and 8.18, constructed to throw some light on the variation of the percentage of Class I nouns with increasing X: the groupings used are those previously employed for Table 6.10 and 6.11, showing the variation with X of the percentage of monosyllabic nouns. As with those tables, the figures are rather puzzling. For Bunyan, Table 8.19, the percentage rises from 41·6 for the once-nouns to 45·6 for nouns with three occurrences, but drops slightly in the group 4–10 (compare the earlier tables cited) and rises to no

TABLE 8.19. Bunyan data: condensed comparison of the distribution for Class I nouns with the distribution for all classed nouns, compiled from Table 8.17

X	All classed nouns	Class I nouns	Percentage of Class I
1	892	371	41·6
2	363	156	43·0
3	193	88	45·6
4– 10	437	184	42·1
11– 20	152	72	47·4
21–100	130	73	56·2
101 up	22	18	81·8
Total	2189	962	43·95

TABLE 8.20. Macaulay data: condensed comparison of the distribution for Class I nouns with the distribution for all classed nouns, compiled from Table 8.18

X	All classed nouns	Class I nouns	Percentage of Class I
1	1385	399	28·8
2	590	159	26·9
3	312	88	28·2
4–10	738	153	20·7
11–20	229	55	24·0
21–59	150	45	30·0
60 up	33	17	51·5
Total	3437	916	26·65

more than 47·4 in the group 11–20. It is the last two groups alone which show substantially increased figures: we might in fact alter the last group to $X = 46$ and upwards and still leave the percentage of Class I nouns as high as 80·8. If we did this, the preceding group would become $X = 21–45$ and it would show a percentage of Class I nouns of no more than 49·0, so that the increase of the percentage in the tail of Table 8.17 is even more abrupt than it looks in Table 8.19. For Macaulay, Table 8.20, the percentages for the first five groups run quite erratically. The figure for once-nouns, 28·8, is actually the *highest* until we come to the penultimate group 21–59 and exceeds that for the group 4–10 by 8·1 points. The standard error of the percentage 28·8 is 1·217, that of the percentage 20·7 is 1·498, making the standard error of the difference 1·925, so that the difference 8·1 is well over four times its standard error and is certainly significant. What does this odd course of the percentages mean? One might surely have expected a smoother and more uniform run of the figures; I myself had looked for a rapid initial increase becoming gradually slower and slower as the percentage asymptotically approached 100.

8.23.   The distributions for monosyllabic nouns in Bunyan and Macaulay were given together in Table 6.9, and it seemed to me that it would be of interest to have an etymological analysis of these distributions on the same lines as that of the distributions for all nouns. The analysis was accordingly carried out and the results are given in Tables 8.21 and 8.22, which are on precisely the same lines as Tables 8.17 and 8.18. Table 8.21 rather closely resembles Table 8.17 in its general features, and Table 8.22 similarly resembles Table 8.18. In Table 8.21 as in Table 8.17 the mean of the Class I distribution is practically double that of the Class II distribution: in Table 8.22 as in Table 8.18 the mean of the Class I distribution is between one-fourth and one-third greater than that of the Class II distribution. In Table 8.21 as in Table 8.17 very few Class II nouns are left in the second half of the table: in Table 8.22 as in Table 8.18 the reduction of Class II nouns in the second half of the table is not nearly so striking. The large share taken in Bunyan's text by monosyllabic nouns of the OE.-Teutonic group is shown by the fact that the occurrences of such nouns amount to no less than 7281 out of the total of 16,056 occurrences (including nouns not classed), or 45·3 per cent. The corresponding figures for Macaulay are 4626 out of 20,178 or 22·9 per cent—only just over half the Bunyan percentage. The proportions of nouns of Class I in the vocabularies of these monosyllabic nouns and amongst occurrences are as follows:

		Monosyllabic nouns		
		Class I nouns	All classed nouns	Percentage of Class I
Bunyan:	S_0: vocabulary	503	716	p_v 70·3
	S_1: occurrences	7281	8843	p_w 82·3
Macaulay:	S_0: vocabulary	469	766	p_v 61·2
	S_1: occurrences	4626	6927	p_w 66·8

These values of p_v and p_w should be compared with those for all nouns given in § 8.21. The percentages of Class I nouns amongst the monosyllables are both considerably higher than amongst nouns in general, the proportions for Bunyan being raised from 43·9 to 70·3 per cent in vocabulary, and from 60·3 to 82·3 per cent amongst occurrences. But for Macaulay the differences

TABLE 8.21. Bunyan data: etymological analysis of the distribution for mono-syllabic nouns of Table 6.9. Class I, OE.-Teutonic. Class II, Latin-Romance

1	2	3	4	5	1	2	3	4
	Number of nouns f_x					Number of nouns f_x		
X	Class I	Class II	Total classed	Not classed	X	Class I	Class II	Total classed
1	156	79	235	7	45	1	—	1
2	82	27	109	3	46	1	—	1
3	48	21	69	1	47	1	—	1
4	30	17	47	2	48	2	—	2
5	18	6	24	—	49	2	2	4
6	24	8	32	—	51	1	—	1
7	9	1	10	—	53	1	—	1
8	11	9	20	—	54	1	—	1
9	11	4	15	—	57	1	—	1
10	3	5	8	—	58	1	—	1
11	5	1	6	—	63	1	—	1
12	5	2	7	1	68	1	—	1
13	8	3	11	—	69	1	—	1
14	5	2	7	—	87	1	—	1
15	5	—	5	—	90	1	—	1
16	4	3	7	—	96	1	—	1
17	3	2	5	—	102	1	—	1
18	4	3	7	—	111	1	—	1
19	4	1	5	—	112	1	—	1
20	4	1	5	—	116	1	—	1
21	4	1	5	—	117	1	—	1
22	5	1	6	—	119	1	—	1
23	2	1	3	—	124	—	1	1
24	—	3	3	—	131	1	—	1
25	2	—	2	—	134	1	—	1
26	2	2	4	—	135	1	—	1
27	—	1	1	—	139	1	—	1
28	—	1	1	—	160	1	—	1
29	1	1	2	—	168	—	1	1
31	2	—	2	—	189	1	—	1
35	2	1	3	—	216	1	—	1
36	1	—	1	—	261	1	—	1
38	1	1	2	—	292	1	—	1
40	2	—	2	—	297	1	—	1
41	1	1	2	—	305	1	—	1
42	3	—	3	—	638	1	—	1
Total	—	—	—	14	Total	503	213	716

Class I: $S_0 = 503,$ $S_1 = 7281,$ $M = 14\cdot475.$
Class II: $S_0 = 213,$ $S_1 = 1562,$ $M = 7\cdot333.$
Not classed: $S_0 = 14,$ $S_1 = 36,$ —

TABLE 8.22. Macaulay data: etymological analysis of the distribution for mono-syllabic nouns of Table 6.9. Class I, OE.-Teutonic. Class II, Latin-Romance

1	2	3	4	5	1	2	3	4
	Number of nouns f_x					Number of nouns f_x		
X	Class I	Class II	Total classed	Not classed	X	Class I	Class II	Total classed
1	162	105	267	8	37	—	1	1
2	82	39	121	1	38	1	—	1
3	51	29	80	1	39	2	—	2
4	24	16	40	1	42	1	—	1
5	19	11	30	1	43	1	—	1
6	14	16	30	—	44	—	1	1
7	9	8	17	1	47	1	—	1
8	9	6	15	—	48	1	1	2
9	12	2	14	—	50	1	—	1
10	5	6	11	—	51	1	1	2
11	9	3	12	—	54	—	1	1
12	3	5	8	—	55	2	—	2
13	3	2	5	—	56	—	1	1
14	7	5	12	—	57	1	—	1
15	4	1	5	—	59	—	1	1
16	4	—	4	—	60	1	1	2
17	4	5	9	—	62	1	—	1
18	2	6	8	—	64	2	—	2
19	3	1	4	—	68	1	—	1
20	—	4	4	—	74	1	1	2
21	1	3	4	—	82	1	—	1
22	—	1	1	—	86	1	—	1
23	1	1	2	—	90	1	—	1
24	2	1	3	—	95	1	—	1
25	2	—	2	—	100	—	1	1
26	1	1	2	—	106	—	1	1
28	1	2	3	—	128	1	—	1
29	1	1	2	—	141	1	—	1
30	3	—	3	—	143	1	—	1
31	2	—	2	—	193	1	—	1
33	1	2	3	—	239	1	—	1
34	—	2	2	—	459	1	—	1
36	—	2	2	—	—	—	—	—
Total	—	—	—	13	Total	469	297	766

Class I: $S_0 = 469$, $S_1 = 4626$, $M = 9.864$
Class II: $S_0 = 297$, $S_1 = 2301$, $M = 7.747$
Not classed: $S_0 = 13$, $S_1 = 29$, —

are   much more striking: p_v is raised from 26·7 to 61·2 per cent, and p_w from 31·9 to 66·8 per cent. Even in Macaulay the *monosyllabic* nouns are in the main Teutonic.

8.24.   In the above we have considered the percentages of monosyllabic nouns which are Teutonic in the vocabularies of the respective authors. Now let us consider the reverse percentages, the percentages of Teutonic nouns (and alternatively of Latin-Romance nouns) which are monosyllabic. The following are the figures:

		Vocabulary		
		Monosyllabic	Total	Percentage of monosyllabic
Class I nouns:	Bunyan	503	962	52·3
	Macaulay	469	916	51·2
Class II nouns:	Bunyan	213	1227	17·4
	Macaulay	297	2521	11·8

For nouns of Class I the figures for the two authors are very concordant: both show that in the Teutonic vocabulary rather more than half the nouns are monosyllabic. For nouns of Class II the agreement is not so close: Bunyan shows over 17 per cent of his nouns monosyllabic, Macaulay barely 12 per cent. It looks as if Bunyan preferred the monosyllable as such and not merely the Teutonic monosyllable. But what are the reasons for this differentiation between nouns of Class I and Class II? One reason seems fairly evident: no noun with a (still recognisable) Latin prefix can be monosyllabic and this of necessity places large numbers of nouns of Class II amongst polysyllables. But the Teutonic group is on the whole the older group of words in our language, and this suggests another probable cause of differentiation. Just as the older pebbles on the beach have had the longer time for (and the better chance of) being worn to rotundity, so the older words in the language have had the longer time for (and the better chance of) being eroded to brevity. It is true that the metaphor of slow attrition will not hold in all instances: *mobile* can hardly have been curtailed to *mob*, or *periwig* decapitated to *wig* save by the happy single act of some individual genius. But even in such instances the longer the time the greater the *chance of occurrence* of some such happy thought and the greater the *chance* of some such happy thought tossing up in an environment so favourable that it attains general acceptance. It is a question not only of time for attrition in some instances, but of time for the occurrence of an unlikely event in others.

8.25.   In Tables 8.23, 8.24 are given condensed groupings of Tables 8.21, 8.22 on the same lines as Tables 8.19, 8.20. Both tables show a very irregular course for the percentage of Class I nouns as X increases, with no substantial rise in the percentage until the tail of the distribution is reached. Thus in the case of Bunyan, Table 8.23, the percentage of Class I nouns for $X = 2$ is 75·2, and this is the highest figure obtained until the 90·0 per cent of the final group, $X = 101$ and upwards, is reached. If, instead of the

TABLE 8.23. Bunyan data: monosyllabic nouns, condensed comparison of the distribution of Class I nouns with the distribution of all classed nouns, compiled from Table 8.21

X	All classed nouns	Class I nouns	Percentage of Class I
1	235	156	66·4
2	109	82	75·2
3	69	48	69·6
4– 10	156	106	67·9
11– 20	65	47	72·3
21–100	62	46	74·2
101 up	20	18	90·0
Total	716	503	70·3

TABLE 8.24. Macaulay data, monosyllabic nouns: condensed comparison of the distribution of Class I nouns with the distribution of all classed nouns, compiled from Table 8.22

X	All classed nouns	Class I nouns	Percentage of Class I
1	267	162	60·7
2	121	82	67·8
3	80	51	63·7
4–10	157	92	58·6
11–20	71	39	54·9
21–59	50	27	54·0
60 up	20	16	80·0
Total	766	469	61·2

grouping given in the table, we had made the last two classes $X = 21$–44, $X = 45$ and upwards, the abruptness of the terminal change in percentage would have been even more evident, for the figures for these groups are 28/42 or 66·7 per cent and 36/40 or 90·0 per cent. For the whole range 1 to 44 the proportion is 467/676 or 69·1 per cent. In the Macaulay table, Table 8.24, we find the highest percentage with the exception of the last again at $X = 2$, and a steady drop from that maximum of 67·8 to the value of 54·0 for the penultimate group $X = 21$–59. Then we have the substantial and sudden rise to 80·0 per cent in the little final group of 20 nouns with 60 occurrences or more. It is of course true that errors of sampling are large, but it remains puzzling that our tables of this type give so little suggestion of continuous, monotonic, change in the percentage with increasing values of X.

REFERENCES

A. STATISTICAL METHOD

§ 8.6. For the theory of correlation and simple explanation of the correlation coefficient see Y & K, Chapter 11 generally; for the rank correlation coefficient, *ibid.* § 13.16. For such tables as Tables 8.3 and 8.5 Kendall and Babington Smith suggested a 'coefficient of concordance', closely related to the coefficient ρ_{mn} of equation (8.3), that some might prefer. I thought it better, for the sake of uniformity, to modify this and to keep to the coefficient of correlation in all cases. The reference is:

(8.1) Kendall, M. G. and Babington Smith, B. (1939). 'The problem of m rankings.' *Annals of Mathematical Statistics*, **10**, 275.

§ 8.9. For the effect of the variation of p on the standard error of sampling, see Y & K, Chapter 19, § 19.32, especially equations (19.9) and (19.10).

B. CITATIONS IN TEXT OR TABLES

(8.2) Onions, C. T. *et al.* (1933). *The Shorter Oxford English Dictionary.* 2 vols. Oxford: Clarendon Press.

Chapter 9

THE *DE IMITATIONE CHRISTI,*
THOMAS À KEMPIS AND GERSON

9.1. Now I come to the work which, as explained in Chapter 1, initiated the whole of these researches; work on that small volume of world-wide fame generally known as the *De Imitatione Christi,* though these words are really only part of the title of Lib. I, cap. i—'De imitatione Christi et contemptu omnium vanitatum mundi.' For the sake of brevity I shall often refer to the book simply as the *Imitatio,* as indeed I have done in previous chapters. The work has been most generally ascribed to the Augustinian Canon Thomas Hemerken or Haemmerlein of Kempen in the diocese of Cologne (1379–1471), or, to give him his familiar title, Thomas à Kempis, and personally I see little reason to doubt that attribution: the proofs, including contemporary evidence, seem to me overwhelming. But the authorship has been most vigorously disputed and still is disputed. The colophon of the *editio princeps* printed by Zainer of Augsburg circa 1472 or 1473 ascribes the book to Thomas, but a large number of the early editions attribute it to Jean Charlier de Gerson (1363–1429), sometime Chancellor of the University of Paris, and place after the *Imitatio* the latter's tract *De meditatione cordis,* as if it were a work of the same author. Others to whom the work has been attributed include St Bernard, St Bonaventure, Pope Innocent III, and an alleged Benedictine Abbot, John Gersen of Vercelli, later proved to have been a sheer invention: the most recent candidate is Gerard Groote, founder of the Brothers of the Common Life (ref. 9.6). The literature of this authorship controversy is now immense—the reader will find some references at the end of the chapter—and I cannot pretend to any real familiarity therewith though interest in the book itself has led me to look into it a little. Amongst other evidence the vocabulary and diction of the *Imitatio* and of admitted works of Thomas have naturally been taken into consideration, but such evidence always seemed to me to concern what might fairly be called *details*—the use of Dutch words or idioms literally translated,* of Italianate words, of words in unusual non-classical senses,

---

* In § 1.3 reference was made, as an illustration, to the use of *exterius* in the sense of 'by heart' in Lib. I, cap. i of the *Imitatio.* It may be of interest to remark that this idiom was certainly known to Thomas à Kempis but is not distinctive of his writing. It occurs twice in the letter of Florentius which is appended to his *Life* by Thomas, Pohl, VII, 197. 5 and 12:

    'quem librum etiam ita discas exterius...'
    'quando prompta consuetudine scis libellum exterius....'

The word is also in Maigne d'Arnis in this sense, with a reference to Busch.

and so forth. In the *Scutum Kempense* of Amort for example, which is included in the editions of 1728 and later of Sommalius's collection of the works (ref. 9.7), a comparison is made between the *Imitatio* and admitted minor works of Thomas à Kempis, and Section 3, 'Similitudo quoad phrases, et verba alioquin barbara, aut minus bonis authoribus usitata', contains a collection of 350 citations from the *Imitatio* showing such peculiarities with either actual statistics of the numbers of times they are found also in the minor works, or just the letters S or SS if they are found 'saepe' or 'saepissime'. Subject to certain conditions which I cannot stay here to discuss (see below §§ 9.20–9.22) such data may afford valid evidence in a matter of controversy—they may, as I suggested in § 1.3, be quite 'useful to the police' in the same sort of way as a wart or a scar or an odd formation of the lobe of the ear may be useful recognition-marks for the identification of an individual. But such data fail entirely to give any notion of the vocabulary as a whole, and indeed may be gravely misleading since all the stress is laid on oddities. It is true, of course, that if any considerable number of the exceptional words fall under the same general description, so as to form a large *class*, that *class* may become characteristic of the author even though each individual word in it is only used once: Latin polysyllables like *impurpurate, rubicund, rubiginous, illuminous, conflagrate, Favonian, occident, inarticulate, corrival, palpitant, transtellar, crocean, reverberant* may be said in this sense to characterise the poems of Francis Thompson, though no one of the words is used at all often, indeed most of them probably no more than once. Barring this special case, the savour of an author's text must, it seemed to me, be determined in the main not by the exceptional words but by the common words, the common everyday working words which the author uses over and over and over again. To get a real picture of the vocabulary of the *Imitatio*—the sort of picture that a man would like of his friend and not the sort of specification that the police would like of a criminal—it would therefore be essential to have not merely a list of the words used by the author, but a complete schedule of the words classified by the number of times each was used—lists of words used once, words used twice, and so forth. It seemed to me that it would be very interesting to draw up such a schedule for the *Imitatio* and see what it was like. And I had dim visions of possibly going further from that stage. If two works in the same field, e.g. two religious works, were written by the same author, was it not probable that his special predilections for particular words would tell in both, so that the correlation between the number of times X that a word was used in the first work and the number of times Y that it was used in the second work would be greater than if the two works had been written by different hands and minds? There might be considerable interest then in drawing up, not only the word-distributions for individual authors, but the correlation tables between them. These were roughly my notions when a start was made at the end of September 1938. This and the first portion of the following chapter give an account of the resulting investigations up to the stage they had reached in June 1939, when they were put aside for a couple of years during which my energies were devoted, not to this special problem, but to clearing up the general properties of statistics of the kind by the work on which the preceding chapters have been founded. Notes will be made as we proceed of any points on which these first investigations seem to require supplementing, and an account will be found of the resulting supplementary investigations in §§ 10.19–10.23.

9.2.   The *Imitatio* was an excellent work on which to begin, for it is not over long and is provided with a concordance, Storr's *Concordance* based on the text of Hirsche (refs. 9.8, 9.9), which greatly lightens the work. It seemed clear that it would be desirable to limit in some respects the words to be included. It would hardly be necessary to include interjections or conjunctions, or perhaps relative or interrogative pronouns: in fact it would seem desirable to limit the scope to definitely significant words. But, on looking through the *Concordance* and forming rough notions as to the numbers of words entered, it seemed to me it would be as well to make some much more drastic limitation, simply in order to keep the work reasonably within the scope of one man working by himself—not forgetting that in other cases there would be no friendly concordance available in which more than half the work had already been done. Such a drastic limitation might be made by restricting the work to verbs, nouns, or adjectives, and might have the further advantage of making the material more homogeneous. Finally I pitched on the nouns, a large group, obviously more numerous than adjectives (cf. Tables 2.1, 2.6, 2.7) and, as I then decided, probably more characteristic of the author than either verbs or adjectives. Whether my decision in this respect was right is a question that has already been raised (§ 2.13): but, having been made, it led to my keeping to nouns for the whole of the work that followed.

9.3.   I bought 1000 cards for a start and began work on the *Concordance*, entering each noun on the top right-hand corner of a card, and the total number of its occurrences on the first line at the left. Almost at once I began to get into difficulties with the question what *is* a noun? The largest class of doubtful cases is that of adjectives or participles used substantivally. They are not treated consistently by Storr in the *Concordance*: *malum* as a sub-stantive receives separate entry, but *bonum* does not; *adversum* used sub-stantivally, generally in the plural, receivès separate entry; for the most part such absolute uses of adjectives either in the neuter or the masculine do not. I fear my treatment has been no more consistent than Storr's, though I have not followed his. For the most part such adjectives and participles seem to have been left out, but some have been included. Writing now more than two years after the work was done it is often difficult to see what decided the event one way or the other in any particular instance, but I think the deciding factor in many instances was this. If the adjective (either in the masculine or neuter) is frequently used both adjectivally and substantivally, it is best omitted altogether, for it will be very troublesome to have to examine every occurrence with care. But if the uses are generally sub-stantival in either gender the word may be included: *adversum* and *domesticus* have, for example, both been included and would fall under this rule. *Pauper* is often used substantivally, but is also often used adjectivally, and so was left out. *Objectum* was admitted: the verb does not otherwise occur. *Parum* was admitted as an indeclinable noun, so it seemed difficult to refuse admission to *modicum*, but *multum* was turned down; it would have been very troublesome to distinguish substantival from adjectival, not to mention purely adverbial uses. There were other cases of difficulty but mostly, I think, affecting only words with comparatively few occurrences and hence not of much importance. *Mane* was counted as a noun if used substantivally, but not if used adverbially, and consequently the adverbial *vespere* was also omitted. *Sponte* was admitted, though very doubtfully: it is always used absolutely in the *Imitatio*, without any possessive pronoun, and for all practical purposes seems to be then really an adverb. There were no special difficulties in the counting, though the reader may be warned as to one trap: with a word of frequent occurrence there may be more than one use of the word in a single quotation, cf. e.g. *sub* 'Nihil et nil', the citations ii. 5. 36, ii. 5. 37, ii. 12. 173, iii. 4. 32, iii. 4. 34 each with two uses of the word. Also as a warning to others I have to confess that, when the whole *Concordance* had been worked through, I did not unfortunately go through it again at once to make sure that no nouns had been overlooked: this was only done at a later date and the check added no less than 22 nouns with nearly 40 occurrences, the bulk of which had been simply passed over unseen, though a few were added on a reconsideration of doubts. Work should always be checked, so far as it can be checked, at once. The resulting frequency dis-tribution with its constants was given as my first example of a word-distribution in Table 2.1, but is repeated for convenience of reference in Table 9.1 below (§ 9.13): the values of the sums S_0, S_1, S_2 together with the mean, standard deviation, characteristic, etc. are given in Table 9.2, but the characteristic had not at this time been invented, see § 9.9.

9.4.   I wish I could recapture and depict for the reader the fascination of these first data. They gave one something entirely new; something— indeed two things, the statistical distribution and the word-schedule—which certainly I, and, so far as I knew, nobody else, had ever looked on before. I could sit and brood over either quite happily by the hour. The distribution itself was quite unexpected in form. I had not seriously thought about the matter and—because I had not done so—had been more or less dimly and quite irrationally looking for a skew distribution with a maximum frequency at some low number of occurrences, say about 2 to 5, with the frequency falling off very rapidly towards lower numbers of occurrences and much more slowly towards the higher values, since it was obvious that nouns like *Deus*, *Dominus* and *homo* occurred very often indeed. But such an expectation *was* irrational. For the number of nouns f_0, in the author's vocabulary but not occurring in this particular work, must clearly be very large, and if f_1, f_2, f_3, form an increasing series there must be a sharp minimum at f_1, or almost a discontinuity between f_0 and f_1. Rational consideration ought to have led one to expect that $f_1, f_2, f_3, f_4, \ldots$ would be a rapidly decreasing series, continuous with the high but otherwise unknown value of f_0. Yet this resulting form had astonishing consequences. The main use of the vocabu- lary was concentrated on to a very small proportion of the whole: the mere handful of 60 nouns (cf. § 2.3) or some 5 per cent of the whole vocabulary would account for half of all the occurrences of a noun in the *Imitatio*. From this point of view language seemed so inefficient. The distribution too had its psychological interest, showing the difficulty of acquiring any extensive vocabulary by simple reading, a point that has been touched on already (§§ 2.20, 2.21).

9.5.   As for the schedule of nouns arranged according to numbers of occurrences, it was noticed first that the bulk of the once-nouns were by no means rare nouns as such, but merely of rare occurrence in this particular work: many of them were in the ordinary sense quite common, though of course this is the class into which the majority of the uncommon words tend to fall and do fall. As one read on through the list and came to the more frequent words it was evident that the proportion of nouns of one or two syllables was increasing and the proportion of more polysyllabic nouns decreasing: the proportion of certain *types* of noun, e.g. nouns of action or faculty in *-tio* or *-sio* and nouns in *-tor* and *-sor* expressing the personal agent, seemed also considerably to fall away. Most forcibly, as one read idly, letting a word here and there recall some familiar passage, was it impressed on one how with accelerating rapidity, as one approached the end, the nouns seemed to become more and more characteristic of the book, until the final dozen or so seemed almost a brief epitome of the book itself—

anima: spiritus: verbum: pax: amor: consolatio: mundus: vita: nihil: cor: gratia: Lominus: homo: Deus.

Nihil? it may be queried—*Nihil* a typical and characteristic word? Yes, surely; a word not merely characteristic of the *Imitatio*, a word occurring very frequently therein, but *distinctive* of the book too, a word of which the writer is definitely fond and that he loves to repeat so that it enters like a little chime into the music of his lines, as in these:

> Nil magnum nil altum,
> nil gratum nil acceptum tibi sit:
> nisi pure Deus aut de Deo sit.　(II. 5. 36–38, Hirsche.)

or again these:

> Nihil dulcius est amore:
> nihil fortius,
> nihil altius nihil latius:
> nihil jucundius nihil plenius nec melius in caelo et in terra:
> quia amor ex Deo natus est;
> nec potest nisi in Deo super omnia creata quiescere.
> 　　　　　　　　　　　　　　　　(III. 5. 37–42.)

or in the more solemn music of:

> O quam humiliter et abjecte mihi de me ipso sentiendum est:
> quam nihil pendendum si quid boni videar habere.
> O quam profunde submittere me debeo sub abyssalibus judiciis tuis Domine:
> ubi nihil aliud me esse invenio,
> quam nihil et nihil.
> O pondus immensum:
> O pelagus intransnatabile;
> ubi nihil de me reperio quam in toto nihil.　(III. 14. 27–34.)

or once more:

> Domine nihil sum,
> nihil possum:
> nihil boni ex me habeo:
> sed in omnibus deficio,
> et ad nihil semper tendo.　　　(III. 40. 8–12.)

When one starts quoting the *Imitatio* it is difficult to stop. Roughly something like two-thirds of the occurrences of *nihil* (*nil, nihilum*) come, not in casual uses, but in passages definitely enforcing the lessons that man is *nothing* before God, that of himself he can do *nothing* good, that the world and its pleasures and honours and all secular knowledge are *nothing*, that *nothing* is of value save God and love and things eternal. Such series of *nihil* or *nil* occur also in the miscellaneous works of Thomas à Kempis, though not so frequently as in the *Imitatio*:

Nil quippe tibi melius, nil salubrius, nil suavius, nil jucundius, nil dignius, nil altius, nil felicius, nil perfectius nil beatius: quam ardentissime amare et altissime laudare Deum.   (*Vallis Liliorum*, Pohl, IV. 109. 14.)

Nil quippe Iesu dulcius, nil salubrius, nil efficacius. Nil Nazareno candidius, nil purius sanctiusque. Nil rege Iudaeorum dignius, nil potentius, nil sublimius.
                                                            (*De passione Christi*, Pohl, V. 150. 2.)

Nil quippe perfectius, nil salubrius, nil utilius, nil laudabilius, nil securius et quietius pro bona conscientia et pace cordis habenda; quam ut religiosus Deo devotus et professus monachus...libenter praelato suo oboediat.
                                                            (*Sermones ad novicios*, Pohl, VI. 147. 25.)

9.6.   The results of the investigation on the *Imitatio* thus proved full of interest and gave plenty of encouragement to proceed further. It seemed to me that two similar investigations ought to be made (1) on the vocabulary of the acknowledged miscellaneous works of Thomas à Kempis, excluding the *Imitatio*, (2) on the vocabulary of the theological works of Gerson. That Gerson could have written the book seemed to me, I must admit, plainly impossible, apart from all questions of style; since it was clearly written for his fellows by one who was leading the monastic life: and from the little that I knew of Gerson's style *that* seemed to me equally incompatible with his authorship. Nevertheless his candidature was still supported by many eminent French critics even in the latter part of the nineteenth century, and he had for long been practically the only opposition candidate remaining in the field. Given the two sets of data one might, I hoped, at least get some interesting comparisons on novel lines. But one could not go ahead so rapidly as with the *Imitatio*, one short work conveniently provided with a complete concordance. The works of Thomas à Kempis in the valuable edition of Pohl (ref. 9.10) run to seven small octavo volumes each of 350 to 400 pages, apart from appendices, the *Imitatio* occupying only the bulk of vol. II. The works of Gerson in the edition used (ref. 9.11) fill four volumes folio. Somehow out of this mass of material one would have in each case to take a manageable sample and preferably a sample of the same size as the *Imitatio* or as near as might be, i.e. about 8200 occurrences, for it was obvious that only samples of the same size could be fully compared.

9.7.   The minor works of Thomas à Kempis were naturally the first to be tackled. Omitting blanks, titles, etc. the *Imitatio* in vol. II of Pohl covers some 248 whole pages net. A sample of some 248 pages spread over the minor works might then be expected to give one something like the same number of occurrences of a noun, at a first rough estimate. How were these pages to be taken? Here I was to some extent guided by experience, having already had the problem of sampling these same works for sentence-length (ref. 9.12). I decided to take sub-samples of *ten pages each* from a number of the minor works, exercising my judgment if necessary as to what should be included, and perhaps taking two such sub-samples from one of the longer works so as to give some weight to its length. It would obviously be necessary to keep an eye on the number of occurrences of a noun being included, and for this purpose the nouns were written out on manuscript sheets and the nouns on each sheet counted as it was completed, a process carried on into most of the subsequent work. The following list shows the works from which the samples were actually taken: it will be seen that two samples were taken from four of the longer works and 1.2 from the tract *De resurrectione Christi*, etc. in vol. V. This last entry means that one sample was taken from that tract in the first instance, but when I had taken twenty-two samples and found my total requirements almost made up I harked back to it for the extra couple of pages necessary, as it was a relatively long work that might well have been represented by two full samples. The pages for a sample were never started on the first page of the work, for that would always be a part-page, but on a near page thereafter, and were continued at such intervals as might spread the sample pages well over the work: e.g. in a short work one might take pp. 83, 85, 87, etc., in a longer work pp. 131, 137, 143, 149, etc., and so on.

The *Cantica* in vol. IV were omitted deliberately, as poetry and prose should in no case be confounded. In vol. VII the second, third and fourth books of the *Dialogi noviciorum* containing the biographies of Gerard Groote, and of Florentius and his disciples, were not used, as purely biographical matter is not properly comparable with the *Imitatio*. The *Chronica montis S. Agnetis*, also in vol. VII, was omitted for similar reasons. It will be seen that my original estimate, that 24 or 25 ten-page samples would be necessary, was excessive. Either the prose of these minor works is more substantival or there is on the whole less waste space on the page.

THOMAS À KEMPIS: works from which ten-page samples were taken

	Volume in Pohl	Title of work	Number of samples
1.	Vol. I	De tribus tabernaculis	1
2.	,,	De vera compunctione cordis	1
3.	,,	Sermones devoti	1
4.	,,	Epistula ad quendam cellerarium	1
5.	,,	Soliloquium animae	2
6.	Vol. III	Meditatio de incarnatione Christi	1
7.	,,	Sermones de vita et passione Domini	2
8.	Vol. IV	Hortulus rosarum	1
9.	,,	Vallis liliorum	1
10.	,,	Consolatio pauperum with Epitaphium monachorum	1
11.	,,	Manuale parvulorum	1
12.	,,	Doctrinale juvenum	1
13.	,,	Hospitale pauperum	1
14.	,,	De solitudine et silentio	1
15.	Vol. V	De vita et beneficiis Salvatoris Jesu Christi, and De passione Christi	2
16.	,,	De resurrectione Christi	1·2
17.	Vol. VI	Sermones ad novicios	2
18.	Vol. VII	Dialogi noviciorum: liber primus. De contemptu mundi	1
		Total samples of 10 pages	22·2

9.8.   When the manuscript sheets of nouns occurring in these samples had been completed, the occurrences of the nouns had to be booked on to cards. For a noun that had already been met with in the *Imitatio* the same card was used, the record being continued on the second line, a tick or stroke being entered on the line for each occurrence and these ticks or strokes being grouped in fives for convenience in counting. When a new noun occurred, its card was begun on the first line with the entry zero for the *Imitatio* so as to keep all cards in the same form. As each occurrence of a noun on the manuscript sheet was booked up, the entry on the sheet was struck through: at least that was the intended rule, but if on looking at a sheet which I thought had been completed a noun was noticed which had not been struck through, the question at once arose whether in fact I had failed to book up the occurrence or whether I had merely failed to delete the noun after making the entry. An error of this kind might result in a noun being entered twice. On the other hand the entry on the sheet might be struck through first, with the intention of making the entry on the card afterwards, and then owing to some distraction the card entry be omitted after all. On the whole, errors of omission for some unknown reason preponderated in this work and continued consistently to preponderate in later work, the total number of occurrences booked on to the cards, which of course could only be known on completion of the word-distribution, always proving fewer, even if by only a few units, than the numbers counted on the sheets. In view of the variability of the author and the rough nature of the sampling process I do not think the error is of any real consequence; in work of this kind one may be quite well content with the sort of accuracy of, say, a Census. Moreover the effect of practice—it is difficult to imagine why—was to reduce the error to quite trifling proportions. When all the nouns had been booked from the sheets on to the cards, the totals had to be entered on the cards and then checked; in view of the large proportions of 0's, 1's, 2's, etc. this was not a very formidable business. The word-distribution was then compiled by dealing the cards into packs according to the totals entered for the occurrences in the miscellaneous works of Thomas à Kempis (0's, i.e. nouns occurring in the *Imitatio* but not found in the samples from the *Miscellanea*, 1's, 2's, 3's, and so on) and then counting the cards in each pack. The cards were checked while counting, to see that no card had got into its wrong pack, and all counts were made at least twice. Only those who have done such work will know how horridly, in spite of checking, errors will at times escape detection and are only discovered, at a later stage, through some accident or by further work that itself effects a check.

9.9. The noun-distribution for these samples from the miscellaneous works of Thomas à Kempis was given as an illustration in Table 2.2, but is repeated for convenience of comparison in Table 9.1 (§ 9.13), the sums S_0, S_1 and S_2, together with the mean, standard deviation, characteristic, etc., being given in Table 9.2. I postpone the discussion of these data for the present; they are all considered together in § 9.13. But it may be mentioned here that the 'characteristic' was devised during the early stages of this work on Thomas à Kempis and the first calculations of a characteristic were made. To see how things were going without waiting till the cards were complete, I booked up a frequency distribution at intervals when I was very roughly one-fourth of the way, half-way and three-fourths of the way through the work. These intermediate distributions, since they were found not by card sorting but merely by bookings on to a sheet (refs. A), are not completely to be trusted, but they are not likely to be at all seriously in error: had I at the time fully realised the interest of the results they would have been more carefully checked. These intermediate distributions and the final distribution gave the following values of the characteristic:

Total occurrences, S_1: 2022, 4373, 6539, 8203.
Characteristic, K: 73·8, 69·8, 65·5, 59·7.

So far from remaining constant, the characteristic shows a steady continuous decrease with increasing size of sample. The result was at first most disturbing—the reader must remember that the experiment in sampling of Chapter 4 was not made till months later—but thinking the matter over I came to the conclusion that it was what one ought to expect as the normal, if not necessary, consequence when a writer kept moving from one part to another of his heterogeneous field. I do not think I can do better than quote the note I made in February 1939: 'Would not this result be natural with non-homogeneous material? As the investigation was pushed into different subdivisions of the field, words that had a very small λ in the first patch might now have a better chance of being taken; others that formerly had a large chance would find it lowered, so the general tendency would be for the relative chances to be levelled up a bit, or v_λ lowered.' It was very pleasing to get the direct confirmation of this conclusion by the work on Macaulay and Bunyan (§§ 6.7 and 6.14) long afterwards in the autumn of 1940.

9.10.   The four folio volumes of the works of Gerson in the edition used are printed in two columns. A column seemed too long to form a convenient small unit for building up a sub-sample, and too variable a unit also, as it is frequently broken up by wide spaces for cross-headings, etc. It was finally decided to proceed here on different lines and make the sub-sample not a specified number of columns or lines but a specified number of occurrences of a noun. If the sub-sample were taken as 333 or 334 occurrences of a noun (one-third of a thousand) this would seem fairly convenient: 24 of such sub-samples, or 6 from each volume, would make up 8000 occurrences and the odd 200 or so could be furnished by a shorter sample either from vol. IV or anywhere else that seemed convenient. In choosing the works to be sampled one had to be careful: some works are included in the volumes that are not, or are only doubtfully, Gerson's; some that have been translated from the vernacular by another hand—I hope I have avoided errors on these heads—and some that are on entirely non-religious subjects (legal, etc.). Obviously, to be fair to Gerson, one must confine oneself to his strictly religious writings and amongst these one ought to give play to a bias in favour of anything at all suggestive, by title or otherwise, of the *Imitatio*. I may not have been very successful in this respect: but if so my lack of success must be ascribed to unfamiliarity with the works and not to intention. The works sampled are stated in the following list: the reference is given by volume, or part, and the column in which the work begins, the volumes being numbered by columns and not by pages. A sample meant usually something like two to four columns, and these were spaced out over the work cited as with the pages in the last case. The total amount sampled came to some 80½ columns, an average of about 3¼ columns per sample.

GERSON: works from which samples were taken
of 333 or 334 occurrences of a noun

	Volume and column	Title of work
1.	I. 233.	*Sermo factus in die Circumcisionis Domini coram Papa apud Tarasconem*
2.	I. 258	*Sermo factus coram Alexandro Papa in die Ascensionis Domini*
3.	I. 317.	*Sermo habitus coram concilio Constantiensi*
4.	I. 460.	*Epistola…super tertia parte libri Ruysbroech, de ornatu spiritualium nuptiarum*
5.	I. 529.	*Tractatus de probatione spirituum*
6.	I. 535.	*Tractatus de examinatione doctrinarum*
7.	II. 376.	*Tractatus de parvulis trahendis ad Christum*
8.	II. 549.	*Sermo de vita clericorum*
9.	II. 572.	*Sermo de poenitentia*
10.	II. 642.	*Sermo de quatuor domibus*
11.	II. 712.	*Sermo factus in die Nativitatis Domini*
12.	II. 718.	*Sermo factus Dominica in Septuagesima*
13.	III. 7.	*De consolatione Theologiae*, prose only
14.	III. 160.	*Liber de vita spirituali animae*
15.	III. 252.	*Considerationes de mystica theologia*
16.	III. 364.	*Tractatulus de meditatione cordis*
17.	III. 534.	*Secretum colloquium hominis contemplativi ad animam suam et animae ad hominem super paupertate et mendicitate spirituali*
18.	III. 600.	*Tractatus de oratione et suo valore*
19.	IV. 81.	*Sermo de coena Domini*
20.	IV. 161.	*Lectiones duae super illud Marci, Poenitemini et credite Evangelio*
21.	IV. 257.	*Sermo factus in secunda feria Pentecostes, de sancto Spiritu*
22.	IV. 316.	*Sermo contra luxuriam*
23.	IV. 573.	*Sermo de conceptione virginis Mariae*
24.	IV. 770.	*Tractatus de consolatione in mortem amicorum*
25.	IV. 829.	*Sermo coram rege pro pace* (short sample)

9.11.   I cannot say I think either the method of sampling used for the works of Thomas à Kempis or that used for the works of Gerson very good.

One ought naturally to weight each work in proportion to its length, but the former especially weights some works far more heavily than others: e.g. a ten-page sample out of the *De vera compunctione cordis* or the *Manuale parvulorum* takes 10 pages out of 16, the two samples from the *Sermones ad novicios* only take 20 out of 308 or 10 out of 154. For Gerson's works I do not think the scatter is quite so great. All that can be said is that the works of Thomas à Kempis are fairly well covered, nearly all that are of importance and properly comparable with the *Imitatio* being represented; and that, while the works of Gerson are far too voluminous to be covered to anything like the same extent, at least the samples are well distributed over every class of his theological writings. It must be remembered that these were early attempts at sampling and I had not the experience since acquired. But even if I had, I should not have cared to attempt in these instances the better methods used, e.g. for Bunyan's works. For them there were cheap editions available, and there was no objection to marking freely with a pencil the working copy bought for that sole purpose: this was very necessary to show the exact lines taken into the sample from every page at each stage. My set of Pohl's edition of the works of Thomas à Kempis on the contrary was valuable, having been procured with difficulty since the first volume to be published (vol. v) was already out of print; and the volumes of Gerson belonged to the College Library, not to me. To cover the pages of either with pencil marks would have been unseemly to say the least.

9.12.   The noun-distribution for Gerson was given as an illustration in Table 2.3, but is repeated in Table 9.1 and the particulars concerning it given in Table 9.2. As with the work on the *Miscellanea* of Thomas à Kempis, when making up the cards for Gerson I drew up rough intermediate distributions when I was about one-fourth, one-half, and three-fourths of the way through the manuscript sheets, the distributions not being checked since I drafted them solely for my own interest and amusement and never realised they might be of sufficient interest for publication. These intermediate distributions and the final data given by card sorting gave the following values for the characteristic:

Total occurrences, S_1: 1999, 4000, 6000, 8196.
Characteristic, K: 41·3, 33·4, 34·0, 35·9.

Like the corresponding figures for the à Kempis *Miscellanea* (§ 9.9) these show a decrease *on the whole*, but there the resemblance ends. The à Kempis figures show a steady and continuous decrease, the numbers falling without a break from the first to the last. Here the first figure is the largest but the second is the lowest; the third is slightly larger than the second, and the fourth than the third. This is a warning that the mixture of heterogeneous material need not *necessarily* lower the characteristic, though that is the most probable result. I cannot fully explain the difference between the course shown by these figures for Gerson and the steady fall exhibited by those for the minor works of Thomas à Kempis, but the difference must in some way be related to the arrangement of their works. From the works of Thomas à Kempis, to begin with, we eliminated some that might well have exhibited marked divergences of vocabulary, the *Cantica*, the Lives and the Chronicle of Mount St Agnes. Of the remainder, most cover a fairly varied ground, though some such as Sermons or Meditations on the Passion might give a distinctly specialised vocabulary. But one of my 'quarters of the whole work' would require five or six samples, and if the reader will refer to the list in § 9.7 I think he will agree that any *five or six* consecutive samples, even if they all come from the same volume, do not show at all a *sharply* specialised character. In fact no one of my 'fourths of the whole work' is differentiated clearly from any other by any *assignable* distinctions. Matters are entirely different in the case of Gerson: 'one-fourth of the whole work' would here mean the samples from one of his volumes, and *each volume contains writings of a particular type*. The last three parts have a description given on the title-page: for the first I fail to find such a description but have borrowed one from the prefatory matter, which seems to apply though written concerning another edition. Here they are:

Prima pars continet ea quae et fidem et ecclesiæ regimen et errores circa illa concernunt.

Secunda pars operum maxime continet, quae ad mores sanctius informandos conducunt.

Tertia pars operum mysticam theologiam et meditandi rationem demonstrat.

Quarta pars operum conciones ad populum praesertim complectitur.

Here we have a quite definite grouping by the type of work, which would be bound to affect the type of vocabulary. The first volume or 'Part', in particular, differs so markedly from the second in vocabulary that one could not help noticing the abrupt change, but change was in some degree conspicuous between the later volumes also. One would notice a word rare in earlier volumes suddenly beginning to build up its score in the last, *amor* I remember was a case in point: or conversely a word common in the first part becoming comparatively rare in the later volumes. It would obviously be possible for these abrupt changes in the vocabulary between successive volumes to take place in such a way as first to lower and then slightly to raise v_λ, with consequent parallel changes in K, and this is what must have happened. With the less formal arrangement of matter in the volumes of Thomas, the variations in vocabulary must have been of a much less systematic, more nearly random, character. This is all, I think, that need be said by way of introduction on the mode in which the samples were taken and the vocabularies taken and recorded.

9.13. Now let us turn to Tables 9.1 and 9.2 and consider together the three distributions at which we have arrived. In the first place we notice that the *Imitatio* exhibits by far the smallest vocabulary of the three, 1168 nouns, as against 1406 for the samples from the miscellaneous works of Thomas à Kempis and 1754 for the samples from the religious works of Gerson. The proportions are 1000:1204:1502, so that the vocabulary of the *Miscellanea* is one-fifth greater than that of the *Imitatio*, and the vocabulary of Gerson one-half greater. The difference between the *Imitatio* and the miscellaneous works of Thomas à Kempis might well be accounted for by the greater heterogeneity of the latter. The *Imitatio* itself, it is true, can hardly be described as completely homogeneous, for Lib. IV (as ordinarily numbered, though in Thomas's autograph manuscript it stands as III) is on a special and limited subject, 'Devota exhortatio ad sacram communionem', with in some degree a special vocabulary of its own. The noun *communio* occurs 27 times in the *Imitatio*, but of these 27 occurrences 26 are in Lib. IV: the noun does occur in the minor works of Thomas à Kempis but was not caught in my samples, nor was it caught in the samples from Gerson—whether it occurs in his works at all I cannot say. Fifteen of the seventeen occurrences of *sacerdos* and *all* the 38 occurrences of *sacramentum* are also in Lib. IV. A certain number of the manuscripts, as is well known, do not contain Lib. IV, and in some of the early printed editions it is given a special title of its own.* But notwithstanding this heterogeneity of the *Imitatio* itself, it is clear that a lot of samples taken from some twenty different works is almost certain to possess a still greater heterogeneity. The first two vocabularies in Table 9.2 are not, therefore, directly comparable with safety. But the last two vocabularies are quite properly comparable, *both* being based on scattered samples from diverse works. We may conclude accordingly that for mixed samples of the kind, totalling to some 8000 occurrences, the

---

* Of the two editions of the Italian translation published by Miscomini at Florence in 1491 and 1493 (de Backer 1474 and 1475) the first treats Lib. IV in the *incipit* as a separate work, not terming it the fourth book; in the second the *incipit* terms the book 'elquarto' but the colophon treats it as a separate work. The third edition alone of 1494 (de Backer 1476) terms the book 'elquarto' and makes no qualification.

TABLE 9.1. Showing the number f_x of nouns occurring X times each (1) in the *De Imitatione Christi* (col. 2); (2) in samples spread over the miscellaneous works of Thomas à Kempis (other than the *Imitatio*), col. 3; (3) in samples spread over the religious works of Gerson, col. 4. (These were also given in Tables 2.1, 2.2, 2.3)

1	2	3	4	1	2	3	4
	f_x for				f_x for		
X	Imitatio	à Kempis	Gerson	X	Imitatio	à Kempis	Gerson
1	520	621	804	48	1	1	—
2	174	216	318	50	1	4	—
3	111	122	164	51	1	—	—
4	70	90	98	52	1	1	2
5	37	66	71	53	1	1	—
6	33	46	46	54	1	—	—
7	20	28	34	56	1	1	1
8	28	30	27	57	2	—	1
9	11	21	25	58	1	—	1
10	14	15	16	59	—	3	—
11	10	11	11	61	1	—	—
12	9	8	8	62	3	—	—
13	11	8	10	63	1	—	1
14	5	7	9	64	—	—	1
15	4	10	6	65	—	1	—
16	7	6	10	66	—	—	1
17	7	7	3	67	—	—	1
18	4	4	2	68	—	1	1
19	5	5	5	69	1	1	—
20	2	6	7	74	—	—	1
21	5	5	4	76	2	—	—
22	1	3	4	79	1	—	—
23	1	2	6	86	—	—	1
24	7	3	1	91	—	1	—
25	2	—	2	92	1	—	1
26	1	5	5	93	—	1	—
27	4	4	7	94	1	—	1
28	3	2	2	95	—	1	—
29	2	3	3	102	1	2	1
30	3	3	2	104	1	—	—
31	1	—	—	105	—	—	1
32	—	3	4	115	—	1	—
33	2	1	—	116	—	1	—
34	2	1	4	135	1	—	—
35	—	—	2	146	1	—	—
36	2	4	1	162	—	1	—
37	5	—	—	172	1	—	—
38	4	3	1	196	1	—	—
39	3	3	2	200	—	1	—
40	1	1	3	210	1	—	—
41	1	—	3	242	1	—	—
42	—	1	2	256	—	—	1
43	2	3	—	369	—	1	—
44	2	1	2	418	1	—	—
45	—	1	1				
46	2	—	1	Total	1168	1406	1754
47	—	3	1				

vocabulary of Gerson is greater than that of Thomas à Kempis by about one-fourth. But we cannot be sure that the excess of the vocabulary for the miscellaneous works of Thomas à Kempis over that for the *Imitatio* is due to anything but the fact that in the former case we are dealing with a hotch-potch of different works, in the latter with a single work. On these figures for vocabulary Gerson, to say the least of it, looks a highly unlikely candidate

TABLE 9.2. The sums and sundry data for the three
word-distributions of Table 9.1

Quantity	*Imitatio*	à Kempis	Gerson
1. Sum S_0, vocabulary	1168	1406	1754
2. Sum S_1, occurrences	8225	8203	8196
3. Sum S_2	577665	409619	248984
4. Mean M	7·042	5·834	4·673
5. 1000 S_0/S_1	142	171	214
6. Variance	444·987	257·298	120·118
7. Standard deviation	21·095	16·045	10·960
8. Percentage of once-nouns	44·5	44·2	45·8
9. Characteristic K	84·2	59·7	35·9

for authorship of the *Imitatio*, but Thomas à Kempis cannot be excluded. In consequence of its low vocabulary the *Imitatio* has the highest mean, 7·042 occurrences against only 4·673 for Gerson, and it has also the highest standard deviation, 21·095 against only 10·960 for Gerson. It may be noted that the respective ranges of the distributions stand in the same order as the standard deviations: the highest number of occurrences is 418 for the *Imitatio*, 369 for the samples from Thomas à Kempis, and 256 for the samples from Gerson. The outstanding substantive is in each instance *Deus*. The percentages of once-nouns on the vocabularies, rather surprisingly in view of the very different dispersions, are very close to one another, ranging only between 44·2 and 45·8, and are of no service for differentiating authorship. Finally we come to the characteristic. Here the *Imitatio* stands well at the top with the high characteristic of 84·2: the *Miscellanea* of Thomas à Kempis come next with 59·7, and the samples from Gerson last with the low figure of 35·9. The last two figures are properly comparable, both being based on a hotch-potch, and we may write down Gerson as being distinguished by a much lower characteristic than Thomas à Kempis. But the first two figures are not properly comparable, the first being based on a single work and the second on a hotch-potch. If we had no other information, all that we could say about the figure 59·7 would be that it was certainly a good deal lower than the mean of the characteristics of the separate works included in the samples (cf. §§ 6.7, 6.14). But in fact we have other information. The *first* batch of samples taken from the minor works of Thomas à Kempis (§ 9.9) gave a characteristic of 73·8, not at all so far off from the value for the *Imitatio*, 84·2: and even this figure 73·8, it must be remembered, will probably be lower than the mean of the characteristics for the works included; the samples were Nos. 1, 2, 3, 4, 5*a* and 6 of the list in § 9.7. The good fortune of having that additional figure, even if we cannot trust it as absolutely correct, enables us to make two pairs of comparisons of which the first is the best that we can do and the second is fair and proper:

De Imitatione Christi, characteristic	84·2
First set of samples from Thomas à Kempis	73·8
Whole set of samples from Thomas à Kempis	59·7
Whole set of samples from Gerson	35·9

The conclusion now seems quite clear though one would like it to be ratified by direct determination of the characteristics for some of the separate minor works of Thomas à Kempis. Thomas à Kempis, we conclude, in some of his works yields a characteristic fairly close to that of the *Imitatio*: Gerson's characteristic, taking his work as a whole, is much lower than that of Thomas. The facts seem all in favour of Thomas as against Gerson. So much for the purely statistical evidence afforded by these distributions.

9.14.   Next let us consider the evidence given by the *nature* of the vocabularies. In order to distinguish certain classes amongst the nouns, I first went through all the cards—2454 of them—with a concordance to the Vulgate (ref. 9.13) and marked each card with a V if the noun were in the Vulgate or a *v* if it were not. I then started again with three dictionaries, Lewis and Short, Maigne d'Arnis' *Lexicon of Mediaeval Latin*, and Baxter and Johnson's *Mediaeval Latin Word-List from British and Irish sources* (refs. 9.14, 9.15, 9.16). If the noun was in Lewis and Short the card was marked with an L, in the contrary case with a λ. In the latter event it was next looked up in Maigne d'Arnis and if found there the card was marked with an M, in the contrary case with a μ. In the latter event the noun was finally looked up in Baxter and Johnson and the card marked with a B or a β according as the noun were or were not found in that most useful list: it was surprising how many gaps it did fill. The presence of a word in, or its absence from, the concordance or one or more of the dictionaries affords a number of possible bases for the formation of word classes by purely objective criteria which are wholly independent of the personality of the investigator, a point the importance of which cannot be too strongly stressed.

9.15. *Nouns not in the Vulgate.* The cards for the non-Vulgate nouns were taken out from the rest and the distributions compiled: they are given in Table 9.3. No non-Vulgate noun has any very high number of occurrences, but it will be seen at a glance that, while the first two distributions are very much alike, the distribution for Gerson differs substantially from both. The highest number of occurrences for a non-Vulgate noun in the *Imitatio*

TABLE 9.3. Nouns not in the Vulgate: table showing the number f_x of such nouns occurring X times each in the *De Imitatione Christi* and in samples from the miscellaneous works of Thomas à Kempis and the religious works of Gerson. (The distribution of col. 4 was given in Table 2.5)

1	2	3	4
	f_x for		
X	*Imitatio*	à Kempis	Gerson
1	143	167	315
2	23	31	69
3	15	5	28
4	7	11	14
5	6	—	6
6	5	1	2
7	—	6	4
8	1	1	1
9	2	1	2
10	—	—	1
12	1	1	—
13	—	—	1
16	1	—	1
19	—	—	1
34	—	—	1
42	—	—	1
Total	204	224	447
S_1	376	365	823
	Percentage of all nouns not in the Vulgate		
Vocabulary	17·5	15·9	25·5
Occurrences	4·57	4·45	10·0

is 16, for a noun in the samples from the miscellaneous works of Thomas à Kempis 12; but the samples from Gerson show nouns with 19, 34 and 42 occurrences. The total numbers of these nouns (the non-Vulgate vocabularies) are 204, 224 and 447, as shown at the foot of the table. The total numbers of occurrences are 376, 365 and 823. Looking up the corresponding totals for all nouns in Table 9.2 we find the percentages given in the last two lines of Table 9.3. For example, for the *Imitatio* the total vocabulary is 1168 and the proportion of non-Vulgate nouns to all nouns is therefore 204/1168 or 17·5 per cent. For the same work the total number of occurrences is 8225, and therefore the proportion of occurrences of non-Vulgate nouns to occurrences of all nouns is 376/8225 or 4·57 per cent. For the samples from the minor works of Thomas à Kempis the corresponding percentages are 15·9 and 4·45, very close indeed to those for the *Imitatio*. But for Gerson we have an entirely different state of affairs. The proportion of non-Vulgate nouns in the vocabulary of the samples from his writings is over 25 per cent, or about half as much again as the proportion for the *Imitatio* or the minor works of Thomas à Kempis: and the proportion of occurrences of non-Vulgate nouns to occurrences of all nouns is 10 per cent, or more than double the corresponding proportions for the *Imitatio* and the minor works of Thomas à Kempis. In this particular point, the proportion of non-Vulgate nouns, the *Imitatio* shows a close resemblance to the miscellaneous works of Thomas à Kempis but an emphatic divergence from the writings of Gerson. One may note in conclusion a rather odd feature of these three distributions. Since Gerson uses *more* non-Vulgate nouns, one might have expected that he would also use them more freely, i.e. that the mean number of occurrences for the distribution of col. 4 would be distinctly greater than the means for cols. 2 and 3. But the three means are 1·84, 1·63, 1·84: the mean for the samples from Gerson is precisely the same as that for the *Imitatio* and only exceeds that for the samples from Thomas à Kempis by a trifle. It is the dispersion, not the mean, that distinguishes the Gerson distribution from those of cols. 2 and 3: the standard deviation is 2·99 against 1·91 for col. 2 and 1·55 for col. 3. The three non-Vulgate nouns in Gerson with 19, 34 and 42 occurrences respectively, which help towards the high dispersion, are *theologus*, *theologia*, and *consideratio*, quite distinctive nouns. *Theologus* does not occur at all in the *Imitatio* and only once in the samples from the miscellaneous works of Thomas à Kempis: *theologia* is not found in either. Neither Thomas à Kempis nor the author of the *Imitatio*— if he is a different individual—cares a whit for the subtleties and riddles of theology, for analysis and definition. The author of the *Imitatio* makes his position clear at once in the first chapter of the first book:

> Quid prodest tibi alta de Trinitate disputare:
> si careas humilitate unde displiceas Trinitati?
> Vere alta verba non faciunt sanctum et justum:
> sed virtuosa vita efficit Deo carum.
> Opto magis sentire compunctionem:
> quam scire ejus definitionem.

And Thomas à Kempis takes a similar stand:

> Qui subtilia cogitat et humilia neglegit:
> foveam parat in quam nescius cadit.
> (Recommendatio humilitatis, Pohl, II. 381. 4–6.)
>
> Nam dulcius est longeque nobilius interiora bona
> experiri quam inde quicquam definire.
> (Sermones devoti, IX, Pohl, I. 127. 26–28.)

But Gerson *was* a theologian and a philosopher, a man of analytic mind, prone to distinguishing and defining, and loving a good long, sustained argument, drilled into order under successive heads, *Consideratio prima, Consideratio secunda, Consideratio tertia*—a thing quite foreign to Thomas à Kempis: and that accounts for the reiterated use of the third word *Consideratio*. Gerson is simply fond of the word: he is very frequently talking about this and that 'consideratio' and thus naturally using the word in crossheadings. In Thomas à Kempis, following the usage of Storr's *Concordance* for the *Imitatio*, I (to the best of my memory) included nouns from headings: but fortunately on coming to Gerson I dropped the practice, foreseeing some difficulties, or the number of occurrences of this word would have run up well over 42. It occurs only 4 times in the *Imitatio* and 7 times in the samples from the miscellaneous works of Thomas à Kempis.

9.16. *Nouns not in the dictionary of Lewis and Short.* The sorting of the cards for these nouns gave the three compact little distributions of Table 9.4, 70 to 80 per cent of them being once-nouns. The table is singularly suggestive of a sort of compressed version of Table 9.3, the means not differing very substantially (1·55, 1·53, 1·60) but the standard deviation for the Gerson distribution being considerably greater than that of either col. 2 or col. 3 (1·14, 0·97, 1·92). Evaluating the proportions of nouns not in Lewis and Short to all nouns (cf. Table 9.2), both for vocabulary and occurrences, we have the percentages shown at the foot of the table. For the proportions based on vocabulary, p_v, the figures for cols. 2 and 3 are a little over and under 3 per cent; the figure for Gerson is 5·76 per cent. For the proportions based on occurrences, p_w, the figures for cols. 2 and 3 are in very close agreement, 0·72 and 0·71, but the figure for Gerson is 1·98, some two and three-quarter times the percentage for the *Imitatio* or for Thomas à Kempis. Once more the *Imitatio* shows a close resemblance to the miscellaneous works of Thomas à Kempis but an emphatic divergence from the works of Gerson. The three substantives occurring 7, 10 and 16 times respectively in the Gerson distribution are *esse* (as a noun), *curatus* and *praelatus*, again rather a characteristic selection—a purely philosophical term and two others that are ecclesiastical rather than religious. Neither *esse* nor *curatus* occurs in the *Imitatio* or in the samples from Thomas à Kempis: *praelatus* occurs 5 times in the first and 4 in the second. The data of Table 9.4 were used for an illustration in § 5.17, with the additional information that the total number of distinct nouns not in Lewis and Short (for the three authors together) was 148.

TABLE 9.4. Nouns not in Lewis and Short's *Latin Dictionary*: table showing the number f_x of such nouns occurring X times each in the *De Imitatione Christi* and in samples from the miscellaneous works of Thomas à Kempis and the religious works of Gerson

1	2	3	4
X	f_x for		
	Imitatio	à Kempis	Gerson
1	28	27	79
2	5	6	12
3	2	1	3
4	—	4	3
5	3	—	1
7	—	—	1
10	—	—	1
16	—	—	1
Total	38	38	101
S_1	59	58	162
	Percentage of nouns not in Lewis and Short's *Dictionary*		
Vocabulary	3·25	2·70	5·76
Occurrences	0·72	0·71	1·98

9.17. *Nouns not in the Vulgate nor traceable in the dictionaries used.* Retaining only nouns not found either in the Vulgate, or in Lewis and Short, or in Maigne d'Arnis, or in Baxter and Johnson, naturally gives one a rather brief list: after some reconsideration of a doubtful case or two there are 31 nouns left, which are listed in Table 9.5 with the number of times each was found in the data from each of our three authors. It will be seen that they are all once-nouns in the respective authors save in a single case, *extersio* occurring twice, in a passage of Gerson (II. 583. A) relating to the washing of the disciples' feet. It may be of interest to run through the list and comment on some of the words. *Ablatrix, auditrix* and *productrix* are simply feminine forms of nouns that are in Lewis and Short, and *secretaria,* a female secretary, 'veritas, nostra secretaria' (Gerson, IV, 582. F), is the feminine of *secretarius*, which is given in Maigne d'Arnis. *Homogeneitas* is dealt with in the notes to Table 9.6. The form *hypocrisia* instead of the usual *hypocrisis* occurs in the *De tribus tabernaculis* (Pohl, I. 20. 6), 'vitium hypo-crisiae'. The occurrence of *insertor* is in the *Soliloquium animae* (Pohl, I. 275. 21–22), 'munditiae amator est et insertor'. The *lactatio* that occurs in Gerson (III. 322. B) is the noun with the sense of *lactation, suckling*, not the noun of the same form with the meaning *allurement*. *Maquerela*, 'heraldi et

TABLE 9.5. Nouns not in the Vulgate, nor in Lewis and Short, nor Maigne d'Arnis, nor Baxter and Johnson (refs. 9.13–9.16). The numbers under A are the numbers of occurrences in the *Imitatio*, under B the numbers of occurrences in the samples from the miscellaneous works of Thomas à Kempis, and under C the numbers of occurrences in the samples from the religious writings of Gerson

	A	B	C		A	B.	C
1. Ablatrix	1	0	0	18. Lactatio	0	0	1
2. Auditrix	0	0	1	19. Luciditas	0	0	1
3. Collapsus-ūs	0	0	1	20. Maquerela	0	0	1
4. Decrepitudo	0	0	1	21. Pigritatio	0	1	0
5. Desiderator	1	1	0	22. Praegustus-ūs	1	0	0
6. Dogmatizatio	0	0	1	23. Producibilitas	0	0	1
7. Edomatio	1	0	0	24. Productrix	1	0	0
8. Elargitio	0	0	1	25. Recollectio	1	1	0
9. Elargitor	0	1	0	26. Sagittator	0	1	0
10. Emundatorium	0	0	1	27. Secretaria	0	0	1
11. Excultura	0	0	1	28. Substomachatio	0	0	1
12. Extensio	0	0	2	29. Superinfusio	0	0	1
13. Formidatio	0	0	1	30. Tetralogus	0	0	1
14. Gloriuncula	0	0	1	31. Unificatio	0	0	1
15. Homogeneitas	0	0	1				
16. Hypocrisia	0	1	0	Total, words	6	7	20
17. Insertor	0	1	0	Total, occurrences	6	7	21

Proportions per 1000 of nouns in the above list to all nouns:

	A	B	C
Vocabulary, p_v	5·14	4·98	11·40
Occurrences, p_w	0·73	0·85	2·56

maquerelae carnis, mundi et diaboli' (Gerson, IV. 588. E) seems evidently a latinisation of the French *maquerelle*. Only two of these nouns are found in Ducange: *maquerela* (*maquerella*) with a quotation of 1350, and *homogeneitas* as a term of chemistry. In all there are 6 of these out-of-the-way nouns in the *Imitatio*, 7 in the samples from Thomas à Kempis, but no less than 20 in the samples from Gerson. The numbers of occurrences are the same as the vocabularies in the first two columns, but we have to substitute 21 for 20 in the last column. Turning these numbers into proportions of the corresponding figures for all nouns (Table 9.2) the figures are just about 5 per thousand of the vocabulary for both the *Imitatio* and the samples from Thomas, but over double this, 11·40 per thousand, for the samples from Gerson. The proportions of occurrences are only 0·73 and 0·85 per thousand for the *Imitatio* and Thomas, 2·56, or nearly three times as much, for the samples from Gerson. For the third time the figures for the *Imitatio* show that it closely resembles the miscellaneous works of Thomas à Kempis but differs entirely from the writings of Gerson.

9.18. *Non-religious, non-Vulgate, non-classical nouns borrowed from the Greek.* Running through the manuscript lists of nouns and the cards again and again, I got a strong impression that Gerson's vocabulary was a far more

TABLE 9.6. Non-Vulgate, non-classical nouns borrowed from the Greek, excluding common religious or ecclesiastical terms: see text. A, occurrences in *Imitatio*; B, occurrences in samples from Thomas à Kempis; C, occurrences in samples from Gerson

	A	B	C		A	B	C
1. Agalma	0	0	1	12. Metaphysica	0	0	1
2. Anagogia	0	0	4	13. Metaphysicus	0	0	1
3. Analogia	0	0	1	14. Metrista	0	1	0
4. Astronomia	0	0	1	15. Praxis	0	0	2
5. Centrum	0	0	1	16. Spasmus	0	0	1
6. Discrasia	0	0	1	17. Tetragonum	0	0	1
7. Epitheton	0	0	1	18. Tetralogus	0	0	1
8. Homogeneitas	0	0	1	19. Tropus	0	0	2
9. Idioma	0	0	2				
10. Latria	0	0	1	Total, words	0	1	18
11. Melancholia	0	0	1	Total, occurrences	0	1	24

Proportions per 1000 of all nouns:

	A	B	C
Vocabulary, p_v	0	0·71	10·26
Occurrences, p_w	0	0·12	2·93

NOTES: 1. Hoc est simulacrum vel conceptum, Gerson, III. 36. A. 2. Mystical interpretation. 6. Febrium discrasia, III. 366. F. 8. The meaning is likeness of kind, not uniformity of composition. 9. Per communicationem idiomatum, I. 238. E. and II. 713. F. 14. Poet or versifier. 18. Multa conquirens...nunc a litera, nunc ab allegoria, nunc a moralitate, nunc ab anagogia in modum tetralogi, I. 322. F.

learned vocabulary than the others—as surely one might expect—and in particular that, apart altogether from familiar religious words or ecclesiastical terms, it showed an exceptional proportion of words borrowed from the Greek. For my own interest I tried to make a list of such words, but it was difficult in this case entirely to eliminate the element of personal judgment. I began by deciding to cut out all words that occurred in the Vulgate: this eliminated the commonest religious words and some others that one would hardly call religious but which might well be acquired by a man like Thomas à Kempis who knew his Vulgate well but had nothing like the extent of classical learning possessed by Gerson. But this still left in a number of religious or ecclesiastical words (*biblia, clericus, canonicus, laicus, monachus, monasterium*, etc. etc.) which are not biblical. These had to be eliminated; but here I could not see my way to any mechanical test: the test had to remain in some degree personal, and I simply cut out all nouns which, in my opinion, could be described as religious or ecclesiastical terms in fairly common use, ultimately leaving in only a couple of terms having any relation to religion, viz. *anagogia* (on the ground that it was a technical term of theology rather than religion) and *latria*. Even then I felt not quite contented with the list remaining, which looked unduly loaded with familiar borrowed Greek words of the classical period, not at all the type of word which had been forced on my attention. Here I was able to fall back on a mechanical test again: I cut out all words in Sir William Smith's *Smaller Latin-English Dictionary* (ref. 9.17), a school dictionary, limited to classical authors. This brought my list down to very modest numbers, but the result (Table 9.6) is extraordinarily striking. No one of the residual nouns occurs in the *Imitatio* and only one in the samples from the miscellaneous works of Thomas à Kempis: on the other hand, 18 of the 19 nouns occur in the samples from Gerson with a total of 24 occurrences. The one word of the class in the samples from Thomas à Kempis is *metrista*, a versifier or poet,

> Dicit metrista devotus monachus factus.
> Hoc est nescire: sine Christo plurima scire.
> (*Doctrinale juvenum*, Pohl, iv. 181.)

The word is in Maigne d'Arnis with a reference to Bernard de Breydenbach (ob. 1497) and in Baxter and Johnson with the dates 15th century and circa 1540, entries which, so far as they go, suggest it was a word of the period. The nouns in Gerson are of a different kind, mostly more or less technical terms of philosophy, theology, rhetoric, etc. Obviously there is no significant disagreement between columns A and B, while yet once again the data for Gerson are entirely divergent.

9.19.   It may be as well to summarise the evidence up to this point. In § 9.13 we discussed the purely statistical evidence afforded by the word-distributions. Difficulties are presented by the fact that the *Imitatio* is a single work, while the samples from Thomas à Kempis and from Gerson are spread over a variety of writings: notwithstanding, the high vocabulary of Gerson makes him a very unlikely candidate for the authorship of the

Imitatio. When we come to the 'Characteristics' of the distributions, the difficulty due to heterogeneity can be partially evaded owing to the happy accident that a characteristic is available for the distribution given by the first quarter of the samples from Thomas à Kempis—not quite so heterogeneous as the totality. This characteristic is 73·8, not greatly below that for the *Imitatio*, 84·2. For the entirety of the samples from Thomas à Kempis the characteristic is 59·7 and for those from Gerson only 35·9. The high vocabulary and low characteristic are all against Gerson: the relatively low vocabulary and high characteristic in favour of Thomas à Kempis. We then proceeded to compare the proportions, both in vocabulary and amongst occurrences, of certain classes of nouns in our three authors (to call them so for the time)—the author of the *Imitatio*, Thomas à Kempis and Gerson— determining those classes as far as possible by purely objective or impersonal tests, i.e. tests independent of the personality of the investigator himself. The said classes of nouns were (1) Nouns not in the Vulgate, § 9.15, Table 9.3; (2) Nouns not in Lewis and Short's *Dictionary*, § 9.16, Table 9.4; (3) Nouns neither in the Vulgate nor in either of three specified dictionaries, § 9.17, Table 9.5; (4) Nouns borrowed from the Greek that are non-Vulgate, non-religious and non-classical, § 9.18, Table 9.6. These four tables gave most consistent results, showing a high degree of similarity between the author of the *Imitatio* and Thomas à Kempis, and a notable divergence on the part of Gerson, the samples from whose works gave in every instance a much higher number or proportion of occurrences of nouns of the classes specified. The totals of occurrences were in fact:

	A	B	C
Table 9.3	376	365	823
Table 9.4	59	58	162
Table 9.5	6	7	21
Table 9.6		1	24

As the total number of occurrences of all nouns is close to 8200 in each case, these figures are fairly comparable with each other. We noted, however, in § 9.13 that for completion of the statistical argument on the basis of the distributions it would be desirable to determine the characteristics for one or two *separate* works of Thomas à Kempis. Perhaps it would also be of interest, though not necessary, to get another classification of nouns. 'Nouns not in Lewis and Short' has no very definite meaning, for the dictionary does not purport to include words up to any definite date: it includes many Vulgate words (but not all, e.g. neither *bravium* (βραβεῖον) nor *gazophylacium*) and also includes large numbers of very late or 'ecclesiastical Latin' words. This inclusiveness results in very short lists of nouns *not* in the dictionary. Would it not be desirable to determine a larger class of 'non-classical' nouns and perhaps as in § 9.18 define this in terms of the school dictionary? The definition is obviously crude but such a dictionary is bound to include the words of the best authors of the classical period, and equally will exclude the 'ecclesiastical' and the mediaeval.

9.20.   In § 9.1 reference was made to the *Scutum Kempense* of Amort. The method used in § 3 of that work is to compare the frequency of 'phrases, et verba alioquin barbara, aut minus bonis authoribus usitata' in the *Imitatio* with their frequency in acknowledged works of Thomas à Kempis. The conclusion reached, on the basis of 350 quotations (which on the one hand overlap a good deal but on the other usually contain more than one marked or italicised word apiece), is: 'Itaque cum haec omnia reperiantur in aliis opusculis Thomae Kemp. non potest esse possibile secundum leges combinatorias quin sit idem author.' I am not happy about this argument and have more than one objection to it as it actually stands. The first, and by far the most important, is on a point of principle; the others on questions of fact. It will be noticed that the form of the argument differs in a very important respect from that of the arguments in this chapter. In every case we have not only compared the *Imitatio* with the minor works of Thomas à Kempis, but also with the works of the other candidate Gerson. The argument is in brief: 'The vocabulary of the *Imitatio* is very much *more* like that of admitted works of Thomas à Kempis than that of the theological works of Gerson.' And surely the double character of this argument is essential. If you want to show that the author of B (not the author of C) is also the author of A, you must show that the vocabularies of A and B are, not merely *alike*, but *more closely alike* than the vocabularies of A and C. There is no explicit second part to Amort's argument, but tacitly it is there—the silent premiss that these words and idioms are such a carefully selected list and so odd that they *couldn't possibly* occur to anything like the same extent in the writings of anyone other than the author of the *Imitatio*, and statistical verification of this premiss is not necessary. The objection in principle to such a simple assumption of one of the premisses is obvious, and is no less valid because Amort really was unable to go further than he did. He was in the main arguing against not Gerson, but Gersen, alleged Benedictine Abbot of Vercelli, and himself brought forward evidence that no such Abbot existed. He could hardly do more: there were no real works of the imaginary Abbot with which he *could* compare the *Imitatio*.

9.21.   But now, given this unhappy state of affairs that no comparison of vocabularies with the second candidate is possible, how ought the list of test-words to be compiled in order that the drawing of such a conclusion as that given by Amort may be as little dangerous as possible? Surely the list should be compiled on some such specification as this: the words, idioms, etc. in question must be (1) not found or exceedingly rarely found in authors of the same epoch writing on similar subjects, and (2) not found in the books which these writers are likely to have read, i.e. books which have served as a foundation for their own vocabulary. If these conditions are fulfilled, then Amort's appeal to the 'laws of combinations' may be justified. The argument, I take it, would be somewhat as follows: (1) For all other authors of the period whose writings we have examined the chances of these words or phrases being used (or their λ's) are exceedingly small. (2) The author of the *Imitatio* appears to be a biased sampler for whom the chances in question are much larger. (3) If then we find any considerable proportion of these words, etc. in any other work, that work is probably by the author of the *Imitatio*, or to put it the other way round the *Imitatio* was probably written by the author of that work.

9.22. Amort does not, however, define his words and idioms in anything like the terms suggested, nor is any evidence given that he has made any special examination of the works of theological writers contemporary with the *Imitatio*. The heading to his § 3 refers to 'phrases et verba alioquin barbara, aut minus bonis authoribus usitata', the heading to par. 23 of his § 4 says that the author of the *Imitatio* 'habet quendam habitum derivandi aut excogitandi novas voces, aut talibus minus usitatis utendi', and proceeds to give illustrations. But surely almost any theological writer of the period may be expected to use 'phrases et verba alioquin barbara'; and as to phrases and words 'minus bonis authoribus usitata'—who are meant by 'good authors'? If the phrase means classical authors, or authors who try to write in a purely classical style, the selection of words 'little used by classical writers' seems misconceived: almost any fifteenth-century writer will be apt to use many such words. If the term does not mean classical writers, it is not clear what it means. In the second heading cited, a precisely similar question arises—What is meant by 'voces...minus usitatae'? words little used by whom? Even a brief inspection of Amort's actual lists does not make one any happier as to his method of selection. It is obvious enough that any theological writer of the period is sure to draw much of his vocabulary from the Vulgate, and that therefore under condition (2) laid down in § 9.21 Vulgate words should be excluded from the test list. Yet on quite a casual inspection of § 3 of the *Scutum* I find italicised (as a marked word) in par. 185 *provisor* (2 Mac. 4. 2), in par. 195 *sufferentia* (Eccli. 16. 14;

Jac. 5. 11), and in par. 321 *susceptor,* which occurs thirteen times in the Psalms. In par. 21 of the same section 'Noli altum *sapere*' (*Imit.* i. 2. 28) is cited, with the verb italicised; but this is a direct quotation from Rom. 11.20, 'Be not highminded'. In par. 23 of the following § 4, the heading of which was cited above, the first example given is a sentence from Lib. i, cap. iv of the *Imitatio,*

longanimiter res est...ponderanda.

Amort does not italicise here, but the only word which can well be regarded as amongst either 'novas voces' or 'voces minus usitatas' is *longanimiter,* and this is found in quite a familiar text,

Et sic longanimiter ferens, adeptus est repromissionem.
And so, after he had patiently endured, he obtained the promise.
(Hebr. 6. 15, A.V.)

Perhaps I misunderstand in some way the point of these quotations of Amort's, but it would almost seem that the worthy Canon did not know his Vulgate very well. His selected list surely requires serious reconsideration and revision.

REFERENCES

A. STATISTICAL METHOD

The method of 'booking up on a sheet' referred to in § 9.9 is that described in Y & K, § 6.8.

B. CITATIONS IN TEXT OR TABLES

§ 9.1. The authorship controversy: the reader will find a brief epitome in (9.2) and more detailed treatment in (9.1), (9.3) and (9.4). If these do not suffice, he can follow up De Backer's Bibliography (9.5), items 3057–3301. Ref. (9.6) gives evidence in favour of Groote.

(9.1) Cruise, F. R. (1887). *Thomas à Kempis.* London: Kegan Paul, Trench. (Part iv deals with the authorship controversy.)

(9.2) Cruise, F. R. (1898). *Who was the author of the Imitation of Christ?* London: Catholic Truth Society. (A brief epitome.)

(9.3) Wheatley, L. A. (1891). *The Story of the Imitatio Christi.* London: Elliot Stock.

(9.4) De Montmorency, J. E. G. (1906). *Thomas à Kempis: his age and book.* London: Methuen.

(9.5) De Backer, Augustin (1864). *Essai bibliographique sur le livre De Imitatione Christi.* Liège: Grandmont-Donders.

(9.6) Van Ginneken, Jac. (1940). *Trois textes pré-Kempistes du premier livre de l'Imitation.* Amsterdam: Koninklijke Nederlandsche Akademie van Wetenschappen.

§ 9.1. For the *Scutum Kempense* of Amort the edition used was:

(9.7) Sommalius, Henricus (1759). *Thomae Malleoli à Kempis Opera Omnia...cui annexum est Scutum Kempense...autore...Eusebio Amort.* Coloniae Agrippinae: apud Viduam Joan. Wilh. Krakamp.

§ 2. For the work on the *Imitatio* the following were used:

(9.8) Storr, Rayner (1911). *Concordantia ad quatuor libros latine scriptos De Imitatione Christi.* Altera editio Oxford: University Press.

(9.9) Hirsche, Carolus (1891). *Thomae Kempensis De Imitatione Christi Libri Quatuor.* Editio altera. Berolini: Habel. (Quotations are made throughout from this edition and reference made by book, chapter and line as numbered by Hirsche.)

§ 9.6. For the work on the miscellaneous writings of Thomas à Kempis and for the work on Gerson the editions used were:

(9.10) Pohl, M. J. (1902–22). *Thomae Hemerken à Kempis Opera Omnia.* 7 vols. Friburgi Brisigavorum: Herder. (References to this edition are given by volume, page and line on the page.)

(9.11) Gersonii, Ioannis (1606). *Opera . . . in partes quatuor distributa.* Parisiis. (References given by volume, column and section of column, A–F.)

(9.12) Yule, G. U. (1939). 'On sentence-length as a statistical characteristic of style in prose: with application to two cases of disputed authorship.' *Biometrika*, **30**, 363. (One of the cases considered is the authorship of the *Imitatio*.)

§§ 9.14 *et seq.* The following were the dictionaries, etc. used:

(9.13) Peultier, Etienne et Gantois (1896). *Concordantiarum universae scripturae sacrae thesaurus.* Parisiis: Lethielleux.

(9.14) Lewis, C. T. and Short, C. (1879 and later impressions). *A Latin Dictionary.* Oxford: Clarendon Press.

(9.15) Maigne d'Arnis, W. H. (1890). *Lexicon Manuale ad Scriptores mediae et infimae Latinitatis.* Parisiis: Garnier Fratres.

(9.16) Baxter, J. H. and Johnson, C. with the assistance of Phyllis Abrahams (1934). *Medieval Latin Word-List from British and Irish sources.* Oxford: University Press.

(9.17) Smith, Sir William and Hall, T. D. (1881, impression of 1901). *A Smaller Latin-English Dictionary.* 2nd edition. London: John Murray.

(9.18) Ducange (ed. Henschel) (1840–) *Glossarium mediae et infimae Latinitatis.* Parisiis: Firmin Didot Fratres.

Chapter 10

THE *DE IMITATIONE CHRISTI*, THOMAS À KEMPIS AND GERSON, *CONTINUED*

10.1.   From the beginning of these investigations, as mentioned in § 9.1, I had looked forward to drafting correlation tables between the number of occurrences of a word in the *Imitatio* and the numbers of its occurrences in the samples from Thomas à Kempis and the samples from Gerson. To save mere duplication of work this was in fact done at once on completion of the cards, so as to get the single-variate word-distributions and the bi-variate distributions or correlation tables by successive sortings. Thus the entire set of 2454 cards, containing the complete vocabulary for our three sets of samples, was first sorted for the number of occurrences in the *Imitatio*. This gave a first block of 1286 cards of nouns *not* occurring in the *Imitatio*, or nouns with 0 occurrences, and then blocks of 520 cards for nouns with 1 occurrence, 174 for nouns with 2 occurrences, 111 for nouns with 3 occurrences, and so on as shown by the frequencies of Table 9.1, col. 2.   Each of these resulting blocks of cards for 0, 1, 2, 3, etc. occurrences in the *Imitatio* was then re-sorted or sub-sorted according to the numbers of occurrences of the nouns in the samples from Thomas à Kempis, and thus the successive columns could be filled in for the correlation table between X_1 = number of occurrences in the *Imitatio*, and X_2 = number of occurrences in the samples from Thomas à Kempis. The X_1-totals having been taken as totals of columns, totalling the rows of this table gave the distribution for the samples from Thomas à Kempis, Table 9.1, col. 3. The cards (after this sub-sorting) having been put back into their blocks for the *Imitatio* distribution, the blocks were then sub-sorted once more according to the numbers of occurrences of the nouns in the samples from Gerson. This gave the correlation table between X_1 = the number of occurrences in the *Imitatio* and X_3 = the number of occurrences in the samples from Gerson, and also the Gerson distribution of Table 9.1, col. 4.   Finally the whole lot of 2454 cards had to be sorted entirely afresh according to the number of occurrences in the samples from Thomas à Kempis, X_2, and the numbers in the resulting blocks checked with those obtained by summing the rows in the first correlation table. The blocks were then sub-sorted according to the numbers of occurrences of the nouns in the samples from Gerson, and thus the correlation table formed for X_2 and X_3. Since each of the three total or single-variate distributions occurs in two of the correlation tables, agreement between these totals affords a check on the correctness of the sorting and counting.

10.2.   The three correlation tables thus formed are very extensive and could only have been given on folding sheets: owing to the present cost of printing they have been omitted. They are in fact, as might have been conjectured from the distributions for the single variates, of the most inconvenient form possible, a form that is at least suggested by the condensed contingency tables, Tables 10.1–10.3 below (§ 10.3). The great bulk of the frequency is concentrated up in the top left-hand or N.W. corner of the table and thence falls away, very rapidly at first and then much more slowly, towards the bottom right or S.E. corner. A great part of the correlation table is occupied only by single scattered units of frequency. To the eye, the run of the frequencies suggested that the trend turned over more and more steeply as we passed from left to right, so that (in technical terms) the regression was far from linear. But this (see below, § 10.7) was an illusion due to the omission of empty rows and columns, an omission which, though essential for condensation, seriously distorts the apparent form of the distribution. Comparing the three tables with each other, it was evident that the second (*Imitatio*-Gerson) and third (Thomas à Kempis-Gerson) presented a distinctly larger proportion of widely outlying frequencies, towards the N.E. and S.W. corners of the table, than the first table (*Imitatio*-Thomas à Kempis). That is to say, when one compared the *Imitatio* with the samples from Thomas à Kempis one found relatively fewer instances where a noun was used rarely in the first but often in the second or vice versa, and relatively more of such wide discrepancies when one compared the *Imitatio* or the samples from Thomas à Kempis with the samples from Gerson. The presence of these scattered outliers made the second and third tables, especially the former, look better covered—more filled up—with scattered units than the first. The second and third distributions are evidently less highly correlated than the first.

10.3.   But though we cannot reproduce the full tables, perhaps some readers, before we proceed to discuss the correlations, may be glad to study the highly condensed versions obtained by grouping rows and columns. A grouping down to a table with seven rows and seven columns was chosen, leading off with the first three arrays, 0, 1 and 2 ungrouped, followed by 3, 4 and 5 grouped together, and then in the case of the *Imitatio* the three groups 6–19, 20–39, 40 and upwards. But for Thomas à Kempis the last three groups were altered to 6–15, 16–34, 35 upwards, and for Gerson to 6–10, 11–24, 25 upwards, so as to make rough allowances for the lower

TABLE 10.1. Contingency table for numbers of occurrences of nouns in
(1) *Imitatio*, (2) samples from Thomas à Kempis

Occurrences in samples from Thomas à Kempis	Occurrences in *Imitatio*							
	0	1	2	3–5	6–19	20–39	40 up	Total
0	683	271	54	37	2	1	—	1048
1	416	110	47	38	10	—	—	621
2	98	52	21	30	15	—	—	216
3–5	75	63	38	59	40	3	—	278
6–15	14	21	12	51	74	10	2	184
16–34	—	2	2	3	26	19	11	63
35 up	—	1	—	—	1	17	25	44
Total	1286	520	174	218	168	50	38	2454

TABLE 10.2. Contingency table for numbers of occurrences of nouns in
(1) *Imitatio*, (2) samples from Gerson

Occurrences in samples from Gerson	Occurrences in *Imitatio*							
	0	1	2	3–5	6–19	20–39	40 up	Total
0	340	251	53	41	14	1	—	700
1	601	101	42	39	19	2	—	804
2	169	73	25	35	13	3	—	318
3–5	135	65	32	57	40	2	2	333
6–10	31	21	13	26	38	13	6	148
11–24	8	7	8	13	28	16	6	86
25 up	2	2	1	7	16	13	24	65
Total	1286	520	174	218	168	50	38	2454

TABLE 10.3. Contingency table for numbers of occurrences of nouns in
samples from (1) Thomas à Kempis, (2) Gerson

Occurrences in samples from Gerson	Occurrences in samples from Thomas à Kempis							
	0	1	2	3–5	6–15	16–34	35 up	Total
0	198	343	87	59	12	1	—	700
1	553	129	44	52	23	3	—	804
2	156	61	29	46	25	1	—	318
3–5	113	59	42	67	45	6	1	333
6–10	24	27	7	32	35	19	4	148
11–24	3	2	6	16	33	15	11	86
25 up	1	—	1	6	11	18	28	65
Total	1048	621	216	278	184	63	44	2454

dispersions of these distributions. The 'contingency tables' resulting from these groupings are given in Tables 10.1, 10.2, and 10.3. The coefficients of contingency (Pearson's coefficient of mean square contingency) for these tables are as follows; a coefficient can only take the value zero for a distribution exhibiting complete independence:

Table 10.1, *Imitatio* and Thomas à Kempis, $C = 0.71$,
Table 10.2, *Imitatio* and Gerson, $C = 0.61$,
Table 10.3, Thomas à Kempis and Gerson, $C = 0.66$.

The coefficient is highest for the *Imitatio* and the samples from Thomas à Kempis, next highest for the samples from Thomas à Kempis and the samples from Gerson, lowest for the *Imitatio* and the samples from Gerson.

10.4.   Reverting now to the correlation tables, the following are the means and standard deviations, the mean deviation-products p and the correlations r for the three tables: the correlations being high, values of $1 - r^2$ have been added. The subscript 1 refers to the *Imitatio*, 2 to the samples from Thomas à Kempis, and 3 to the samples from Gerson. *All* the cards were booked into each table so that the number of observations was 2454 in each case: the values of the sums S_1 and S_2, as given in Table 9.2, are unaltered by the inclusion of the f_0 frequencies, and the new means, etc. are to be obtained by substituting $S_0 = 2454$ in each case for the value of S_0 in Table 9.2:

$$M_1 = \ \ 3.351671, \qquad M_2 = \ \ 3.342706, \qquad M_3 = \ \ 3.339853.$$
$$\sigma_1 = \ \ 14.9721, \qquad\quad \sigma_2 = \ \ 12.4798, \qquad\quad \sigma_3 = \ \ 9.50294.$$
$$p_{12} = 169.2026, \qquad\quad p_{13} = 114.7301, \qquad\quad p_{23} = 99.2271.$$

$$r_{12} = 0.9056, \qquad\qquad 1 - r_{12}^2 = 0.1799.$$
$$r_{13} = 0.8064, \qquad\qquad 1 - r_{13}^2 = 0.3497.$$
$$r_{23} = 0.8367, \qquad\qquad 1 - r_{23}^2 = 0.2999.$$

The three correlations stand then in exactly the same order as the coefficients of contingency, but are all rather higher. The correlation between the number of occurrences of a noun in the *Imitatio* and the number of its occurrences in the samples from Thomas à Kempis is substantially higher than the correlation between the number of occurrences in the *Imitatio* and the number of occurrences in samples from Gerson: the value of $1 - r^2$ in the latter case is nearly double its value in the former. Differences are not so striking as some of those in the preceding chapter for, owing to similarity of subject, all the correlations are inevitably high, but once more the resemblance of the *Imitatio* to the works of Thomas à Kempis is much closer than its resemblance to the works of Gerson.

10.5. It is obvious that the few nouns with very high numbers of occurrences must greatly influence the value of the mean deviation-product p and hence the value of the correlation r. As a matter of curiosity and to see whether it would appreciably affect the *relative* values of the correlations, I repeated the calculations omitting the noun *Deus*, the noun with the greatest number of occurrences in each distribution. The resulting correlations were

$$r_{12} = 0{\cdot}8607, \qquad r_{13} = 0{\cdot}7237, \qquad r_{23} = 0{\cdot}7639.$$

They are all a little smaller than before, but stand in the same order.

10.6. It is also obvious that there is a certain element of arbitrariness in the magnitude of the $(0, 0)$ frequencies, the frequencies in the top left-hand cells of the tables. They are determined solely by the fact that our vocabulary is limited to that in the three sets of samples. But the vocabulary might have been extended to cover a much wider field, or on the other hand it might have been limited in each table to the total vocabulary of the particular pair concerned. To test the stability of the correlations against arbitrary changes of this kind, the effect was tried of the second alteration suggested, i.e. limiting the vocabulary in each table to the total vocabulary of the particular pair of samples concerned. This merely amounts to putting zero for the frequency in the top left-hand cell of each table. The change only makes slight alterations in the third place of decimals of the correlations, the new values being:

$$r_{12} = 0{\cdot}9037, \qquad r_{13} = 0{\cdot}8050, \qquad r_{23} = 0{\cdot}8356.$$

As before, the correlations stand in precisely the same order. These results give one some confidence in the reasonable stability of the correlations towards either small changes in the frequencies—though indeed the omission of the most frequently occurring noun can hardly be called a *small* change—and towards more or less arbitrary alterations in the field that fixes the total vocabulary.

10.7. Some test of the linearity of the regression (the form of the relationship between the two variables of any table) seemed desirable, and the graphic test was judged quite adequate to give all that was wanted. It has been applied to one regression line only in each table. Figs. 10.1, 10.2 and 10.3 correspond to the tables for r_{12}, r_{13} and r_{23}, and each shows the means of columns or groups of columns, as used for the corresponding contingency tables 10.1, 10.2, 10.3, plotted to the means of the row-variable given by the totals of the columns in the group. Thus taking the table for r_{12} for example, there is no difficulty about columns 0, 1 and 2 which are taken singly in the contingency table (Table 10.1): the mean of col. 0 is plotted to $X_1 = 0$, the mean of col. 1 to $X_1 = 1$ and the mean of col. 2 to $X_1 = 2$. But as will be seen from the contingency table we then come to a group of columns, cols. 3, 4 and 5, the total frequency in which is $111 + 70 + 37 = 218$. The value of the sum S_1 for the three columns together was found to be 833,

Occurrences in the *Imitatio*

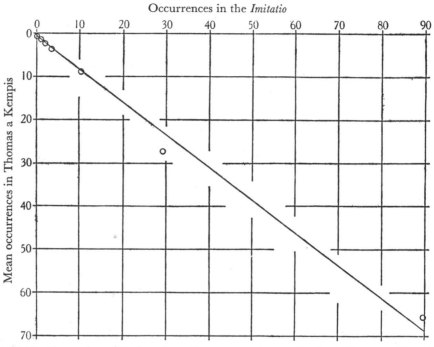

Fig. 10.1. Regression of X_2 (number of occurrences in samples from Thomas à Kempis) on X_1 (number of occurrences in the *Imitatio*). Cf. § 10.7.

whence the mean value of X_2 is $833/218 = 3.82$. This has to be plotted to the mean value of X_1 for the three columns, and this is

$$\{(111 \times 3) + (70 \times 4) + (37 \times 5)\}/218 = 798/218 = 3.66.$$

The remaining points are calculated in the same way. Superposed on the points are the corresponding lines of regression calculated from the constants given in § 10.4. The equations are:

$$\text{Fig. 10.1: } X_2 = 0.8128 + 0.7548X_1,$$
$$\text{Fig. 10.2: } X_3 = 1.6245 + 0.5118X_1,$$
$$\text{Fig. 10.3: } X_3 = 1.2102 + 0.6371X_2,$$

where X_1 = number of occurrences in the *Imitatio*, X_2 = number of occurrences in the samples from Thomas à Kempis and X_3 = number of occur-

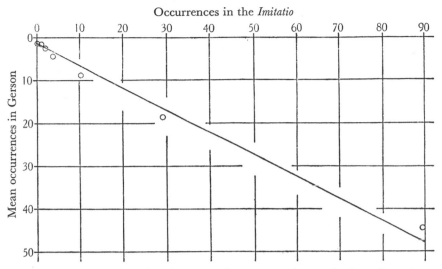

Fig. 10.2. Regression of X_3 (number of occurrences in samples from Gerson) on X_1 (number of occurrences in the *Imitatio*). Cf. § 10.7.

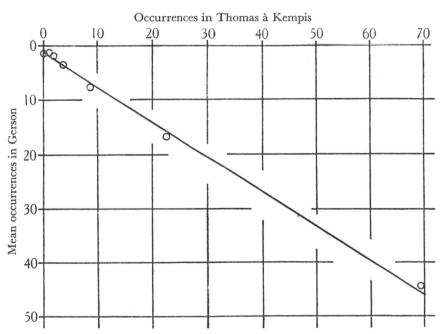

Fig. 10.3. Regression of X_3 (number of occurrences in samples from Gerson) on X_2 (number of occurrences in samples from Thomas à Kempis). Cf. § 10.7.

rences in the samples from Gerson. Given any one of these charts alone, I do not think it would have suggested any definite evidence of non-linearity of regression, but taking them together there is a certain likeness that makes one more doubtful. At the top end there is some irregularity owing to the erratic values of the (0, 0) frequencies, but of the first three points either all three are above the line, or that for the zero column is below and the next two are above. Then follow three points all below the line in each chart, and the final point above the line in each chart. On the whole it looks as if the curve of regression might be of a very flat S-shape like a reversed sign of integration lying on its side, a common form of non-linear regression. The divergence from linear regression is, however, evidently very slight and of no material consequence.

10.8.   The preceding paragraphs may have been rather over-technical for the general reader. Let us look at the correlation tables in another and quite elementary way. Suppose we define nouns occurring a certain number of times or more as 'frequent' nouns and ask ourselves how many of the 'frequent' nouns in, say, the *Imitatio* are also 'frequent' nouns in the samples from Thomas à Kempis or the samples from Gerson, and so forth. Evidently the answers to such questions will throw a good deal of light on the similarity or dissimilarity between the more often used components of the vocabularies of our authors: and the answers can be obtained very readily from the correlation tables. Twenty occurrences was considered a convenient limit to take for 'frequent', particularly as it happens to give nearly the same number of 'frequent' nouns for each of our authors: there are 88 nouns with 20 or more occurrences in the *Imitatio*, 85 in the samples from Thomas à Kempis, and 87 in the samples from Gerson. Taking the first correlation table and dividing it vertically between cols. 19 and 20 and horizontally between rows 19 and 20, 21 nouns were counted in the upper right-hand quadrant, and 18 in the lower left-hand quadrant. That is $88 - 21 = 67$ of the frequent nouns in the *Imitatio* are frequent also in the samples from Thomas à .Kempis, or conversely, $85 - 18 = 67$ of the nouns that are frequent in the samples from Thomas à Kempis are frequent also in the *Imitatio*; they are the 67 nouns common to the two lists of frequent nouns, and roughly we may say amount to three-quarters of the total of either list. Treating the second table in the same way, one found a very different story: there were 43 nouns in the upper right-hand quadrant and 42 in the lower left-hand; that is to say, only $88 - 43 = 87 - 42 = 45$, or roundly about one-half, of the frequent nouns in the lists for the *Imitatio* and the samples from Gerson proved common to the two. Finally from the third table one got much the same figures as from the second: 42 nouns in the upper right-hand quadrant and 44 in the lower left-hand, or $85-42 = 87-44 = 43$, or again roundly one-half of the nouns in each list, for the samples from Thomas à Kempis and the samples from Gerson, were common to the two. Thus the lists of commonly used or 'frequent' nouns showed once again a comparatively close resemblance between the *Imitatio* and the acknowledged writings of Thomas à Kempis, but a much lower degree of resemblance between the *Imitatio* (or the writings of Thomas à Kempis) and Gerson.

10.9. Let us now bring these purely statistical results into relation with the actual vocabularies. Tables 10.4, 10.5 and 10.6 give the nouns with 20 occurrences or more arranged according to the respective word-distributions, and to facilitate comparisons the numbers of occurrences in the two other distributions have been placed *after* each noun. Thus in Table 10.4 we see that *nomen* occurs 22 times in the *Imitatio*, and from the figures following that there are 42 occurrences in the samples from Thomas à Kempis and 23 in the samples from Gerson. Again in Table 10.6 *aqua* occurs 23 times in the samples from Gerson, but 4 times only in the *Imitatio* and 8 times in the samples from Thomas à Kempis. The two columns on the right of each table have been compiled from the figures following the nouns. Thus in the first line of Table 10.4 *discipulus* occurs more than 20 times in the samples from Thomas à Kempis, but *libertas* does not: there is therefore only one noun 'found also in the list for Thomas à Kempis'. But neither *discipulus* nor *libertas* is 'frequent' in Gerson, so the column on the right under 'G.' is blank. The totals of these columns must of course check with the figures given in § 10.8. In view of the fact that only 43 or 45 nouns are common to the list for Gerson and the list for Thomas à Kempis or for the *Imitatio*, it is rather remarkable that no less than 38 nouns are common to all three lists. These are as follows in the order in which they occur in the *Imitatio* list, Table 10.4:

Nomen: locus: pater: regnum: angelus: fides: mors: oratio: oculus: amicus: caritas: opus: peccatum: salus: spes: terra: caro: dies: corpus: tempus: virtus: caelum: res: filius: gloria: anima: spiritus: verbum: pax: amor: mundus: vita: nihil: cor: gratia: dominus: homo: deus.

No one of these nouns, obviously, can be taken as distinctive of any one of the authors; so that when, as mentioned in § 9.5, it seemed to me on obtaining the *Imitatio* distribution that the last 14 words, from *anima* onwards, were almost a brief epitome of the book itself, I was mistaken in so specialised an interpretation. All the 14 nouns save one are common to all three lists.

TABLE 10.4. Nouns of 20 occurrences or more in the *Imitatio*,
ranked as in the tail of the word-distribution

The number before the noun is the number of occurrences in the *Imitatio*, the numbers
following it the numbers of occurrences in the samples from Thomas à Kempis and in the
samples from Gerson. The two columns on the right show the numbers of nouns on the
same line found also in the corresponding lists (Tables 10.5 and 10.6) for the samples from
Thomas à Kempis and the samples from Gerson.

	Numbers of nouns found also in lists for	
	T. à K.	G.
20. Discipulus, 29, 7: libertas, 3, 6	1	—
21. Cogitatio, 13, 26: donum, 9, 4: intentio, 5, 10:	—	1
necessitas, 11, 20: sapientia, 19, 32	—	2
22. Nomen, 42, 23. 23. Timor, 18, 7	1	1
24. Amator, 13, 1: locus, 50, 34: manus, 26, 19:	2	1
misericordia, 21, 11: pater, 59, 56: regnum, 50, 20:	3	2
vitium, 28, 9	1	—
25. Parum, 8, 2: saeculum, 38, 8. 26. Vanitas, 9, 4	1	—
27. Angelus, 59, 21: communio, 0, 0: profectus, 4, 2:	1	1
vox, 28, 16	1	—
28. Humilitas, 36, 13: meritum, 14, 10: os (oris), 47, 10	2	—
29. Fides, 39, 52: sensus, 15, 29	1	2
30. Hora, 23, 13: mors, 47, 66: solatium, 20, 1	3	1
31. Oratio, 29, 30. 33. Nemo, 27, 16: patientia, 26, 2	3	1
34. Gaudium, 33, 8: laus, 32, 9	2	—
36. Dolor, 43, 7: oculus, 36, 44	2	1
37. Amicus, 38, 29: caritas, 43, 20: conscientia, 22, 7:	3	2
natura, 11, 23: passio, 43, 16	1	1
38. Judicium, 19, 36: labor, 38, 9: opus, 44, 27:	2	2
sacramentum, 7, 11	—	—
39. Finis, 27, 18: honor, 27, 16: peccatum, 30, 64	3	1
40. Salus, 36, 20. 41. Spes, 21, 26	2	2
43. Devotio, 21, 12: terra, 53, 34	2	1
44. Mens, 39, 16: servus, 26, 8	2	—
46. Affectus, 8, 15: via, 39, 13	1	—
48. Caro, 47, 46. 50. Dies, 48, 39. 51. Creatura, 10, 6	2	2
52. Corpus, 29, 40. 53. Voluntas, 16, 9	1	1
54. Desiderium, 27, 9. 56. Tempus, 50, 38	2	1
57. Tribulatio, 22, 7: virtus, 65, 40	2	1
58. Tentatio, 21, 3. 61. Caelum, 91, 28	2	1
62. Crux, 59, 3: res, 24, 44: veritas, 19, 47	2	2
63. Filius, 68, 41. 69. Gloria, 56, 22	2	2
76. Anima, 102, 102: spiritus, 69, 86	2	2
79. Verbum, 116, 92. 92. Pax, 50, 41	2	2
94. Amor, 52, 45. 102. Consolatio, 32, 7	2	1
104. Mundus, 102, 26. 135. Vita, 95, 67	2	2
146. Nihil, 40, 63. 172. Cor, 162, 74	2	2
196. Gratia, 93, 68. 210. Dominus, 200, 94	2	2
242. Homo, 115, 105. 418. Deus, 369, 256	2	2
Totals found in corresponding lists	67	45
Totals not found in corresponding lists	21	43
Total in above list for *Imitatio*	88	88

The one exception is *consolatio*, frequent only in the *Imitatio* and the samples from Thomas à Kempis but distinctive for its very high frequency (102) in the former.

10.10.   Let us now take Table 10.4 and study the 43 nouns which, while frequent in the *Imitatio*, are not frequent in Gerson—nouns that are in that sense distinctive of the *Imitatio*: the reader may find it desirable to extract the list. Of these 43 nouns, I think he will find, 29, or roundly two-thirds, are frequent in the samples from Thomas à Kempis, so the list is largely distinctive of Thomas à Kempis as well as of the *Imitatio*. To descend to particulars, the first thing I noted was an oddity—the quasi-noun *parum* with 25 occurrences in the *Imitatio*, but only recorded 8 times in the samples from Thomas à Kempis and twice in the samples from Gerson. Oddities of the kind—'indifferent' nouns not specially related to any particular subject but of frequent occurrence simply owing to the author's idiosyncrasies, his fondness for this or that particular idiom—might obviously be of importance in deciding a question of authorship, but I am not inclined to lay too much stress on this particular one. Such quasi-nouns are, in my experience, rather easily missed and I feel some uncomfortable doubt as to the completeness of my record for Thomas à Kempis and Gerson. Next there are two words, 27. *Communio* and 38. *Sacramentum*, which as already noticed (§ 9.13) are specially distinctive of Lib. IV of the *Imitatio* and may be put aside. Reading through the remainder of the list more than once, it seemed to me to consist to a surprising extent of words related, to the Christian religion indeed, but to simple personal religion, the relation between man and God, with little reference to the Church or its offices or doctrine, or any elaborations of theology, and but little reference even to monasticism. Thus we have the following general terms, taken as they occur in Table 10.4:

23. Timor. 24. Amator. 24. Misericordia. 24. Vitium. 25. Saeculum. 26. Vanitas. 28. Humilitas. 33. Patientia. 37. Conscientia. 39. Finis. 43. Devotio. 44. Servus. 46. Via. 62. Crux. (14)

Of these 14 nouns only *saeculum* seems to me to have a touch of the monastic from its frequent use in the sense of the *world* in contrast to the religious life, but of course it also occurs in other senses, *ante saecula, in saecula, usque in saeculum* and so forth. Then we have the griefs and trials of life:

36. Dolor. 38. Labor. 57. Tribulatio. 58. Tentatio. (4)

the consolation that will be given:

30. Solatium. 102. Consolatio. (2)

TABLE 10.5. Nouns of 20 occurrences or more in the samples from
Thomas à Kempis, ranked as in the word-distribution

The number before the noun is the number of occurrences in the samples from Thomas à Kempis, the numbers following it the numbers of occurrences in the *Imitatio* and in the samples from Gerson. The two columns on the right show the numbers of nouns on the same line found also in the corresponding lists (Tables 10.4 and 10.6) for the *Imitatio* and the samples from Gerson.

	Numbers of nouns found also in lists for	
	Imit.	G.
20. Animus, 10, 12: dulcedo, 17, 1: laetitia, 19, 9	—	—
ordo, 2, 13: periculum, 7, 12: solatium, 30, 1	1	—
21. Devotio, 43, 12: misericordia, 24, 11:	2	—
obedientia, 10, 8: spes, 41, 26: tentatio, 58, 3	2	1
22. Conscientia, 37, 7: superbia, 8, 8:	1	—
tribulatio, 57, 7	1	—
23. Hora, 30, 13: sermo, 10, 19	1	—
24. Propheta, 13, 23: res, 62, 44: silentium, 7, 6	1	2
26. Manus, 24, 19: patientia, 33, 2: rex, 8, 30:	2	1
servus, 44, 8: virgo, 3, 7	1	—
27. Desiderium, 54, 9: finis, 39, 18: honor, 39, 16:	3	—
nemo, 33, 16	1	—
28. Vitium, 24, 9: vox, 27, 16	2	—
29. Corpus, 52, 40: discipulus, 20, 7: oratio, 31, 30	3	2
30. Apostolus, 4, 32: exemplum, 12, 35: peccatum, 39, 64	1	3
32. Consolatio, 102, 7: facies, 17, 9: laus, 34, 9	2	—
33. Gaudium, 34, 8. 34. Diabolus, 8, 5	1	—
36. Humilitas, 28, 13: mater, 1, 27: oculus, 36, 44:	2	2
salus, 40, 20	1	1
38. Amicus, 37, 29: labor, 38, 9: saeculum, 25, 8	3	1
39. Fides, 29, 52: mens, 44, 16: via, 46, 13	3	1
40. Nihil, 146, 63. 42. Nomen, 22, 23	2	2
43. Caritas, 37, 20: dolor, 36, 7: passio, 37, 16	3	1
44. Opus, 38, 27. 45. Frater, 6, 11	1	1
47. Caro, 48, 46: mors, 30, 66: os (oris), 28, 10	3	2
48. Dies, 50, 39. 50. Locus, 24, 34	2	2
pax, 92, 41: regnum, 24, 20: tempus, 56, 38	3	3
52. Amor, 94, 45. 53. Terra, 43, 34	2	2
56. Gloria, 69, 22	1	1
59. Angelus, 27, 21: crux, 62, 3: pater, 24, 56	3	2
65. Virtus, 57, 40. 68. Filius, 63, 41	2	2
69. Spiritus, 76, 86. 91. Caelum, 61, 28	2	2
93. Gratia, 196, 68. 95. Vita, 135, 67	2	2
102. Anima, 76, 102: mundus, 104, 26	2	2
115. Homo, 242, 105. 116. Verbum, 79, 92	2	2
162. Cor, 172, 74. 200. Dominus, 210, 94	2	2
369. Deus, 418, 256	1	1
Totals found in corresponding lists	67	43
Totals not found in corresponding lists	18	42
Total in above list for Thomas à Kempis	85	85

and the joy and praise that should follow:

34. Gaudium. 34. Laus. 39. Honor. (3)

I have included *honor* with *laus* as some two-thirds of the uses in the *Imitatio* occur in phrases such as *ad Dei honorem, pro honore Dei, tibi debetur laus honor et gloria*, and so forth, but of course it occurs also in the secular sense of worldly honours—*vanitas est honores ambire*, etc. Not a single one of the 9 nouns in these last three short lists has any flavour of monasticism. It is true that these are only 23 nouns out of the 40 left when we had put aside *parum*, *communio*, and *sacramentum*, but they were the nouns that seemed to me to fall readily into a class and it is surely noteworthy how little mark of the institutional they bear about them. There are a few more nouns that might perhaps be brought in, but I do not think they would appreciably alter the character of the list; the reader has the data and can make out his own list of such words if he pleases. Many of the excluded words, such as *donum, vox, meritum, os, hora, nemo, mens, affectus, desiderium*, seemed to me too miscellaneous to bring together under any classification.

10.11. There is one other point that may be noted concerning this list. If the reader adds up the occurrences of the 23 nouns he will find they amount to 906 in the *Imitatio*, 651 in the samples from Thomas à Kempis and 183 in the samples from Gerson. That is to say, dividing by 23, the mean occurrences are 39·4 in the *Imitatio*, 28·3 in the samples from Thomas à Kempis and 8·0 in the samples from Gerson. Now from the regression equation for fig. 10.1 (§ 10.7) we have for the mean number of occurrences in Thomas à Kempis corresponding to 39·4 in the *Imitatio*,

$$X_2 = 0{\cdot}8128 + 0{\cdot}7548 \,(39{\cdot}4) = 30{\cdot}6.$$

The observed mean 28·3 is but little less than this and I think may be taken as consistent with it. But from the regression equation for fig. 10.2 (§ 10.7) we have for the mean number of occurrences in Gerson corresponding to 39·4 in the *Imitatio*,

$$X_3 = 1{\cdot}6245 + 0{\cdot}5118 \,(39{\cdot}4) = 21{\cdot}8,$$

against 8·0 only observed. Although then (as was to be expected from the mode of its formation) the occurrences in Gerson of the nouns in this list are far below what would be estimated from their occurrences in the *Imitatio*, yet the occurrences in the samples from Thomas à Kempis differ but little from their estimated number on the same basis. Even in this special group of nouns the similarity between the *Imitatio* and the writings of Thomas à Kempis is still outstanding. Of the 23 nouns considered 20 are in fact frequent also in the samples from Thomas à Kempis. The exceptions are 23. *Timor*, 24. *Amator* and 26. *Vanitas*, which show only 18, 13 and 9 occurrences respectively in the samples from Thomas.

10.12.   Let us now turn to Table 10.6 and treat it in corresponding fashion, selecting out of it the list of nouns which, though frequent in Gerson, are not frequent in the *Imitatio*. The reader will, I think, agree with me that the list is very heterogeneous and rather difficult to classify. We have far more of what I can only call sheer oddities or idiosyncrasies: 22. *Actus*, 23. *Ars*, 27. *Materia*, 41. *Persona*, 42. *Consideratio*, 52. *Pars*, 57. *Modus*, are examples. *Actus*, with 22 occurrences in Gerson, is only found 6 times in the *Imitatio* and 7 times in the samples from Thomas à Kempis, although *actio* is almost equally frequent in the three (12 in *Imitatio*, 11 in Thomas à Kempis, 10 in Gerson). *Ars* seems to occur in quite a scattered way with nothing special in its use: phrases noted are such as *sine arte, in arte divina, in sua arte peritus, per modum artis, ars artium est regimen animarum*. *Materia* occurs frequently in the literary sense, *invectionis materiam habebimus*, but also in senses that denote the philosopher: *anima in esse suo naturali considerata, imaginanda est tanquam materia nudata*. *Persona, consideratio* (cf. § 9.15), *pars* and *modus* seem pure idiosyncrasies. If our standard for a 'frequent' noun had been rather lower, we might have included *pactum* as an idiosyncrasy also: it occurs 14 times in the samples from Gerson, in such phrases as *quo pacto, eo pacto, nullo pacto*, etc., but there is not a single occurrence in the *Imitatio* or in the samples from Thomas à Kempis. Substantives with definite religious associations one can hardly class as pure idiosyncrasies: 21. *Vinea* (the parable of the vineyard), 23. *Aqua*, 25. *Vinum*, 32. *Pes* (the washing of the feet), are instances in point. References to the parable of the vineyard account for part, but only part, of the relatively high frequency of *vinea*, and the fact that the marriage at Cana of Galilee was the subject of sample No. 3 (§ 9.10) for part but only part of the relatively high frequency of *vinum*. *Aqua* is in part associated with the water of baptism (*baptismus* occurs 12 times in the samples from Gerson, but was not met with in the samples from either the *Imitatio* or Thomas à Kempis), but I think the largest single contribution comes from the sermon *De Poenitentia* (sample 9). The text of the sermon is taken from the washing of the feet, and this is used as a metaphor for the cleansing of the soul *per aquam contritionis*, so that the word *aqua* and the phrase *aqua contritionis* keep on recurring throughout the sermon. The largest contribution to the occurrences of *pes* comes, not from this sermon, I think, but from the sermon *De coena Domini* (sample 19, § 9.10). In that sermon Gerson tells of the soul's approach to God by the two *feet*,

TABLE 10.6. Nouns of 20 occurrences or more in the samples
from Gerson, ranked as in the word-distribution

The number before the noun is the number of occurrences in the samples from Gerson, the numbers following it the numbers of occurrences in the *Imitatio* and in the samples from Thomas à Kempis. The two columns on the right show the numbers of nouns on the same line found also in the corresponding lists (Tables 10.4 and 10.5) for the *Imitatio* and the samples from Thomas à Kempis.

	Numbers of nouns found also in lists for	
	Imit.	T. à K.
20. Caritas, 37, 43: domus, 6, 17: miraculum, 2, 2:	1	1
necessitas, 21, 11: regnum, 24, 50: salus, 40, 36:	3	2
scientia, 18, 6	—	—
21. Angelus, 27, 59: litera, 1, 6: puer, 0, 5: vinea, 1, 3	1	1
22. Actus, 6, 7: gloria, 69, 56: intellectus, 10, 8:	1	1
vir, 14, 11	—	—
23. Aqua, 4, 8: ars, 4, 3: contemplatio, 8, 6:	—	—
natura, 37, 11: nomen, 22, 42: propheta, 13, 24	2	2
24. Cognitio, 4, 2	—	—
25. Confessio, 6, 2: vinum, 1, 7	—	—
26. Cogitatio, 21, 13: filia, 0, 5: mundus, 104, 102:	2	1
sententia, 3, 5: spes, 41, 21	1	1
27. Mater, 1, 36: materia, 6, 5: mos, 7, 19: opus, 38, 44:	1	2
parvulus, 8, 12: scriptura, 9, 16: status, 13, 17	—	—
28. Caelum, 61, 91: justitia, 2, 6	1	1
29. Amicus, 37, 38: causa, 11, 18: sensus, 29, 15	2	1
30. Oratio, 31, 29: rex, 8, 26	1	2
32. Apostolus, 4, 30: pes, 5, 19: sapientia, 21, 19:	1	1
visio, 4, 5	—	—
34. Doctrina, 10, 12: locus, 24, 50: terra, 43, 53:	2	2
theologia, 0, 0	—	—
35. Exemplum, 12, 30: meditatio, 3, 10	—	1
36. Judicium, 38, 19. 38. Tempus, 56, 50	2	1
39. Dies, 50, 48: lex, 13, 18	1	1
40. Corpus, 52, 29: poenitentia, 7, 8: virtus, 57, 65	2	2
41. Filius, 63, 68: pax, 92, 50: persona, 7, 4	2	2
42. Consideratio, 4, 7: ratio, 16, 3	—	—
44. Oculus, 36, 36: res, 62, 24	2	2
45. Amor, 94, 52. 46. Caro, 48, 47	2	2
47. Veritas, 62, 19. 52. Fides, 29, 39: pars, 7, 9	2	1
56. Pater, 24, 59. 57. Modus, 19, 16	1	1
58. Ecclesia, 4, 11. 63. Nihil, 146, 40	1	1
64. Peccatum, 39, 30. 66. Mors, 30, 47	2	2
67. Vita, 135, 95. 68. Gratia, 196, 93	2	2
74. Cor, 172, 162. 86. Spiritus, 76, 69	2	2
92. Verbum, 79, 116. 94. Dominus, 210, 200	2	2
102. Anima, 76, 102. 105. Homo, 242, 115	2	2
256. Deus, 418, 369	1	1
Totals found in corresponding lists	45	43
Totals not found in corresponding lists	42	44
Total in above list for Gerson	87	87

the right foot of love (*pes amoris*) and the left foot of knowledge (*pes cognitionis*). This very clumsy metaphor is worked to death in quite characteristic fashion through the whole nine columns of the sermon, with complete lack of humour. It inevitably leads to some rather startling pictures. There are the scholars with very unequal feet or only one foot:

Claudicant vero omnes literati habentes magnum pedem cognitionis, qui amoris pede vel carent, vel breviorem eum nimis habent (IV. 86. E);

and there are awkward situations that may arise when the two feet are at cross-purposes:

Pes amoris in via hac Dei saepe intrat ubi cognitionis pes foris stat (IV. 87. A).

Thomas à Kempis rarely works a metaphor to death like this; the only instance of such tediousness I recall at the moment is that of the three garments of St Agnes (*Sermones ad Novicios*, XXVI). For the most part his similes, whether they come singly or in flocks, flit past and are gone. Gerson holds on to the metaphor, and this conservatism of his is a real danger to the statistician, especially with samples as large as ours. The use of one metaphor throughout a whole sample may mean a very substantial contribution of some one word to the total of its occurrences, and the chance inclusion of that one sample may raise it well into the class of 'frequent' nouns. The conservatism implies in fact large and erratic fluctuations of sampling.

10.13.   Returning to our study of the list of words frequent in Gerson but not in the *Imitatio*, nouns like 22. *Intellectus*, 24. *Cognitio*, 29. *Causa*, 42. *Ratio* suggest the philosopher in Gerson: 23. *Contemplatio*, 34. *Doctrina*, 34. *Theologia*, 35. *Meditatio*, the theologian. *Theologus*, with 19 occurrences in the samples from Gerson, is just below our standard for a 'frequent' noun, but only occurs once in the samples from Thomas à Kempis and not at all in the *Imitatio*. It is surprising how little we hear of the Church in the *Imitatio* or the writings of Thomas à Kempis: *ecclesia* occurs only 4 times in the former and 11 times in the samples from the latter. Its occurrence no less than 58 times in the samples from Gerson clearly marks the ecclesiastic. *Confessio* with 25 occurrences (against 6 and 2) and *poenitentia* with 40 (against 7 and 8) also mark the offices of the Church. How relatively little, both in the *Imitatio* and in Thomas à Kempis, we hear of the officers and offices of the Church (with the exception of *communio*, *sacerdos* and *sacramentum* in Lib. IV of the *Imitatio*) or of its troubles or scandals, is shown by the following supplementary list of nouns that occur but are not 'frequent' in the samples from Gerson:

| | | Occurrences in | |
	Imitatio	Thomas à Kempis	Gerson
Absolutio	0	0	2
Archiepiscopus	0	0	2
Baptismus	0	0	12
Commenda	0	0	1
Curatus	0	0	10
Dioecesis	0	0	3
Episcopus	1	0	3
Eucharistia	1	0	3
Haeresis	0	1	9
Papa	1	1	9
Papatus	0	0	1
Pluralitas	0	0	1
Pontifex	0	1	6
Primas	0	0	1
Schisma	0	0	7
Simonia	0	0	1
Synodus	0	0	2
Total occurrences	3	3	73

By such touches Gerson has stamped 'ecclesiastic' all over his vocabulary. Finally, 28. *Justitia* and 39. *Lex* suggest the lawyer in him, and to these might perhaps be added 26. *Sententia*, which occurs several times at least in the sense of a judicial sentence.

10.14.   This survey has now, I think, brought out fairly well the classes of words which are distinctive of the *Imitatio* (and of Thomas à Kempis) as against Gerson, and of Gerson as against the author of the *Imitatio* (and Thomas à Kempis). The words *distinctive* of the *Imitatio* and Thomas à Kempis are largely words relating to simple personal (not institutional) religion, the most surprising inclusion amongst these being *crux* with 62 occurrences in the *Imitatio* and 59 in the samples from Thomas à Kempis *but only 3 in the samples from Gerson.* There are few mere oddities or idiosyncrasies; *parum* was the only one noticed. Theological or philosophical terms are conspicuously rare, as are most terms relating to the Church and its offices or officers or troubles with only two or three exceptions. Do not these facts go some way to explain the universal appeal of the *Imitatio*, though it was written for the narrow class of Roman Catholic monastics? With Gerson, on the other hand, oddities or idiosyncrasies are much more numerous, especially if we may include under this head a few words with religious associations which come in for repeated use owing to the over-driving of metaphors (cf. *pes, filia*). Gerson was at once theologian, philosopher, ecclesiastic and lawyer, and all these aspects of his personality are reflected in some degree in his vocabulary by theological, philosophical, ecclesiastical and legal terms. Terms of simple personal religion are mostly of much less frequent occurrence. The respective vocabularies are quite in keeping with the characters of the men and their respective approaches to religion: that of Gerson intellectual and institutional, that of Thomas à Kempis personal, emotional. This discussion exemplifies very happily the usefulness of the vocabulary classified by frequency.

ASSOCIATIONS

10.15.   In Tables 10.1, 10.2, 10.3 (§ 10.3) we gave condensations of our correlation tables to contingency tables with seven rows and seven columns. Now let us group them right down, so as to retain only the zero row and column against all the rest, and we have the three association tables, Tables 10.7, 10.8, 10.9, for association between the presence of a noun in any one of our vocabularies and its presence in another, the 'universe' (or total vocabulary to which we are limited, cf. § 7.14) being the total vocabulary for the *Imitatio* and the samples from Thomas à Kempis and Gerson together.   Let us study the associations shown by these tables by the methods of §§ 7.13–7.15, and take first the simple method of comparison of proportions. Taking Table 10.7 and comparing proportions by columns, we have:

Proportion of nouns not in *Imitatio* but in Thomas à Kempis $= 603/1286 = 0\cdot4689$
Proportion of nouns in *Imitatio* and also in Thomas à Kempis $= 803/1168 = 0\cdot6875$

Difference $+0\cdot2186$

There is clearly a fairly high association (positive association) between the presence of a noun in the vocabulary of the *Imitatio* and its presence in the samples from Thomas à Kempis. Taking next Table 10.8, we have:

Proportion of nouns not in *Imitatio* but in Gerson $= 946/1286 = 0\cdot7356$
Proportion of nouns in *Imitatio* and also in Gerson $= 808/1168 = 0\cdot6918$

Difference $-0\cdot0438$

Here there is a small negative association: if a noun is *not* in the vocabulary of the *Imitatio* its chance of being in the Gerson vocabulary is slightly greater than in the contrary case.   Finally, taking Table 10.9, we have:

Proportion of nouns not in Thomas à Kempis but in Gerson $= 850/1048 = 0\cdot8111$
Proportion of nouns in Thomas à Kempis and also in Gerson $= 904/1406 = 0\cdot6430$

Difference $-0\cdot1681$

Here we have quite a considerable negative association.   Only 64 per cent of the nouns in the vocabulary of the samples from Thomas à Kempis are found in the vocabulary of the samples from Gerson, as against 81 per cent of the nouns *not* in the vocabulary of Thomas à Kempis: the difference is quite substantial. The association coefficients for the three tables are:

$$\text{Table 10.7, } Q = +0\cdot427,$$
$$\text{Table 10.8, } Q = -0\cdot107,$$
$$\text{Table 10.9, } Q = -0\cdot409.$$

TABLE 10.7. Association table between presence of a noun in the vocabulary of (1) the *Imitatio*, (2) the samples from Thomas à Kempis

In Thomas à Kempis noun is	In *Imitatio* noun is		Total
	Absent	Present	
Absent	683	365	1048
Present	603	803	1406
Total	1286	1168	2454

TABLE 10.8. Association table between the presence of a noun in the vocabulary of (1) the *Imitatio*, (2) the samples from Gerson

In Gerson noun is	In *Imitatio* noun is		Total
	Absent	Present	
Absent	340	360	700
Present	946	808	1754
Total	1286	1168	2454

TABLE 10.9. Association table between the presence of a noun in the vocabulary of (1) the samples from Thomas à Kempis, (2) the samples from Gerson

In Gerson noun is	In Thomas à Kempis noun is		Total
	Absent	Present	
Absent	198	502	700
Present	850	904	1754
Total	1048	1406	2454

These associations are striking, bringing out very clearly the likeness between the vocabularies of the *Imitatio* and of Thomas à Kempis and the unlikeness, or comparative unlikeness, of the pairs *Imitatio*-Gerson, Thomas à Kempis-Gerson. Both in magnitude and range the coefficients differ signally from those for the four samples from Macaulay and the four samples from Bunyan in Table 7.12 (§ 7.15). In that table the coefficients for Macaulay ranged from $-0 \cdot 080$ to $+0 \cdot 216$ only, and those for Bunyan from $-0 \cdot 046$ to $+0 \cdot 310$, the last figure being the association for the two parts of the *Pilgrim's Progress*.

10.16. Association tables can of course be formed for any of the special classes of words of §§ 9.15 *et seq.*, and I happen to have drawn up the tables for the 'nouns not in Lewis and Short's *Dictionary*' of § 9.16. These are

TABLE 10.10. Nouns not in Lewis and Short: association table between presence of a noun in the vocabulary of (1) the *Imitatio*, (2) the samples from Thomas à Kempis

In Thomas à Kempis noun is	In *Imitatio* noun is		Total
	Absent	Present	
Absent	84	26	110
Present	26	12	38
Total	110	38	148

TABLE 10.11. Nouns not in Lewis and Short only: association table between presence of a noun in the vocabulary of (1) the *Imitatio*, (2) the samples from Gerson. This may also be read as the association table between presence of a noun in the vocabulary of (1) the samples from Thomas à Kempis, (2) the samples from Gerson, the figures being the same

In Gerson noun is	In *Imitatio* noun is		Total
	Absent	Present	
Absent	20	27	47
Present	90	11	101
Total	110	38	148

Tables 10.10 and 10.11, the latter serving as association table both for (1) the *Imitatio* and Gerson, and (2) the samples from Thomas à Kempis and Gerson, the figures being the same. For Table 10.10, $Q = +0 \cdot 197$; for Table 10.11, $Q = -0 \cdot 834$; again an emphatic contrast.

10.17. Surveying briefly the work of the preceding paragraphs, I think it must be admitted that the correlation tables themselves, though supporting and fortifying the general conclusions, did not throw very much further light on the matter. Paragraphs 10.8 *et seq.* were very illuminating but, though we did in fact relate them to the correlation tables, all the information given could be quite readily obtained by simple comparison of the word-distributions. It would not be necessary, for work on such lines, to draw up the correlation tables, though it might be judicious as a check. And finally the association tables, Tables 10.7–10.9, afforded a striking contrast that put the correlation tables altogether in the shade. Taken in conjunction with the work of Chapter 7 (cf. especially § 7.15 and § 7.18) this looks as if the association for presence or absence of a word from the vocabulary were likely to prove a more useful method of investigation than correlation between numbers of occurrences. This conclusion I find a little disappointing, for work with vocabulary always has its special risks of fallacy, and also somewhat puzzling, since the reason for the more emphatic results given by associations is not clear.

10.18.   Before passing on to the supplementary investigations, however, we may deal briefly with the alphabetical distributions of these vocabularies.

TABLE 10.12. Showing the alphabetical distributions of the nouns in the *Imitatio*, the samples from Thomas à Kempis, the samples from Gerson, and the total combined vocabulary

1	2	3	4	5
	Number of nouns with the initial in			
Initial of noun	*Imitatio*	Samples from Thomas à Kempis	Samples from Gerson	Total vocabulary
A	96	112	152	211
B	15	25	19	35
C	138	169	202	293
D	81	97	117	164
E	41	48	73	95
F	62	65	85	120
G	20	26	27	42
H	22	27	37	50
I	88	82	116	169
J	15	19	24	28
L	48	62	70	102
M	72	90	111	148
N	26	34	39	55
O	42	46	56	77
P	129	150	207	276
Q	7	8	7	12
R	45	61	74	108
S	113	135	174	239
T	42	62	77	107
U	8	18	14	23
V	56	69	71	97
Z	2	1	2	3
Total	1168	1406	1754	2454

Cols. 2, 3 and 4 of Table 10.12 show the alphabetical distributions for the *Imitatio*, the samples from Thomas à Kempis and the samples from Gerson respectively, and col. 5 the alphabetical distribution for the total vocabulary. It is evident that they all closely resemble one another. Taking cols. 2, 3 and 4 alone and forming the correlation between all possible pairs after reducing them to the same totals, in the manner described in § 8.6, I find $r = 0.9896$. For the corresponding correlation for the four samples from Bunyan we found the value 0.9779 (§ 8.6, correlation 2) and for the four samples from Macaulay 0.9880 (§ 8.6, correlation 3). Our three Latin alphabetical distributions are then more like each other, by this measure, than four samples from one and the same author in two examples from English literature. There is clearly no important difference between them, and we should hardly have expected any. The ranking of col. 3, Table 8.16, was based on col. 5 of Table 10.12. It should be mentioned that the correlation 0.9896 for all possible pairs of cols. 2, 3 and 4 of Table 10.12 is based on the 22 letters of the alphabet of that table, omitting K, W, X, Y altogether.

SUPPLEMENTARY INVESTIGATIONS

10.19. Two suggestions were made in § 9.19 for supplementary investigations. It was suggested that the characteristics should be determined for one or two separate works of Thomas à Kempis, and it was suggested that a larger class of 'non-classical' nouns might be sorted out from our vocabularies, using non-inclusion in a school Latin dictionary as a criterion. The latter is obviously much the less formidable business of the two, and was undertaken first. I should again have used, as in § 9.18, the 2nd edition of Smith's *Smaller Latin-English Dictionary*, which was on my shelves, but it was suggested that I should do better to use the recent greatly revised edition (ref. 10.1). I accordingly got a copy of the latter, and went through the 2454 cards of the joint vocabulary, marking each one with an S if the noun were found in the dictionary or with a σ if it were not found there. The new edition of the dictionary was no doubt the better to use from the standpoint of vocabulary, but was exceedingly troublesome owing to its adoption of revised spelling, *adfectio, conloquium, inlusio, inrisio* and so forth for the *affectio, colloquium, illusio* and *irrisio* to which one was accustomed. This not only greatly increased the time and trouble spent on the work but, obviously enough, the risk of error also—the risk of a card being marked in error with a σ when the noun was not found at once under its accustomed form. When all the cards had been marked, the σ-cards were extracted, and found to number 565 in all; 23·02 per cent of the vocabulary. They were then sorted in succession according to the numbers of occurrences X in the *Imitatio*, in the samples from Thomas à Kempis and in the samples from Gerson, and yielded the three distributions shown in Table 10.13. There proved to be 212 of these 'non-classical' nouns in the *Imitatio*, 230 in the samples from Thomas à Kempis and 376 in the samples from Gerson, or expressing these figures as percentages of the respective total vocabularies (Table 9.2) 18·2 per cent, 16·4 per cent and 21·4 per cent. The total numbers of occurrences are as shown on the line S_1, and expressing these as percentages of the total occurrences (Table 9.2) we obtain the figures in the last line of the table, 8·16, 8·64 and 11·13. We have then a result similar to that of the corresponding Tables 9.3 and 9.4—the data for the *Imitatio* and for Thomas à Kempis in fairly close agreement but Gerson divergent—only the contrast between Gerson on the one hand and the *Imitatio* and Thomas à Kempis on the other is not so striking. There is also another point of difference. In both Tables 9.3 and 9.4 there is no great difference between the means of the three distributions, but the standard deviation of the Gerson distribution is considerably greater than that of either of the other two, so that it extends to higher values of X, this greater extension catching the eye at once. In Table 10.13 we have precisely the reverse. The distributions of cols. 2 and 3 are notably the more extended, running up to nouns with 50 or more occurrences: the Gerson distribution of col. 4 stops short at nouns of 32 and 34 occurrences. The means and standard deviations are in fact:

De Imitatione Christi:	Mean = 3·17, s.d. = 6·43,
Samples from Thomas à Kempis:	Mean = 3·08, s.d. = 6·15,
Samples from Gerson:	Mean = 2·43, s.d. = 3·53.

In this instance both the mean and the standard deviation of the Gerson distribution are low compared with the other values, which are fairly closely in concordance with each other. We have now the results of five separate tests for comparison of the proportions of 'out of the way' nouns in the *Imitatio*, the samples from Thomas à Kempis and the samples from Gerson, the criteria being (1) nouns not in the Vulgate (Table 9.3), (2) nouns not in Lewis and Short (Table 9.4), (3) nouns not in the Vulgate nor the three dictionaries used (Table 9.5), (4) non-Vulgate, non-classical nouns borrowed from the Greek, excluding common religious or ecclesiastical terms (Table 9.6), (5) nouns not in Smith's *Smaller Latin-English Dictionary*, revised edition (Table 10.13). The results of all these tests are astonishingly concurrent. We may repeat the totals of occurrences as in § 9.19, adding at

TABLE 10.13. Nouns not in Sir William Smith's *Smaller Latin-English Dictionary* (revised edition 1933): table showing the number f_x of such nouns occurring X times each in the *De Imitatione Christi* and in samples from the miscellaneous works of Thomas à Kempis and the religious works of Gerson

1	2	3	4
	f_x for		
X	*Imitatio*	Thomas à Kempis	Gerson
1	123	132	224
2	36	43	65
3	14	13	28
4	9	15	19
5	7	6	11
6	6	1	4
7	—	2	7
8	3	2	1
9	1	2	4
10	2	3	1
11	1	2	3
12	1	1	1
13	2	—	1
15	—	1	—
16	1	—	3
17	—	1	—
18	1	—	—
19	1	—	—
21	—	—	1
22	—	1	—
23	—	—	1
24	—	1	—
27	1	—	—
30	—	1	—
32	—	—	1
34	—	1	1
37	1	—	—
43	—	1	—
51	1	—	—
57	1	—	—
59	—	1	—
Total	212	230	376
S_1	671	709	912
	Percentage of nouns not in Smith		
Vocabulary	18·2	16·4	21·4
Occurrences	8·16	8·64	11·13

the head those from our new table, these absolute figures being quite fairly comparable since the total number of occurrences of all nouns is approximately 8200 in each instance:

	Total occurrences of the special nouns in		
	Imitatio	Thomas à Kempis	Gerson
Table 10.13	671	709	912
Table 9.3	376	365	823
Table 9.4	59	58	162
Table 9.5	6	7	21
Table 9.6	0	1	24

These totals are not only remarkably concordant in showing the similarity of the *Imitatio* and the writings of Thomas à Kempis, and the divergence of Gerson from both, but also suggest that Gerson diverges the more, the more stringent the test defining the class, i.e. the fewer the nouns left in the class. For Table 10.13 the Gerson total only exceeds the other totals by some 30 per cent: in Table 9.3 it is more than double the other totals, in Tables 9.4 and 9.5 some three times the other totals, and in Table 9.6—what shall we say—48 to 1? It seems to me rather remarkable that the author who was far more familiar with the classics than Thomas à Kempis or the author of the *Imitatio*, and whose writings are full of quotations from them, should also be the writer to exhibit by far the larger proportion of out-of-the-way late, non-classical nouns in those writings. So much has been said of the barbarisms of Thomas à Kempis that the result came moreover as a considerable surprise.

10.20. The question of determining the characteristics for one or two separate works of Thomas à Kempis was next considered. Here I had a good deal of difficulty. Many of the little works are so brief that they are far too short for our purpose. The sampling experiment of Chapter 4 showed that reasonably trustworthy values of the characteristic could be obtained from distributions based on 2000 occurrences or so of a noun, but it would hardly be desirable to go much below this. Many of Thomas à Kempis's works would give nothing like such a figure. Again, many of Thomas à Kempis's writings which are gathered under a single title, e.g. sermons or meditations, are collections rather than homogeneous works and hardly comparable with the *Imitatio*, while his biographies and the Chronicle are barred by their total dissimilarity of matter and aim. In the end I was left with only four works which seemed to me reasonably suitable for the purpose, viz. to test whether works admitted to be by Thomas à Kempis and in matter and aim somewhat similar to the *Imitatio* would give values of the characteristic comparable with that obtained for the latter work (84·2). The four works in question are:

A. *De paupertate humilitate et patientia sive De tribus tabernaculis.* (Pohl, I.)
B. *Hortulus rosarum in valle lacrimarum.* (Pohl, IV.)
C. *Vallis liliorum ad laudem Dei pro solacio tribulatorum.* (Pohl, IV.)
D. *Soliloquium animae.* (Pohl, I.)

Of these the *Hortulus rosarum* is the shortest, the *De tribus tabernaculis* coming next: a rough estimate suggested that the former would yield in all probability rather less than the desired 2000 occurrences of a noun, but the latter rather more. Both, however, are so brief that it was obviously essential to take the works as wholes and not merely samples therefrom. They were therefore dealt with first, the resulting distributions being given in Table 10.14, cols. 2 and 3. From Table 10.15 it will be seen that the estimates of lengths, in terms of numbers of occurrences of a noun, were not far out: the *Hortulus rosarum* gave 1806 and the *De tribus tabernaculis* 2245 occurrences. Having disposed of these, I had to decide whether to content myself with samples of some 2000 occurrences from the longer works or to take them also as wholes, and finally screwed up my courage to the more complete procedure. These distributions are shown in cols. 4 and 5 of Table 10.14: from Table 10.15 it will be seen that the *Vallis liliorum* yielded 3143 occurrences and the *Soliloquium animae* 4811. The latter figure proved a good deal lower than I had expected from the mere length of the work in pages, the majority of chapters in the *Soliloquium* being appreciably less substantival in style than the three other works.

10.21. The four characteristics are given in the last column of Table 10.15. The first three, it will be seen, are surprisingly self-consistent, ranging only between 100 and 114. When the first two had proved so close to one another it became rather exciting to see what the third would give. When this again had proved so close to the first two I did wonder how the fourth would turn out, and whether perhaps, contrary to the experience with Macaulay and Bunyan, it would lie in a bunch with the first three. But even while writing out the manuscript lists of nouns I began to doubt this, for the *Soliloquium* is in some respects rather heterogeneous, and changes of subject involving changes of vocabulary tend to lower the characteristic. Actually the characteristic for this work came out, it will be seen, at only 66·9. But the arithmetic mean of the four characteristics is 97·9, against the value of 84·2 found for the *Imitatio* (§ 9.13), and three of the four are greater than the latter value. There can be no doubt at all then that works admitted to be by Thomas à Kempis give values of the characteristic quite comparable with,

TABLE 10.14. Showing the number f_x of nouns occurring X times each in four of the works of Thomas à Kempis. A. *De Tribus tabernaculis*; B. *Hortulus rosarum*; C. *Vallis liliorum*; D. *Soliloquium animae*

1	2	3	4	5	1	2	3	4	5
	f_x for the work					f_x for the work			
X	A	B	C	D	X	A	B	C	D
1	319	299	369	493	34	1	—	—	1
2	107	94	137	177	35	—	1	—	2
3	41	35	62	98	36	1	—	1	—
4	27	32	32	58	38	—	—	—	1
5	20	19	34	48	39	1	—	—	2
6	15	16	17	13	40	—	—	2	—
7	6	5	17	17	41	1	—	1	—
8	7	11	6	13	42	—	—	—	2
9	5	5	8	4	43	—	—	1	—
10	4	2	4	7	44	—	—	1	—
11	4	2	5	8	48	1	—	1	—
12	4	2	7	5	49	—	—	—	1
13	4	1	3	9	52	—	—	1	1
14	4	3	7	6	53	—	—	—	1
15	—	—	8	5	55	—	—	—	2
16	—	5	4	5	60	—	—	—	1
17	1	2	3	5	64	—	—	1	—
18	5	2	1	2	69	—	—	1	—
19	—	1	1	3	72	—	—	—	1
20	—	2	—	2	78	1	—	—	—
21	1	—	1	2	80	1	—	—	—
22	—	1	1	2	81	—	—	1	—
23	—	—	2	1	104	—	—	—	1
24	3	1	2	4	115	—	—	—	1
25	—	1	1	2	116	—	—	—	1
26	—	1	2	3	120	—	—	—	1
27	3	—	—	1	122	1	—	—	—
28	2	—	1	2	148	—	1	—	—
29	—	3	—	1	188	—	—	—	1
30	1	1	—	4	254	—	—	1	—
31	1	—	—	1					
32	1	—	—	2	Total	593	548	748	1025
33	—	—	1	2					

TABLE 10.15. Values of the sums S_0, S_1, S_2 and of the characteristic for the four distributions of Table 10.17. A. *De tribus tabernaculis*; B. *Hortulus rosarum*; C. *Vallis liliorum*; D. *Soliloquium animae*

Work	S_0	S_1	S_2	Characteristic K
A	593	2245	52699	100·1
B	548	1806	37974	110·9
C	748	3143	115471	113·7
D	1025	4811	159629	66·9

or even higher than the value for the *Imitatio*: a result entirely consistent with his authorship of that famous work. The reader will see very clearly how the characteristics for the *Imitatio*, Thomas à Kempis and Gerson stand in relation to each other from the chart facing p. 284.

10.22.   It may be noted that, if we use 3 as the divisor of the sum of squares of deviations and not 4, the estimated standard deviation of the four characteristics is 21·5, or roundly 22 per cent of the mean, and this confirms our very tentative estimate that the standard deviation of the characteristic for a set of similar works by the same author is likely to be some 20 to 25 per cent of the mean (§ 6.12).

10.23.   This concludes my work on the problem of the authorship of the *Imitatio*, from which the whole of the work in this book originated. The results, it seems to me, almost exclude the possibility of Gerson as the author, but are entirely consistent with the authorship of Thomas à Kempis. One cannot of course go further and say that the authorship of Thomas à Kempis is proved, for statistical data can only balance the claims of one author against those of another: but our evidence quite confirms the poetic simile of Rosweyd in his *Vindiciae Kempenses* (ref. 10.2): 'Non rosa rosam magis redolet, quam liber *de Imitatione Christi* similis est reliquis Thomae à Kempis scriptionibus.'

10.24.   The evidence from vocabulary is also entirely consistent with the evidence from sentence-length discussed in a paper to which reference has already been made (ref. 10.3). It will be seen from Table II of that paper that the mean length of sentence in samples from the *Imitatio* came out at 16·2 words, in samples from the miscellaneous works of Thomas à Kempis at 17·9 words and in samples from the writings of Gerson taken by two different methods at 23·4 and 22·7. But the difference is best brought out by some measure more sensitive to the proportion of long sentences, such as the *ninth decile*, i.e. the value of the variable X only exceeded by one-tenth of the observations. The mean value of the ninth decile in the samples from the *Imitatio* is 27·7 words, in the samples from the miscellaneous works of Thomas à Kempis 31·0, in the samples from the writings of Gerson 44·0 and 43·5. For some discussion of the special difficulties of work on sentence-length, and warnings as to the considerable element of personal judgment that may affect the data based on badly and arbitrarily punctuated work, the reader must be referred to the original paper.

10.25.   Comment may be made in conclusion on the argument sometimes brought forward, that the *Imitatio* can hardly be the work of Thomas à Kempis, since it is so very much better than anything that is certainly known to be his. This form of argument is not uncommon in connection with questions of authorship, but is of little weight. If all the works of an author could be assigned valid marks for their quality, it is probable that these marks would fall into a frequency distribution, not like those with which we have been dealing, but either of the symmetrical or more probably the moderately asymmetrical form with the shorter tail towards low marks or zero and the longer tail towards high marks. In the extreme tails of such distributions, where the theoretical or 'expected' frequencies are falling away to lower and lower values, the last few observations are inevitably scattered, and tend to be scattered at wider and wider intervals. That is to

TABLE 10.16. Showing the three largest values of the number of occurrences X in each of the tables of Chapter 2 (except the roundly estimated figures of Table 2.8), together with the differences between them

Table	The three largest values of X			Differences	
	First	Second	Third	$1-2$	$2-3$
2·1	418	242	210	176	32
2·2	369	200	162	169	38
2·3	256	105	102	151	3
2·4	255	89	81	166	8
2·5	42	34	19	8	15
2·6	586	227	210	359	17
2·7	225	206	196	19	10
2·9	149	139	90	10	49
2·10	145	137	83	8	54
Total	2445	1379	1153	1066	226
Mean	—	—	—	118·4	25·1

say the difference between the extreme value observed and the second *tends* to be greater than the difference between the second and the third: the difference between the marks of the first prize man and the marks of the second prize man *tends*, for example, to be greater than the difference between the marks of the second man and the marks of the third. One can only say *tends* to be greater, or will be greater on the average, for fluctuations of sampling may be large and the statistical rule may not hold in every individual case. Our distributions in this book are single-tailed (nobody I think has yet termed them *monocercous*) but will serve quite well to illustrate the principle. Table 10.16 shows, for each of the tables of Chapter 2 except Table 2.8 (where the numbers of occurrences are partly estimated) the greatest or extreme value of the number of occurrences X, the second and the third; say X_1, X_2 and X_3. In the last two columns are given the values of the differences $X_1 - X_2$ and $X_2 - X_3$. It will be seen that in six cases out of the nine the first difference exceeds the second, and for every table of the six except Table 2.7 the excess of the first over the second is very large. As regards the exceptions, Table 2.5 is based on only 447 non-Vulgate nouns, and Tables 2.9 and 2.10 on only 296 and 353 nouns respectively. The last two tables, moreover, do not give independent evidence, for both refer to the Gospel according to St John (Basic Version and A.V. respectively) and the two most frequent nouns are the same in both. If we average the results of the nine tables, the mean difference between X_1 and X_2 is 118·4 and the mean difference between X_2 and X_3 only 25·1: the former is between four and five times the latter. We should always expect an author's best work to exceed his second best by far more than the second best exceeds the third. His best work *should* normally stand out well above the rest. It might be added that his worst work might be expected similarly to stand conspicuously below the rest, but we are usually less interested in such failures.

REFERENCES

A. Statistical Method

§§ 10.1–10.7. For the theory of correlation see Y & K, Chapter 11; for the coefficient of contingency used in § 10.3, see Y & K, §§ 5.9 *et seq.*, 10.15, 10.16; for the theory of association, and the association coefficient used, see Y & K, Chapter 3. § 10.24. Percentiles, Y & K, §§ 8.22 and 8.30. § 10.25. Forms of frequency distribution, see Y & K, Chapter 6.

B. Citations in Text or Tables

It is hardly necessary to repeat the general references at the end of the last chapter. For the investigation of § 10.19 the dictionary used was:

(10.1) Smith, Sir William, and Lockwood, J. F. (1933). *A Smaller Latin-English Dictionary.* Revised edition. London: John Murray.

(10.2) Rosweyd, H. (1617, etc.). *Vindiciae Kempenses,* first published in full according to De Backer with the edition of the *De Imitatione Christi* printed at the Plantin Press, Antwerp, in 1617 (De Backer 161). Also included as an item with *Chronicon Canonicorum regularium ordinis Sancti Augustini Capituli Windesemiensis* auctore Joanne Buschio, Antwerp, 1621 (De Backer 2926) of which there is said to be also a separate issue of the same date (De Backer 3061).

(10.3) Yule, G. U. (1939). 'On sentence-length as a statistical characteristic of style in prose: with application to two cases of disputed authorship.' *Biometrika,* **30**, 363.

Chapter 11

VALEDICTORY

11.1. I know this work is in many respects incomplete, but it seemed better to bring it to a halt in the hope, already expressed in the introductory chapter, that others might aid in correcting errors, supplying omissions and making further advances. The most conspicuous limitation of my work is perhaps its limitation to nouns, with the exception of a single table for adjectives in the *Imitatio* and another for verbs in the same book (Tables 2.6 and 2.7). Obviously further investigations on both adjectives and verbs are desirable, preferably for writings the nouns of which have also been dealt with, so as to throw light on the relations between the three and on the answers to such questions as the following: If author A cannot be clearly differentiated from B on the basis of nouns, can he be differentiated on the basis of verbs or adjectives? If A's vocabulary considerably exceed B's for nouns, is it probable that it will also exceed in the case of verbs and adjectives? or do such vocabularies vary to some considerable extent independently of one another?

11.2. We judged that it was best, if fairly trustworthy results were wanted, not to take a sample of much less than some 2000 occurrences of a noun. This would imply a sample of something like 10,000 words, more or less. But many works the authorship of which is disputed are brief tracts far shorter than this. We shall obviously be broadening the basis of our work if we bring in adjectives and verbs as well as nouns. But even this may only utilise some half of all the words available (§ 3.19). Would it be of service to include other words? if so, should it be *all* other words or should there be some specified exceptions, such as say the definite and indefinite article in English, or auxiliary verbs? My impression is that the inclusion of all words without exception would be a mistake; that the inclusion of *a* and *the* and *is* and the like, each with a very large number of occurrences in *any author*, would merely tend to obscure differences, and it would be best to limit data to what are in some sense 'significant words'. But this is pure speculation. Only investigation of a test case by varied methods can throw real light on the matter and suggest the best rules for practice.

11.3. I hope, however, that the methods developed will not be used solely or even mainly for endeavours to solve controverted questions of authorship or chronological order or the like. They are methods for studying language-in-use, as distinct from the anatomized bones of language in the dictionary, and ought to find their due position in the study of the living tongue, past and present. Personally I found the investigation of the language of Bunyan and Macaulay—unrelated to any question of controversy —one of the most interesting pieces of the whole work, limited though it was to nouns; and of especial interest the analysis of that language into the two streams of OE.-Teutonic and Latin-Romance. The analysis would have been of more interest still if we had had more knowledge of the background against which it should be viewed; similar, if better, studies not only of their contemporaries but of writers before Bunyan and of the period between him and Macaulay. We cannot at present, so far as I know, give definite answers to even the most obvious questions. How far does the vocabulary of Bunyan's other writings differ from that of the tales here considered? Is the vocabulary of the tales exceptionally Teutonic even for his epoch? Is Macaulay in his epoch exceptional in the degree of latinisation of his language, as compared with writers on similar subjects? Was there, between the seventeenth and nineteenth centuries, anything like a continuous change in the degree of latinisation of the literary language in the direction suggested by a comparison of Bunyan and Macaulay? Or do even contemporary writers differ so greatly from one another that no general statement can safely or usefully be made?

11.4.   Again, the spoken language of any epoch differs greatly from the written language, even amongst the well educated. Can we, from written records, get any nearer to the former? Many collections of letters are available. In so far as they are personal friendly letters, not formal or official, would not the language of such letters come a good deal nearer than the literary language to the ordinary speech of the writers? Would not a descriptive analysis of the language of such personal letters between friends, at different epochs, be both interesting and illuminating? Nowadays, and for a comparatively brief period of the past, we have novels. Could the dialogue in carefully selected novels dealing with the contemporary scene be taken in some degree as evidence of contemporary speech? It must be admitted that the novels would require *very* careful selection.

11.5.   Of problems purely for the theoretical statistician I have noted only two or three in passing: the problem of characteristics of higher order (§ 3.25); the problem of standard errors when it is S_1 and not S_0 that is arbitrarily fixed (§ 3.26); and the question of the mathematical form of the word-distribution (§ 3.27).

11.6.   But these are all only problems for solution or possible lines of work that one can see from the position at present reached—portions of the view from one's present standpoint on the road. Even from that standpoint, others more clear-sighted than I may see much more. Always, moreover, as one goes on, the view changes and develops; as more work is done, new problems and fresh lines of work will become obvious. I hope that the methods and ideas of the preceding chapters may prove interesting to others as they have been to myself, and fruitful in their hands.

11.7. **Theorem on the Characteristic.** Let me here insert as a final postscript a theorem that is helpful in the practical interpretation of the characteristic as a measure of concentration. If to any word-distribution we add one more word with X occurrences, this will add X to the value of S_1 and X^2 to the value of S_2. According to the value of X the added word may either increase or decrease the characteristic. Let us ask ourselves what must be the value of X such that the addition of the new word just leaves the characteristic unaltered. If X_s is this *stable value* or *stable point* the condition is

$$\frac{S_2 - S_1 + X_s^2 - X_s}{(S_1 + X_s)^2} = \frac{S_2 - S_1}{S_1^2},$$

which gives on reduction

$$X_s = \frac{S_1(2S_2 - S_1)}{S_1^2 - (S_2 - S_1)}. \tag{11.1}$$

This may be put in the form

$$X_s = 2\frac{S_2}{S_1}\frac{1 - \dfrac{S_1}{2S_2}}{1 - \dfrac{S_2 - S_1}{S_1^2}}. \tag{11.2}$$

Since both S_1/S_2 and $(S_2 - S_1)/S_1^2$ are in general small fractions, we have as an approximation to X_s

$$X_s' = 2\frac{S_2}{S_1}. \tag{11.3}$$

X_s', it may be noted, may be either rather larger or rather smaller than X_s. If we take as an example the distribution of nouns in the *Imitatio* (Table 2.1 or Table 9.1), $X_s = 140 \cdot 6$. The addition of a word of 141 occurrences will *just* raise the characteristic, very minutely, the addition of a word of 140 occurrences will just lower it. Equation (11.3) gives $X_s' = 140 \cdot 5$, a very close approximation. Taking the distribution for Macaulay's essay on Bacon as a second illustration (Table 2.4 or Table 4.4), I find for the stable point $X_s = 44 \cdot 9$ only, and (11.3) gives the much less close approximation $X_s' = 45 \cdot 7$.

DATA FOR THE OPPOSITE CHART OF
CHARACTERISTICS FOR NOUNS

In order that the data may be set out clearly, a separate column of the chart has been allotted to each group of characteristics as below.

Author	Work	Characteristic and reference	
Macaulay	Four essays	20·1	Table 6.4
	Essay on Milton	17·9	Table 6.2
	Essay on Frederic	21·8	Table 6.2
	Essay on Bacon	27·2	Table 4.5
	Essay on Hampden	34·1	Table 6.2
Bunyan	Four works	51·3	Table 6.7
	Pilgrim's Progress, Part II	56·5	Table 6.6
	Pilgrim's Progress, Part I	66·9	Table 6.6
	Mr Badman	80·6	Table 6.6
	Holy War	88·0	Table 6.6
Gerson	Works	35·9	Table 9.2
à Kempis	Works	59·7	Table 9.2
	Soliloquium animae	66·9	Table 10.15
——	*De Imitatione Christi*	84·2	Table 9.2
à Kempis	*De tribus tabernaculis*	100·1	Table 10.15
	Hortulus rosarum	110·9	Table 10.15
	Vallis liliorum	113·7	Table 10.15
St John's Gospel	Basic English	141·5	§ 4.1
	A.V. all nouns	161·5	§ 4.1
	A.V. select nouns	177·9	§ 4.1

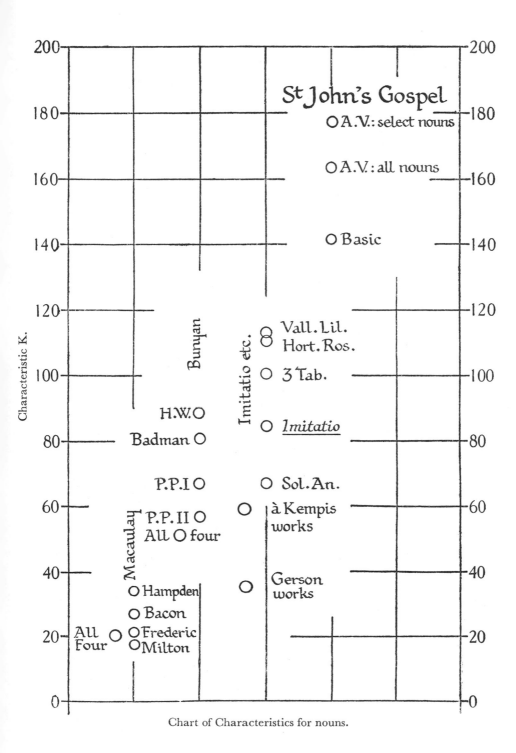

Chart of Characteristics for nouns.

APPENDIX I. BUNYAN

A. *PILGRIM'S PROGRESS*, PART I

Lists of the nouns in the sample from the *Pilgrim's Progress*, Part I, grouped according to the numbers of their occurrences, the first list giving the nouns occurring only once in the sample, the next those occurring twice, and so on. For the numerical distribution see Table 6.5. For notes on words see p. 298, following Appendix IV.

1. Abundance: acceptance: accomplishment: account: ado: adultery: advantage: advice: air: alien: amaze: amazement: amendment: amity: ancestor: annoyance: apparel: appearance: applause: arm: army: arrow: ascent: assurance: authority: awakening: backsliding: badness: band: bank: beck: bedlam: bee: beggar: behaviour: benefice: billow: birth: bit: bitterness: blasphemy: blot: boat: boldness: bolt: bond: border: bottle: bowel: bravado: break: breaking: brimstone: brow: brunt: brush: brute: bush: business: candle: carefulness: catechiser: cave: chaff: chain: chair: chance: change: chariot: cheek: chief: church: churl: clambering: closet: clout: club: cluster: coal: cogitation: colour: comforter: commodity: commotion: compass: complaint: conceit: confederate: conference: confusion: congregation: contempt: content: contents: contrary: conversion: cord: courage: court: covenant: coward: cowardliness: creator: cry: cunning: curse: customer: dainty: damnation: damp: damsel: daybreak: daytime: debate: deceitfulness: deceiving: degree: demonstration: derision: descent: desert: design: despair: destroyer: difference: disciple: discontent: discoursing: dislike: distemper: distinction: disturbance: division: dog: dominion: doom: doorway: drink: drinking: drop: drought: dump: dunghill: dwelling: edge: edification: egg: employ: encouragement: endeavour: estate: esteem: eternity: example: experience: extravagance: eyesight: fairness: farthing: fashion: fat (1): fault: favour: feat: feather: fence: ferryman: fierceness: filth: finding: finger: firmament: flight: flock: flood: flower: flying: folly: fondness: footman: fountain: fraud: fray: friendship: fright: fulfilling: furnace: gallows: garner: gazing: gesture: ghost: gin: gladness: glass: goodness: government: grandfather: grave: greatness: groan: groaning: guess: guide: gulf: hail: half: halt: hanging: hap: happiness: hay: heat: heedlessness: helper: hillside: hobgoblin: hold: host (1): howling: hunger: ignominy: image: immortality: impediment: improvement: indignation: inditing: industry: inheritance: iniquity: injury: ink-horn: innocence: inscription: instance: instrument: insufficiency: jaw-bone: jealousy: jot: justifier: knave: knocker: labourer: labouring: lad: lake: language: lap: leap: lesson: lily: limb: lineage: load: lodge: loser: lucre: lying: male: market: match: meat: medicine: meekness: merchandise: middle: midway: might: mile: ministration: mistake: mistress: mode: moment: monument: moon: morrow: motion: much: music: naming: nature: need: news:

nickname: nobility: nobleman: nostril: notice: object: obtaining: offence: overthrow: owner: ox: painfulness: painter: pang: paper: pardon: parish: parson: parting: passenger: patch: pathway: pause: pearl: penalty: penny: peril: philistine: pillar: pitch: pitfall: plague: plat: plume: poison: pound: practice: praying: prediction: present: presumption: prison: proceeding: process: promotion: prophecy: prospect: protection: proverb: providence: pull: quality: rabblement: railer: rain: raisin: rarity: rate: reach: rebel: recantation: record: reference: reforming: refreshing: refreshment: refuge: region: rejoicing: remainder: repentance: reply: request: resurrection: revelling: revenge: review: reward: riches: ridicule: rioting: rise: roaring: robber: robbery: rod: ruin: running: sabbath: salt: salutation: satyr: saving: saviour: savour: scar: science: score: scrub: scum: sea: seal: secret: sequel: sermon: serpent: setting: shelter: shelving: shoulder: shouting: sigh: singing: sister: skull: slander: slave: sling: slipper: slut: smell: smile: spark: spear: spectacle: speculation: speech: spoiling: sport: stain: stalking-horse: start: steadiness: steepness: stir: stocks: story: strangeness: stream: stripe: struggle: stubble: sunbeam: sun-rising: supposition: surfeit: surveyor: sway: swearer: swearing: swoon: tale: talker: tare: tent: term: text: threshold: thunder: tide: tidings: tittle: toil: token: tooth: torment: townsman: trade: tradesman: treason: trembling: trespass: tribulation: triumph: trumpeter: turk: turn: turncoat: turning: turtle: twitch: vain-glory: vale: value: violence: virtue: walk: walking: wane: warrior: watching: wave: weariness: wearisomeness: week: weeping: well-doing: wheat: whip: whistle: whit: white: whore: wickedness: window: winter: wish: witch: witness: worker: working: worst: wound: writing.

2. Abuse: admittance: affection: affront: apostle: appetite: ash: assault: babe: bag: bar: bear: beast: behalf: blow: bone: brain: bread: brink: captain: care: catch: cause: caution: certificate: cheer: christian: christianity: condemnation: confidence: confirmation: corruption: countenance: couple: course: creature: crime: cut: dark: dart: dealing: deliverance: depth: detestation: dirt: disease: ditch: doing: duty: effect: enough: error: escape: evidence: examination: fall: fiend: form: giant: girl: goad: governor: grief: guilt: halter: hardship: hare: harvest: hearkening: heir: history: hole: hour: hubbub: hurt: ignorance: imagination: infirmity: instruction: invitation: knee: knife: laughter: leaf: lip: loaf: lock: loin: loss: majesty: malice: manhood: marvel: miracle: money: murder: murderer: nap: nation: necessity: nobody: notion: obedience: objection: occasion: orchard: ordinance: original: pace: pain: palace: parlour: patience: perdition: plight: pocket: prey: professor: promise: proof: prophet: purpose: purse: railing: reading: relation: remedy: report: reproach: robe: row: rule: saint: scripture: season: sentence: shadow: sharer: shell: shield: shop: shopkeeper: smoke: spring: stand: standing: state: step: stone: subject: suffering: sunshine: supper: temper: terror: thanks: throne: tomb: transgressor: trap: travel: treasure: trespassing: trial: uncleanness: use: victor: vileness: virgin: want: weakness: weather: wind: wine: wing: wise: worship: yelling: youth.

3. Acquaintance: action: affliction: anything: apprehension: arbour: armour: battle: believing: bell: belly: call: chamber: charge: coming: confession: con-

versation: conviction: countryman: cross: deal: debt: den: discovery: distress: doctrine: ear: entrance: evil: field: fight: flame: forehead: garden: harp: haste: haven: hearing: help: honour: kindred: lane: leave: look: lot: lust: mark: meaning: mine: minister: mire: mischief: mother: mystery: nakedness: order: party: performance: picture: plain: point: presence: profession: profit: rage: reflection: rest (1): rogue: safety: security: sense: sickness: sleeping: something: substance: table: threatening: tongue: traveller: understanding: village: villain: vineyard: ware: wisdom: woman: wrath.

4. Act: angel: bed: beginning: bird: birthright: case: champion: combat: condition: cud: darkness: deed: delight: despite: direction: dragon: dungeon: dust: earth: fit: going: hazard: home: hoof: justification: key: kindness: master: mercy: midst: misery: peace: prayer: principle: prisoner: relief: remembrance: revelation: road: room: sake: sign: silver: snare: speed: stile: strength: trouble: view: wayside: while: wicket-gate: yard (1).

5. Blessing: cage: coat: conscience: destruction: doubt: garment: gospel: heed: iron: judge: kind: meadow: means: net: note: opinion: opportunity: porter: power: service: slough: sound: stranger: top: tree: trumpet: voice: will.

6. Body: castle: cloud: custom: discourse: flatterer: highway: jewel: kingdom: land: liberty: love: matter: noise: pleasure: raiment: saying: skill: son: sort: street: sword: tear: testimony: wage: wall: wilderness.

7. Blood: bosom: crown: family: father: fruit: gold: hell: holiness: hope: joy: light: little: morning: piece: roll: salvation: servant: vanity: wonder: year.

8. Comfort: desire: devil: enemy: face: mouth: pit: rag: river: sinner: spirit: sun: thief.

9. Answer: distance: ease: fire: good: knowledge: pilgrimage: rest (2): sorrow: talk.

10. Companion: difficulty: gentleman: journey: night: people.

11. Flesh: foot: glory: lion: manner: path: prince: question.

12. Bottom: child: counsel: neighbour: shame: sleep: thought.

13. Fool: person: righteousness: water.

14. Back: end: judgment: mountain: sight.

15. Burden: eye: nothing: shepherd: wife.

16. Door: friend: ground: king: valley.

17. Book: grace: head. 18. Interpreter: part: soul: truth. 19. City: danger: fellow: reason: town. 20. Mind: religion. 22. Brother: country: fear: law. 23. Company: heaven: side: work. 24. Death: fair. 26. Dream. 27. House. 28. Sin. 30. Faith. 31. Life. 32. Hill: name. 33. Day: word. 34. Hand: pilgrim. 35. World. 36. Gate. 38. Time. 41. Lord. 43. Heart. 50. Place. 59. God. 99. Thing. 131. Way. 197. Man.

APPENDIX II. BUNYAN

B. *PILGRIM'S PROGRESS*, PART II

Lists of the nouns in the sample from the *Pilgrim's Progress*, Part II, grouped according to the numbers of their occurrences. For the numerical distribution see Table 6.5. For notes on words see p. 298, following Appendix IV.

1. Ability: abundance: acceptance: acquaintance: action: admittance: ado: advantage: adventure: affair: affection: alarm: allowance: altar: anchor: antidote: appetite: approach: aptness: arm: army: arrival: assault: author: authority: badness: bar: basket: bawling: beam: beckon: bed-side: beholder: belief: bemoaning: bench: bible: bidding: bill: biting: blank: blessing: blushing: bond: border: bowl: bowshot: box: bracelet: branch: brass: breadth: breast: breeding: bridle: brunt: busybody: butcher: by-end: by-path: cage: calf: calling: capacity: case: caul: ceremony: chapter: cheating: check: cheer: chief: choice: civet-box: closet: clutch: coal: coast: colour: comeliness: coming: commandment: commendation: commission: commodity: compass: compassion: complexion: concern: confession: consent: contentment: contents: contrary: cote: couch: counselling: couple: course: covenant: craft: credit: crime: crop: crumb: crust: curse: dame: dark: decay: deceiver: deep: defender: dejection: delusion: demolishing: demonstration: den: denial: derision: design: destruction: detriment: devil: digestion: discouragement: dissimulation: distance: distress: doubting: due: dung: dungeon: dunghill: duty: eater: eating: ebbing: edge: edifying: endeavour: enduring: enough: entreaty: errand: escape: essay: evening: example: excrement: exploit: fainting: fall: fancy: fat (2): fault: feather: feeding: field: fierceness: finger: firebrand: fish: flash: flowing: foe: fog: folk: force: forehead: forerunner: forgetfulness: form: foundation: fountain: fray: frying-pan: fulfilling: fullness: gain: game: generals: generation: gentlewoman: gift: gin: gladness: goddess: grass: grasshopper: grave: greens: grief: groan: guess: guilt: gunshot: habitation: half: halter: hammer: handkerchief: hap: hardness: hardship: haunt: hazard: health: heap: hearing: hearsay: heart's-ease: heave-shoulder: hedge: helmet: hen: herb: heritage: hissing: history: honesty: horn: hospital: housewife: husk: ice: illumination: immortality: imperfection: inclination: incoherency: incommodity: indignity: infirmity: influence: information: inheritance: iniquity: innkeeper: innocence: innocency: inquiry: instant: intercession: interest: intimation: jaw-bone: jew: jewel: joint: juniper: justice: kidnapper: kindred: kiss: knife: knock: knowledge: labourer: lady: language: lantern: lap: lass: laughing: laying: laziness: leak: leap: leave: length: let: lightning: limner: line: load: lodge: look: loser: loss: main: maintenance: map: mast: mastiff: match: matron: meanness: mediation: merit: method: midwife: might: mine: mistress: mite: mixture: mole: month: moon: mortal: motion: muck: mud: murmuring: musician: nativity: neglect: net: news:

nobody: noon-day: northward: nosegay: novelty: nut: obedience: obeisance: objection: offence: offer: opportunity: ordinance: ornament: orphan: oversight: owlet: ox: pace: pain: pair: parlour: particulars: patience: pause: pay: pearl: pelican: perfection: perfume: peril: pharisee: plain: plate: plum: pocket: point: poison: pole (1): pole (2): pond: post (1): posterity: pot: potion: praise: preaching: preparation: preservation: pretence: prey: price: pride: principle: print: prisoner: profession: proffer: profit: prophet: protection: protector: providence: provision: publican: purge: purity: quietness: rag: rain: rap: rarity: reader: rear: rebellion: reckoning: redemption: reference: refuge: rejoicing: reliance: renovation: rent: reproach: repulse: request: resting: resurrection: revenue: rewarder: rib: right: ring: roar: roaring: robbery: roll: rote: rudeness: ruffian: sack: salutation: samaritan: sap: satisfaction: scar: screen: scripture: seed: sentence: sepulchre: service: settle: sex: shame: shape: sharer: sheaf: shield: shift: shipmaster: shouting: sickness: silence: silk: sincerity: singing: sitting: skull: slaughter: slaughterhouse: slave: slaying: sleeper: slough: sociableness: sorcery: sore: sorrow: sovereign: sow: speed: spite: staff: stead: stile: sting: stitch: store: street: succour: suffering: summons: sunshine: supporting: surfeit: surprise: swoon: tale: temple: temptation: testament: thaw: theft: thirst: thunderbolt: tidings: tinder: tinder-box: tip: toleration: trap: trial: troubler: trumpeter: turning: tyrant: unbeliever: understanding: valour: value: veil: velvet: venom: villain: virginals: wain: washing: wasp: wave: wayside: weakening: weed: week: weight: welfare: well: well-wisher: whelp: white: whole: wilderness: window: wisdom: wit: worthy: wretch: writing: wrong.

2. Act: air: arrow: ass: attire: back: bank: beast: behalf: being: bit: blade: board: book: break: breath: bridge: brink: butter: by-way: call: carriage: chain: character: charge: chariot: charity: chicken: churl: city: cloth: cloud: combat: command: complaint: conclusion: cook: cord: corruption: counsel: countryman: crowing: dancing: darling: deal: degree: delight: departure: dining-room: disciple: disease: doctrine: doubt: dragon: dwelling: earring: entertainment: esteem: fame: fashion: feature: fight: fold: forgiveness: glory: gold: goodness: goodwill: gripes: guest: guile: happiness: harbour: harp: havoc: hope: horse: hose: hour: hypocrite: ignorance: injury: inn: inside: keeper: knocking: lad: lamb: lamp: landlord: liberty: lust: meaning: meat: middle: mile: minister: mire: mist: notice: opposition: orchard: order: outside: owner: palace: palate: paradise: partaker: passage: path: performance: persuasion: physician: picture: pillar: pool: power: presence: present: process: professor: progress: proof: quality: quarrel: rainbow: reliever: repentance: resistance: respect: retreat: return: reward: riches: ruin: sacrifice: salt: saying: seal: serpent: ship: shoe: shoulder: sign: silver: similitude: sister: slip: sloth: smile: sound: stick (1): stick (2): stomach: storm: straw: strength: summer: sweat: taste: terror: thanks: top: townsman: train: transgression: travelling: trembling: union: verse: vessel: vision: war: weakness: well-being: witch: witness: wound.

3. Advice: attempt: barking: benefit: bird: bliss: blow: bottom: bread: caution: cave: chamber: clothes: club: cock: creature: dish: disparagement: ditch: dust: ear: evil: experience: feast: flower: folly: ghost: godhead: guard:

heat: hole: honey: host (2): iron: judgment: knee: labour: leaf: lip: maid: manhood: manner: marvel: meadow: message: messenger: mischief: money: monument: mountain: muck-rake: neck: office: outcry: physic: pit: post (2): proverb: purpose: purse: reception: record: riddle: salvation: setting: sinner: skill: song: spot: stand: state: thief: thorn: thought: throne: traveller: trencher: trumpet: vineyard: warning: weapon: weather: wicket-gate: wind: wing: yard (1): year.

4. Answer: argument: babe: bath: beginning: bone: bosom: bottle: bowel: burden: church: conduct: cross: custom: deliverance: difficulty: doing: ease: encouragement: entrance: fire: fool: garment: glass: going: heed: hobgoblin: kind: kingdom: ladder: law: lodging: lot: mark: occasion: piece: pill: pleasure: question: relief: religion: robin: season: spring: stage: tongue: vice: victory: visitor: voice: wish: wood.

5. Account: age: angel: arbour: business: castle: cause: courage: face: farewell: favour: fellow: fiend: food: haste: help: hold: land: letter: means: monster: morning: much: note: peace: promise: report: sake: saviour: sheep: sleep: sort: spider: stone: story: stranger: table: token: travel: tree: want: work.

6. Countenance: crown: crutch: danger: flesh: garden: hell: home: hurt: matter: mercy: music: person: porter: prayer: relation: sea: wall: will.

7. Anything: apple: bed: brother: comfort: condition: damsel: darkness: discourse: family: heaven: highway: kindness: pardon: rest (1): servant: sword: virtue.

8. Blood: body: deed: desire: dirt: earth: gentleman: mouth: nature: noise: prince: rest (2): road: snare: step: tear: water.

9. Battle: faith: fruit: good: love: night: soul: sun: talk: truth.

10. Companion: enemy: light: little: need: opinion: reason: supper: trouble.

11. Neighbour: part: something.

12. Conductor: eye: joy: side: sin.

13. Country: master: shepherd: sight: spirit.

14. Daughter: dream: room: valley: wife.

15. Dog: fear: while.   16. Death: hill: people.   17. Foot: giant: ground: interpreter: river.   18. Grace: son.   19. End: journey: world.   20. Company: friend: lion.   21. Town.   22. Door.   23. Head: nothing.   24. Mother: righteousness.   25. King.   26. Father.   28. Name: word.   31. Hand. 33. Gate: heart.   34. Mind.   35. House: pilgrimage.   36. Husband. 37. Guide.   38. Day.   39. Boy.   40. Woman.   43. Life.   45. Lord. 46. Time.   57. Child.   61. God.   62. Thing.   68. Place.   96. Way. 99. Pilgrim.   133. Man.

APPENDIX III. BUNYAN

C. *MR BADMAN*

Lists of the nouns in the sample from the *Life and Death of Mr Badman*, grouped according to the numbers of their occurrences. For the numerical distribution see Table 6.5. For notes on words see p. 298, following Appendix IV.

1. Abomination: accuser: accustoming: actor: adulteress: affair: affection: affinity: affirmative: agony: agreement: air: amazement: answering: appearance: apprenticeship: arm: arrogancy: arrow: ash: assault: assembly: assistance: assize: assurance: astonishment: attesting: author: avoucher: babe: bacon: bag: bailiff: bar: bearer: beauty: beer: beggar: beggary: being: blasphemy: blindness: bondage: bonnet: borrower: bottom: bound: bowshot: box: bracelet: brag: bravery: breach: breast: breeding: brevity: bridegroom: bridle: brimstone: brotherhood: brute: bull: bump: burden: burning: canker: carcase: career: cash-box: catalogue: cattle: caul: chance: change: chapter: check: cheese: chest: chief: chrisom-child: christian: circumstance: clerk: cogitation: colour: coming: commandment: commonwealth: complaint: completing: compliment: composition: conceit: concern: concord: conduit: congregation: constable: controversy: corn: corner: corrector: council: counsellor: countenance: country: county: courage: cousin: creator: crime: crook: cross: cry: crying: cup: damn-me-blade: darling: dart: daughter: deal: debauchery: debtor: decking: decoy: delight: deluder: delusion: deportment: depth: description: destruction: devotion: diet: disadvantage: disguise: disobedience: disparagement: displeasure: disquietment: disquietness: distemper: dog: door: dread: drinking: drollery: drowsiness: duchy: due: dunce: earning: earring: ease: edge: egg: element: encouragement: engine: enmity: entreaty: ephah: equity: error: evil-doer: excellency: excuse: exercise: exhortation: experience: extravagancy: fact: faithfulness: farthing: fashion: fatness: fault: favour: feast: feeding: felicity: fireside: firstborn: fish: forbidding: foretop: form: formality: fornication: fornicator: fortune: foulness: fraudulency: freedom: frenzy: fullness: funeral: fury: future: gallows: generation: gentleman: gentleness: getter: getting: gift: girl: glass: glutton: gospel: gourd: government: governor: grape: grass: groom: guard: guess: guilt: habitation: hair: half-crown: halfpennyworth: handiwork: hangman: hap: happiness: hardening: hatful: hay: hazarding: headband: heat: heathen: hectoring: hedge: heed: heir: heresy: hin: hoarder: hoarding: honouring: hood: hook: horror: hour: howlet: humour: hunger: hungering: idleness: idolater: impairing: impediment: incitement: inconsiderateness: inconvenience: indignation: industry: infidel: information: inhabitant: injustice: ink: innocency: instruction: interest: intermission: interrogatory: intimate: invention: inventor: jade: jew: jewel: journey: judge: juggle: keeper: kindness: knave: labour: lad: lady: land:

lasciviousness: leave: leisure: length: life-time: likelihood: linen: lip: little: liver: look: losing: loss: lot: loving: luck: maid: maintaining: maker: malice: management: manifestation: mantle: margin: market: mass: mast: masterpiece: match: maturity: meekness: meeting: memory: mending: meteyard: midst: midwife: mile: milk: mincing: miscreant: misery: mistress: mistrust: mixture: mock: mocking: moderation: molestation: mood: moon: mourning: muffler: multitude: naught: neighbourhood: net: news: noble: noise: nose: nostril: notion: number: nurse: object: observer: odds: offspring: oil: opinion: oppression: orchard: order: ordinance: outcry: ox: page: pap: party: passion: path: pattern: pawn: peal: pen: performance: perplexity: personage: pest: piece: pilot: pipe: pit: plot: ploughing: point: possession: pot: prank: praying: preacher: precept: preparing: present: pretence: principal: prison: prize: probability: prodigal: profaneness: prognostic: protection: psalm: pullen: purse: putting: quart: rag: rain: rank: reading: rebellion: redeemer: rein: relater: relating: release: remark: repute: respect: restitution: resurrection: revelling: reverence: reward: ribaldry: right: righteousness: ring: ripeness: rising: road: robbery: rod: rogue: roguery: romance: roof: rottenness: rule: ruler: rush: safety: satisfaction: savour: say: scales: scandal: scorner: sea: search: season: seat: security: sedition: seed: sepulchre: severity: shape: shekel: shift: ship: shopkeeper: shoulder: sieve: silver: sinning: skull: slander: slaughter: slavery: slut: snake: society: song: sot: spawn: speaking: spectacle: spectator: sport: stamp: stand: steeple: stocks: stone: stop: stranger: stripling: strumpet: study: stumbling-block: stupidity: suit: suitableness: summer: sunday: supply: swearer: swing: sword: tablet: taking: tang: tax: tear: temptation: tendency: tent: term: thieving: thinking: thirsting: thorn: threatening: thunder: tire: token: top: torment: tradesman: transgression: transgressor: treasure: trial: trick: trifle: understanding: undoing: unequality: unrighteousness: vail: vapour: vineyard: violence: vizard: vomit: walk: wall: wantonness: ware: wave: wealth: web: wedding: welfare: wholesale: whoredom: whoring: wimple: wind: wine: wisdom: woe: worker: working: worldling: worship: worth: writ.

2. Abundance: abuse: action: adorning: adulterer: age: alteration: amendment: angel: antagonist: apostle: apparel: appointment: apprentice: artist: authority: back: band: behaviour: beholder: bell: benefit: bowel: brain: brat: buyer: capacity: captain: caution: chamber: charge: childhood: church: city: command: communion: conclusion: contrary: control: conversation: conviction: cord: corruption: course: covetousness: cow: craft: creature: cruelty: cunning: custom: damage: dame: damsel: design: desperateness: disgrace: dislike: dispensation: distance: distress: drink: dust: endeavour: expression: extortioner: feather: fellowship: foot: forehead: forgiveness: game: gang: garden: garment: generals: ghost: goodness: greatness: grief: half: hardness: haunt: hazard: hypocrisy: hypocrite: ignorance: inclination: informer: instance: jest: jesting: joy: kinswoman: lamentation: liar: light: lightness: loin: looking-glass: lover: magistrate: marvel: mention: month: morrow: murderer: note: oath: paper: physic: picking: pin: pleasure: portion: pound: poverty: praise: presence: purpose: quean: rage: reformation: reply: restraint: ringleader: root: sanctuary:

seller: sleep: sorrow: sort: sound: soundness: spider: stealing: stitch: stroke: struggling: sun: tale: temper: theft: trespass: tribunal: tub: unsuitableness: using: vermin: virtue: want: waster: water: wheat: whole: will: window: witchcraft: witness: wrong.

3. Account: acquaintance: act: advice: affliction: argument: bastard: beast: blow: business: care: chain: chapman: cheat: clothes: consideration: consternation: contempt: conversion: correction: credit: danger: deed: dishonour: dissimulation: doctor: doctrine: doubt: dying: enemy: fancy: fellow: finger: fondness: going: health: height: help: hurt: idol: iniquity: justice: lamb: living: madness: majesty: means: mischief: miss: much: objection: ornament: payment: pennyworth: plague: pox: profession: profit: question: quietness: reference: relation: remorse: riches: robbing: sabbath: sake: saying: sentence: serpent: service: show: sigh: snare: stalking-horse: substance: survivor: talk: villain: warning: week: wish: wit: worm: worshipper: wound: wretch: yard (2).

4. Adultery: anything: art: atheist: aught: balance: bosom: carriage: customer: despair: dissembling: drunkenness: effect: envy: estate: flesh: foolishness: glory: godliness: hearing: hold: holiness: image: language: liberty: minister: occasion: opportunity: pain: particular: power: promise: proof: providence: reproach: rest (1): rest (2): selling: sermon: shame: skill: son: strength: testament: thief: trouble: uncleanness: value: vice.

5. Advantage: ale-house: bird: blessing: bone: buying: case: commission: doing: drunkard: duty: friend: fruit: gain: gate: grace: grave: ground: inheritance: knowledge: murder: necessity: pocket: practice: prey: price: remembrance: scorn: whore: wonder: youth.

6. Answer: boy: brother: comfort: debt: deceit: discourse: earth: family: fit: home: horse: kingdom: law: lying: morning: mouth: night: penny: punishment: sense: shop: town: trade: villainy: while: wrath.

7. Breaking: calling: cause: counsel: desire: faith: fire: marriage: measure: notice: part: scripture: step: use: year.

8. Charity: ear: face: fool: husband: kind: prayer: saint: something: state: text: tongue.

9. Badness: curse: dealing: disease: nature: sickness.

10. Anger: bed: commodity: company: damnation: fear: good: hope: leg: neck: nothing: prophet: servant: sight: sign: work.

11. Creditor: head: love: money: parent: peace: person: professor: religion: salvation.

12. Beginning: book: thought: truth: weight.

13. Condition: example: lust: spirit: story: woman.

14. Body: cursing: matter: mother: repentance.

15. Mercy: sinner: swearing. 16. Manner. 17. Companion: end: heaven: mind. 18. Lie: people. 19. Place. 20. Name. 22. Evil: reason. 24. Eye: pride. 25. Father. 26. Devil: lord. 27. Conscience: day: house. 28. Hell: wickedness. 29. Hand. 31. Neighbour: soul. 32. World. 34. Word. 37. Wife. 39. Child. 40. Death: way. 42. Judgment. 43. Master. 47. Life. 55. Heart. 57. Time. 67. Thing. 86. Sin. 178. God. 206. Man.

APPENDIX IV. BUNYAN

D. *HOLY WAR*

Lists of the nouns in the sample from the *Holy War*, grouped according to the numbers of their occurrences. For the numerical distribution see Table 6.5. For notes on words see p. 298, following this Appendix.

1. Abasing: abhorrence: abject: abode: absence: abuse: acclamation: account: achievement: ado: affliction: affront: age: agreement: ambush: amendment: amends: ancient: anger: annoyance: apology: apostasy: apparel: approach: argument: arrow: ash: associate: assurance: auditory: axe: backsliding: banner: bear: behaviour: benefit: bidding: bird: birth: black: blasphemy: blessing: boast: boasting: bond: boot (1): boot (2): bosom: bottom: bout: bracelet: bramble: bread: breadth: breaker: breastplate: brier: broil: brother: brunt: brute: builder: building: burden: burgess: by-place: calling: card: cavil: chamber: chance: change: chastisement: chiding: claim: clause: clemency: clipper: close: closing: comforter: commodity: comparison: compunction: conclave: conclusion: conference: consumption: contrivance: conversing: conviction: cornet: correction: cost: county: couple: courtier: coward: cross: crown: cry: cumber: damning: danger: dart: daughter: decay: deceiver: declining: deep: defection: defiance: delicacy: delicate: deluder: departing: deportment: descent: despair: devising: dictator: dinner: dint: direction: dirt: discomfort: disgrace: dishonour: disorder: disposition: distaste: distress: document: doer: dread: dunghill: durance: dust: duty: earring: eating: emblem: employ: employment: encounter: encouragement: endeavour: engagement: engine: enlargement: enmity: enough: ensign: enterprise: entertainer: equipage: errand: evening: evil-doing: excellency: exhortation: extravagancy: fainting: faithfulness: fame: fancy: fashion: fatherhood: fault: fawning: fetter: fickleness: fidelity: fight: fig-tree: firebrand: firmament: flood: flower: folk: fool: foolishness: foreigner: forgiveness: form: former: fornicator: fortification: foundation: founder: freedom: freeholder: friendship: fright: fury: garland: getting: ghost: gift: giving: gladness: glittering: gorge: grape: grave: greeting: groan: gun: hair: handling: hap: harm: hater: havoc: headpiece: heap: heaviness: heel: heir: hill: homage: honey: horse: hubbub: humiliation: ignorance: image: impediment: impenitency: industry: iniquity: injury: innocency: innocent: instance: insurrection: intention: interfering: interim: interpretation: invasion: inventing: invitation: issue: jar: journey: justifying: justness: keeper: kinswoman: knee: knot: labour: lamb: league: leaguer: leg: leisure: lengthening: liar: life-guard: lifetime: lightning: lock: lodging: look: lust: magazine: making: malapertness: management: maxim: meadow: meat: member: memory: mention: mettle: midnight: mightiness: ministry: minute: mixture: modelling: moment: monster: morals: mountain: multitude: musician: mutiny: nation: naughtypack: neck: net: nobody: nose: notice: nourisher: obdurateness: objection: observation:

occasion: odds: offer: ointment: opposition: oracle: orator: orb: original: ornament: oven: overseer: pain: paper: parleying: parlour: pastime: peer: penance: pepper: perplexity: petitioner: piece: plague: plaster: play: plenty: plight: pole (2): policy: portion: post (1): postern: powder: practice: praise: prank: preference: preparation: prey: producing: profit: promoting: prophet: protection: providing: provision: provocation: punishment: purport: pursuing: rabble: reach: rear: receiver: receptacle: reckoning: reflection: reformade: region: relation: relief: religion: repentance: reply: reproof: repulse: resistance: result: retreat: retribution: revelation: reward: riddle: righteousness: rite: river: robe: rock: roof: root: ruggedness: rule: runagate: sabbath: saddle: safety: saint: satisfaction: sceptre: scout: scoutmaster: sea: seal: secrecy: secret: seer: sense: sergeant: setting: shake: shaking: share: shift: shock: shot: shout: show: silver: simplicity: sinew: sitting: skull: slaughter: slave: slavery: sleep: slinger: slip: sluice: sow: spectacle: sprat: standing: star: station: statute: stealth: stomachfulness: struggle: subject: sufficiency: suit: sum: summoner: swearer: tabor: talk: teacher: teaching: tear: temper: tendency: tenor: testament: theme: thinking: thorn: threatening: throne: throng: timber: toe: trader: transformation: travail: travel: treason: treasure: trench: trial: tribe: troop: troth: turn: tyranny: uncle: under-officer: understanding: undertaking: unrighteousness: unruliness: uproar: vagabond: valley: valour: van: variety: vice: viceregent: victory: vigilance: villain: villainy: vindication: viper: virtue: visit: volunteer: waiting-man: ward: warehouse: warning: warrant: watchfulness: watching: water: wave: waving: weariness: weed: week: whale: whip: wilderness: willingness: wind: window: wine: wing: wish: withdrawing: wrong: yard (1): zeal.

2. Abundance: acquaintance: addition: affair: anguish: appearance: arm: back: badge: battlement: beast: beauty: being: bit: bolt: bone: bough: boy: breast: case: circumstance: cloud: comfort: commander: communion: compassion: confusion: conscience: consequence: consolation: consultation: contempt: converse: corner: countenance: covenant: crew: damage: darkness: debate: degree: demand: deputy: desolation: devil: doctrine: dragon: drummer: dwelling: dying: eagerness: ease: entrance: escape: expectation: fast: feast: fit: flag: folly: food: fox: government: guard: guile: guilt: guise: habitation: happiness: harbour: helmet: inclination: intent: intruder: jewel: judge: justice: kind: kindred: lackey: lecture: legion: lent: lieutenant: lion: livery: loss: madness: meaning: molestation: monument: morning: motion: much: music: need: neighbour: nought: number: oath: obedience: obeisance: oil: opportunity: palace: paradise: parley: party: pavilion: pity: plain: plea: plot: point: potentate: price: promise: proof: proposal: proviso: quarter: readiness: rebel: rebuke: record: reference: remains: remembrance: remorse: rest (1): sake: sally-port: severity: shire: sign: situation: skill: skirmish: smile: song: stomach: story: stoutness: stranger: subjection: success: sun: taking: tale: tent: tower: unbelief: verdict: view: weapon: white: whole: woman: working.

3. Angel: arms: band: battering-ram: bell: boldness: bowel: carriage: concern: consent: continent: council: course: craft: custody: deceit: deliverance:

desire: discouragement: effect: end: faith: favour: fellow: fire: fort: fountain: garrison: gentry: goodness: governor: grief: harness: heed: home: host (1): hour: hurt: leave: length: liberty: lie: light: lip: little: lover: market: message: method: midst: might: mourning: mystery: native: necessity: offence: oration: posture: principle: privilege: project: ram: request: return: ruin: saying: security: shame: shield: sorrow: speed: substance: subtlety: terror: text: threat: title: tongue: traitor: triumph: trust: welfare: wife: wonder.

4. Anything: attempt: audience: beginning: blow: bondage: cave: ceremony: chain: child: clerk: command: contents: defence: distance: ear: earth: feat: flesh: greatness: ground: hearing: hell: help: highness: hole: iron: lordship: march: mount: mouth: noise: office: person: pit: presence: present: reason: reformation: room: service: sickness: siege: something: sort: stone: tidings: token: top: trouble: use: vassal: wickedness: witness.

5. Act: advantage: alarm: bearer: blood: coming: companion: counsel: cunning: destruction: doing: face: gold: half: haste: heaven: jury: opinion: part: possession: question: rage: rope: sentence: sermon: sight: silence: spirit: sword: table: townsfolk: watch: wisdom: year.

6. Assault: authority: care: cause: corporation: delight: drum: elder: evil: gaoler: knowledge: language: majesty: mischief: news: night: note: pleasure: prison: side: street: wound.

7. Action: advice: commandment: country: door: eye: fear: foe: fruit: giant: god: honour: hope: inhabitant: nature: peace: preacher: rebellion: sound: speech: standard: stronghold: transgression: tree: trumpeter: voice.

8. Armour: battle: body: foot: general: hold: joy: letter: means: messenger: officer: purpose: sling: thought: will.

9. Commission: condition: den: grace: indictment: judgment: kingdom: order: pardon: scutcheon: state.

10. Courage: death: execution: garment: matter: soul: summons: trumpet: truth: tyrant: while: world.

11. Company: design: glory: mercy.

12. Answer: business: field: head: manner: nothing.

13. Secretary: servant: sin: strength: townsman: work.

14. Bar: good: life: love: rest (2).

16. Friend: law: master: mind: soldier: wall.

17. Camp: charge: court.   18. Colour.   19. People.   20. Recorder: son. 21. Petition: word.   22. Force: house.   23. Enemy: prisoner.   24. Gentle-man: mayor: power.   26. Army.   29. Heart.   30. Way.   31. Place. 33. Thing.   34. War.   36. Day: father.   37. Hand.   38. Castle.   39. Name. 43. Gate.   48. Time.   61. King.   102. Man.   104. Lord.   105. Captain: prince.   246. Town.

NOTES ON CERTAIN WORDS IN THE PRECEDING APPENDICES

In the following notes a brief explanation is given of the meaning of some of the preceding words, either (1) to distinguish homonyms; as *cock, gallus*, not hay-cock, cock of the hat etc.; *rush*, quick movement, not the plant. If a pair of homonyms occurs, they are numbered, cf. *rest, stick*: (2) simply as a matter of interest, to give the meaning of an archaic word or a word used in an archaic sense, or the particular meaning of a word used in very diverse senses. In a few instances of biblical words references are given, to the Authorised Version unless otherwise stated.

Actor, one who does something: **air**, atmosphere: **arm**, the limb: **arms**, weapons: **ash(es)**, cinders: **beck**, nod, command: **bedlam**, a lunatic: **bill**, of a bird: **bit**, piece: **boot** (1), 'to boot': **boot** (2), the foot-covering: **breaker**, in phrase 'sabbath-breaker': **breaking**, in A sabbath-breaking, in C bankruptcy and breaking-open: **brush**, a short fight: **calf**, of the lips, Hos. 14. 2: **carriage**, the usual sense is 'bearing', only once in C a vehicle: **charge**, all senses: **chest**, of the body: **clipper**, of promises: **cock**, *gallus*: **colour**, in D flag: **compass**, in A a circuit, in B magnetic compass: **consumption**, the disease: **content**, satisfaction: **contents**, that which is contained: **converse**, conversation: **cornet**, the officer: **cote**, for sheep: **crook**, in phrase by hook or crook: **crop**, agricultural: **damn-me-blade**, a roystering, swearing fellow: **deal**, in phrase 'a great deal', etc.: **desert**, wilderness: **dump**, fit of depression: **engine**, in C trickery, in D engine of war: **ensign**, the officer: **ephah**, Lev. 19. 36: **fat** (1), a vessel, vat, cf. Isa. 63. 2 or Mark 12. 1: **fat** (2), of meat or tropically in the sense 'plenty': **fit**, of apoplexy, depression, etc.: **flag**, military, etc.: **fold**, for sheep: **foretop**, a lock of hair on the forehead: **former**, maker, used of the deity, cf. Jer. 10. 16: **haunt**, place of resort, once in C habit: **heart's-ease**, pansy or wall-flower: **heave-shoulder**, Lev. 7. 34: **hin**, Lev. 19. 36: **host** (1), army: **host** (2), entertainer: **innocent**, silly person: **iron(s)**, mostly in sense 'fetters': **jade**, horse, in proverbial saying 'jades there be of all colours': **jar**, a quarrel: **juniper**, cited from Psalm 120. 4: **knocker**, one who knocks: **lap**, of person seated: **laying**, of trenchers on the table: **league**, a compact, agreement: **lent**, the fast: **let**, hindrance: **lie**, false statement: **liver**, the organ: **lock**, of door: **magazine**, military: **main**, principle matter: **march**, of army: **mass**, the sacrament: **mast**, of ship: **meteyard**, a yardstick, cf. Lev. 19. 35: **mincing**, gait: **miss**, young woman, mistress: **mole**, the animal: **nap**, sleep: **naughtypack**, a bad character: **noble**, the coin: **original**, origin: **page**, of book: **pap**, teat: **pitch**, the resinous substance: **plat**, plot of ground: **plot**, a scheme: **point(s)**, laces: **pole** (1), of wood: **pole** (2) of the earth or heavens: **post** (1), of wood: **post** (2), letter-post: **pound**, money: **present**, time: **professor**, professing Christian: **pullen**, poultry: **quarter**, all senses: **ram**, battering-ram: **recorder**, law-officer: **reformade**, volunteer without commission: **rein**, in phrase 'reins on their neck': **relation**, all senses: **rent**, result of rending: **rest** (1), repose: **rest** (2), remainder: **riddle**, problem: **robin**, including 'robin-redbreast': **rote**, in phrase 'by rote': **row**, of houses, street: **runagate**, Psalm 68. 6 in Prayerbook version (Coverdale or Great Bible): **rush**, quick movement: **sap**, in phrase 'sap and spirit': **scales**, for weighing: **score**, debt: **scrub**, insignificant fellow: **seal**, as on documents, etc.: **setting**, including 'setting-out': **share**, portion: **spring**, all senses: **standard**, flag: **state**, all senses: **stick** (1), difficulty: **stick** (2), of wood: **stitch**, in B a distance, in C a pain in the side: **stomachfulness**, obstinacy, anger: **stripe(s)**, lashes: **suit**, all senses: **tear**, *lacrima*: **tire**, head-dress, Isa. 3. 18: **top**, highest part: **train**, of people: **turtle**, dove: **vail**, for veil, Isa. 3. 23: **van**, forefront: **wain**, the group of stars Charles's Wain in the Great Bear: **weed(s)**, clothing: **will**, the faculty and the legal deed: **wise**, manner: **yard** (1), enclosure: **yard** (2), the measure, or a yardstick.

Index